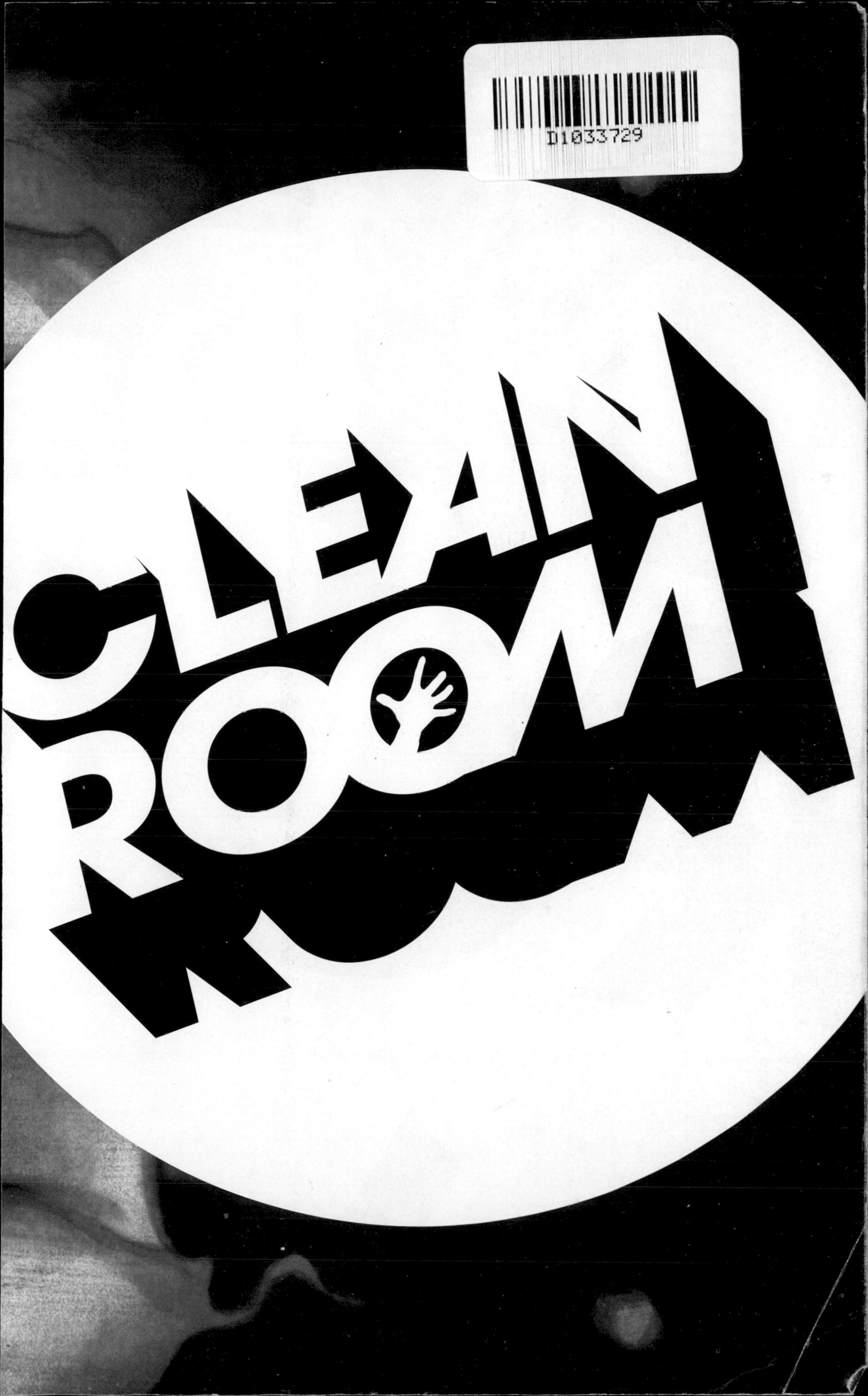
CLEAN
ROOM

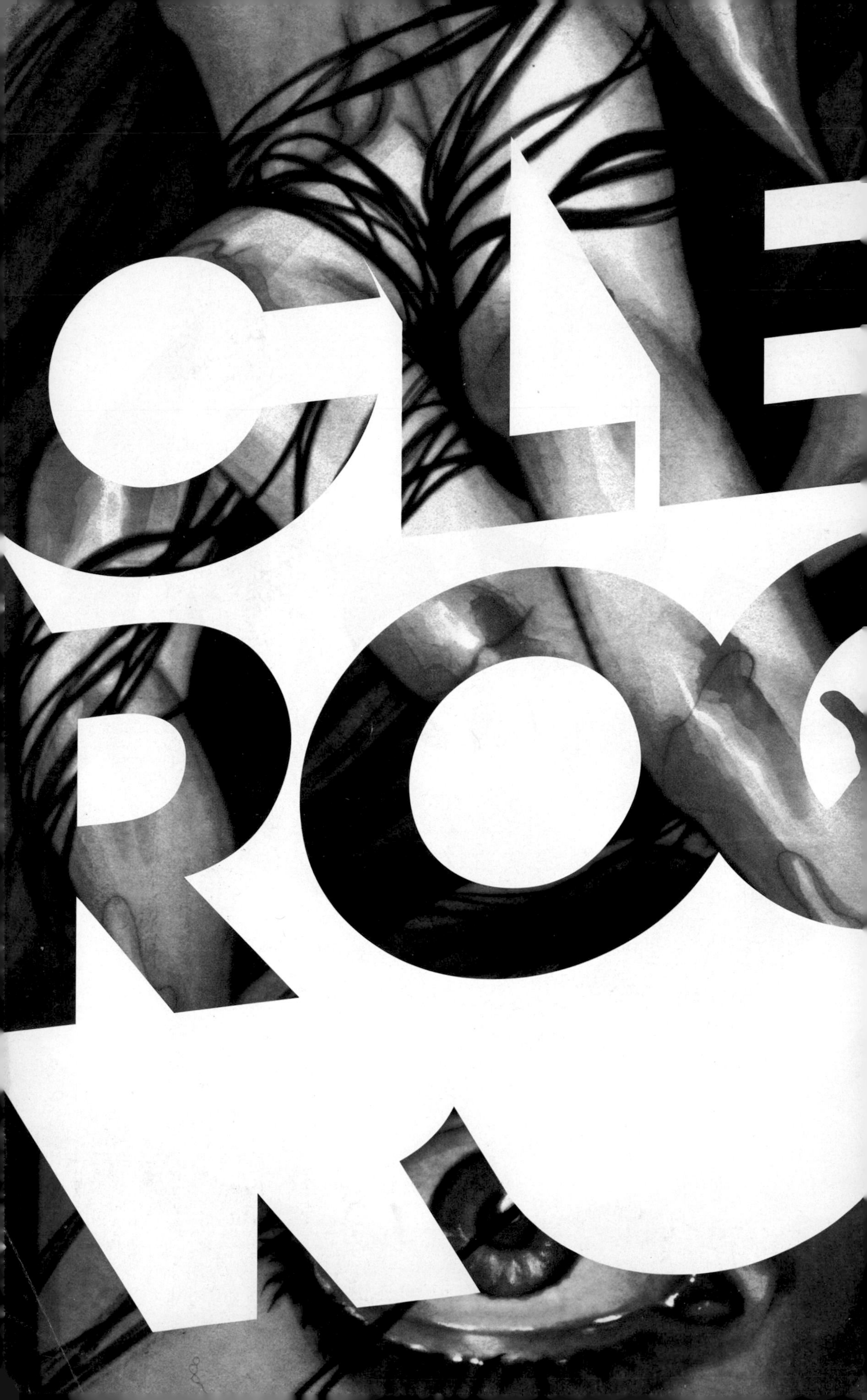

IMMACULATE CONCEPTION

Gail Simone Writer   Jon Davis-Hunt Artist   Quinton Winter Jon Davis-Hunt Colorists

Todd Klein Letterer   Jenny Frison Cover Art and Original Series Covers

CLEAN ROOM created by Gail Simone

SHELLY BOND Editor - Original Series
ROWENA YOW Associate Editor - Original Series
JEB WOODARD Group Editor - Collected Editions
SCOTT NYBAKKEN Editor - Collected Edition
STEVE COOK Design Director - Books
LOUIS PRANDI Publication Design

SHELLY BOND VP & Executive Editor - Vertigo

DIANE NELSON President
DAN DIDIO and JIM LEE Co-Publishers
GEOFF JOHNS Chief Creative Officer
AMIT DESAI Senior VP - Marketing & Global Franchise Management
NAIRI GARDINER Senior VP - Finance
SAM ADES VP - Digital Marketing
BOBBIE CHASE VP - Talent Development
MARK CHIARELLO Senior VP - Art, Design & Collected Editions
JOHN CUNNINGHAM VP - Content Strategy
ANNE DEPIES VP - Strategy Planning & Reporting
DON FALLETTI VP - Manufacturing Operations
LAWRENCE GANEM VP - Editorial Administration & Talent Relations
ALISON GILL Senior VP - Manufacturing & Operations
HANK KANALZ Senior VP - Editorial Strategy & Administration
JAY KOGAN VP - Legal Affairs
DEREK MADDALENA Senior VP - Sales & Business Development
JACK MAHAN VP - Business Affairs
DAN MIRON VP - Sales Planning & Trade Development
NICK NAPOLITANO VP - Manufacturing Administration
CAROL ROEDER VP - Marketing
EDDIE SCANNELL VP - Mass Account & Digital Sales
COURTNEY SIMMONS Senior VP - Publicity & Communications
JIM (SKI) SOKOLOWSKI VP - Comic Book Specialty & Newsstand Sales
SANDY YI Senior VP - Global Franchise Management

CLEAN ROOM: IMMACULATE CONCEPTION

DC Comics
2900 West Alameda Avenue
Burbank, CA 91505
Printed in the USA. First Printing.
ISBN: 978-1-4012-6275-4

Logo design by STEVE COOK

Library of Congress Cataloging-in-Publication
Data is available.

PEFC Certified

Printed on paper from
sustainably managed
forests and controlled
sources

PEFC/29-31-75   www.pefc.org

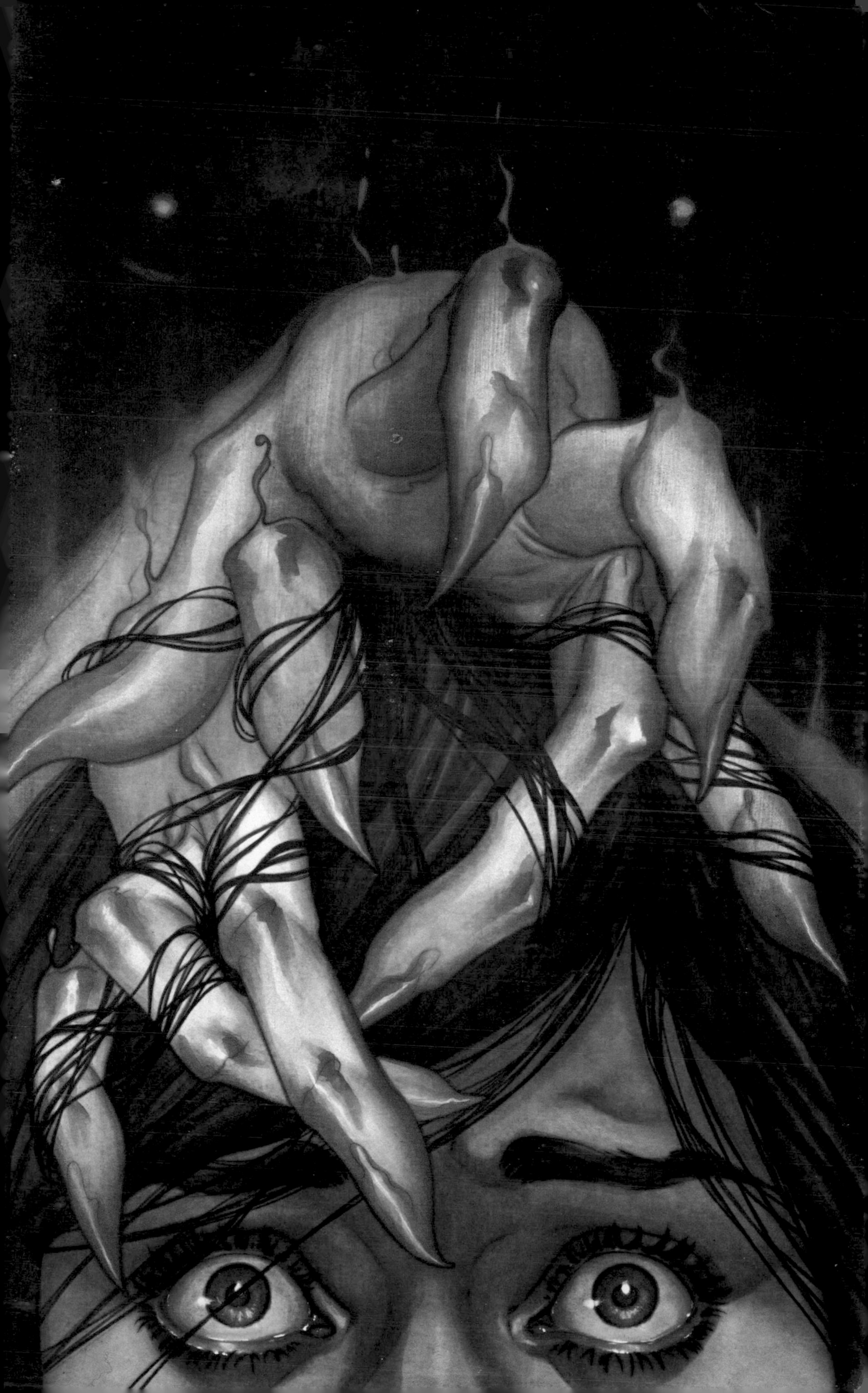

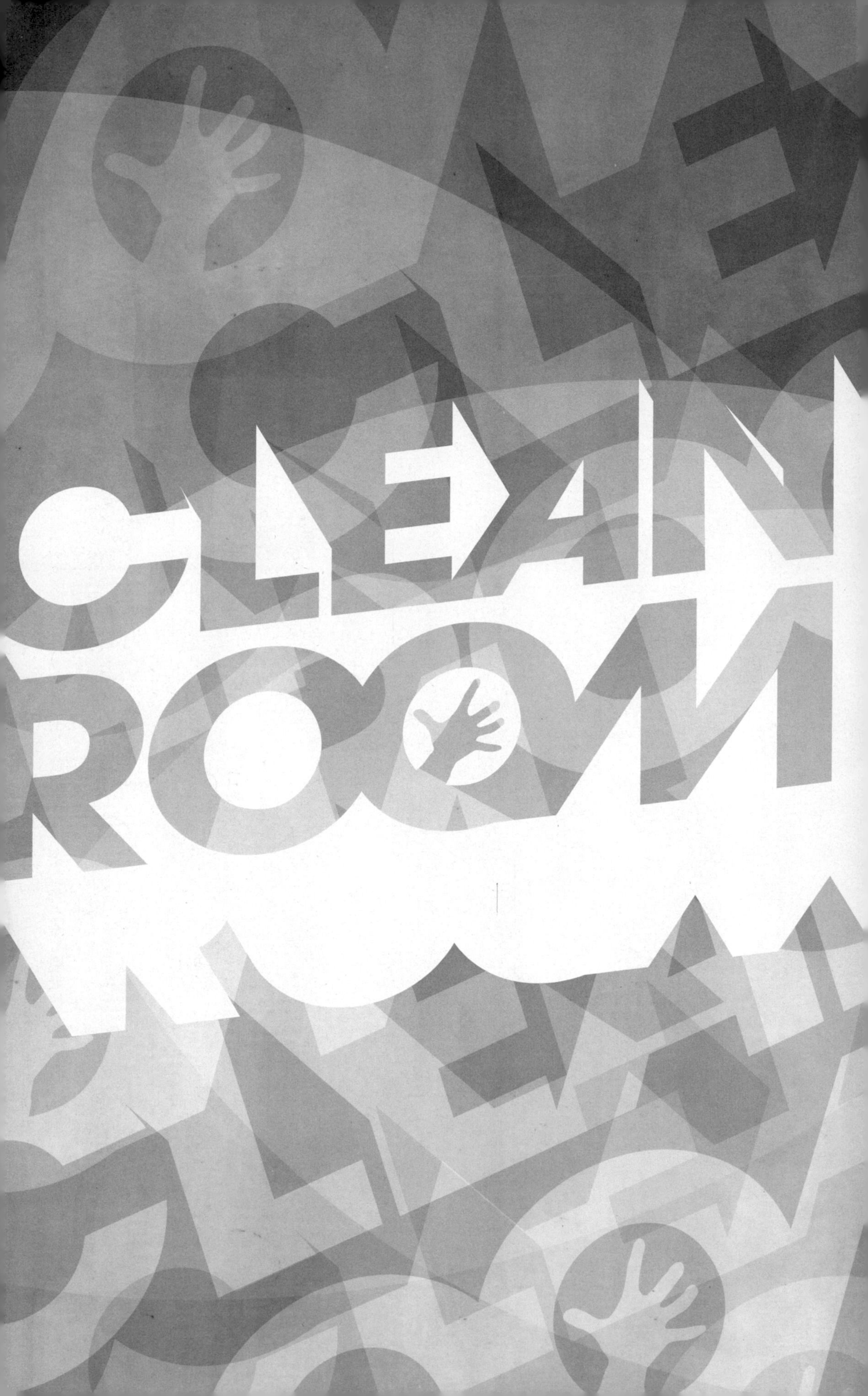
CLEAN
ROOM

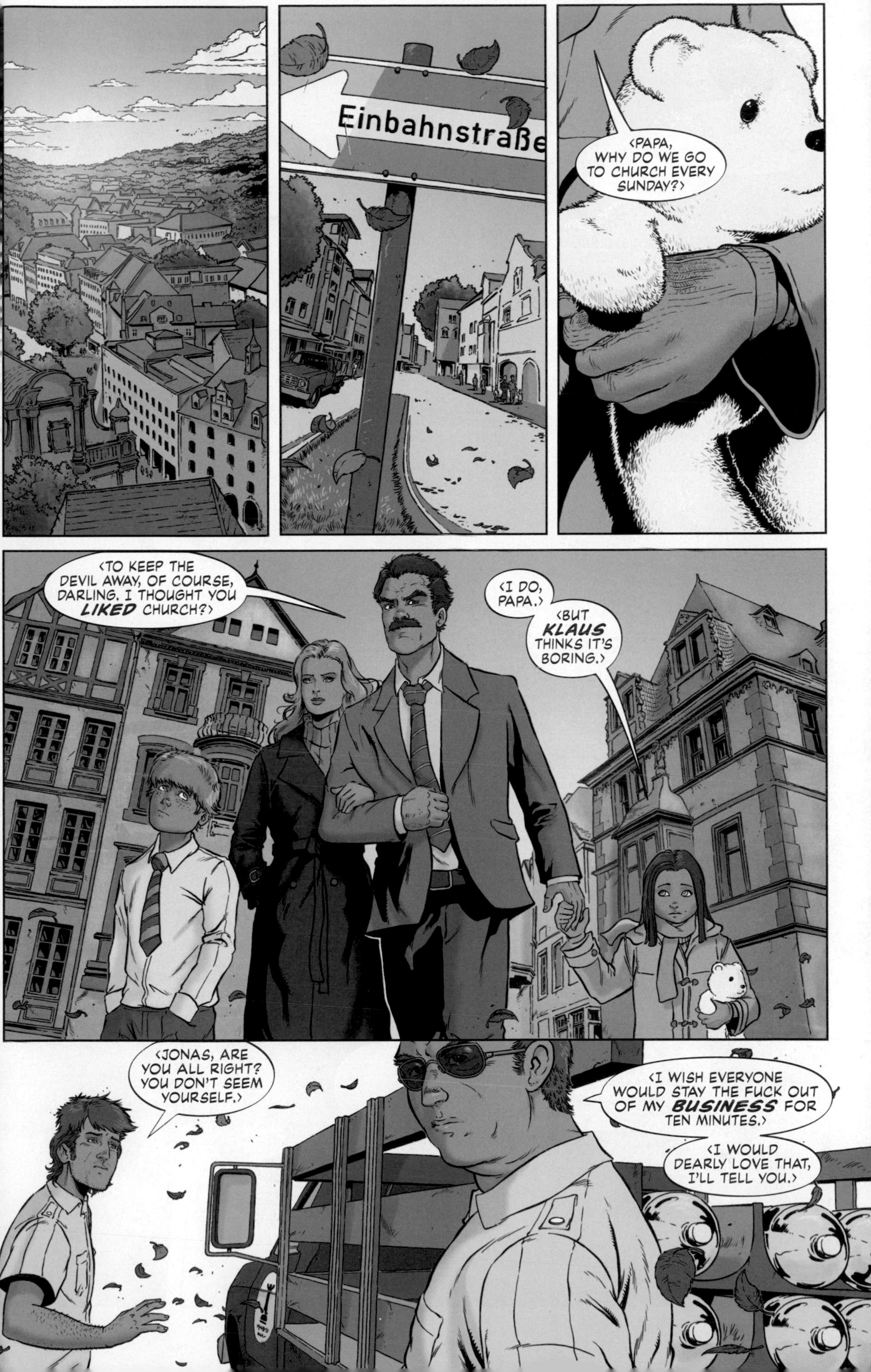
Einbahnstraße
<PAPA, WHY DO WE GO TO CHURCH EVERY SUNDAY?>
<TO KEEP THE DEVIL AWAY, OF COURSE, DARLING. I THOUGHT YOU LIKED CHURCH?>
<I DO, PAPA.>
<BUT KLAUS THINKS IT'S BORING.>
<JONAS, ARE YOU ALL RIGHT? YOU DON'T SEEM YOURSELF.>
<I WISH EVERYONE WOULD STAY THE FUCK OUT OF MY BUSINESS FOR TEN MINUTES.>
<I WOULD DEARLY LOVE THAT, I'LL TELL YOU.>

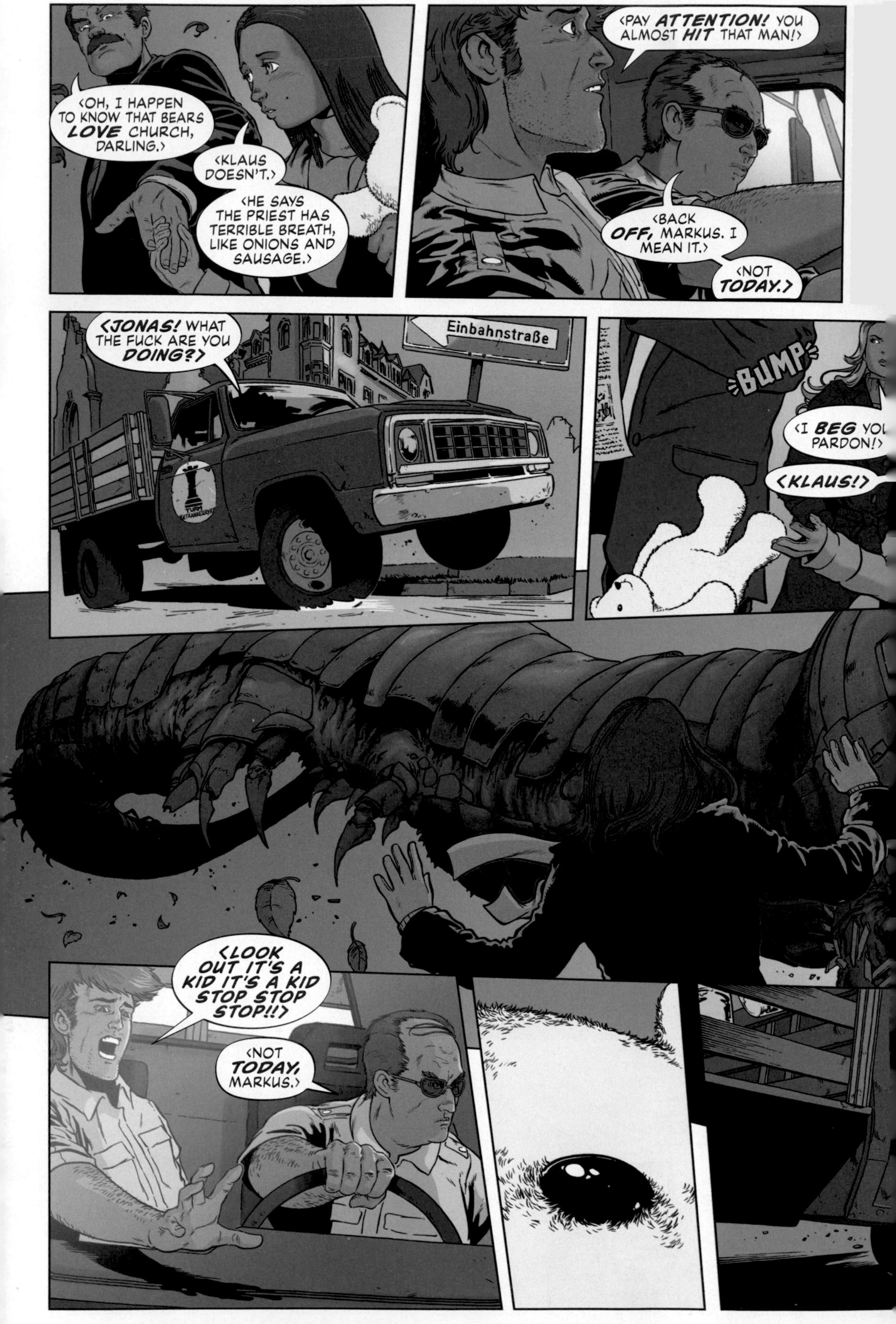
‹OH, I HAPPEN TO KNOW THAT BEARS LOVE CHURCH, DARLING.›
‹KLAUS DOESN'T.›
‹HE SAYS THE PRIEST HAS TERRIBLE BREATH, LIKE ONIONS AND SAUSAGE.›
‹PAY ATTENTION! YOU ALMOST HIT THAT MAN!›
‹BACK OFF, MARKUS. I MEAN IT.›
‹NOT TODAY.›
‹JONAS! WHAT THE FUCK ARE YOU DOING?›
Einbahnstraße
BUMP
‹I BEG YOU PARDON!›
‹KLAUS!›
‹LOOK OUT IT'S A KID IT'S A KID STOP STOP STOP!!›
‹NOT TODAY, MARKUS.›

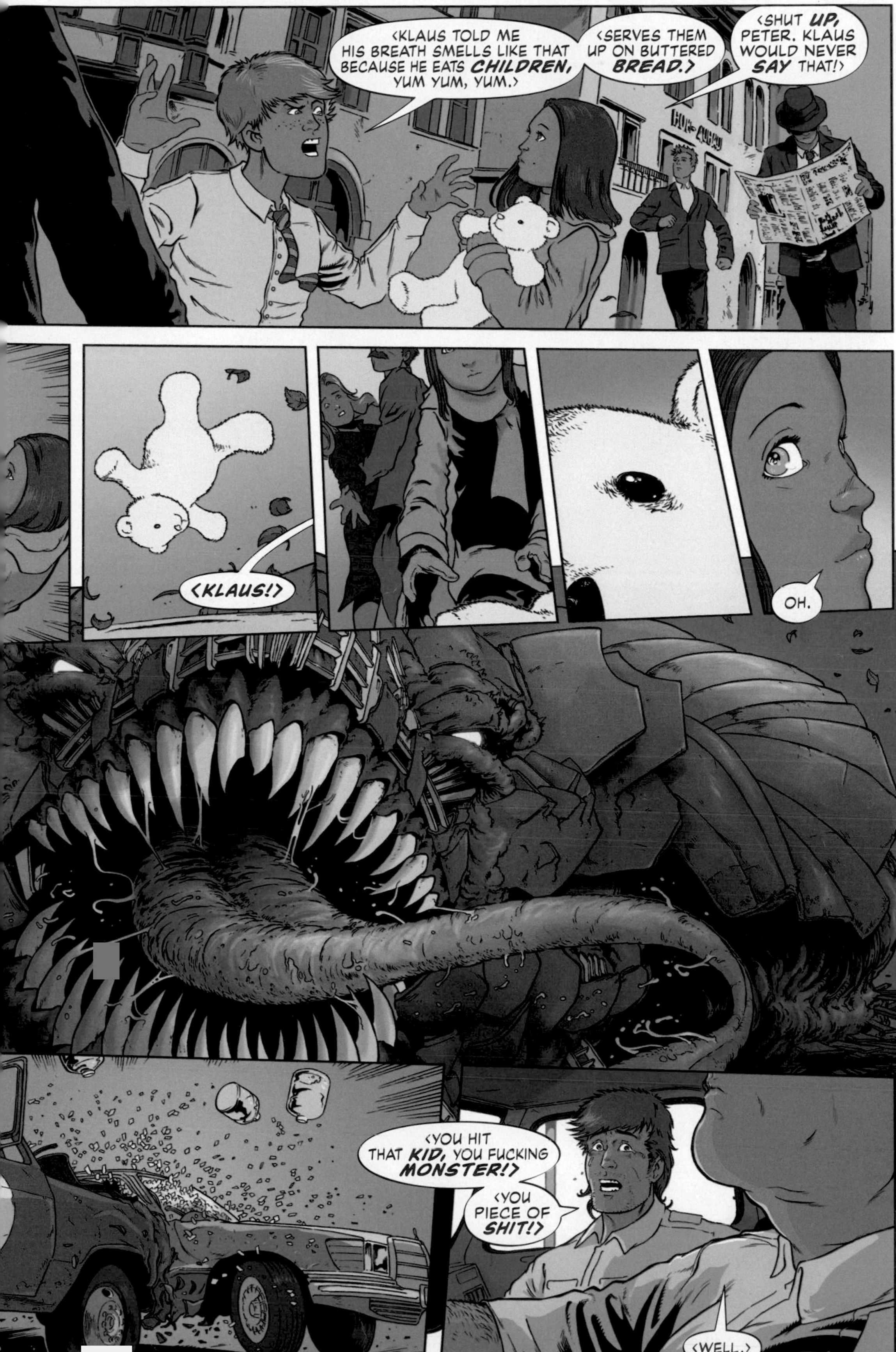

‹KLAUS TOLD ME HIS BREATH SMELLS LIKE THAT BECAUSE HE EATS CHILDREN, YUM YUM, YUM.›
‹SERVES THEM UP ON BUTTERED BREAD.›
‹SHUT UP, PETER. KLAUS WOULD NEVER SAY THAT!›
‹KLAUS!›
OH.
‹YOU HIT THAT KID, YOU FUCKING MONSTER!›
‹YOU PIECE OF SHIT!›
‹WELL.›

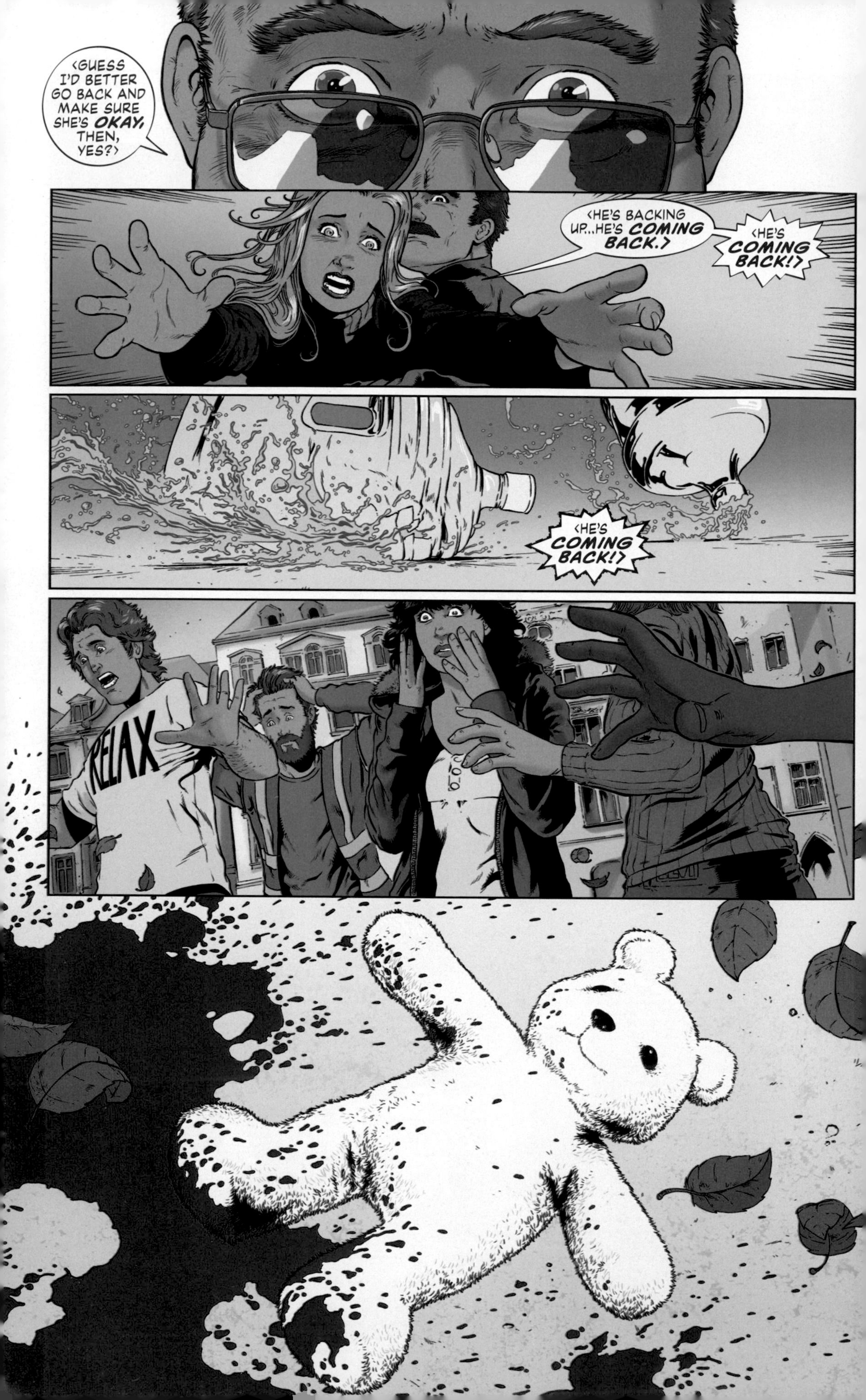
‹GUESS I'D BETTER GO BACK AND MAKE SURE SHE'S OKAY, THEN, YES?›
‹HE'S BACKING UP...HE'S COMING BACK.›
‹HE'S COMING BACK!›
‹HE'S COMING BACK!›
RELAX

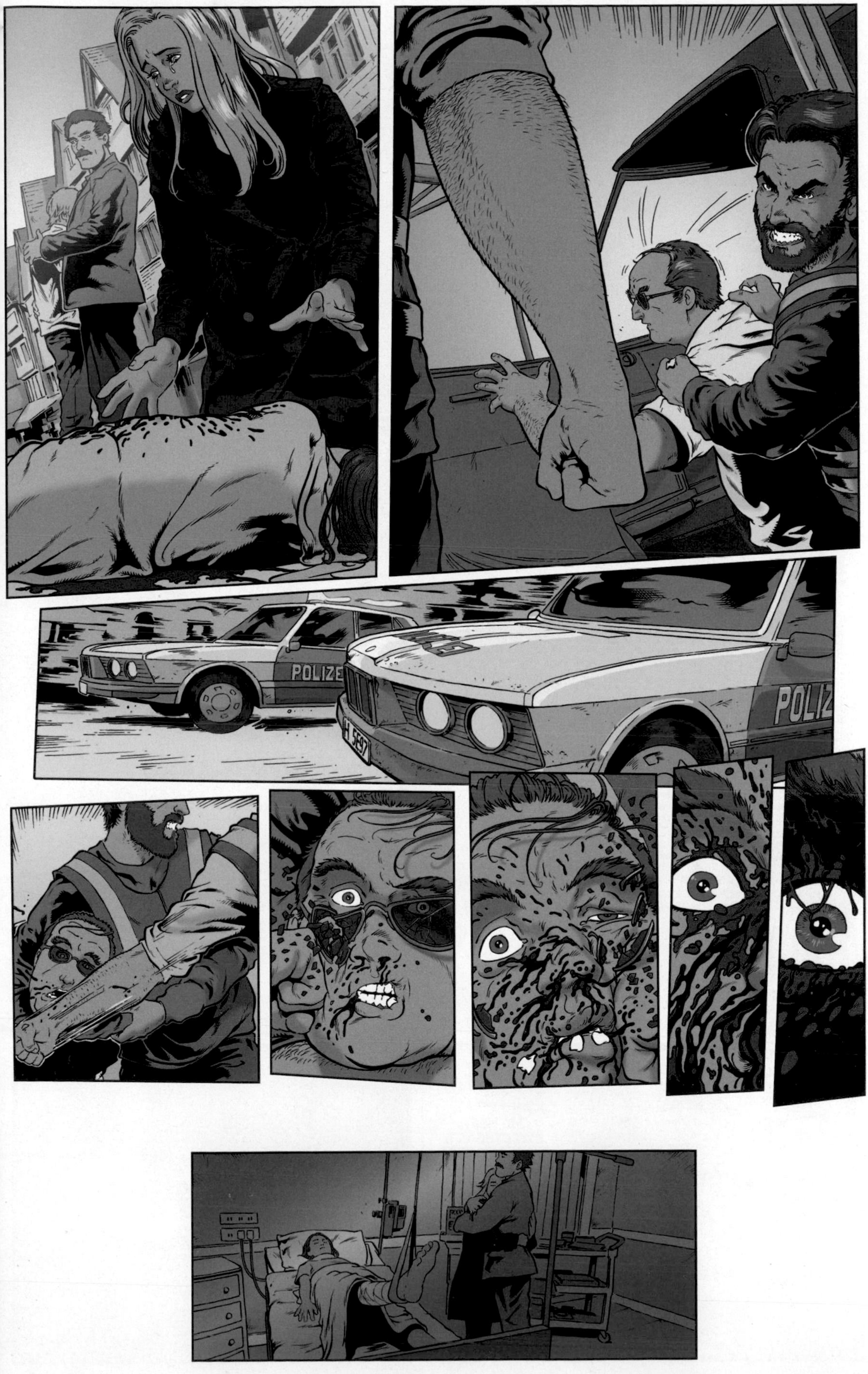
POLIZE
POLIZ

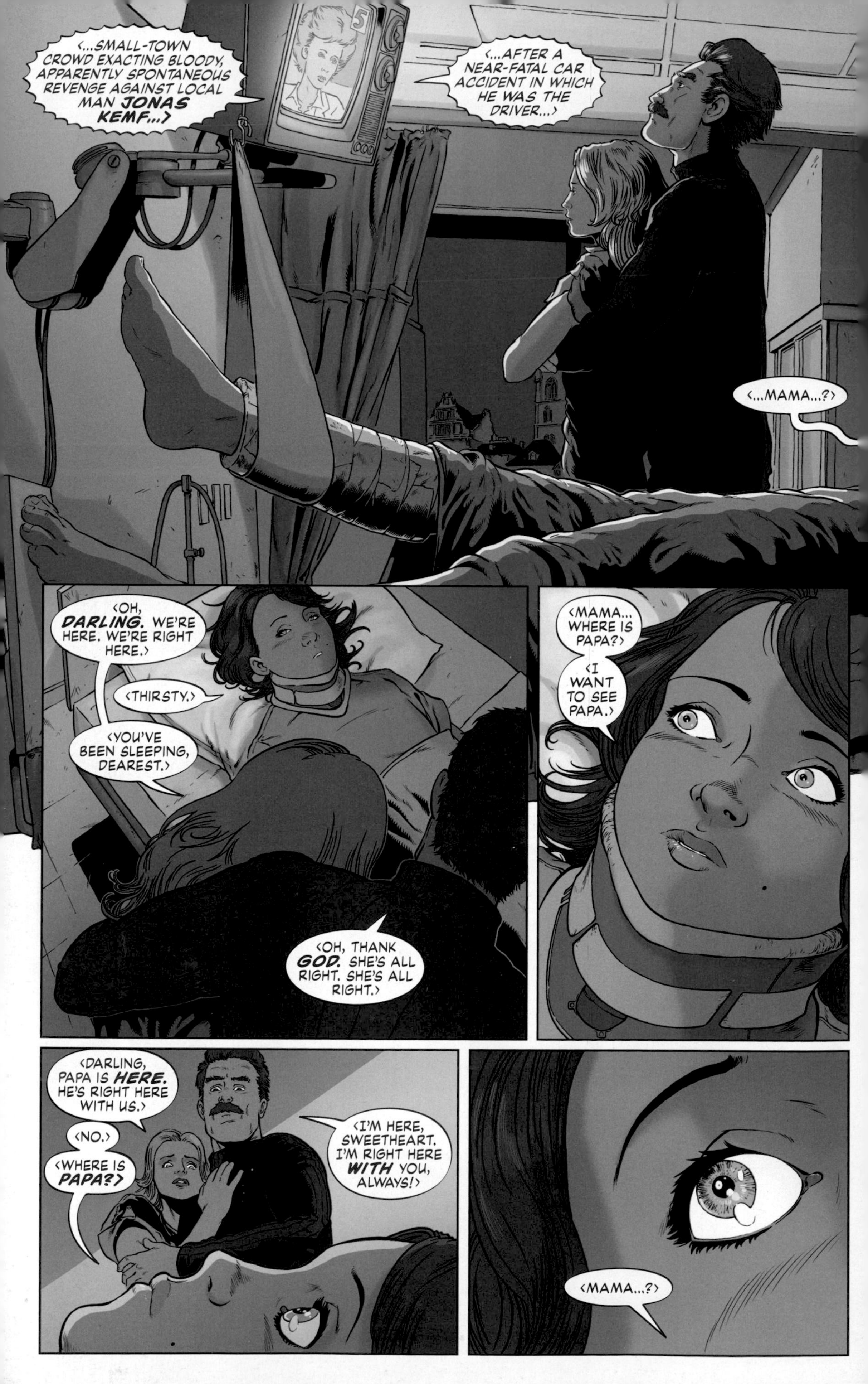

<...SMALL-TOWN CROWD EXACTING BLOODY, APPARENTLY SPONTANEOUS REVENGE AGAINST LOCAL MAN JONAS KEMF...>
<...AFTER A NEAR-FATAL CAR ACCIDENT IN WHICH HE WAS THE DRIVER...>
<...MAMA...?>
<OH, DARLING. WE'RE HERE. WE'RE RIGHT HERE.>
<THIRSTY.>
<YOU'VE BEEN SLEEPING, DEAREST.>
<OH, THANK GOD. SHE'S ALL RIGHT. SHE'S ALL RIGHT.>
<MAMA... WHERE IS PAPA?>
<I WANT TO SEE PAPA.>
<DARLING, PAPA IS HERE. HE'S RIGHT HERE WITH US.>
<NO.>
<WHERE IS PAPA?>
<I'M HERE, SWEETHEART. I'M RIGHT HERE WITH YOU, ALWAYS!>
<MAMA...?>

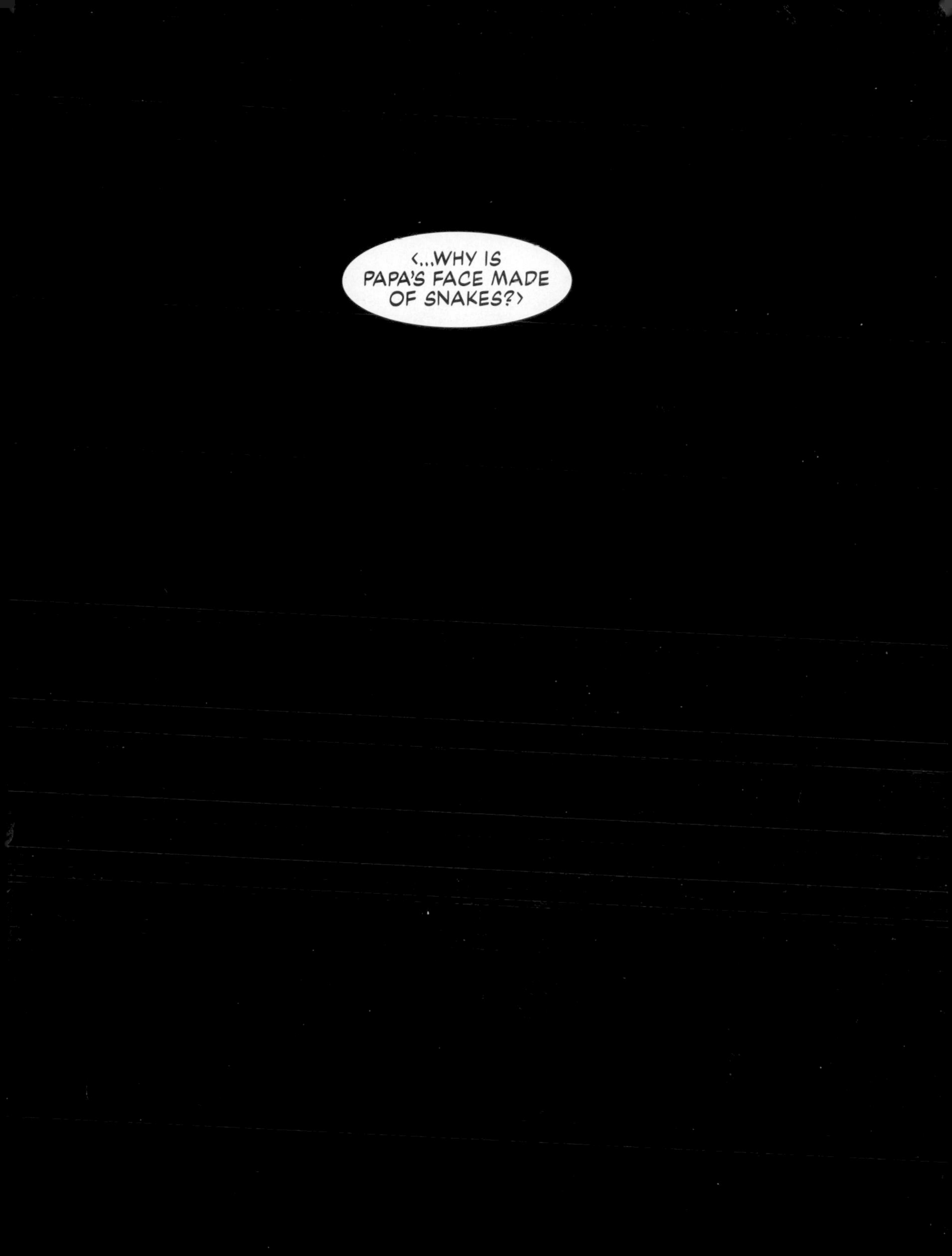
‹...WHY IS PAPA'S FACE MADE OF SNAKES?›

SPRING CLEANING

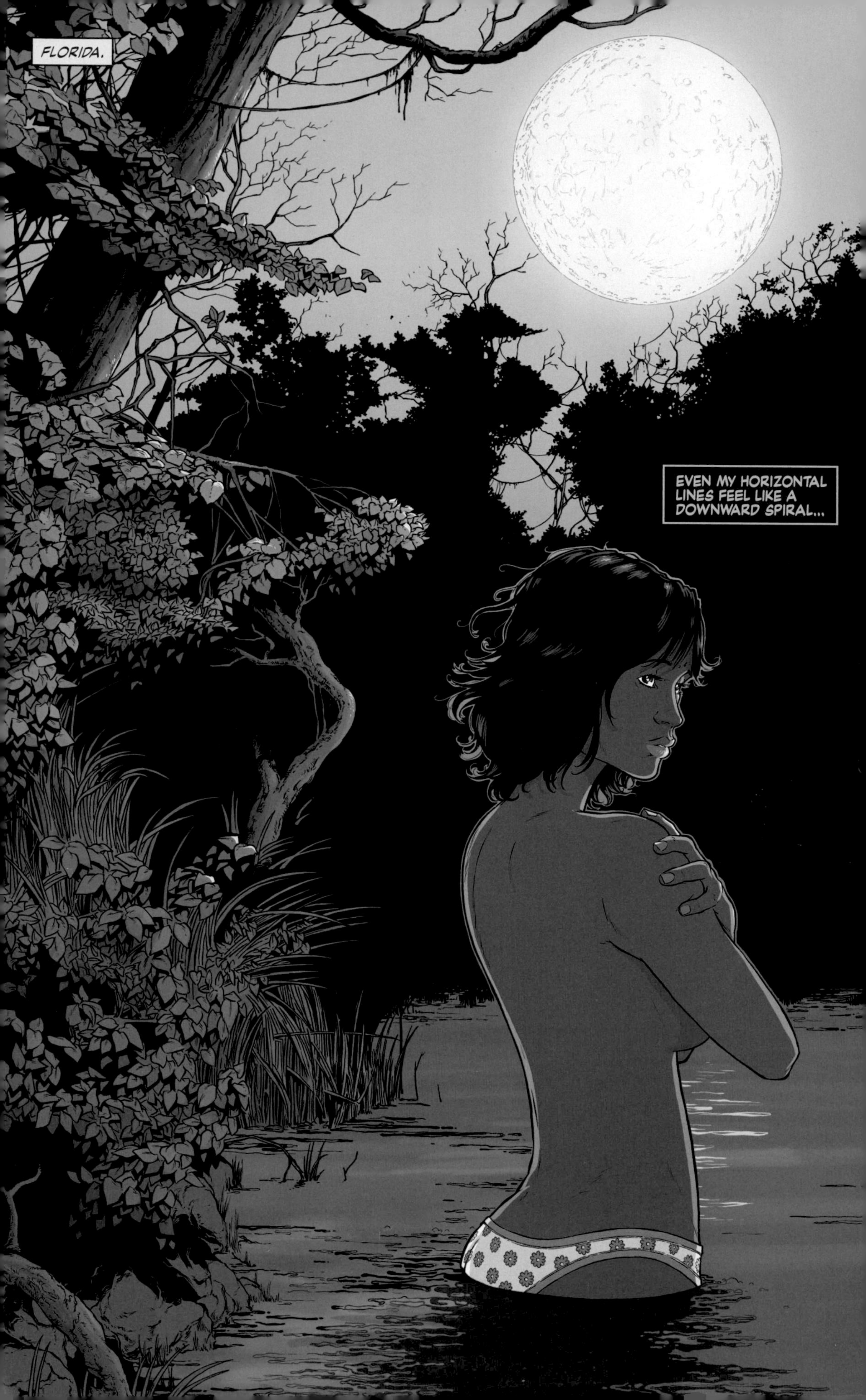
FLORIDA.
EVEN MY HORIZONTAL LINES FEEL LIKE A DOWNWARD SPIRAL...

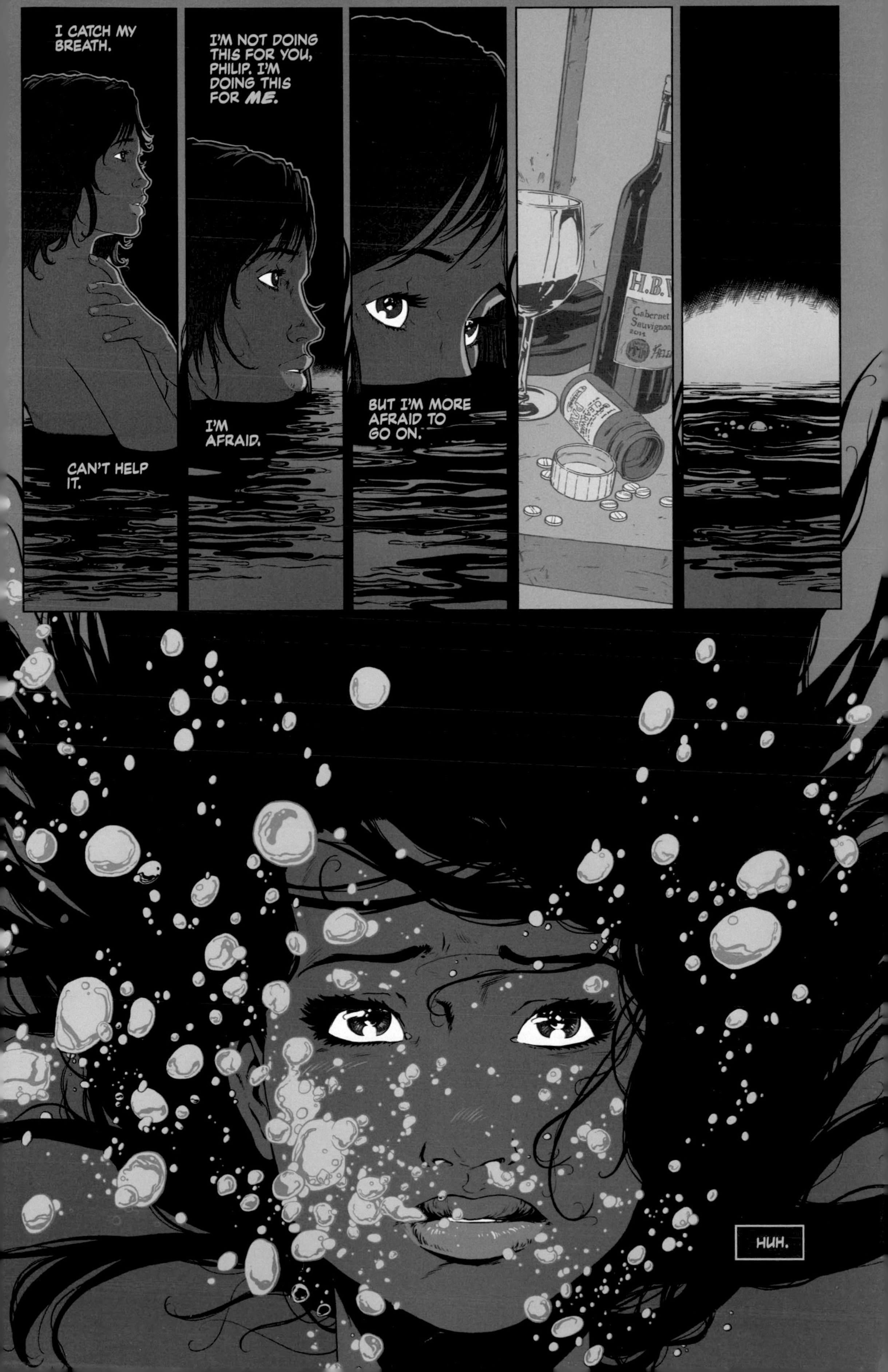
I CATCH MY BREATH.
CAN'T HELP IT.
I'M NOT DOING THIS FOR YOU, PHILIP. I'M DOING THIS FOR ME.
I'M AFRAID.
BUT I'M MORE AFRAID TO GO ON.
H.B.V
Cabernet Sauvignon
2011
HUH.

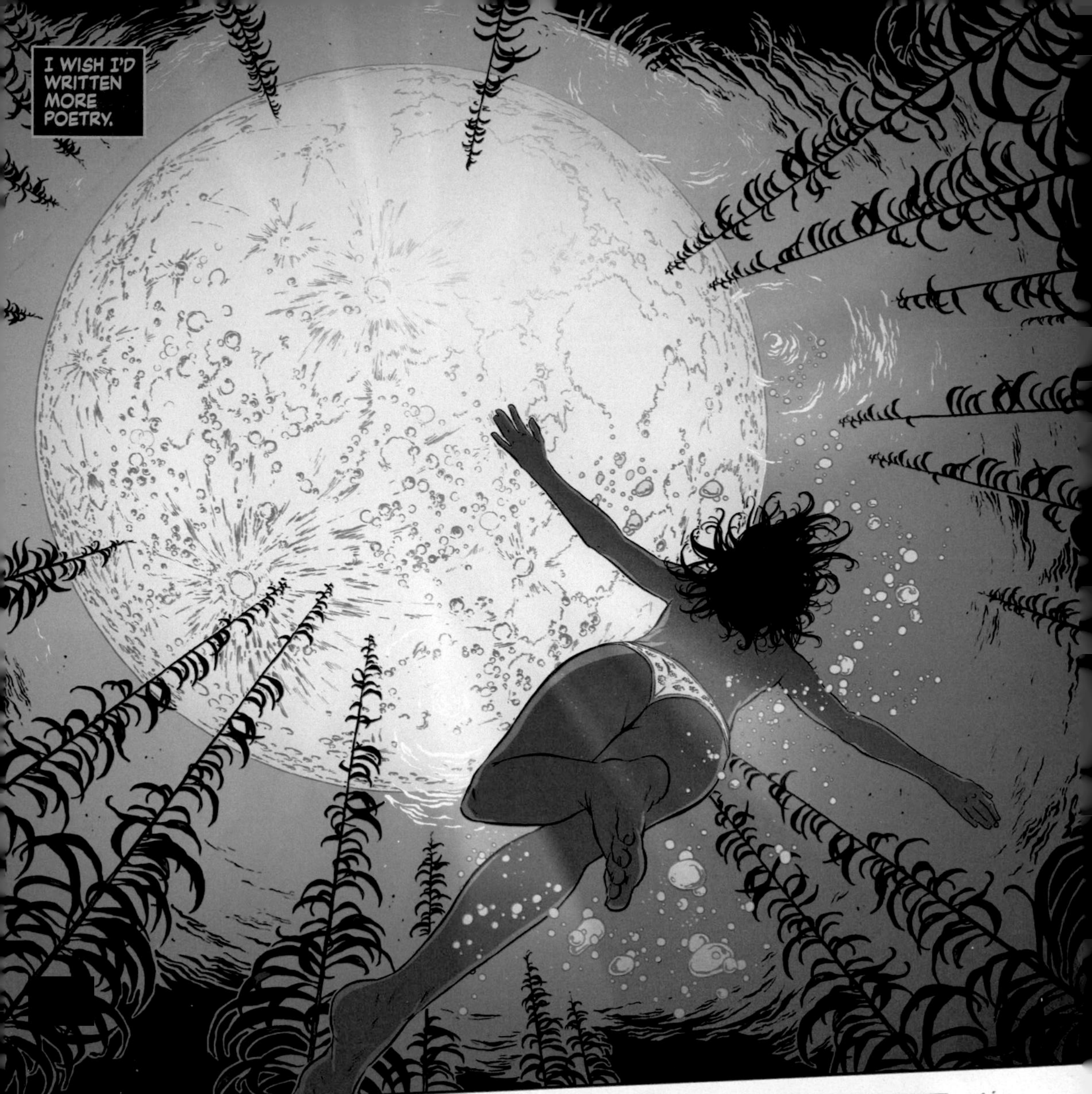
I WISH I'D WRITTEN MORE POETRY.

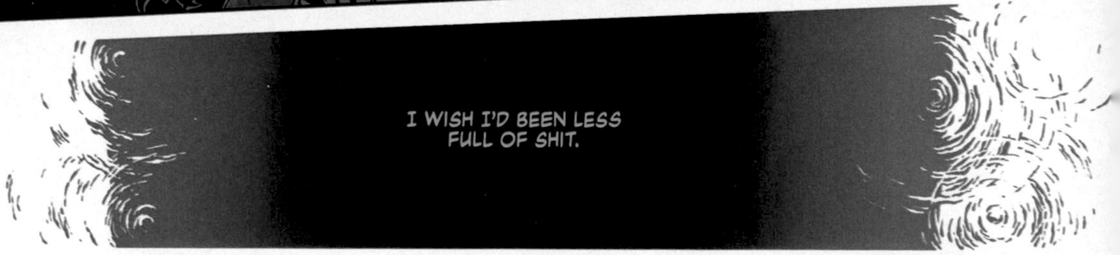
I WISH I'D BEEN LESS FULL OF SHIT.

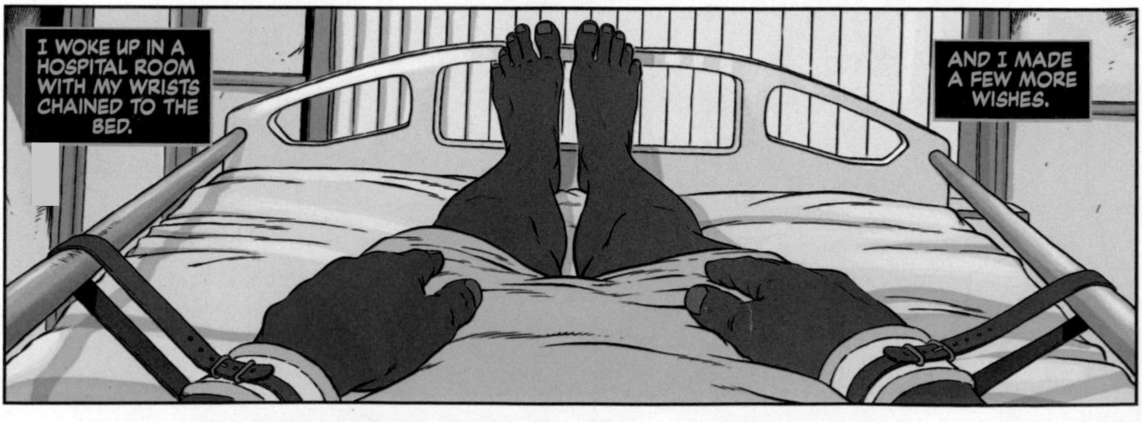
I WOKE UP IN A HOSPITAL ROOM WITH MY WRISTS CHAINED TO THE BED.
AND I MADE A FEW MORE WISHES.

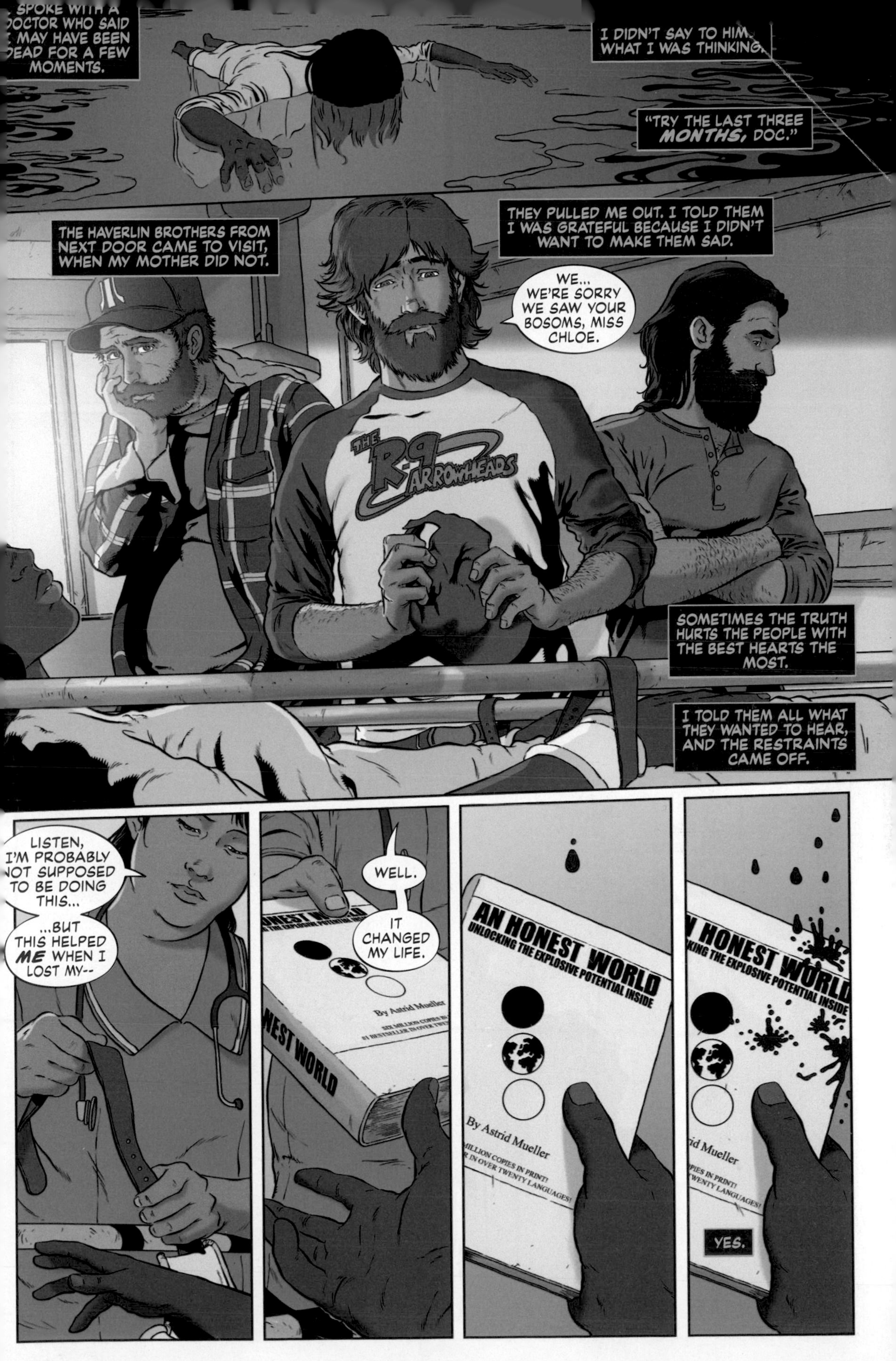
SPOKE WITH A DOCTOR WHO SAID I MAY HAVE BEEN DEAD FOR A FEW MOMENTS.
I DIDN'T SAY TO HIM WHAT I WAS THINKING.
"TRY THE LAST THREE MONTHS, DOC."
THE HAVERLIN BROTHERS FROM NEXT DOOR CAME TO VISIT, WHEN MY MOTHER DID NOT.
THEY PULLED ME OUT. I TOLD THEM I WAS GRATEFUL BECAUSE I DIDN'T WANT TO MAKE THEM SAD.
WE... WE'RE SORRY WE SAW YOUR BOSOMS, MISS CHLOE.
THE R-9 ARROWHEADS
SOMETIMES THE TRUTH HURTS THE PEOPLE WITH THE BEST HEARTS THE MOST.
I TOLD THEM ALL WHAT THEY WANTED TO HEAR, AND THE RESTRAINTS CAME OFF.
LISTEN, I'M PROBABLY NOT SUPPOSED TO BE DOING THIS...
...BUT THIS HELPED ME WHEN I LOST MY--
WELL.
IT CHANGED MY LIFE.
AN HONEST WORLD
UNLOCKING THE EXPLOSIVE POTENTIAL INSIDE
By Astrid Mueller
MILLION COPIES IN PRINT!
IN OVER TWENTY LANGUAGES!
YES.

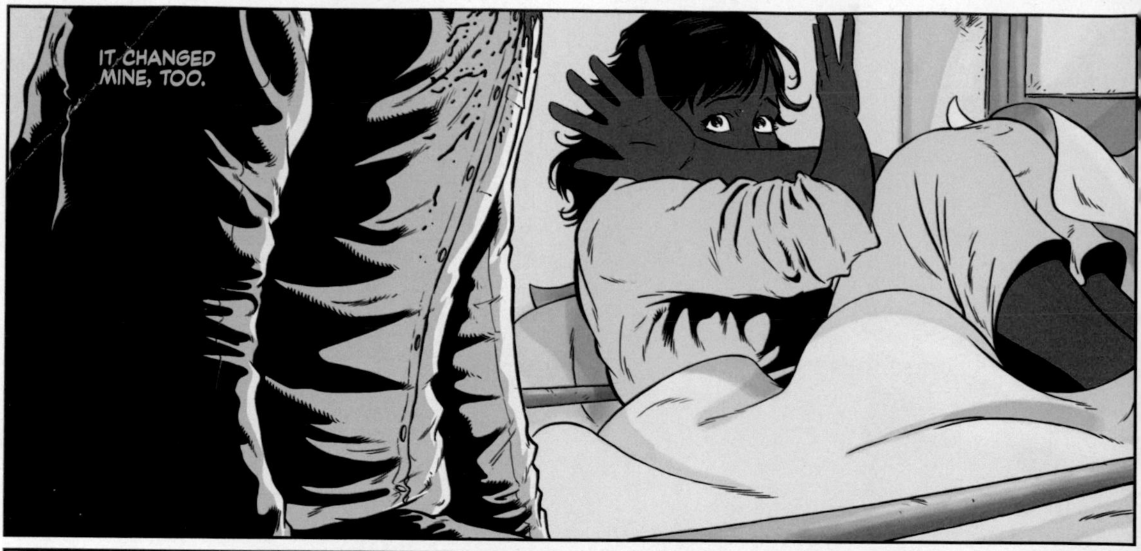
IT CHANGED MINE, TOO.

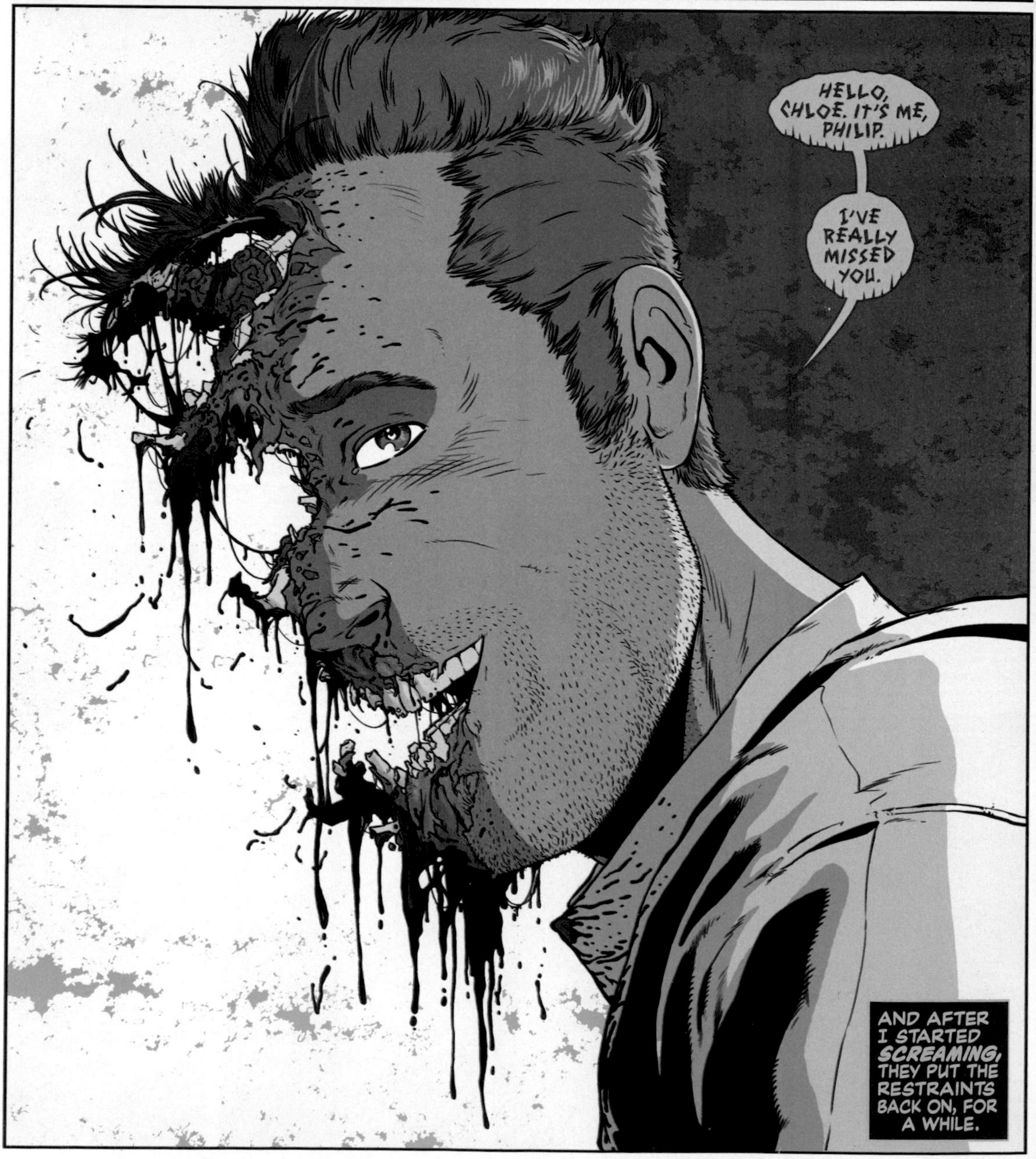
HELLO, CHLOE. IT'S ME, PHILIP.
I'VE REALLY MISSED YOU.
AND AFTER I STARTED *SCREAMING,* THEY PUT THE RESTRAINTS BACK ON, FOR A WHILE.

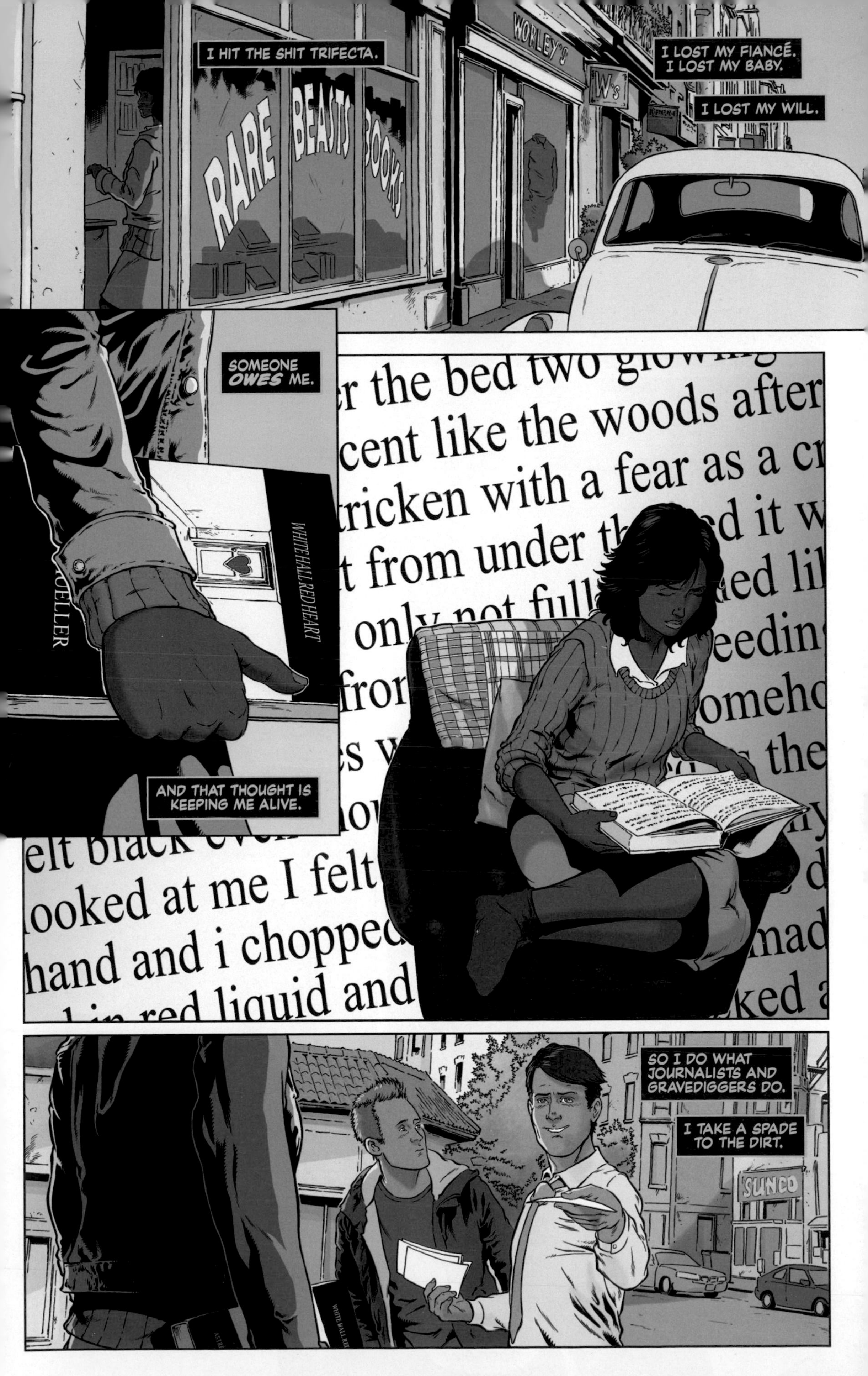

I HIT THE SHIT TRIFECTA.
RARE BEASTS BOOKS
WORLEY'S
W's
I LOST MY FIANCÉ. I LOST MY BABY.
I LOST MY WILL.
SOMEONE OWES ME.
WHITEHALL RED HEART
AND THAT THOUGHT IS KEEPING ME ALIVE.
SO I DO WHAT JOURNALISTS AND GRAVEDIGGERS DO.
I TAKE A SPADE TO THE DIRT.
SUNCO

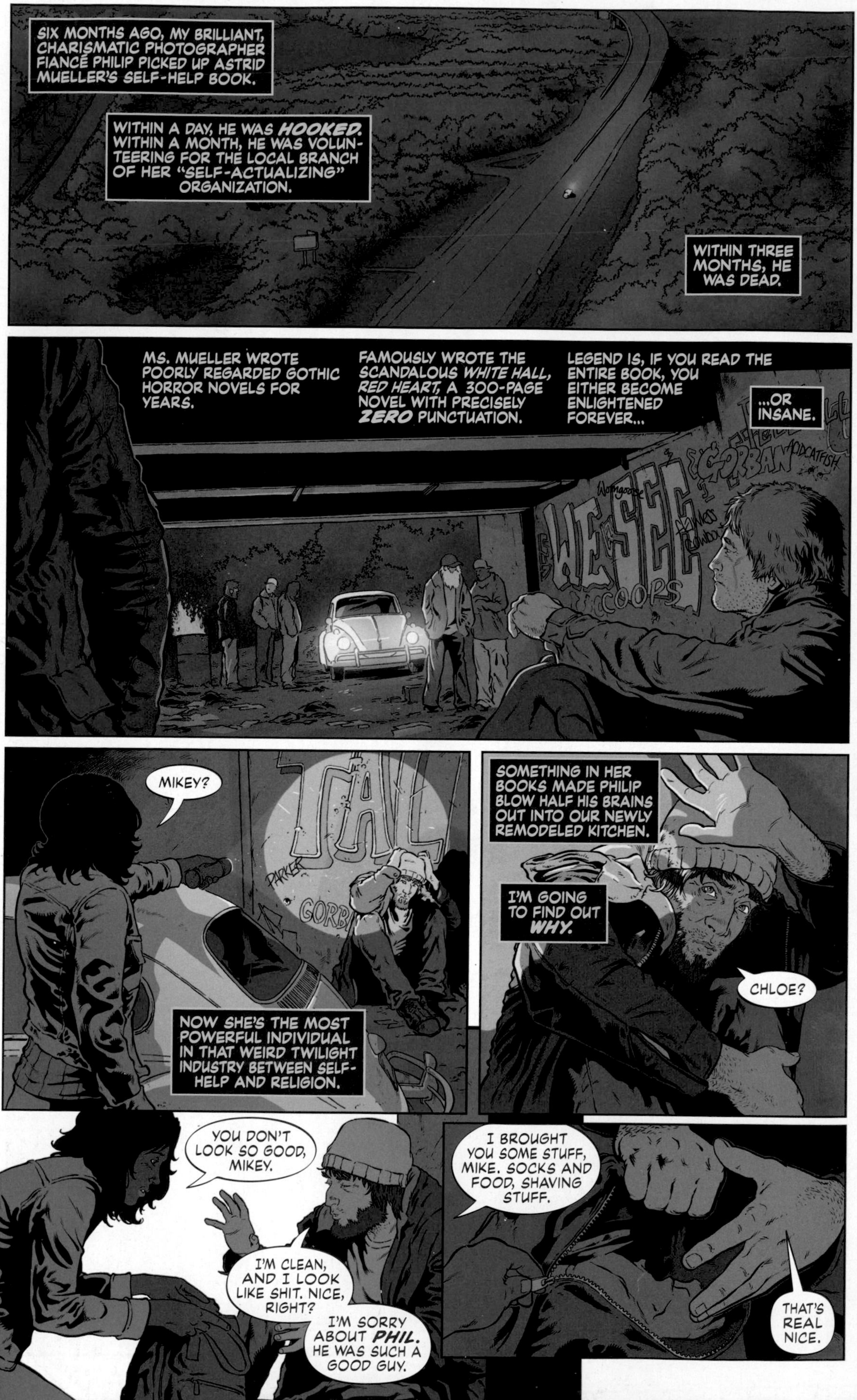
SIX MONTHS AGO, MY BRILLIANT, CHARISMATIC PHOTOGRAPHER FIANCÉ PHILIP PICKED UP ASTRID MUELLER'S SELF-HELP BOOK.
WITHIN A DAY, HE WAS HOOKED. WITHIN A MONTH, HE WAS VOLUNTEERING FOR THE LOCAL BRANCH OF HER "SELF-ACTUALIZING" ORGANIZATION.
WITHIN THREE MONTHS, HE WAS DEAD.
MS. MUELLER WROTE POORLY REGARDED GOTHIC HORROR NOVELS FOR YEARS.
FAMOUSLY WROTE THE SCANDALOUS WHITE HALL, RED HEART, A 300-PAGE NOVEL WITH PRECISELY ZERO PUNCTUATION.
LEGEND IS, IF YOU READ THE ENTIRE BOOK, YOU EITHER BECOME ENLIGHTENED FOREVER...
...OR INSANE.
MIKEY?
NOW SHE'S THE MOST POWERFUL INDIVIDUAL IN THAT WEIRD TWILIGHT INDUSTRY BETWEEN SELF-HELP AND RELIGION.
SOMETHING IN HER BOOKS MADE PHILIP BLOW HALF HIS BRAINS OUT INTO OUR NEWLY REMODELED KITCHEN.
I'M GOING TO FIND OUT WHY.
CHLOE?
YOU DON'T LOOK SO GOOD, MIKEY.
I'M CLEAN, AND I LOOK LIKE SHIT. NICE, RIGHT?
I'M SORRY ABOUT PHIL. HE WAS SUCH A GOOD GUY.
I BROUGHT YOU SOME STUFF, MIKE. SOCKS AND FOOD, SHAVING STUFF.
THAT'S REAL NICE.

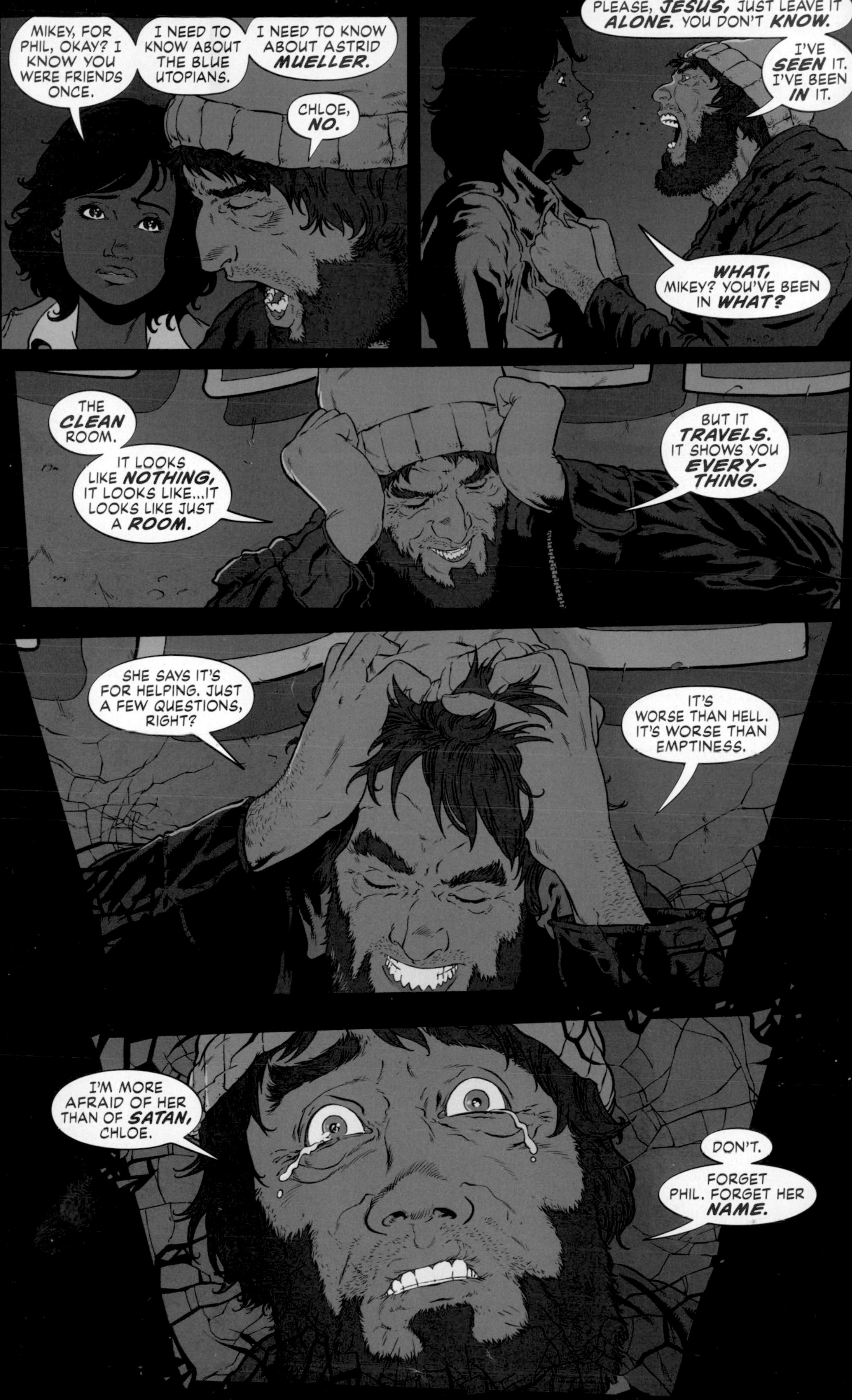
MIKEY, FOR PHIL, OKAY? I KNOW YOU WERE FRIENDS ONCE.
I NEED TO KNOW ABOUT THE BLUE UTOPIANS.
I NEED TO KNOW ABOUT ASTRID MUELLER.
CHLOE, NO.
PLEASE, JESUS, JUST LEAVE IT ALONE. YOU DON'T KNOW.
I'VE SEEN IT. I'VE BEEN IN IT.
WHAT, MIKEY? YOU'VE BEEN IN WHAT?
THE CLEAN ROOM.
IT LOOKS LIKE NOTHING, IT LOOKS LIKE...IT LOOKS LIKE JUST A ROOM.
BUT IT TRAVELS. IT SHOWS YOU EVERY-THING.
SHE SAYS IT'S FOR HELPING. JUST A FEW QUESTIONS, RIGHT?
IT'S WORSE THAN HELL. IT'S WORSE THAN EMPTINESS.
I'M MORE AFRAID OF HER THAN OF SATAN, CHLOE.
DON'T.
FORGET PHIL. FORGET HER NAME.

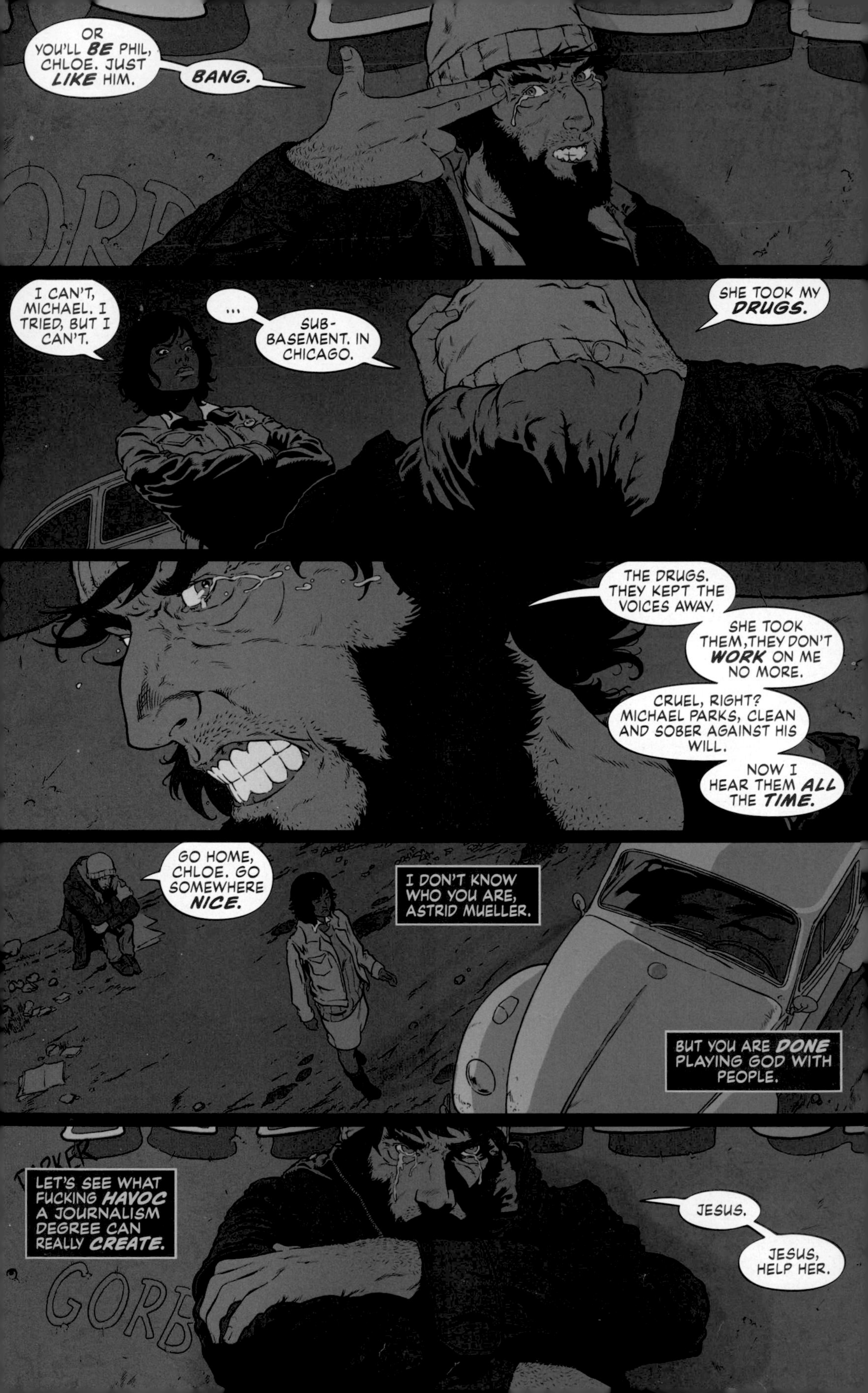

OR YOU'LL BE PHIL, CHLOE. JUST LIKE HIM.
BANG.
I CAN'T, MICHAEL. I TRIED, BUT I CAN'T.
...
SUB-BASEMENT. IN CHICAGO.
SHE TOOK MY DRUGS.
THE DRUGS. THEY KEPT THE VOICES AWAY.
SHE TOOK THEM, THEY DON'T WORK ON ME NO MORE.
CRUEL, RIGHT? MICHAEL PARKS, CLEAN AND SOBER AGAINST HIS WILL.
NOW I HEAR THEM ALL THE TIME.
GO HOME, CHLOE. GO SOMEWHERE NICE.
I DON'T KNOW WHO YOU ARE, ASTRID MUELLER.
BUT YOU ARE DONE PLAYING GOD WITH PEOPLE.
LET'S SEE WHAT FUCKING HAVOC A JOURNALISM DEGREE CAN REALLY CREATE.
JESUS.
JESUS, HELP HER.

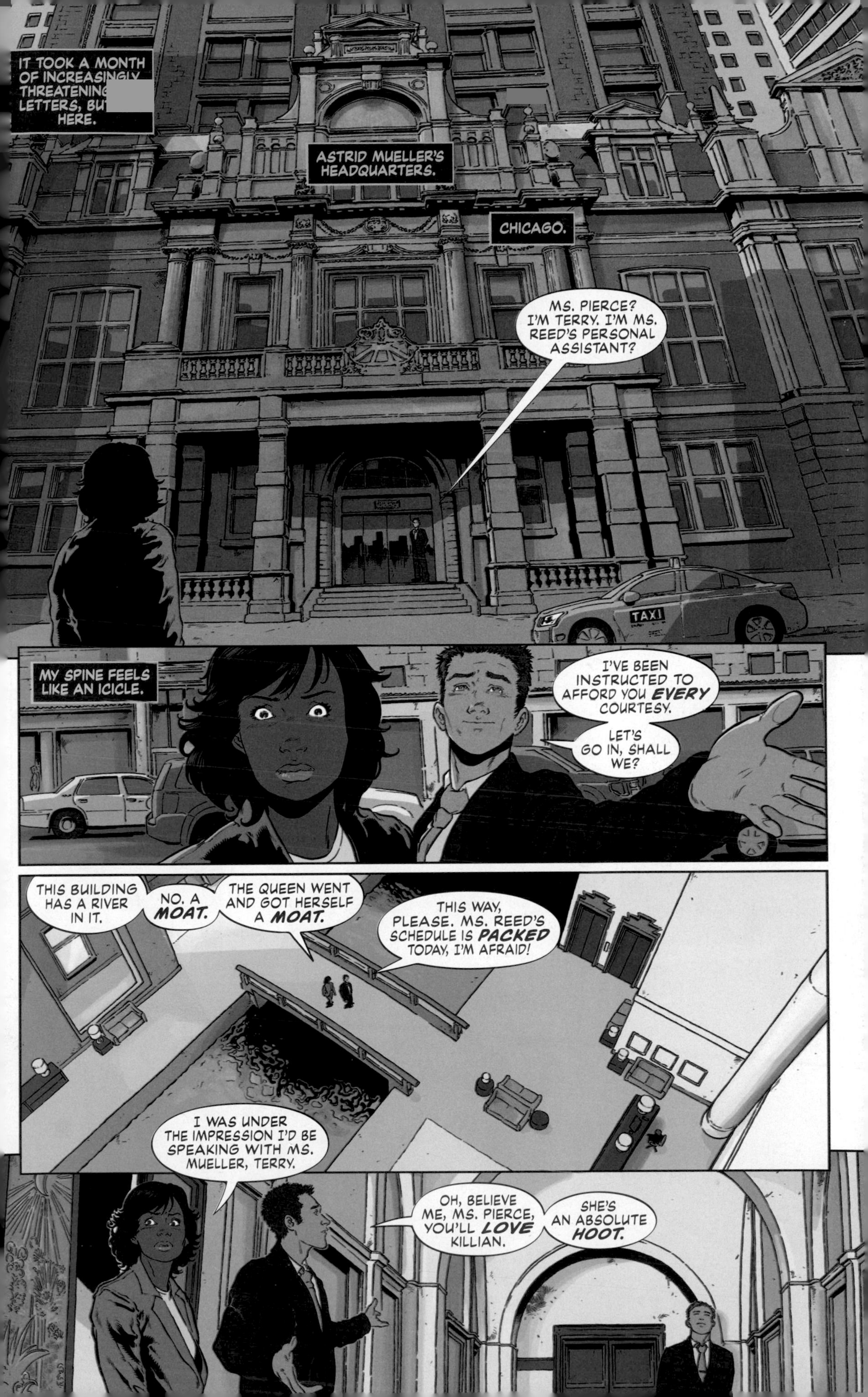
IT TOOK A MONTH OF INCREASINGLY THREATENING LETTERS, BU HERE.
ASTRID MUELLER'S HEADQUARTERS.
CHICAGO.
MS. PIERCE? I'M TERRY. I'M MS. REED'S PERSONAL ASSISTANT?
TAXI
MY SPINE FEELS LIKE AN ICICLE.
I'VE BEEN INSTRUCTED TO AFFORD YOU **EVERY** COURTESY.
LET'S GO IN, SHALL WE?
THIS BUILDING HAS A RIVER IN IT.
NO. A **MOAT.**
THE QUEEN WENT AND GOT HERSELF A **MOAT.**
THIS WAY, PLEASE. MS. REED'S SCHEDULE IS **PACKED** TODAY, I'M AFRAID!
I WAS UNDER THE IMPRESSION I'D BE SPEAKING WITH MS. MUELLER, TERRY.
OH, BELIEVE ME, MS. PIERCE, YOU'LL **LOVE** KILLIAN.
SHE'S AN ABSOLUTE **HOOT.**

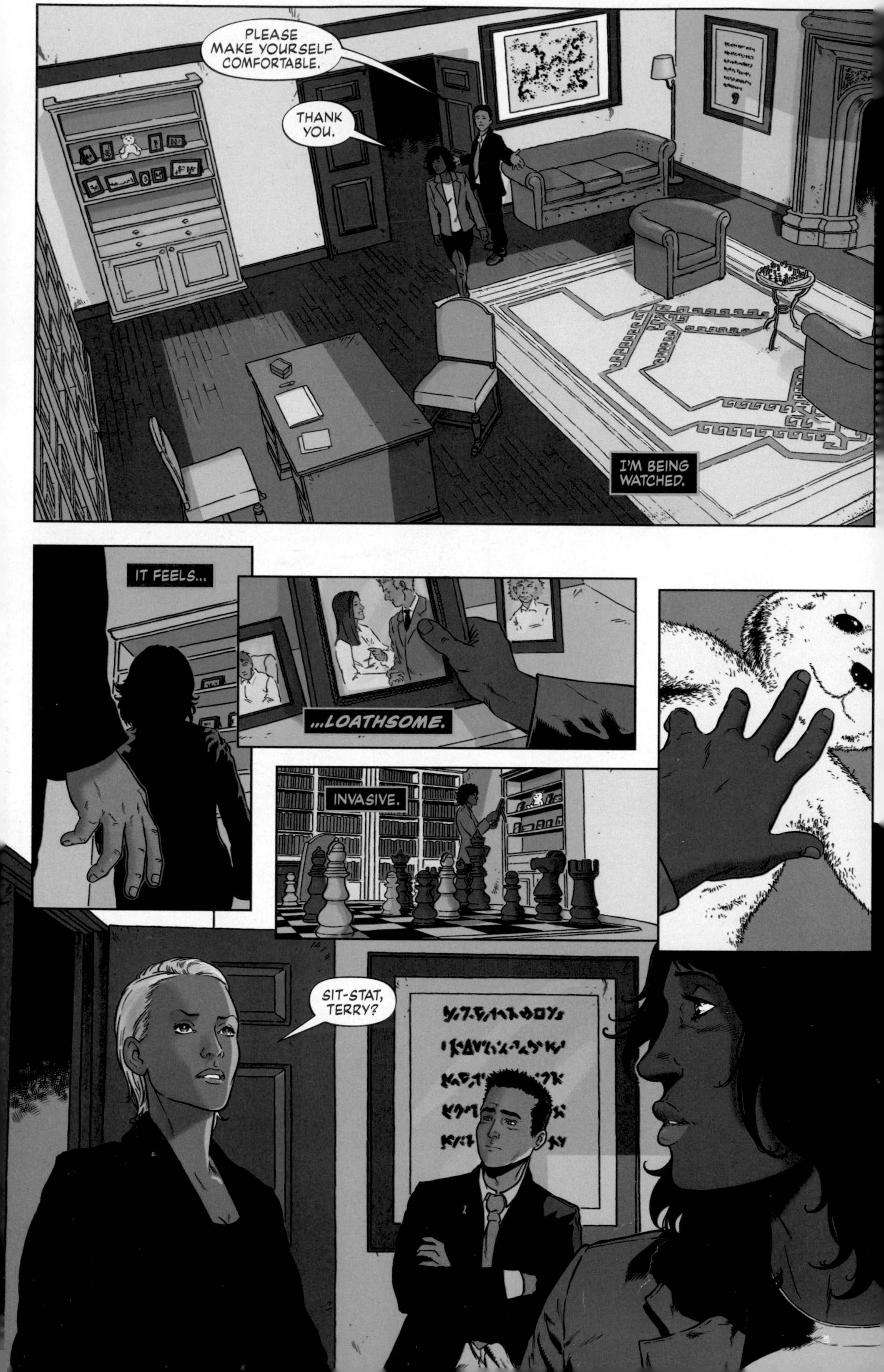
PLEASE MAKE YOURSELF COMFORTABLE.
THANK YOU.
I'M BEING WATCHED.
IT FEELS...
...LOATHSOME.
INVASIVE.
SIT-STAT, TERRY?

HH IS HIGH.

ONE OF THE NONES, DEFINITELY PRE-EMOTIC, POSSIBLE GAMING.

THANK YOU. THAT WILL BE ALL.

MS. PIERCE. IT'S A DELIGHT TO MEET YOU!

AFTER SO MANY REQUESTS, I FEEL LIKE I KNOW YOU.

AND WHAT WAS THIS INTERVIEW FOR, AGAIN, MAY I ASK?

THE *GREENWATER TRIBUNE*, MS. REED. IS MS. *MUELLER* AVAILABLE, PLEASE? I'VE COME A LONG WAY.

THE THING IS, WE GET LITERALLY *THOUSANDS* OF REQUESTS, CHLOE.

AND YOUR CIRCULATION, WELL...

HOW ABOUT A COMPROMISE...WE GIVE YOU AN EXCLUSIVE ON THIS OFFICE, YOU TAKE ALL THE PHOTOS YOU WANT. IT'S MS. MUELLER'S *PRIVATE* OFFICE...

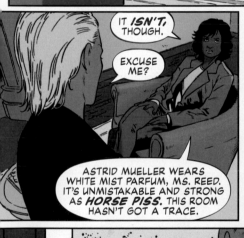

IT *ISN'T*, THOUGH.

EXCUSE ME?

ASTRID MUELLER WEARS WHITE MIST PARFUM, MS. REED. IT'S UNMISTAKABLE AND STRONG AS *HORSE PISS*. THIS ROOM HASN'T GOT A TRACE.

AND THERE ARE TOO MANY *ROOKS* ON THE CHESSBOARD.

IT'S A FAKE.

MAYBE MS. MUELLER'S OPPONENT DOESN'T LIKE TO PLAY FAIR, CHLOE.

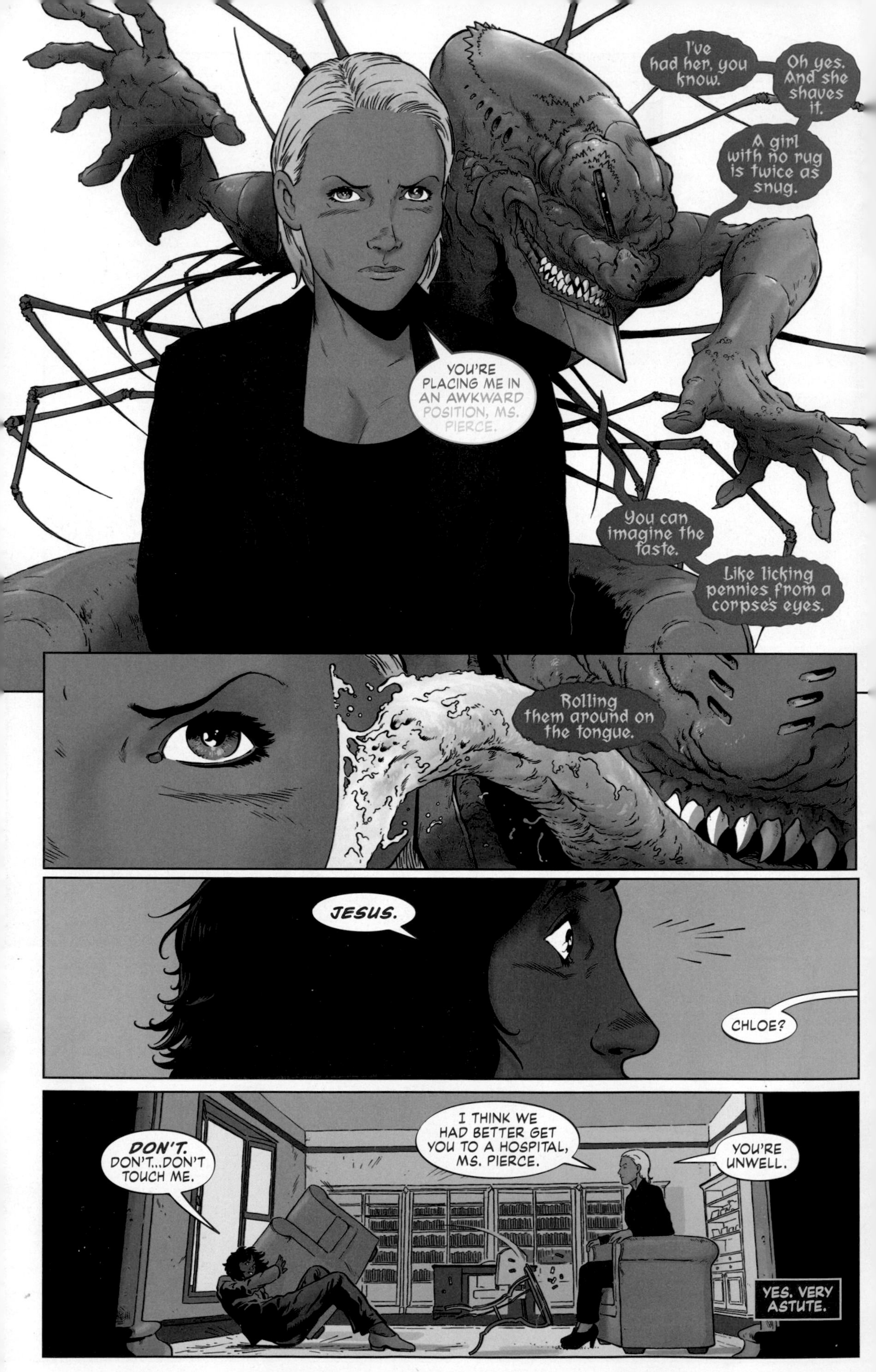
I've had her, you know.
Oh yes. And she shaves it.
A girl with no rug is twice as snug.
YOU'RE PLACING ME IN AN AWKWARD POSITION, MS. PIERCE.
You can imagine the taste.
Like licking pennies from a corpse's eyes.
Rolling them around on the tongue.
JESUS.
CHLOE?
DON'T. DON'T...DON'T TOUCH ME.
I THINK WE HAD BETTER GET YOU TO A HOSPITAL, MS. PIERCE.
YOU'RE UNWELL.
YES. VERY ASTUTE.

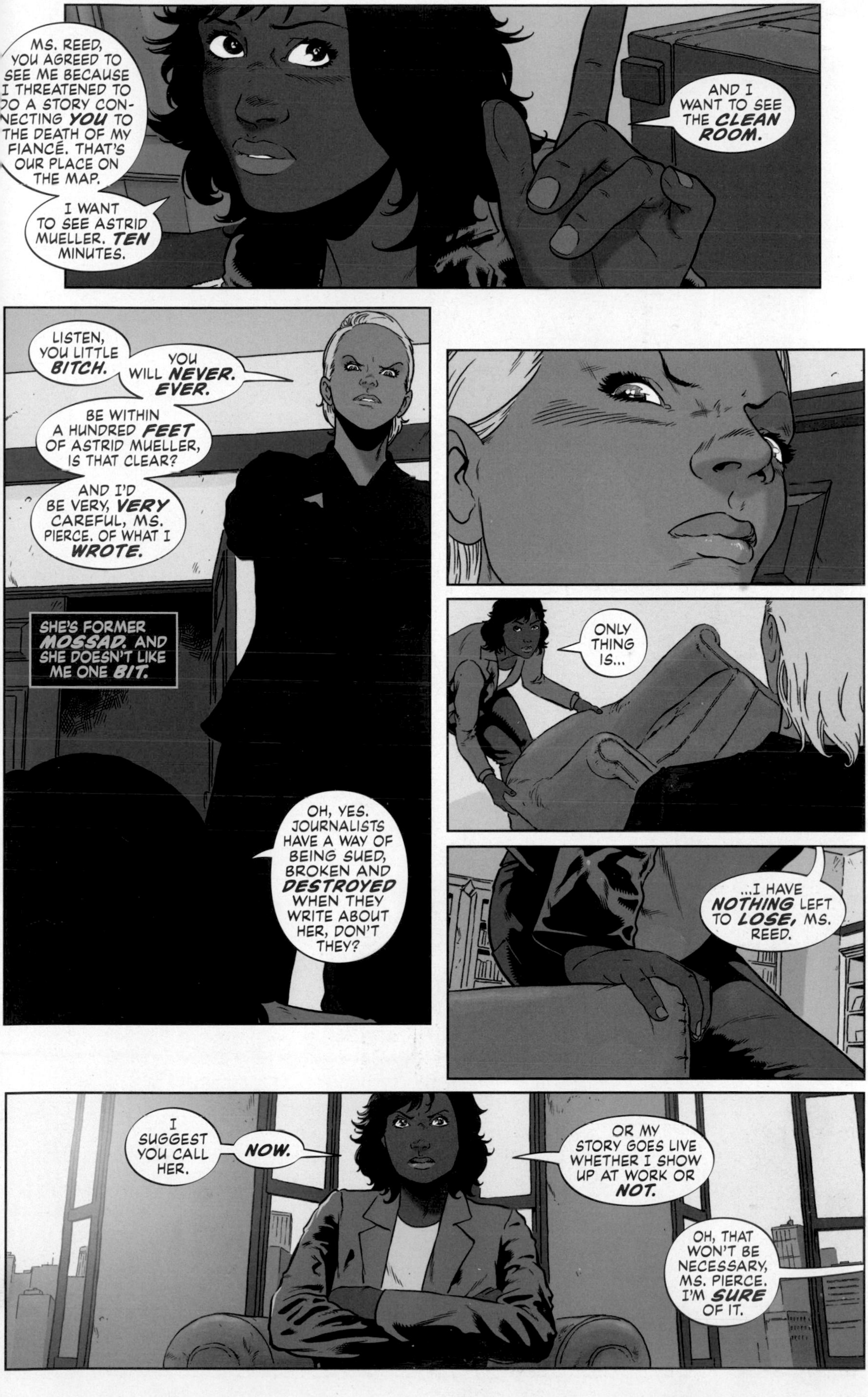
MS. REED, YOU AGREED TO SEE ME BECAUSE I THREATENED TO DO A STORY CONNECTING YOU TO THE DEATH OF MY FIANCÉ. THAT'S OUR PLACE ON THE MAP.
I WANT TO SEE ASTRID MUELLER. TEN MINUTES.
AND I WANT TO SEE THE CLEAN ROOM.
LISTEN, YOU LITTLE BITCH.
YOU WILL NEVER. EVER.
BE WITHIN A HUNDRED FEET OF ASTRID MUELLER, IS THAT CLEAR?
AND I'D BE VERY, VERY CAREFUL, MS. PIERCE. OF WHAT I WROTE.
SHE'S FORMER MOSSAD. AND SHE DOESN'T LIKE ME ONE BIT.
OH, YES. JOURNALISTS HAVE A WAY OF BEING SUED, BROKEN AND DESTROYED WHEN THEY WRITE ABOUT HER, DON'T THEY?
ONLY THING IS...
...I HAVE NOTHING LEFT TO LOSE, MS. REED.
I SUGGEST YOU CALL HER.
NOW.
OR MY STORY GOES LIVE WHETHER I SHOW UP AT WORK OR NOT.
OH, THAT WON'T BE NECESSARY, MS. PIERCE. I'M SURE OF IT.

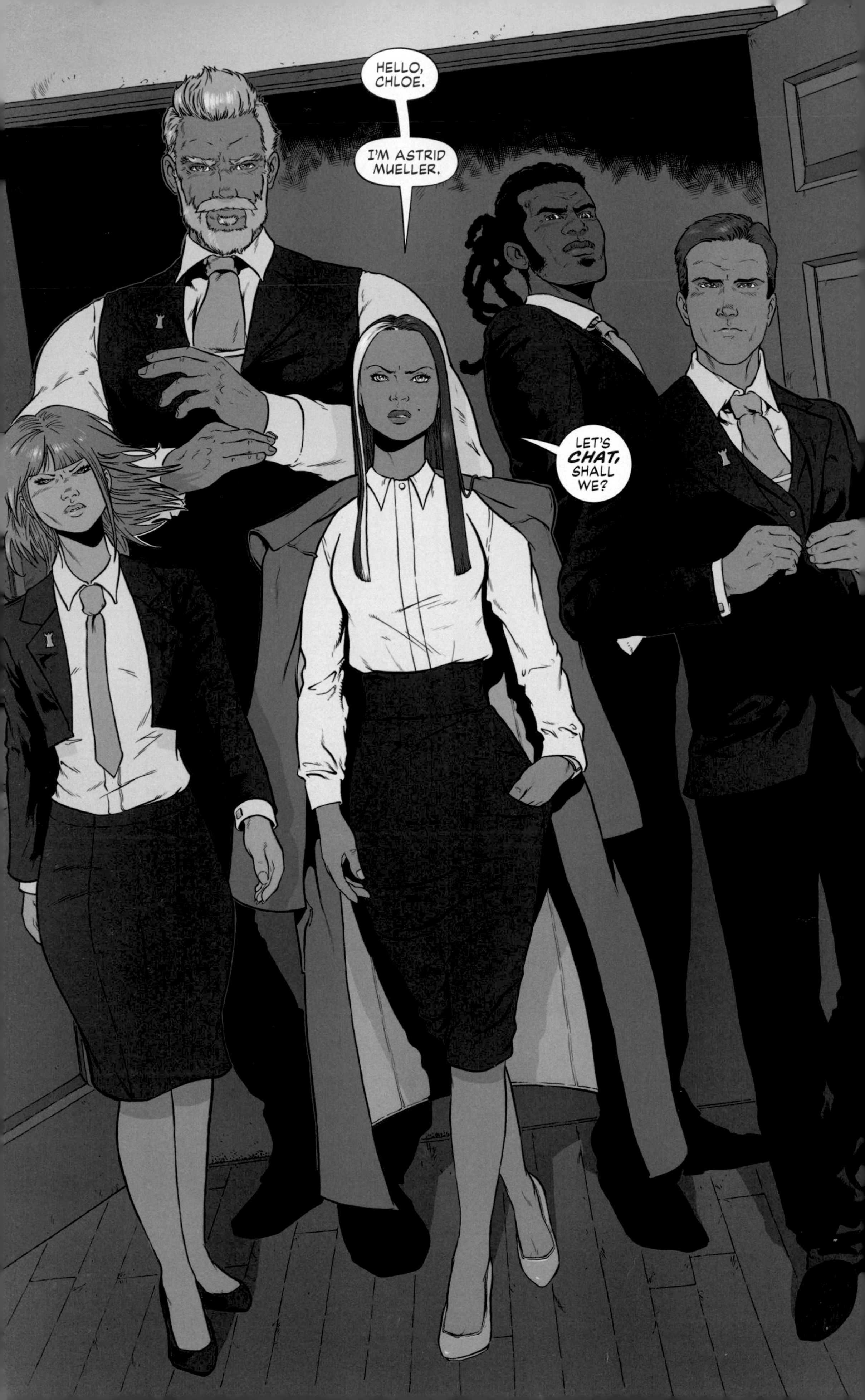
HELLO, CHLOE.
I'M ASTRID MUELLER.
LET'S CHAT, SHALL WE?

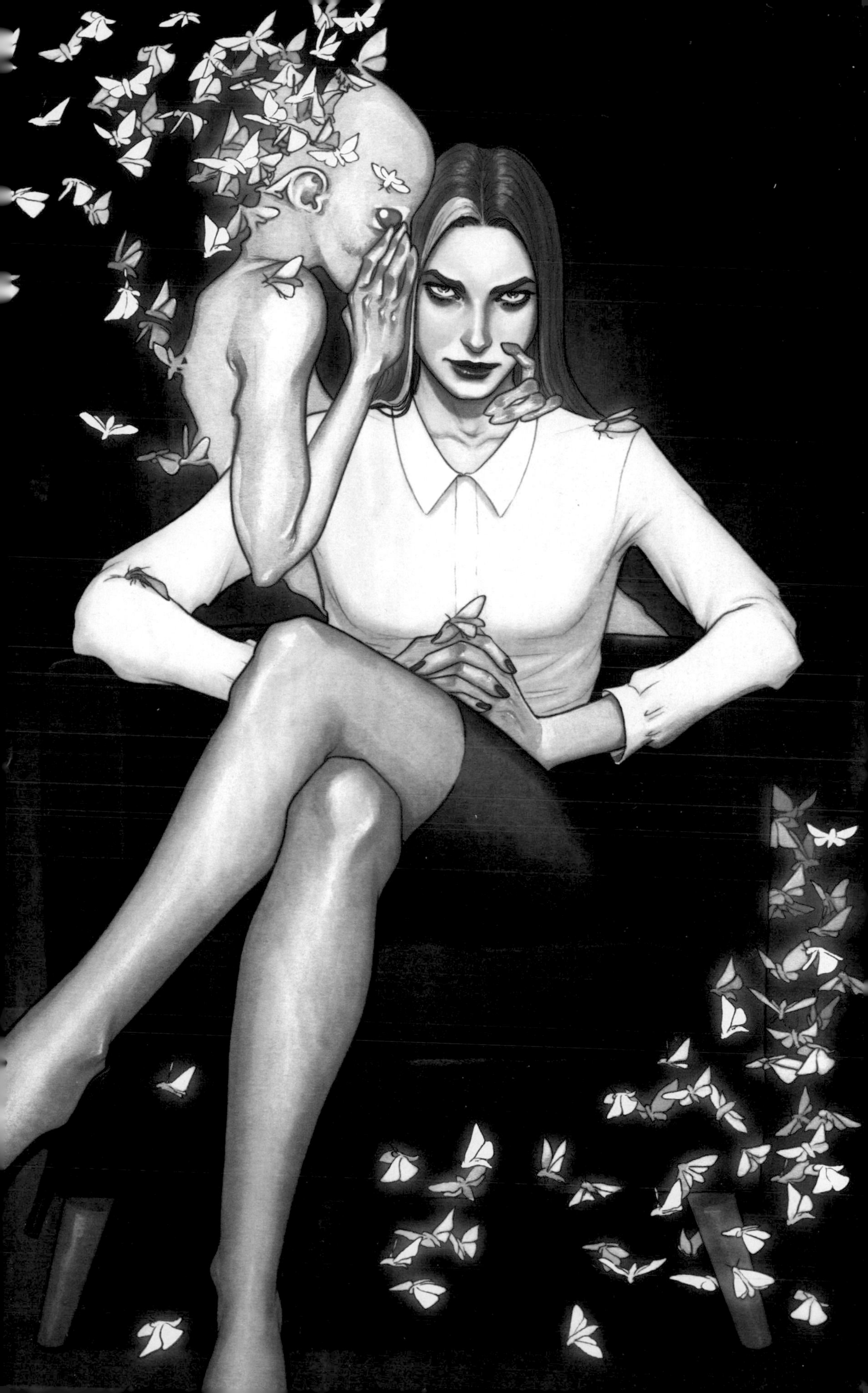

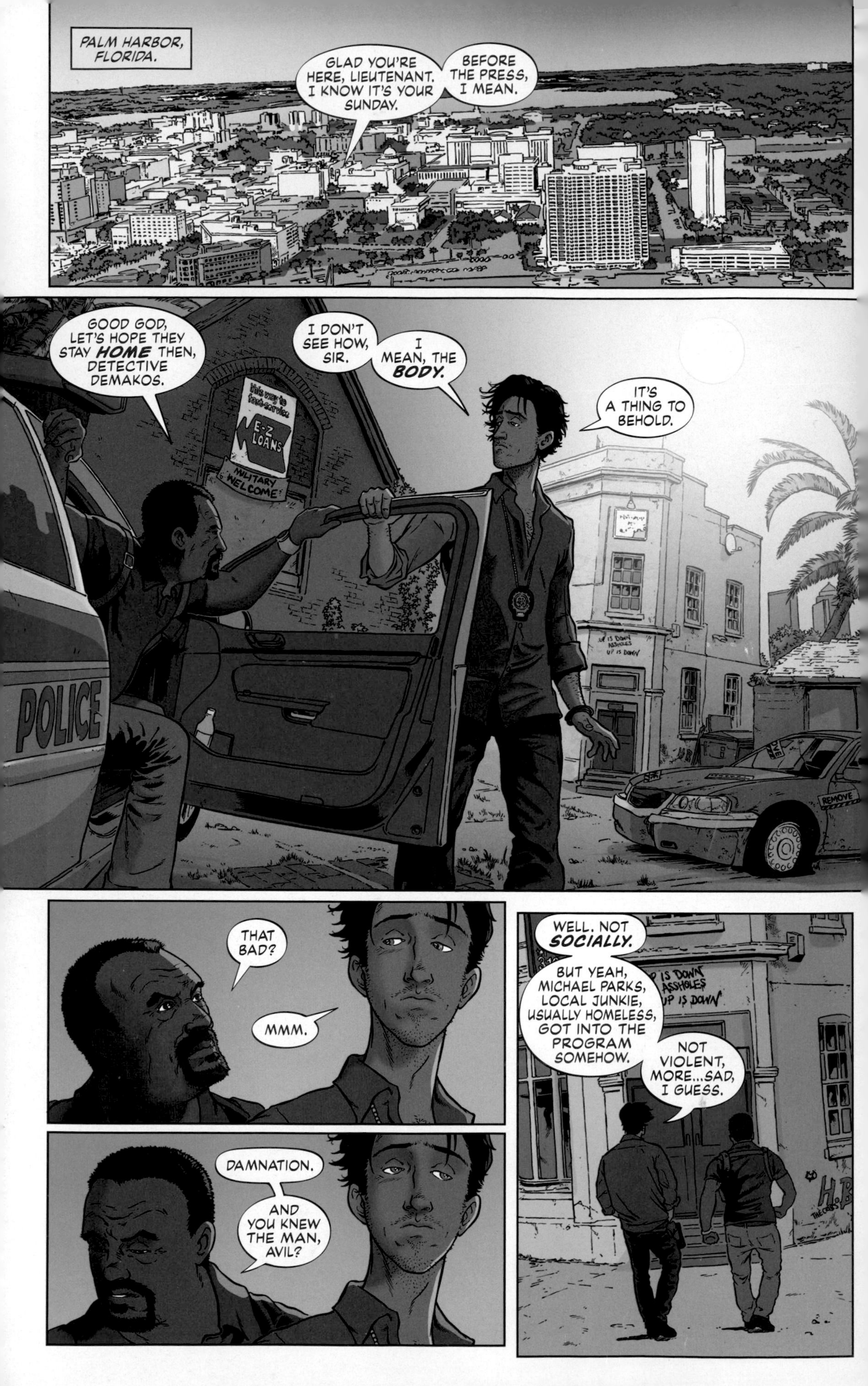
PALM HARBOR, FLORIDA.
GLAD YOU'RE HERE, LIEUTENANT. I KNOW IT'S YOUR SUNDAY.
BEFORE THE PRESS, I MEAN.
GOOD GOD, LET'S HOPE THEY STAY HOME THEN, DETECTIVE DEMAKOS.
I DON'T SEE HOW, SIR.
I MEAN, THE BODY.
IT'S A THING TO BEHOLD.
E-Z LOANS
MILITARY WELCOME
POLICE
REMOVE
THAT BAD?
MMM.
DAMNATION.
AND YOU KNEW THE MAN, AVIL?
WELL. NOT SOCIALLY.
BUT YEAH, MICHAEL PARKS, LOCAL JUNKIE, USUALLY HOMELESS, GOT INTO THE PROGRAM SOMEHOW.
NOT VIOLENT, MORE...SAD, I GUESS.
IS DOWN ASSHOLES UP IS DOWN

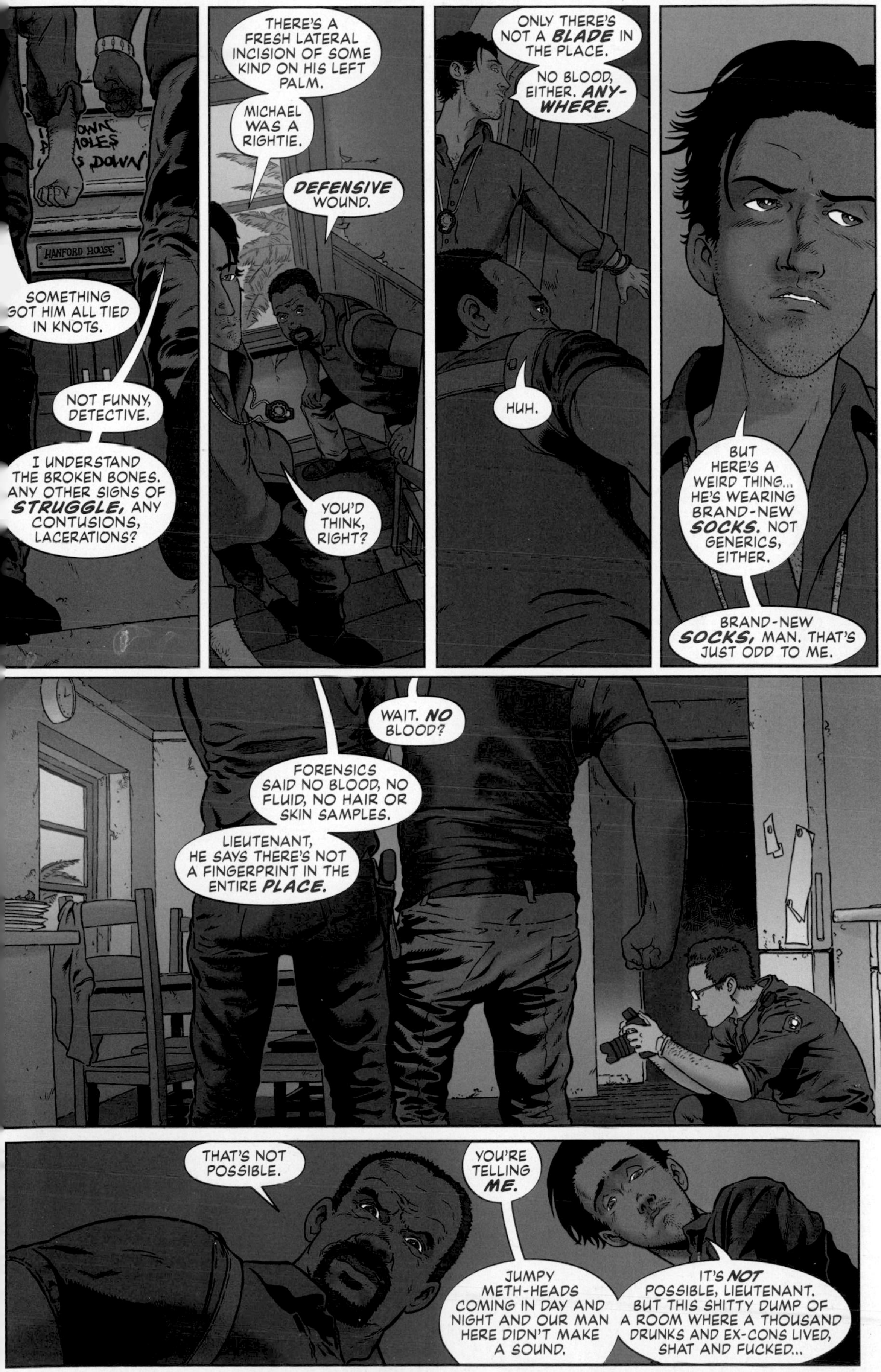

SOMETHING GOT HIM ALL TIED IN KNOTS.
NOT FUNNY, DETECTIVE.
I UNDERSTAND THE BROKEN BONES. ANY OTHER SIGNS OF STRUGGLE, ANY CONTUSIONS, LACERATIONS?
HANFORD HOUSE
THERE'S A FRESH LATERAL INCISION OF SOME KIND ON HIS LEFT PALM.
MICHAEL WAS A RIGHTIE.
DEFENSIVE WOUND.
YOU'D THINK, RIGHT?
ONLY THERE'S NOT A BLADE IN THE PLACE.
NO BLOOD, EITHER. ANY-WHERE.
HUH.
BUT HERE'S A WEIRD THING... HE'S WEARING BRAND-NEW SOCKS. NOT GENERICS, EITHER.
BRAND-NEW SOCKS, MAN. THAT'S JUST ODD TO ME.
WAIT. NO BLOOD?
FORENSICS SAID NO BLOOD, NO FLUID, NO HAIR OR SKIN SAMPLES.
LIEUTENANT, HE SAYS THERE'S NOT A FINGERPRINT IN THE ENTIRE PLACE.
THAT'S NOT POSSIBLE.
YOU'RE TELLING ME.
JUMPY METH-HEADS COMING IN DAY AND NIGHT AND OUR MAN HERE DIDN'T MAKE A SOUND.
IT'S NOT POSSIBLE, LIEUTENANT. BUT THIS SHITTY DUMP OF A ROOM WHERE A THOUSAND DRUNKS AND EX-CONS LIVED, SHAT AND FUCKED...

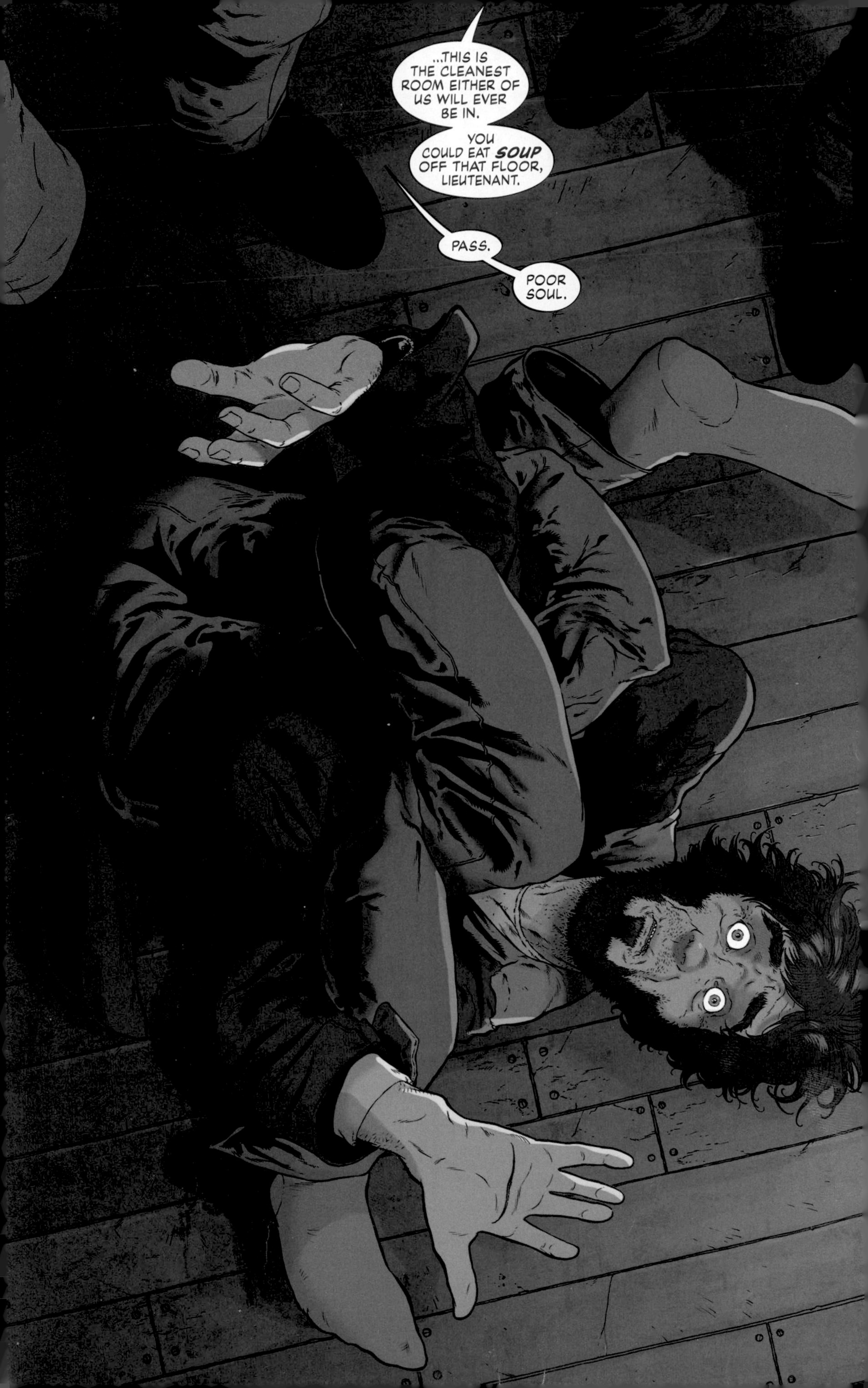
...THIS IS THE CLEANEST ROOM EITHER OF US WILL EVER BE IN.
YOU COULD EAT **SOUP** OFF THAT FLOOR, LIEUTENANT.
PASS.
POOR SOUL.

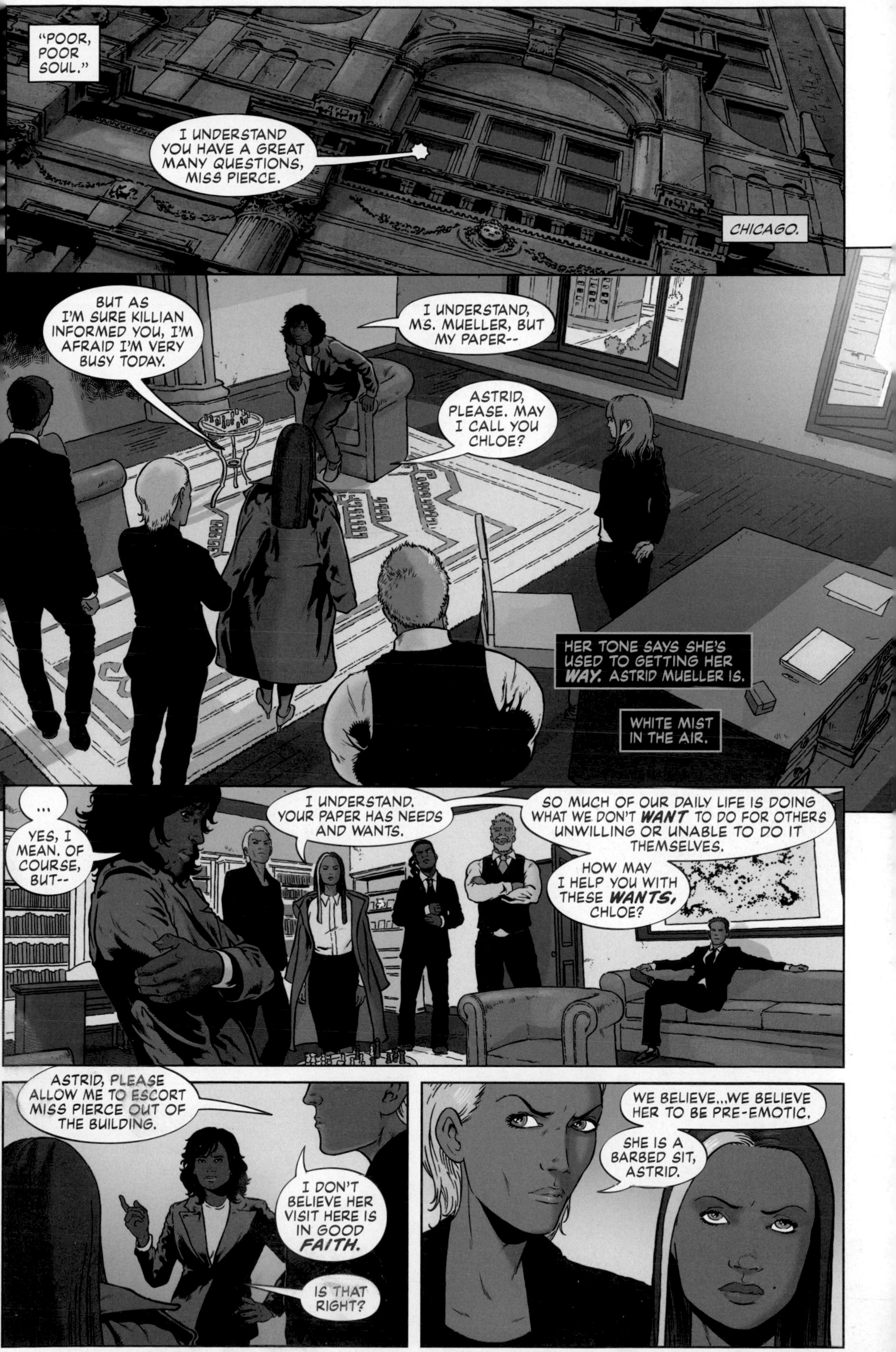
"POOR, POOR SOUL."
I UNDERSTAND YOU HAVE A GREAT MANY QUESTIONS, MISS PIERCE.
CHICAGO.
BUT AS I'M SURE KILLIAN INFORMED YOU, I'M AFRAID I'M VERY BUSY TODAY.
I UNDERSTAND, MS. MUELLER, BUT MY PAPER--
ASTRID, PLEASE. MAY I CALL YOU CHLOE?
HER TONE SAYS SHE'S USED TO GETTING HER WAY. ASTRID MUELLER IS.
WHITE MIST IN THE AIR.
...
YES, I MEAN. OF COURSE, BUT--
I UNDERSTAND. YOUR PAPER HAS NEEDS AND WANTS.
SO MUCH OF OUR DAILY LIFE IS DOING WHAT WE DON'T WANT TO DO FOR OTHERS UNWILLING OR UNABLE TO DO IT THEMSELVES.
HOW MAY I HELP YOU WITH THESE WANTS, CHLOE?
ASTRID, PLEASE ALLOW ME TO ESCORT MISS PIERCE OUT OF THE BUILDING.
I DON'T BELIEVE HER VISIT HERE IS IN GOOD FAITH.
IS THAT RIGHT?
WE BELIEVE...WE BELIEVE HER TO BE PRE-EMOTIC.
SHE IS A BARBED SIT, ASTRID.

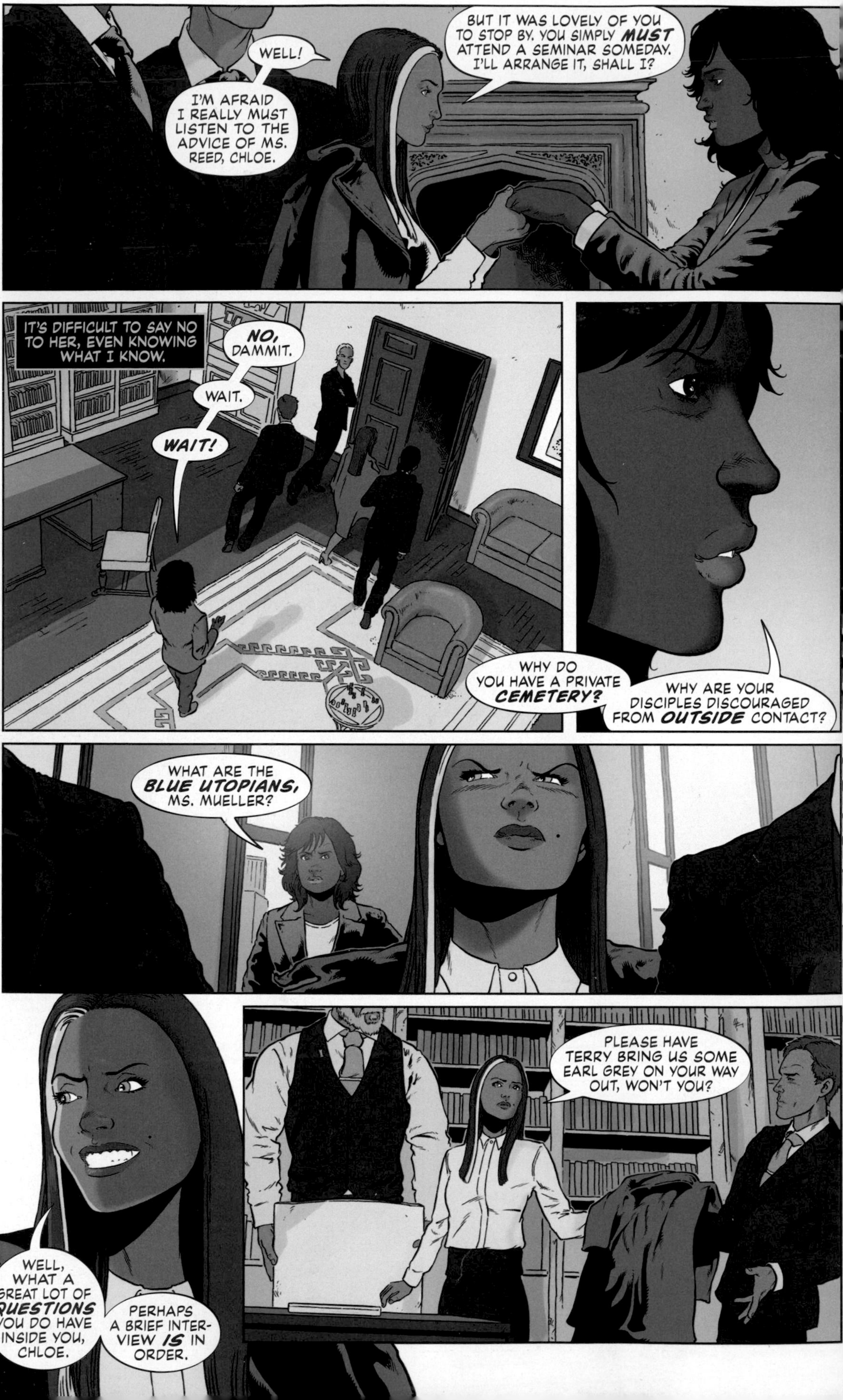
WELL!
I'M AFRAID I REALLY MUST LISTEN TO THE ADVICE OF MS. REED, CHLOE.
BUT IT WAS LOVELY OF YOU TO STOP BY. YOU SIMPLY MUST ATTEND A SEMINAR SOMEDAY. I'LL ARRANGE IT, SHALL I?
IT'S DIFFICULT TO SAY NO TO HER, EVEN KNOWING WHAT I KNOW.
NO, DAMMIT.
WAIT.
WAIT!
WHY DO YOU HAVE A PRIVATE CEMETERY?
WHY ARE YOUR DISCIPLES DISCOURAGED FROM OUTSIDE CONTACT?
WHAT ARE THE BLUE UTOPIANS, MS. MUELLER?
PLEASE HAVE TERRY BRING US SOME EARL GREY ON YOUR WAY OUT, WON'T YOU?
WELL, WHAT A GREAT LOT OF QUESTIONS YOU DO HAVE INSIDE YOU, CHLOE.
PERHAPS A BRIEF INTERVIEW IS IN ORDER.

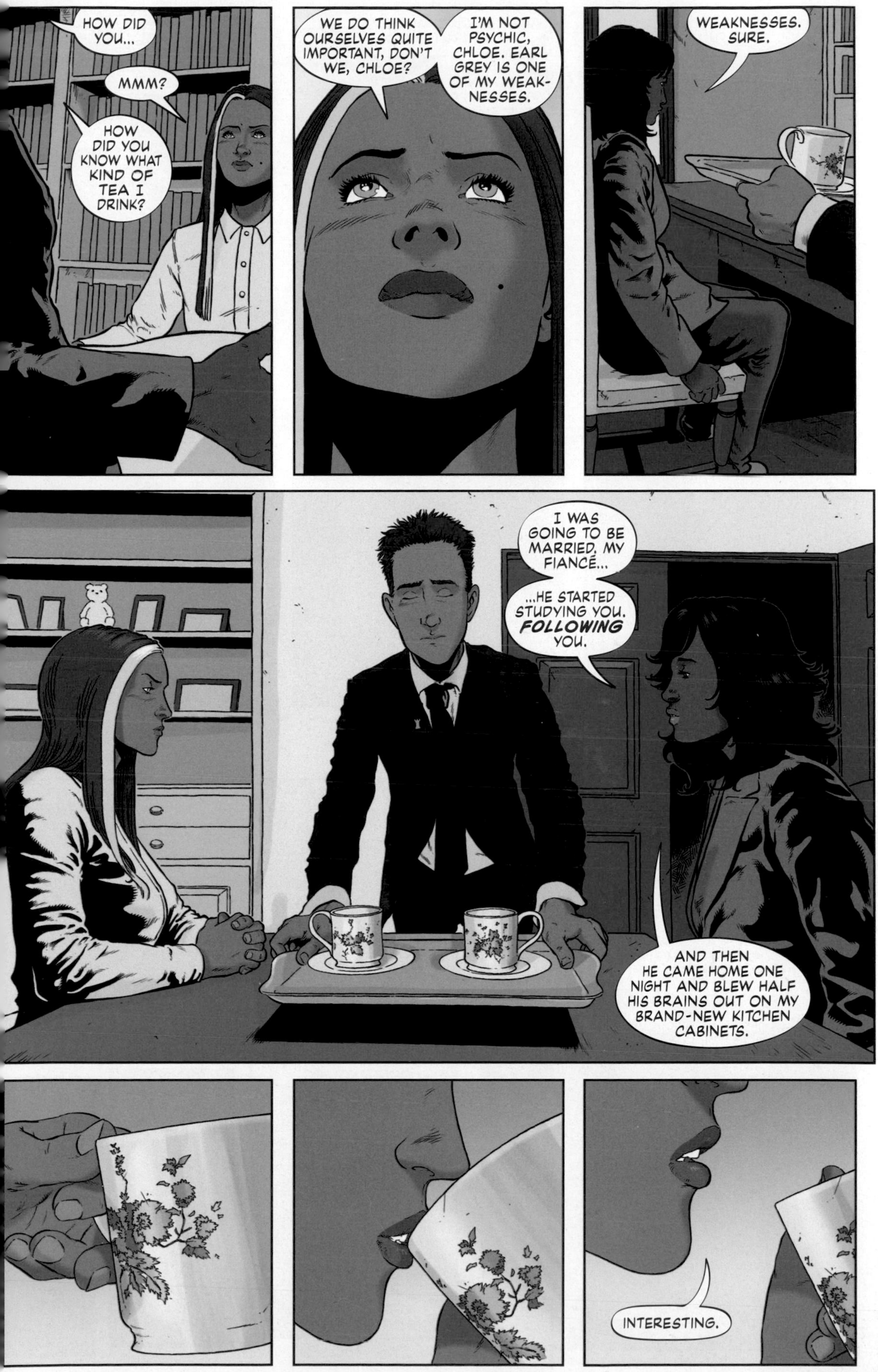
HOW DID YOU...
MMM?
HOW DID YOU KNOW WHAT KIND OF TEA I DRINK?
WE DO THINK OURSELVES QUITE IMPORTANT, DON'T WE, CHLOE?
I'M NOT PSYCHIC, CHLOE. EARL GREY IS ONE OF MY WEAK-NESSES.
WEAKNESSES. SURE.
I WAS GOING TO BE MARRIED. MY FIANCÉ...
...HE STARTED STUDYING YOU. FOLLOWING YOU.
AND THEN HE CAME HOME ONE NIGHT AND BLEW HALF HIS BRAINS OUT ON MY BRAND-NEW KITCHEN CABINETS.
INTERESTING.

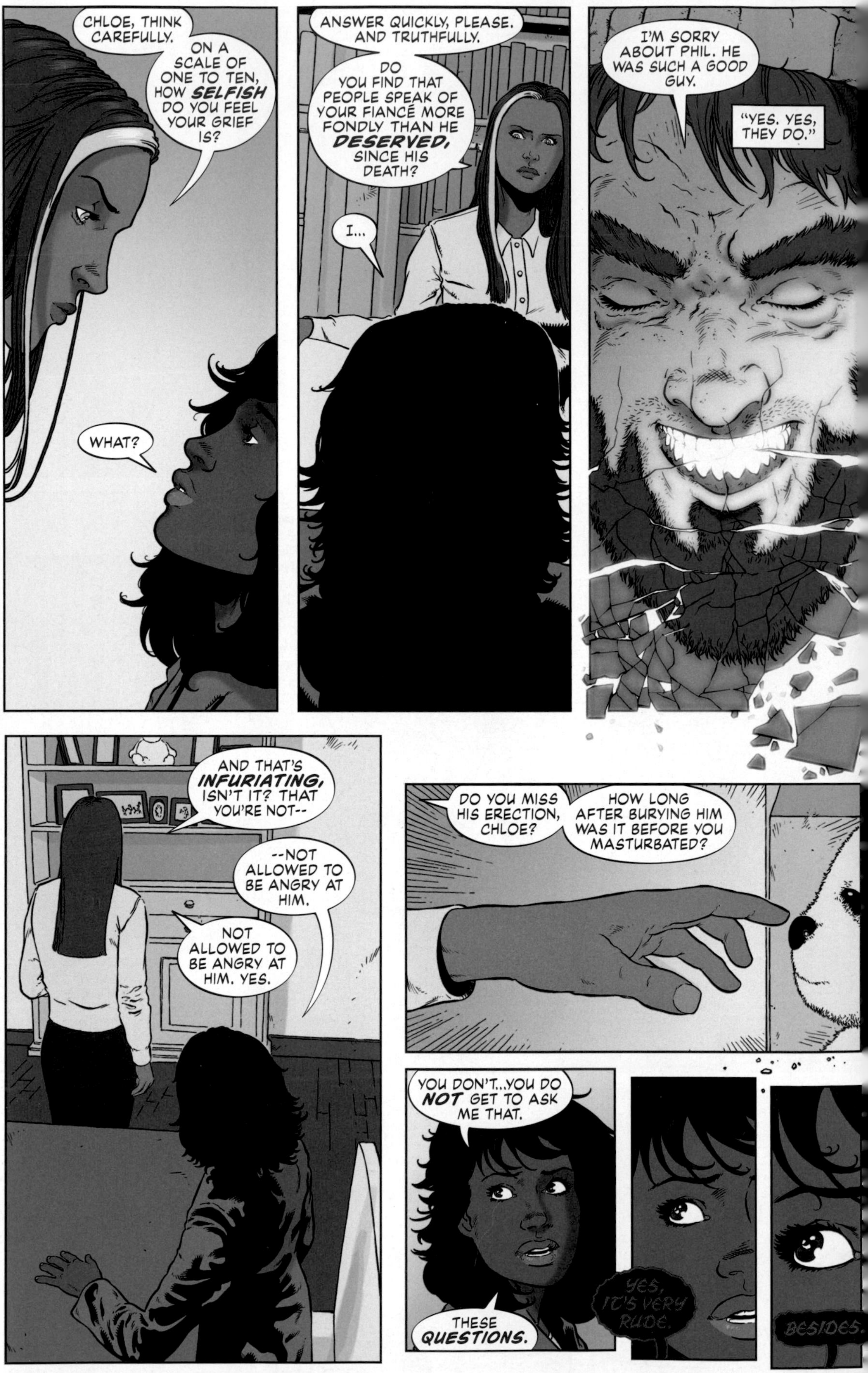
CHLOE, THINK CAREFULLY.
ON A SCALE OF ONE TO TEN, HOW *SELFISH* DO YOU FEEL YOUR GRIEF IS?
WHAT?
ANSWER QUICKLY, PLEASE. AND TRUTHFULLY.
DO YOU FIND THAT PEOPLE SPEAK OF YOUR FIANCÉ MORE FONDLY THAN HE *DESERVED,* SINCE HIS DEATH?
I...
I'M SORRY ABOUT PHIL. HE WAS SUCH A GOOD GUY.
"YES. YES, THEY DO."
AND THAT'S *INFURIATING,* ISN'T IT? THAT YOU'RE NOT--
--NOT ALLOWED TO BE ANGRY AT HIM.
NOT ALLOWED TO BE ANGRY AT HIM. YES.
DO YOU MISS HIS ERECTION, CHLOE?
HOW LONG AFTER BURYING HIM WAS IT BEFORE YOU MASTURBATED?
YOU DON'T...YOU DO *NOT* GET TO ASK ME THAT.
THESE *QUESTIONS.*
YES, IT'S VERY RUDE.
BESIDES.

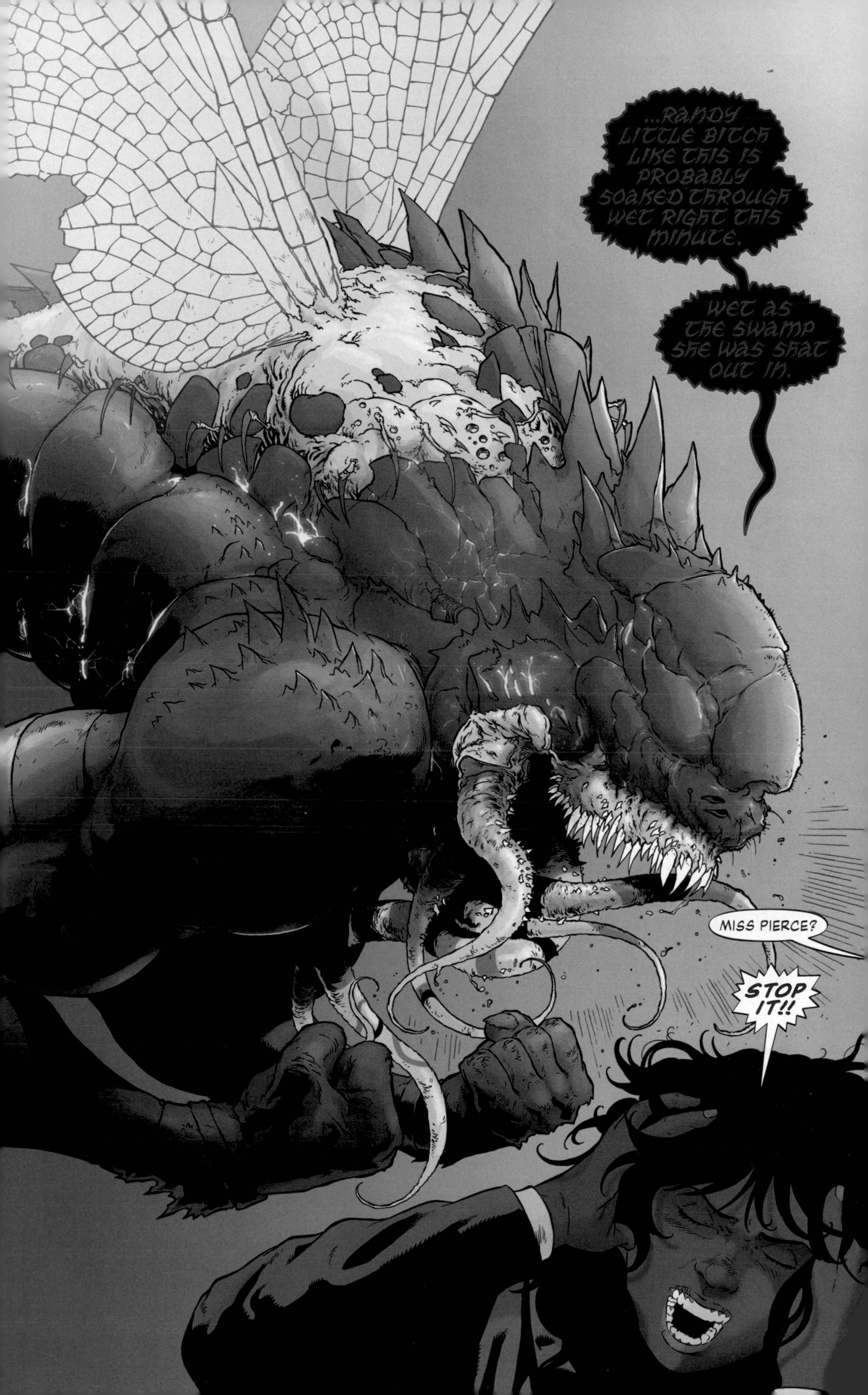
...RANDY LITTLE BITCH LIKE THIS IS PROBABLY SOAKED THROUGH WET RIGHT THIS MINUTE.
WET AS THE SWAMP SHE WAS SHAT OUT IN.
MISS PIERCE?
STOP IT!!

YOU SAW SOMETHING, CHLOE. WHAT DID YOU *SEE?*

...

NOTHING.

I DIDN'T SEE *ANYTHING.*

SHE'S LOOKING AT ME.

NEVER WANTED TO HIDE SO MUCH IN MY LIFE.

FAIRY PIECES.

EXCUSE ME?

FAIRY PIECES, THAT'S WHAT THE EXTRA *ROOKS* ON MY CHESSBOARD ARE, MISS PIERCE.

FOR CENTURIES, THERE HAVE BEEN CHESS *ENTHUSIASTS,* LET'S CALL THEM...

...WHO PLAY WITH IRREGULAR PIECES. THERE ARE OVER TWELVE HUNDRED.

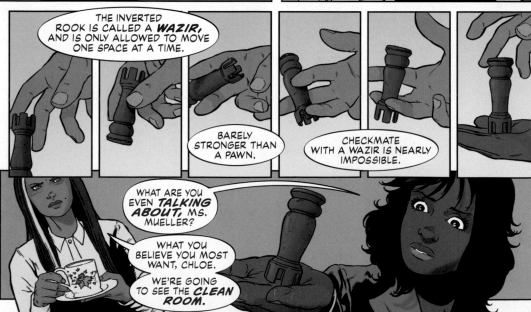

THE INVERTED ROOK IS CALLED A *WAZIR,* AND IS ONLY ALLOWED TO MOVE ONE SPACE AT A TIME.

BARELY STRONGER THAN A PAWN.

CHECKMATE WITH A WAZIR IS NEARLY IMPOSSIBLE.

WHAT ARE YOU EVEN *TALKING ABOUT,* MS. MUELLER?

WHAT YOU BELIEVE YOU MOST WANT, CHLOE.

WE'RE GOING TO SEE THE *CLEAN ROOM.*

THIS IS YOUR *LAST* CHANCE TO GO HOME UN-CHANGED, MISS PIERCE.

HOME?

MY HOME IS A *GRAVE* THAT HASN'T HAD THE DIRT TOSSED BACK IN YET.

I'M FINE.

LET'S DO THIS.

AND THEN I'M TAKEN TO A ROOM ALL TOO SIMILAR TO THE HOSPITALS WHERE I WENT DURING MY RECOVERY.

THE ELEVATOR HAD NO FLOOR MARKINGS.

I'VE NEVER HAD TO PEE SO BADLY IN MY LIFE.

IT FEELS A LITTLE LIKE REBELLION TO NOT DO IT IN FRONT OF THESE TWO.

MY HAIR IS WASHED AND BLOWN DRY.

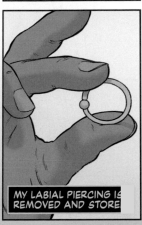

MY LABIAL PIERCING IS REMOVED AND STORE

I AM ALLOWED TO WASH WITH A POWERFUL SOAP THAT SMELLS OF VINEGAR.

SOAP

ISOPROPYL ALCOHOL IS USED ON MY FINGERNAILS AND CUTICLES.

YOU ARE NOT TO *SPEAK,* MISS PIERCE, IS THAT CLEAR?

REGARDLESS OF WHAT YOU SEE.

FINE.

THERE MIGHT BE ANOTHER REASON.

THAT I CAN'T SPEAK BECAUSE I'M *TERRIFIED.*

WHAT...

...WHAT ARE YOU TRYING TO KEEP OUT, MISS MUELLER?

MM? KEEP *OUT*?

NOTHING.

NOTHING AT ALL.

SHALL WE?

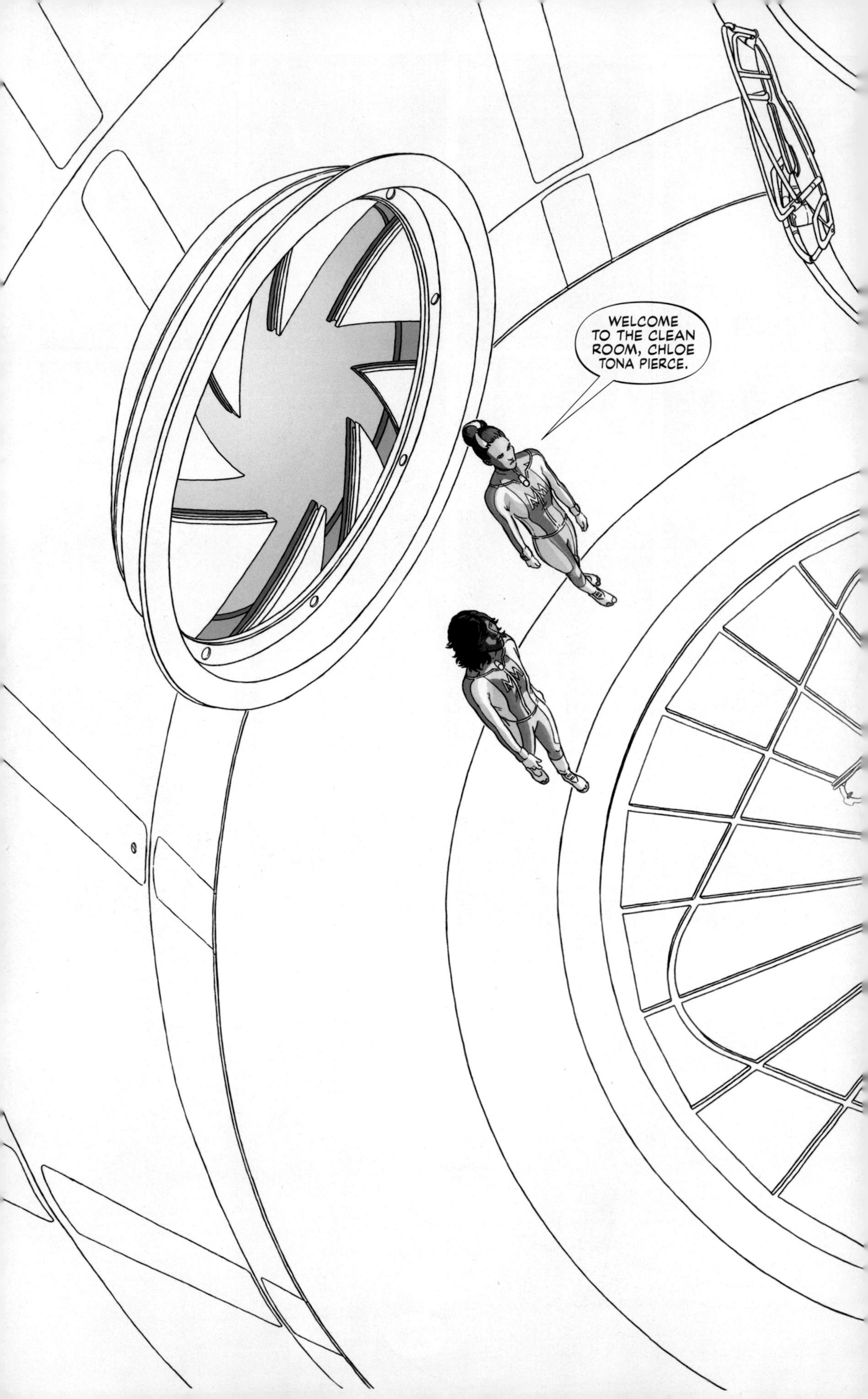
WELCOME TO THE CLEAN ROOM, CHLOE TONA PIERCE.

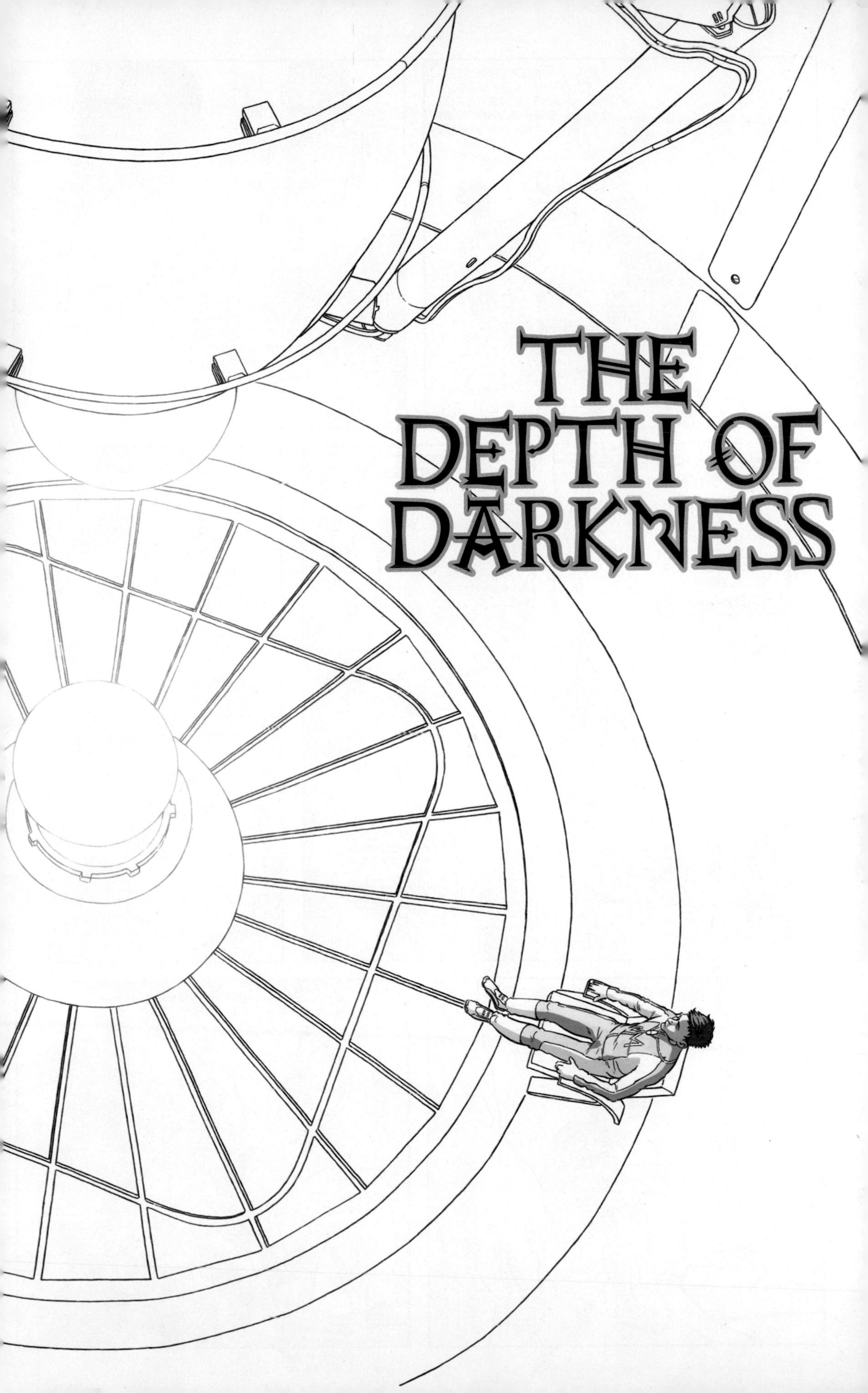
THE DEPTH OF DARKNESS

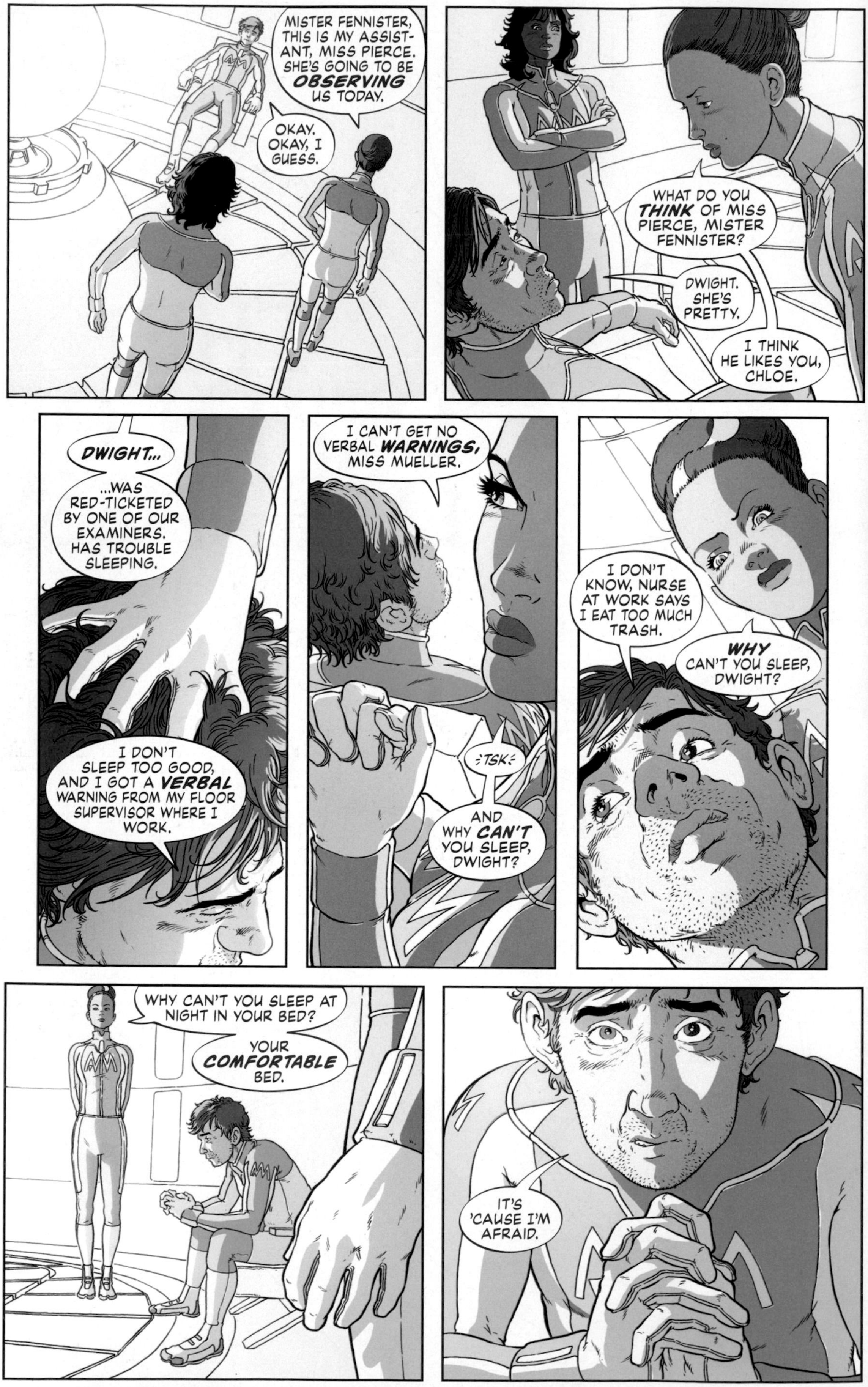
MISTER FENNISTER, THIS IS MY ASSISTANT, MISS PIERCE. SHE'S GOING TO BE **OBSERVING** US TODAY.
OKAY. OKAY, I GUESS.
WHAT DO YOU **THINK** OF MISS PIERCE, MISTER FENNISTER?
DWIGHT. SHE'S PRETTY.
I THINK HE LIKES YOU, CHLOE.
DWIGHT...
...WAS RED-TICKETED BY ONE OF OUR EXAMINERS. HAS TROUBLE SLEEPING.
I DON'T SLEEP TOO GOOD, AND I GOT A **VERBAL** WARNING FROM MY FLOOR SUPERVISOR WHERE I WORK.
I CAN'T GET NO VERBAL **WARNINGS,** MISS MUELLER.
TSK
AND WHY **CAN'T** YOU SLEEP, DWIGHT?
I DON'T KNOW, NURSE AT WORK SAYS I EAT TOO MUCH TRASH.
WHY CAN'T YOU SLEEP, DWIGHT?
WHY CAN'T YOU SLEEP AT NIGHT IN YOUR BED?
YOUR **COMFORTABLE** BED.
IT'S 'CAUSE I'M AFRAID.

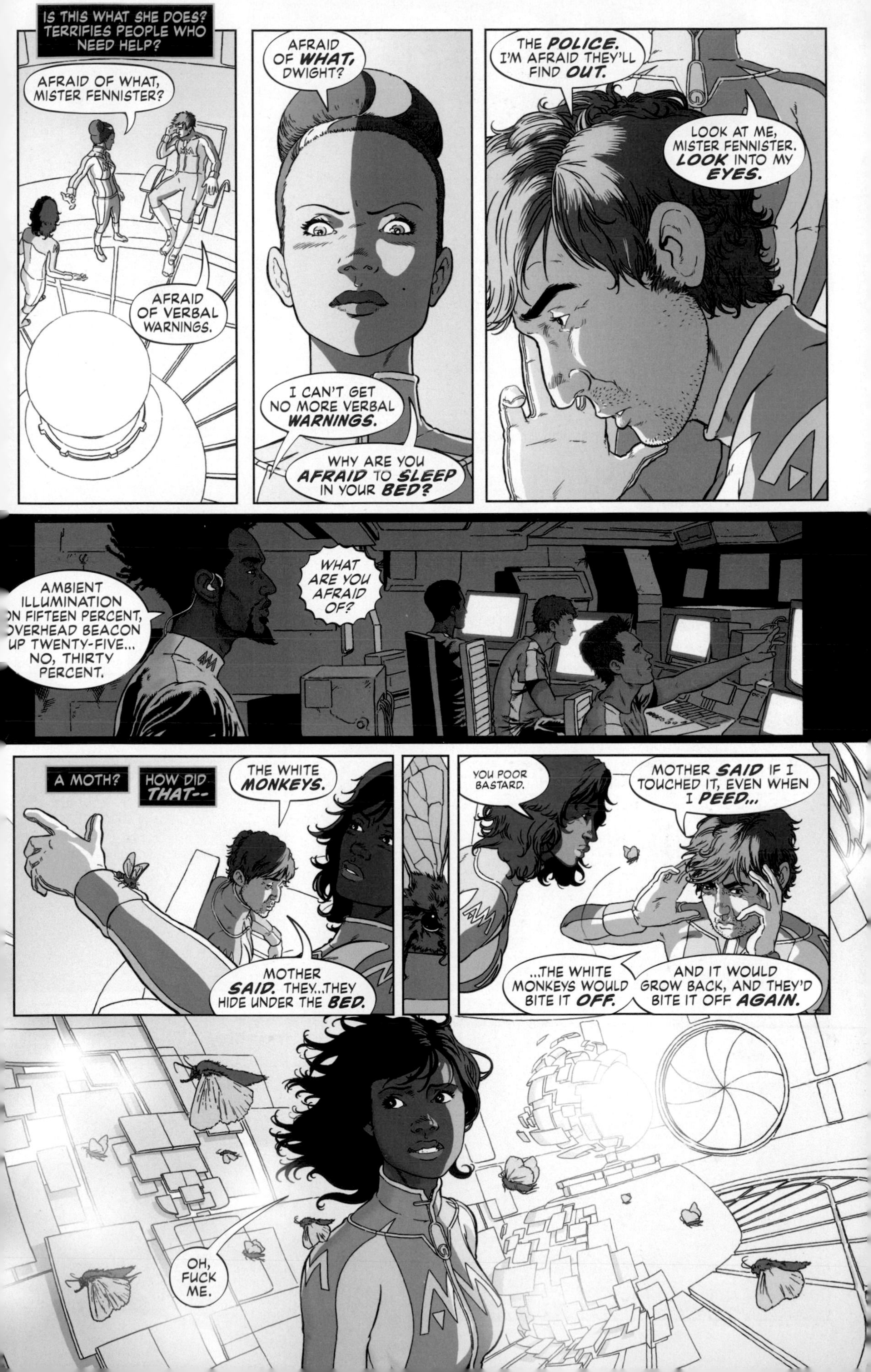
IS THIS WHAT SHE DOES? TERRIFIES PEOPLE WHO NEED HELP?
AFRAID OF WHAT, MISTER FENNISTER?
AFRAID OF VERBAL WARNINGS.
AFRAID OF WHAT, DWIGHT?
I CAN'T GET NO MORE VERBAL WARNINGS.
WHY ARE YOU AFRAID TO SLEEP IN YOUR BED?
THE POLICE. I'M AFRAID THEY'LL FIND OUT.
LOOK AT ME, MISTER FENNISTER. LOOK INTO MY EYES.
AMBIENT ILLUMINATION ON FIFTEEN PERCENT, OVERHEAD BEACON UP TWENTY-FIVE... NO, THIRTY PERCENT.
WHAT ARE YOU AFRAID OF?
A MOTH?
HOW DID THAT--
THE WHITE MONKEYS.
MOTHER SAID. THEY...THEY HIDE UNDER THE BED.
YOU POOR BASTARD.
MOTHER SAID IF I TOUCHED IT, EVEN WHEN I PEED...
...THE WHITE MONKEYS WOULD BITE IT OFF.
AND IT WOULD GROW BACK, AND THEY'D BITE IT OFF AGAIN.
OH, FUCK ME.

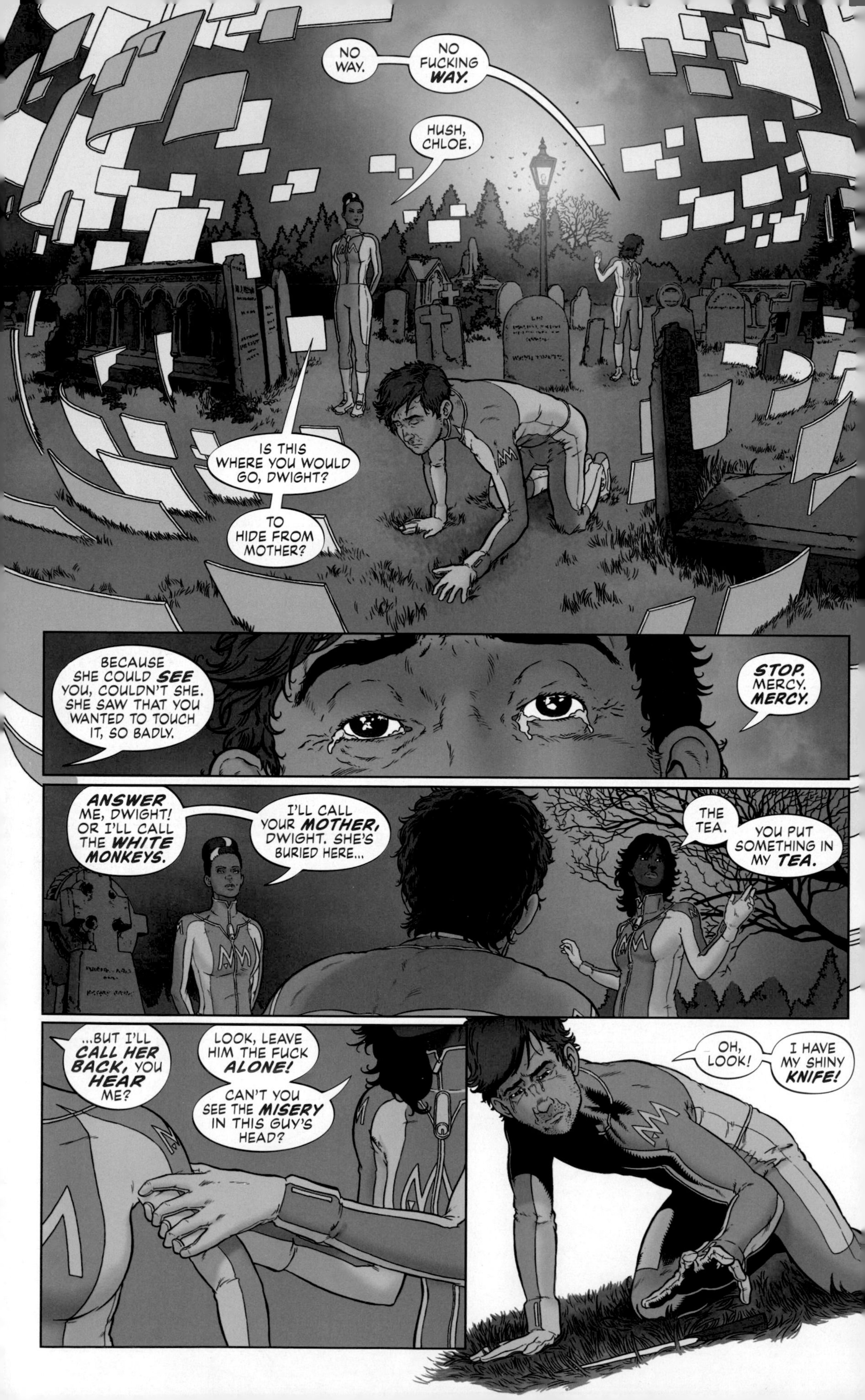
NO WAY.
NO FUCKING **WAY.**
HUSH, CHLOE.
IS THIS WHERE YOU WOULD GO, DWIGHT?
TO HIDE FROM MOTHER?
BECAUSE SHE COULD **SEE** YOU, COULDN'T SHE. SHE SAW THAT YOU WANTED TO TOUCH IT, SO BADLY.
STOP. MERCY. **MERCY.**
ANSWER ME, DWIGHT! OR I'LL CALL THE **WHITE MONKEYS.**
I'LL CALL YOUR **MOTHER,** DWIGHT. SHE'S BURIED HERE...
THE TEA.
YOU PUT SOMETHING IN MY **TEA.**
...BUT I'LL **CALL HER BACK,** YOU **HEAR** ME?
LOOK, LEAVE HIM THE FUCK **ALONE!**
CAN'T YOU SEE THE **MISERY** IN THIS GUY'S HEAD?
OH, LOOK!
I HAVE MY SHINY **KNIFE!**

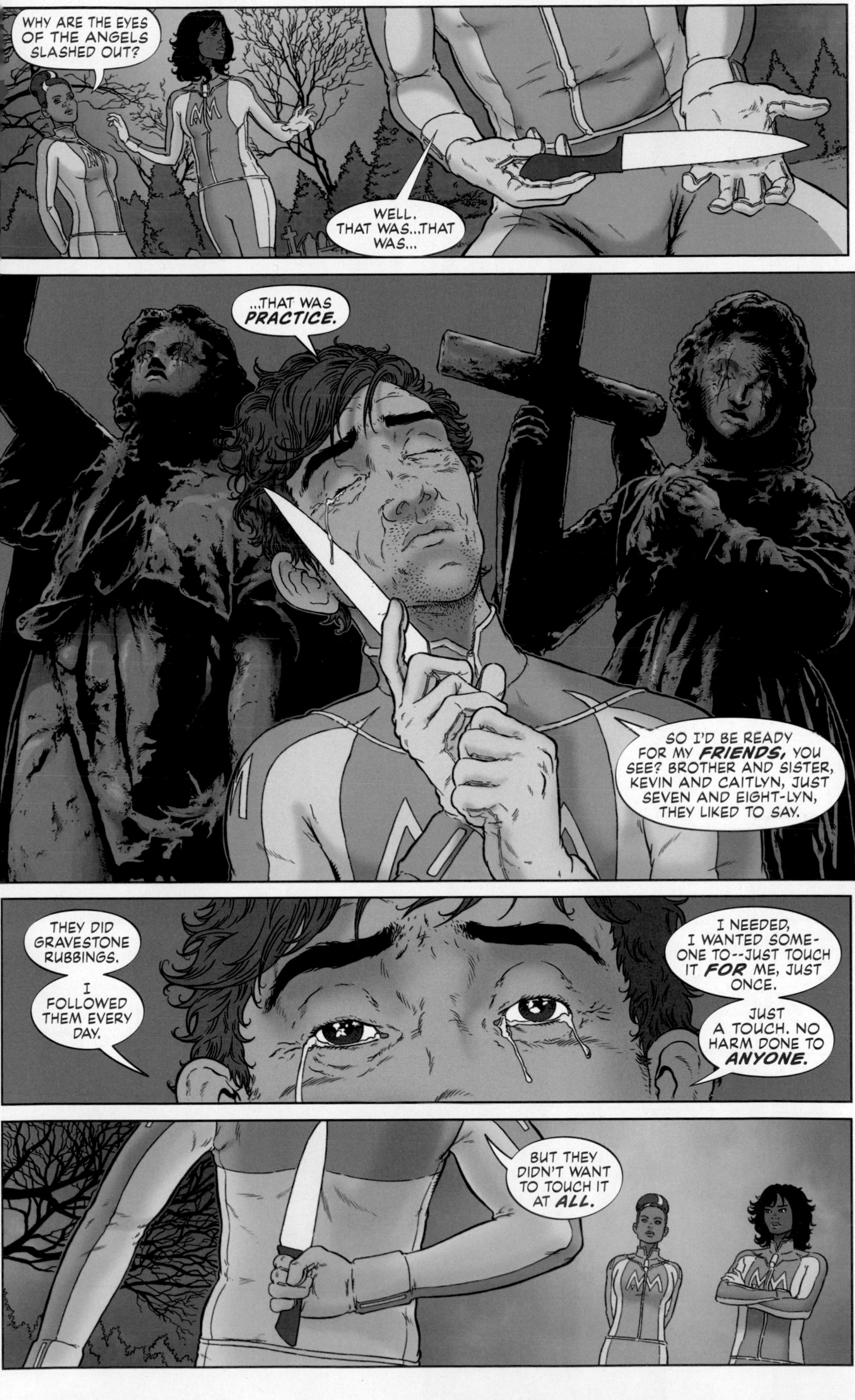
WHY ARE THE EYES OF THE ANGELS SLASHED OUT?
WELL. THAT WAS...THAT WAS...
...THAT WAS *PRACTICE.*
SO I'D BE READY FOR MY *FRIENDS,* YOU SEE? BROTHER AND SISTER, KEVIN AND CAITLYN, JUST SEVEN AND EIGHT-LYN, THEY LIKED TO SAY.
THEY DID GRAVESTONE RUBBINGS.
I FOLLOWED THEM EVERY DAY.
I NEEDED, I WANTED SOME-ONE TO--JUST TOUCH IT *FOR* ME, JUST ONCE.
JUST A TOUCH. NO HARM DONE TO *ANYONE.*
BUT THEY DIDN'T WANT TO TOUCH IT AT *ALL.*

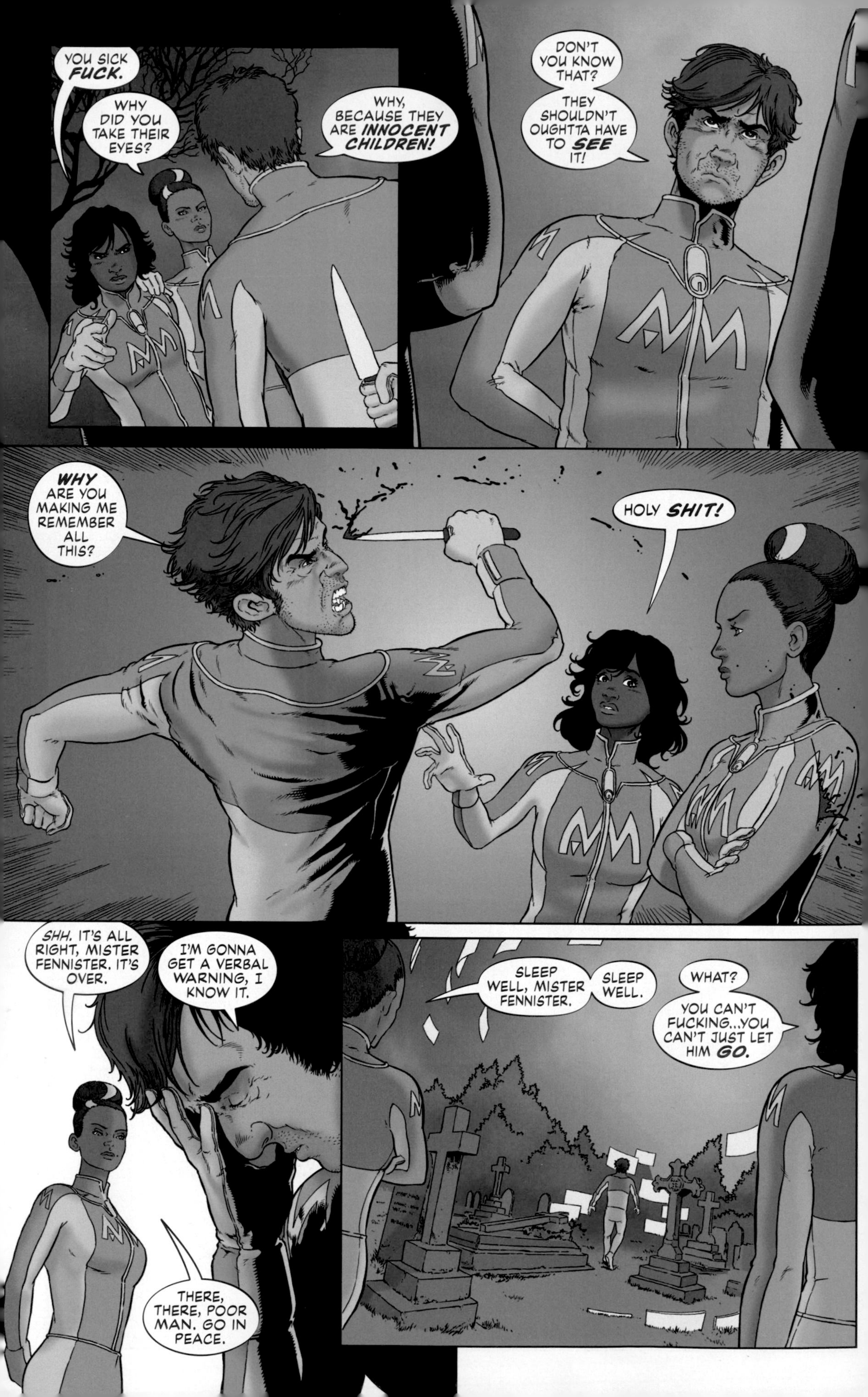
YOU SICK FUCK.
WHY DID YOU TAKE THEIR EYES?
WHY, BECAUSE THEY ARE INNOCENT CHILDREN!
DON'T YOU KNOW THAT?
THEY SHOULDN'T OUGHTTA HAVE TO SEE IT!
WHY ARE YOU MAKING ME REMEMBER ALL THIS?
HOLY SHIT!
SHH. IT'S ALL RIGHT, MISTER FENNISTER. IT'S OVER.
I'M GONNA GET A VERBAL WARNING, I KNOW IT.
THERE, THERE, POOR MAN. GO IN PEACE.
SLEEP WELL, MISTER FENNISTER.
SLEEP WELL.
WHAT?
YOU CAN'T FUCKING...YOU CAN'T JUST LET HIM GO.

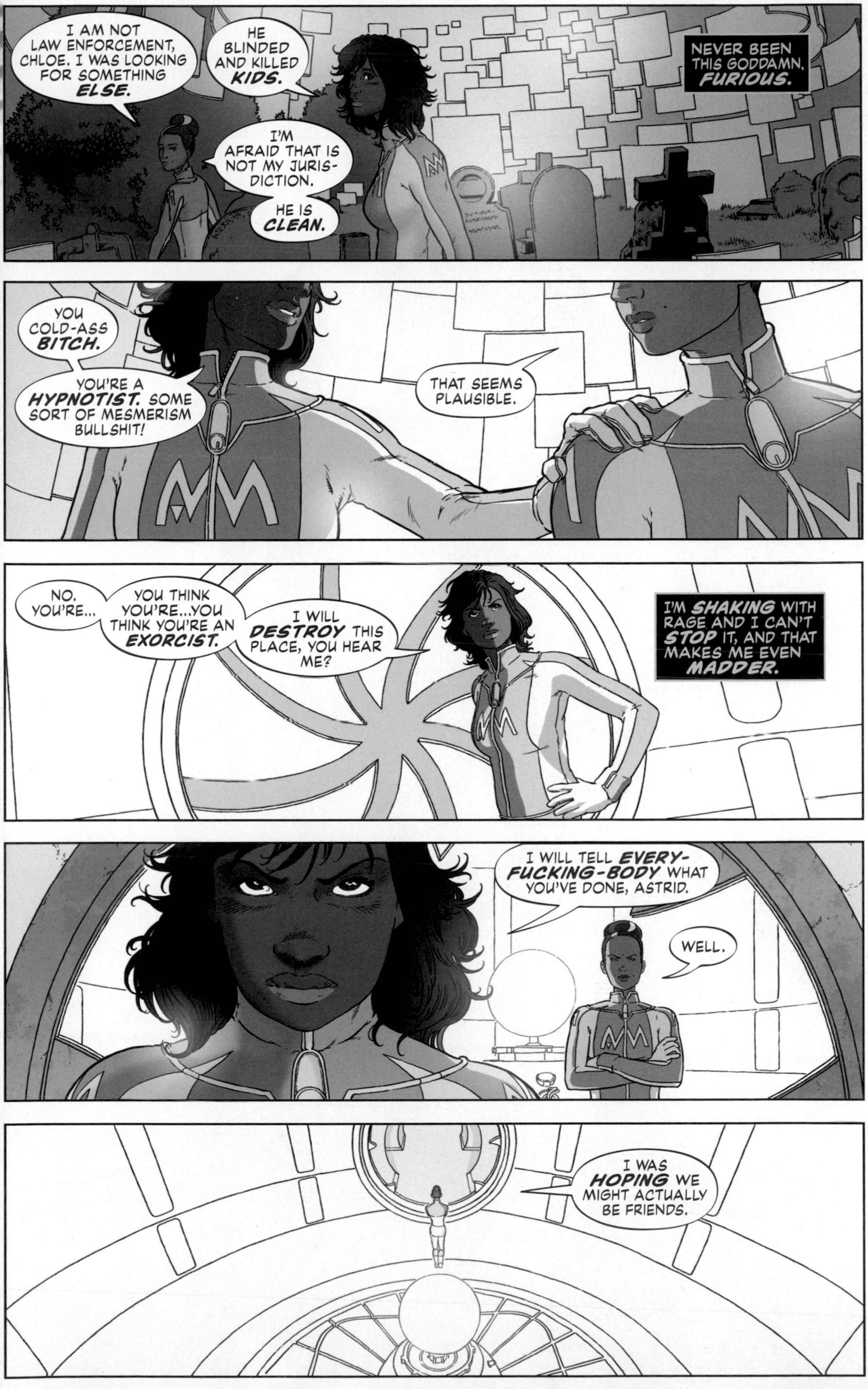
I AM NOT LAW ENFORCEMENT, CHLOE. I WAS LOOKING FOR SOMETHING ELSE.
HE BLINDED AND KILLED KIDS.
I'M AFRAID THAT IS NOT MY JURIS-DICTION.
HE IS CLEAN.
NEVER BEEN THIS GODDAMN. FURIOUS.
YOU COLD-ASS BITCH.
YOU'RE A HYPNOTIST. SOME SORT OF MESMERISM BULLSHIT!
THAT SEEMS PLAUSIBLE.
NO. YOU'RE...
YOU THINK YOU'RE...YOU THINK YOU'RE AN EXORCIST.
I WILL DESTROY THIS PLACE, YOU HEAR ME?
I'M SHAKING WITH RAGE AND I CAN'T STOP IT, AND THAT MAKES ME EVEN MADDER.
I WILL TELL EVERY-FUCKING-BODY WHAT YOU'VE DONE, ASTRID.
WELL.
I WAS HOPING WE MIGHT ACTUALLY BE FRIENDS.

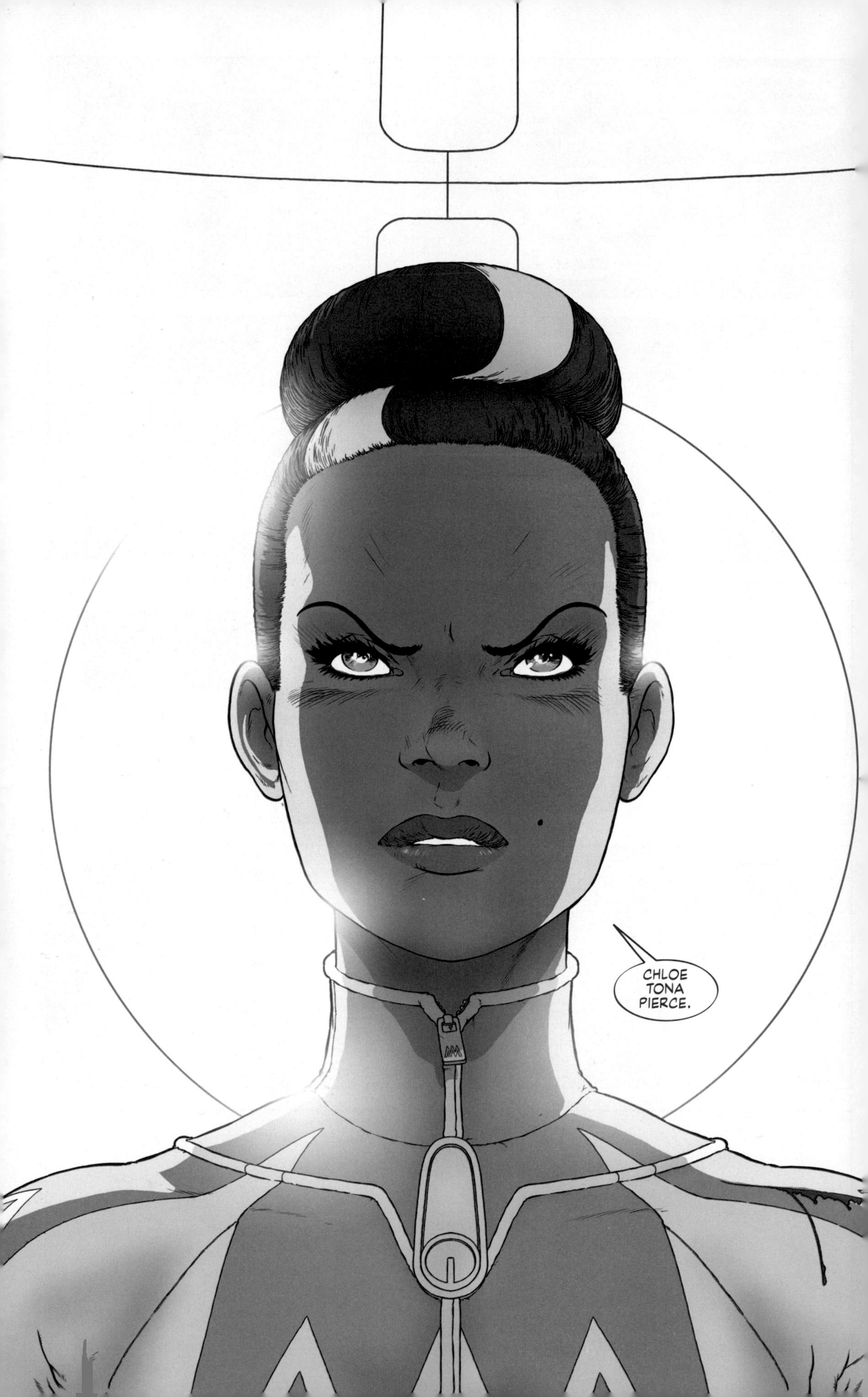
CHLOE TONA PIERCE.

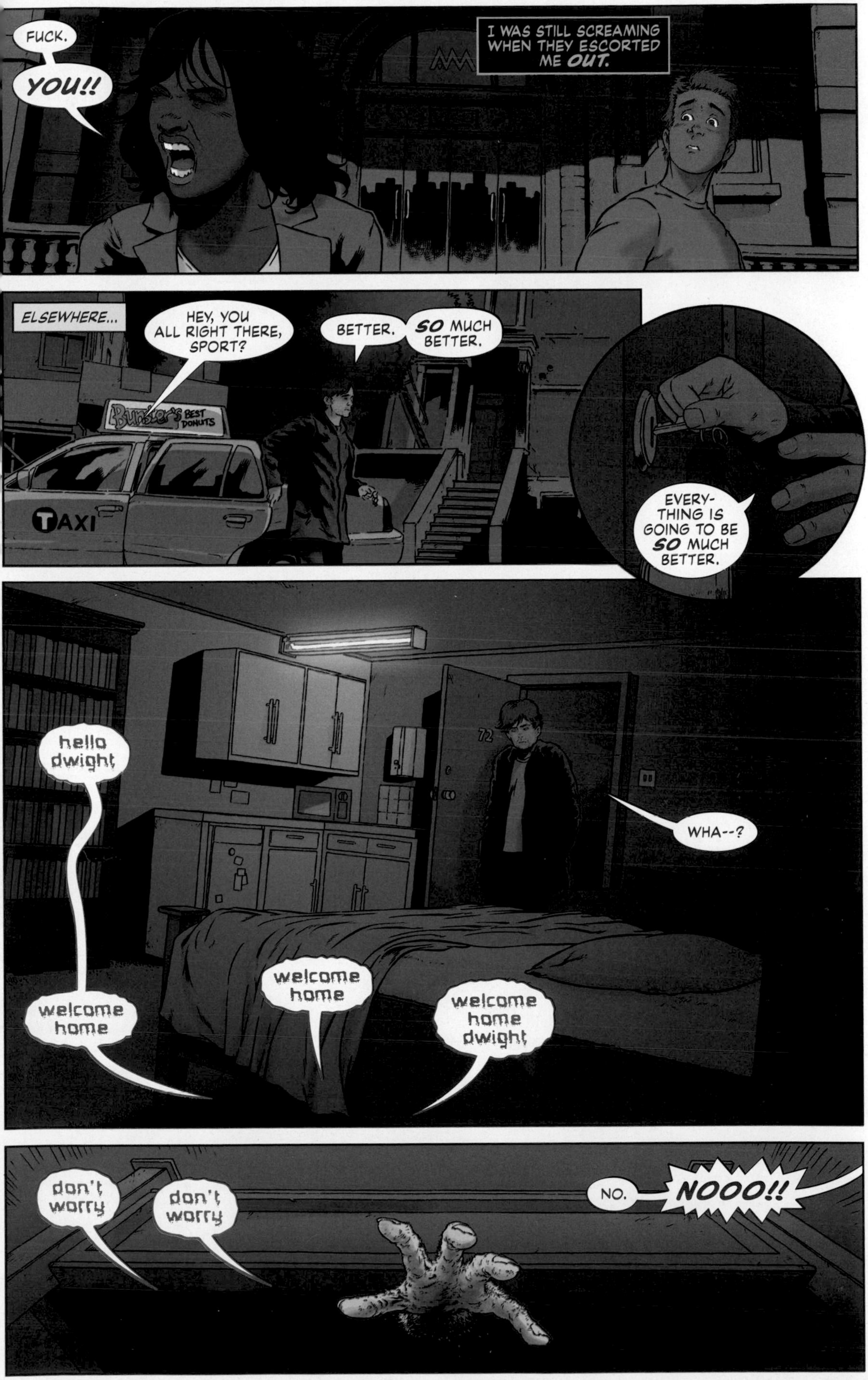
FUCK.
YOU!!
I WAS STILL SCREAMING WHEN THEY ESCORTED ME OUT.
ELSEWHERE...
HEY, YOU ALL RIGHT THERE, SPORT?
BETTER.
SO MUCH BETTER.
Bunser's BEST DONUTS
TAXI
EVERY-THING IS GOING TO BE SO MUCH BETTER.
72
hello dwight
WHA--?
welcome home
welcome home
welcome home dwight
don't worry
don't worry
NO.
NOOO!!

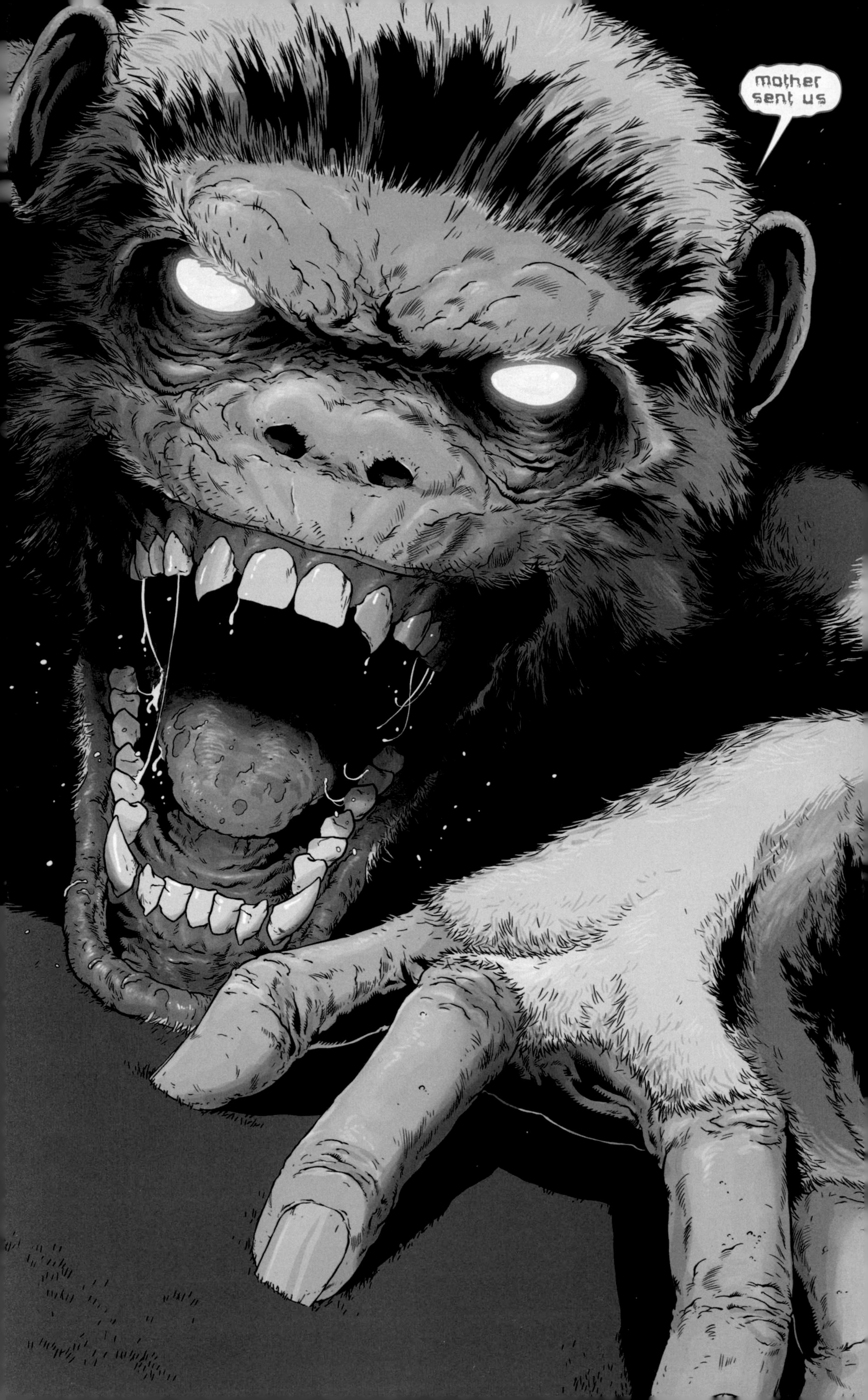
mother sent us

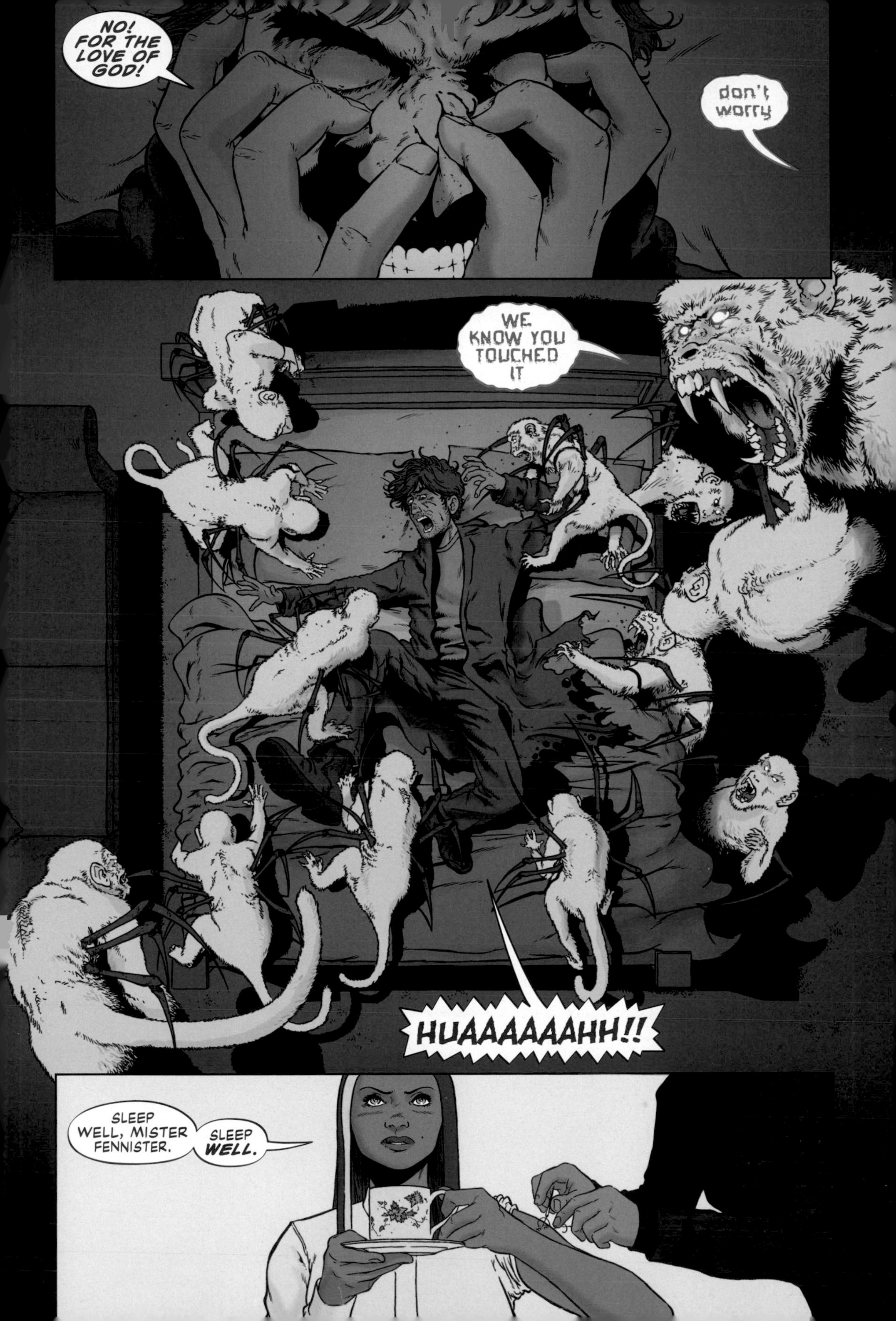
NO! FOR THE LOVE OF GOD!
don't worry
WE KNOW YOU TOUCHED IT
HUAAAAAAAHH!!
SLEEP WELL, MISTER FENNISTER.
SLEEP WELL.

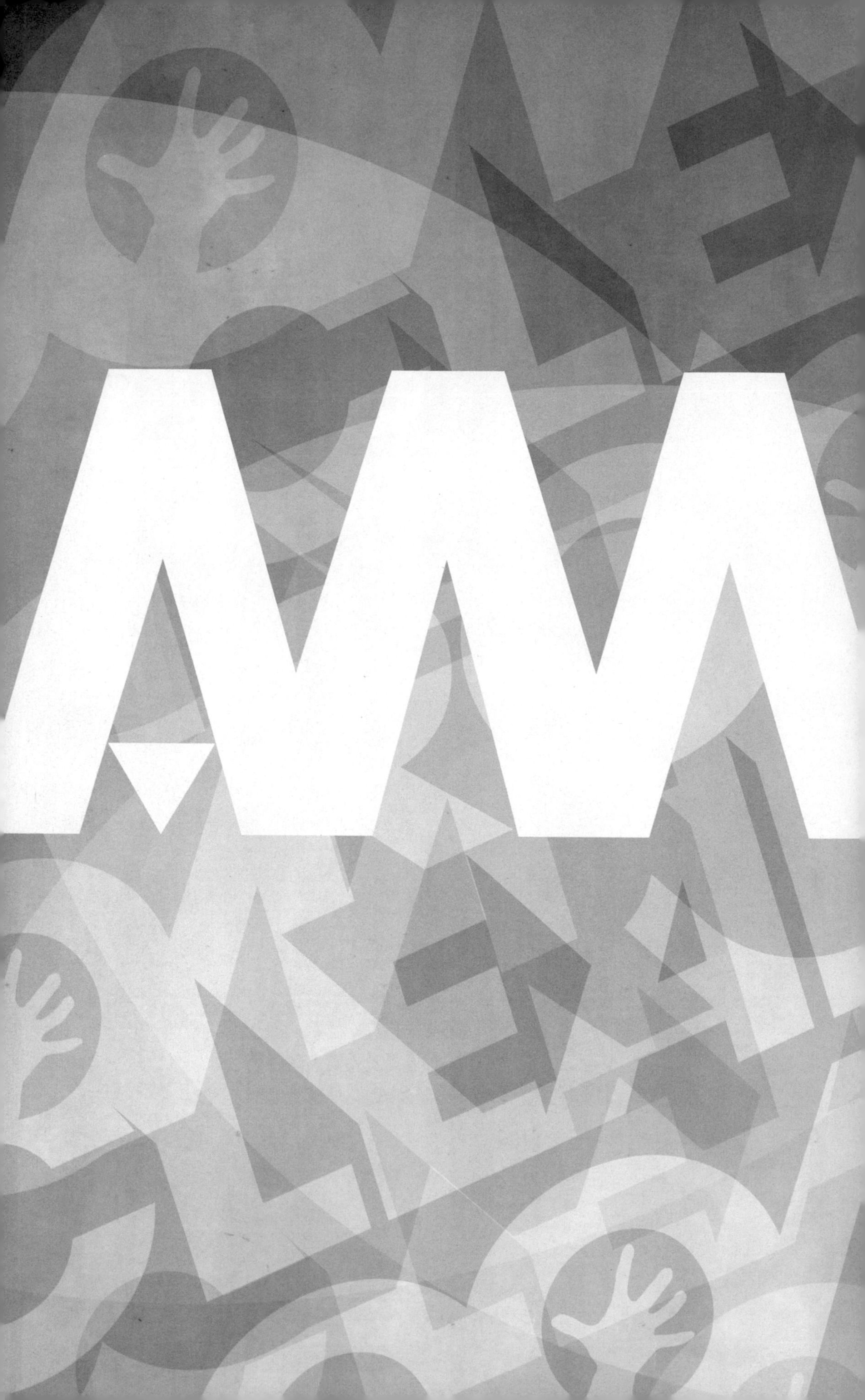

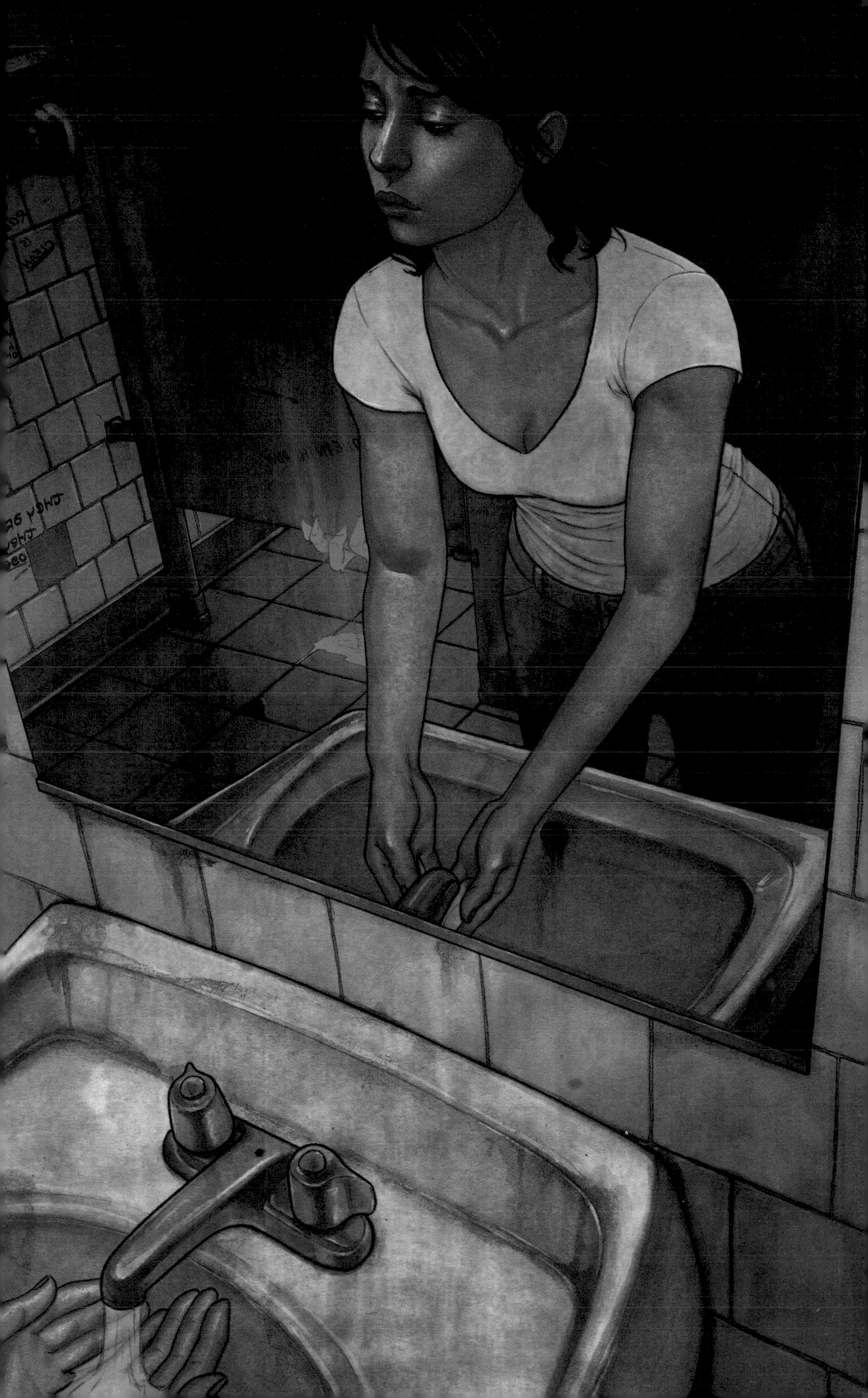

GOOD THINGS

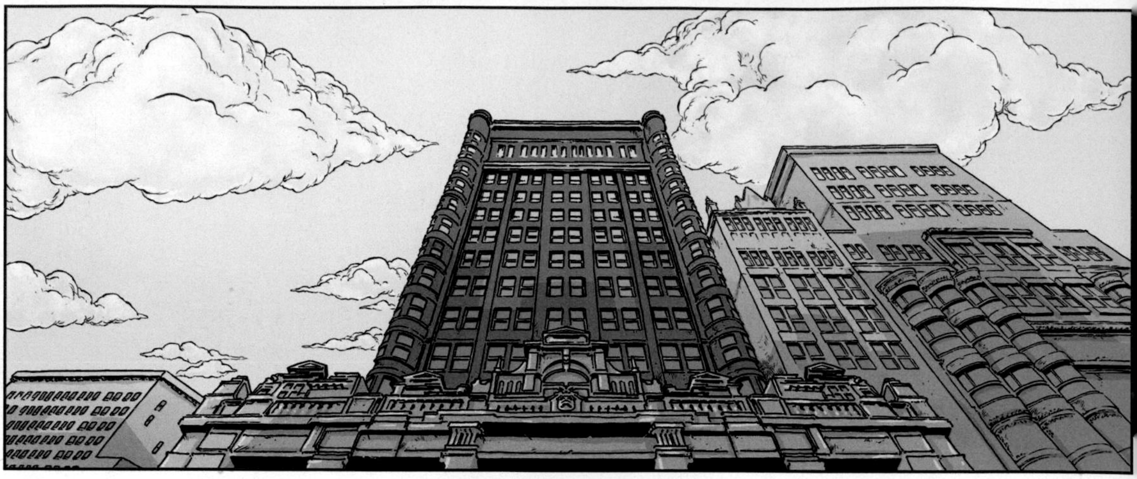

AND

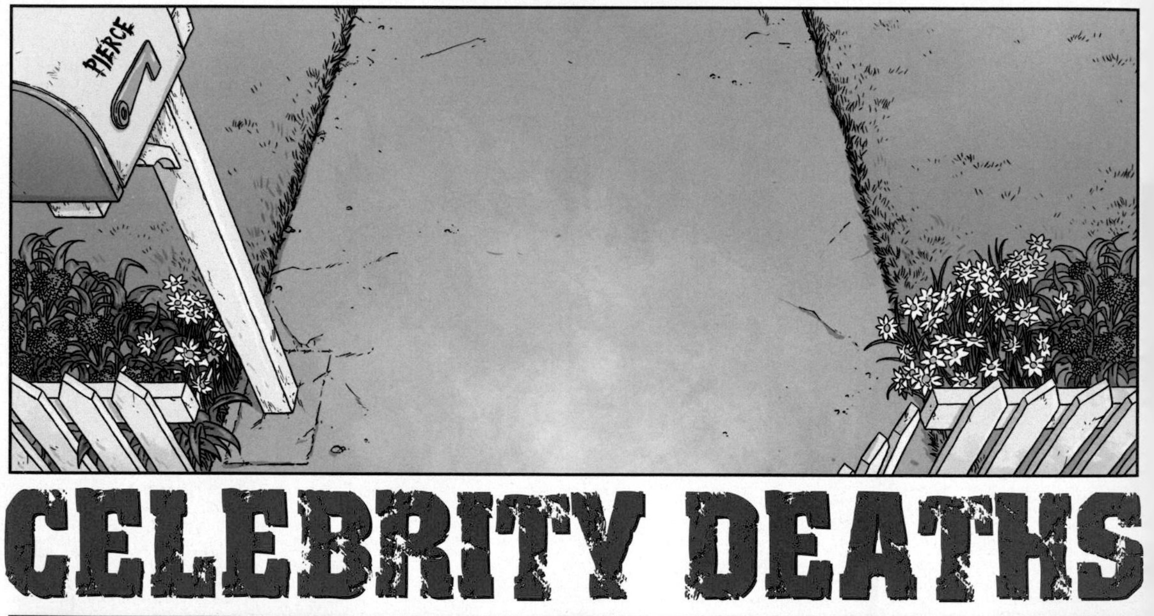
PIERCE
7

CELEBRITY DEATHS

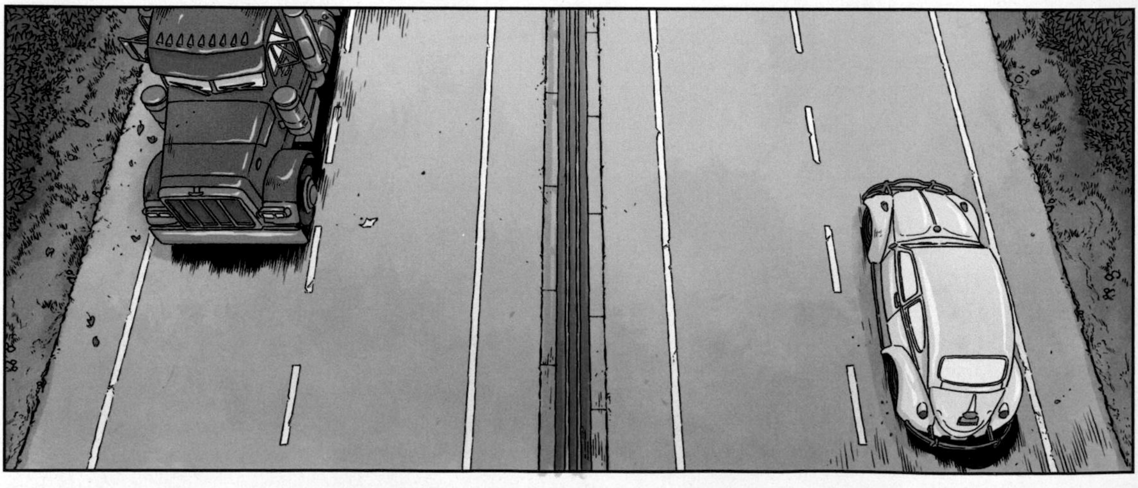

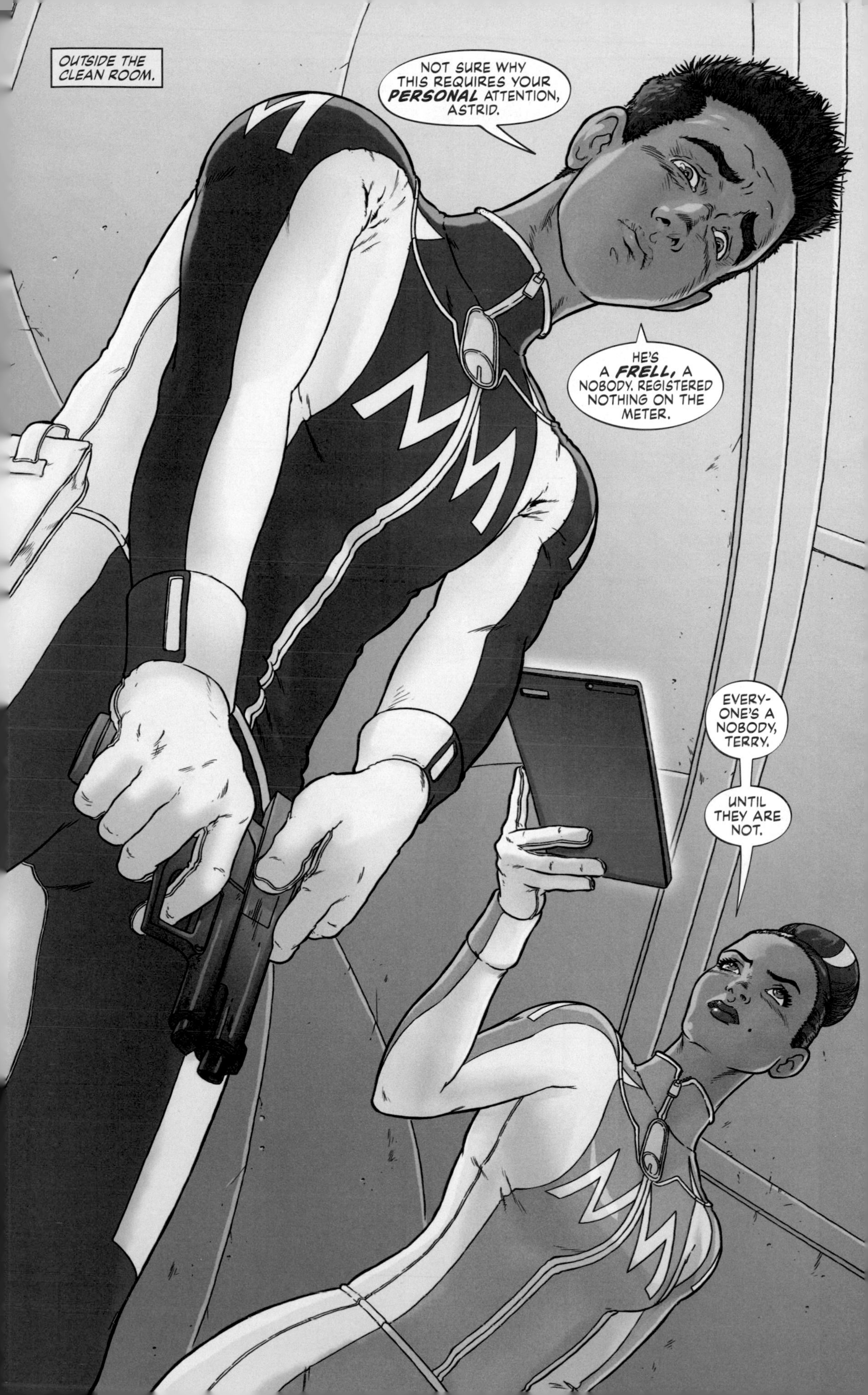
OUTSIDE THE CLEAN ROOM.
NOT SURE WHY THIS REQUIRES YOUR PERSONAL ATTENTION, ASTRID.
HE'S A FRELL, A NOBODY. REGISTERED NOTHING ON THE METER.
EVERY-ONE'S A NOBODY, TERRY.
UNTIL THEY ARE NOT.

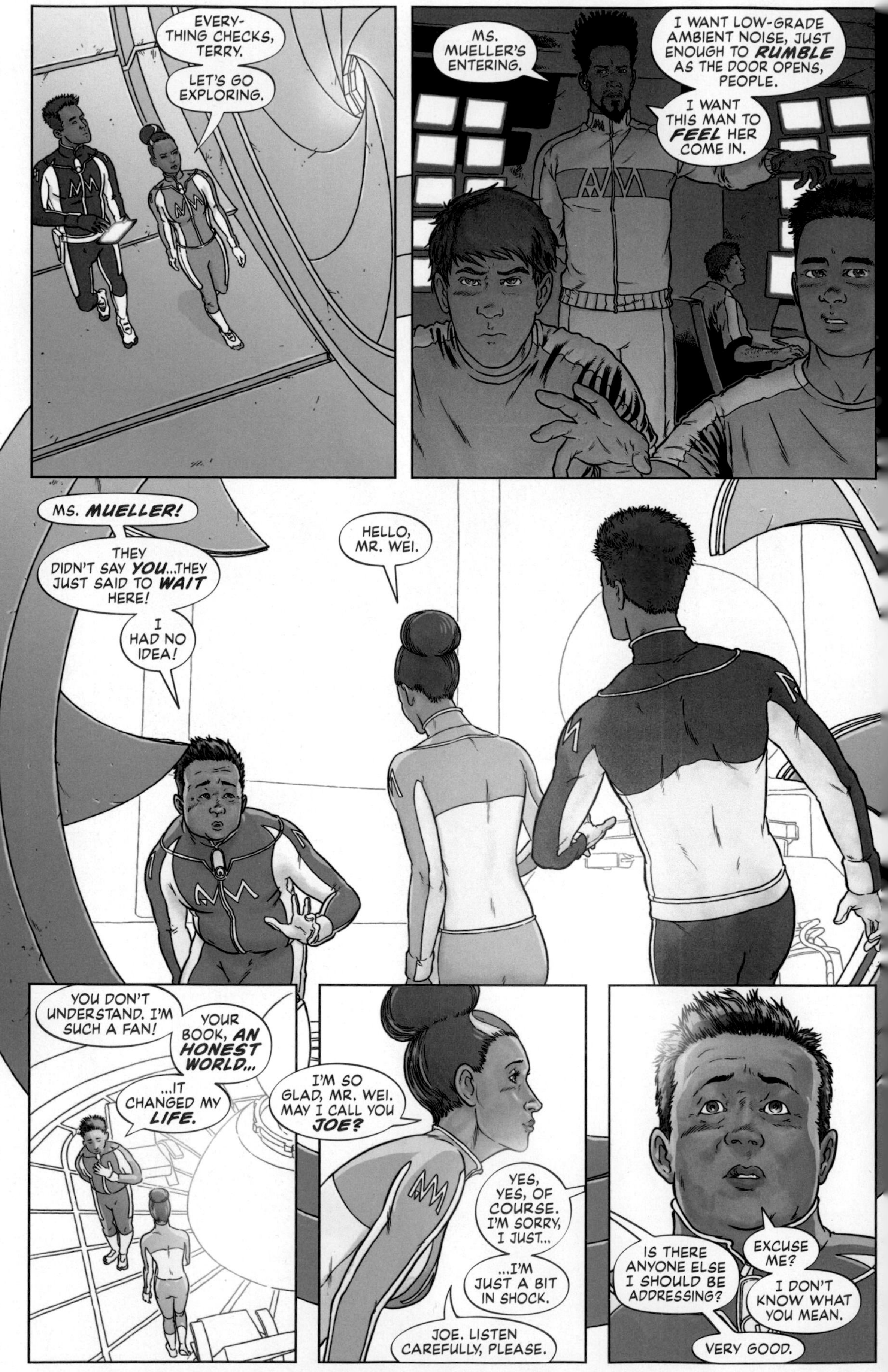
EVERY-THING CHECKS, TERRY.
LET'S GO EXPLORING.
MS. MUELLER'S ENTERING.
I WANT LOW-GRADE AMBIENT NOISE, JUST ENOUGH TO RUMBLE AS THE DOOR OPENS, PEOPLE.
I WANT THIS MAN TO FEEL HER COME IN.
MS. MUELLER!
THEY DIDN'T SAY YOU...THEY JUST SAID TO WAIT HERE!
I HAD NO IDEA!
HELLO, MR. WEI.
YOU DON'T UNDERSTAND. I'M SUCH A FAN!
YOUR BOOK, AN HONEST WORLD...
...IT CHANGED MY LIFE.
I'M SO GLAD, MR. WEI. MAY I CALL YOU JOE?
YES, YES, OF COURSE. I'M SORRY, I JUST...
...I'M JUST A BIT IN SHOCK.
JOE. LISTEN CAREFULLY, PLEASE.
IS THERE ANYONE ELSE I SHOULD BE ADDRESSING?
EXCUSE ME?
I DON'T KNOW WHAT YOU MEAN.
VERY GOOD.

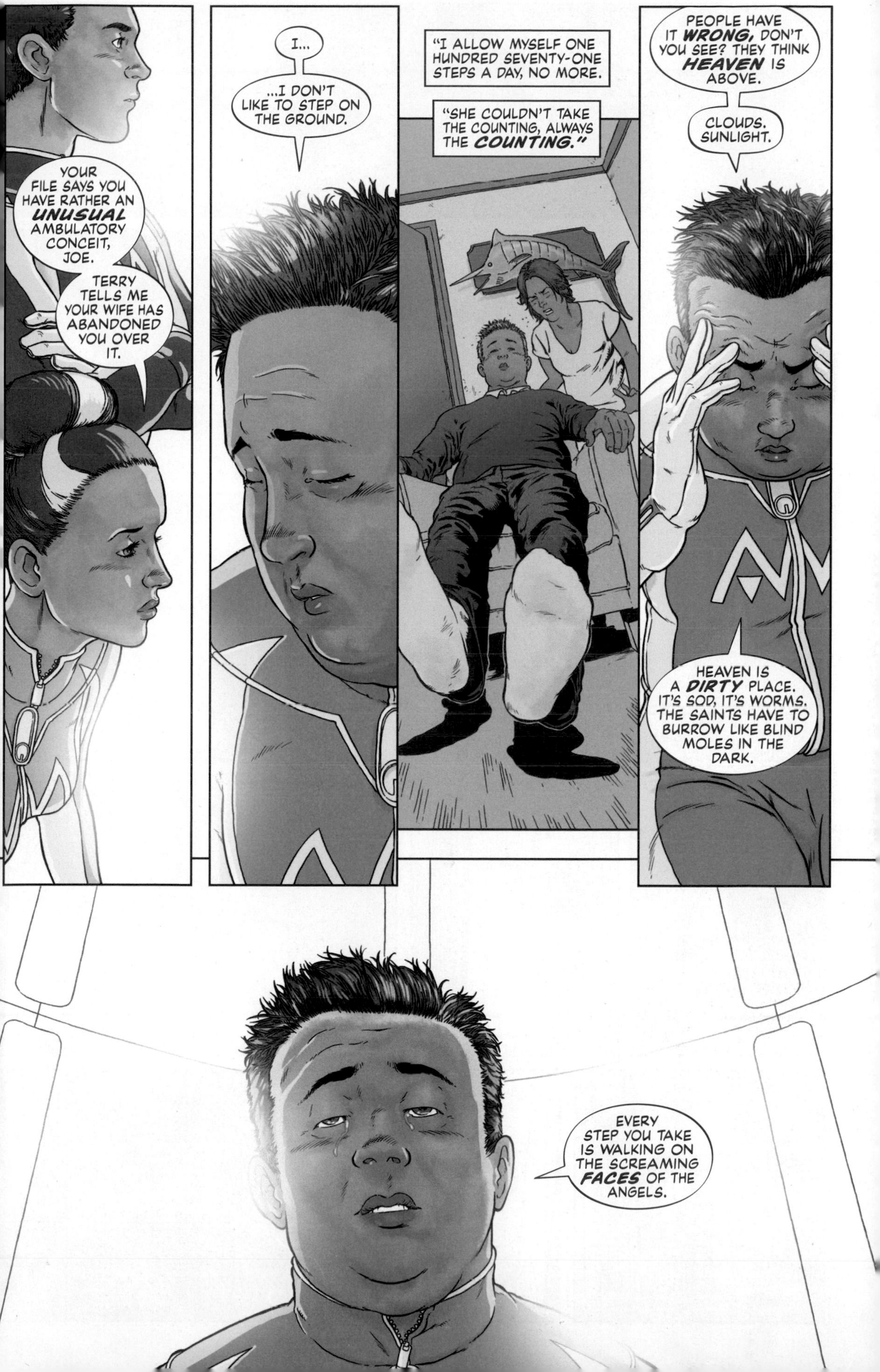
YOUR FILE SAYS YOU HAVE RATHER AN UNUSUAL AMBULATORY CONCEIT, JOE.
TERRY TELLS ME YOUR WIFE HAS ABANDONED YOU OVER IT.
I...
...I DON'T LIKE TO STEP ON THE GROUND.
"I ALLOW MYSELF ONE HUNDRED SEVENTY-ONE STEPS A DAY, NO MORE.
"SHE COULDN'T TAKE THE COUNTING, ALWAYS THE COUNTING."
PEOPLE HAVE IT WRONG, DON'T YOU SEE? THEY THINK HEAVEN IS ABOVE.
CLOUDS. SUNLIGHT.
HEAVEN IS A DIRTY PLACE. IT'S SOD, IT'S WORMS. THE SAINTS HAVE TO BURROW LIKE BLIND MOLES IN THE DARK.
EVERY STEP YOU TAKE IS WALKING ON THE SCREAMING FACES OF THE ANGELS.

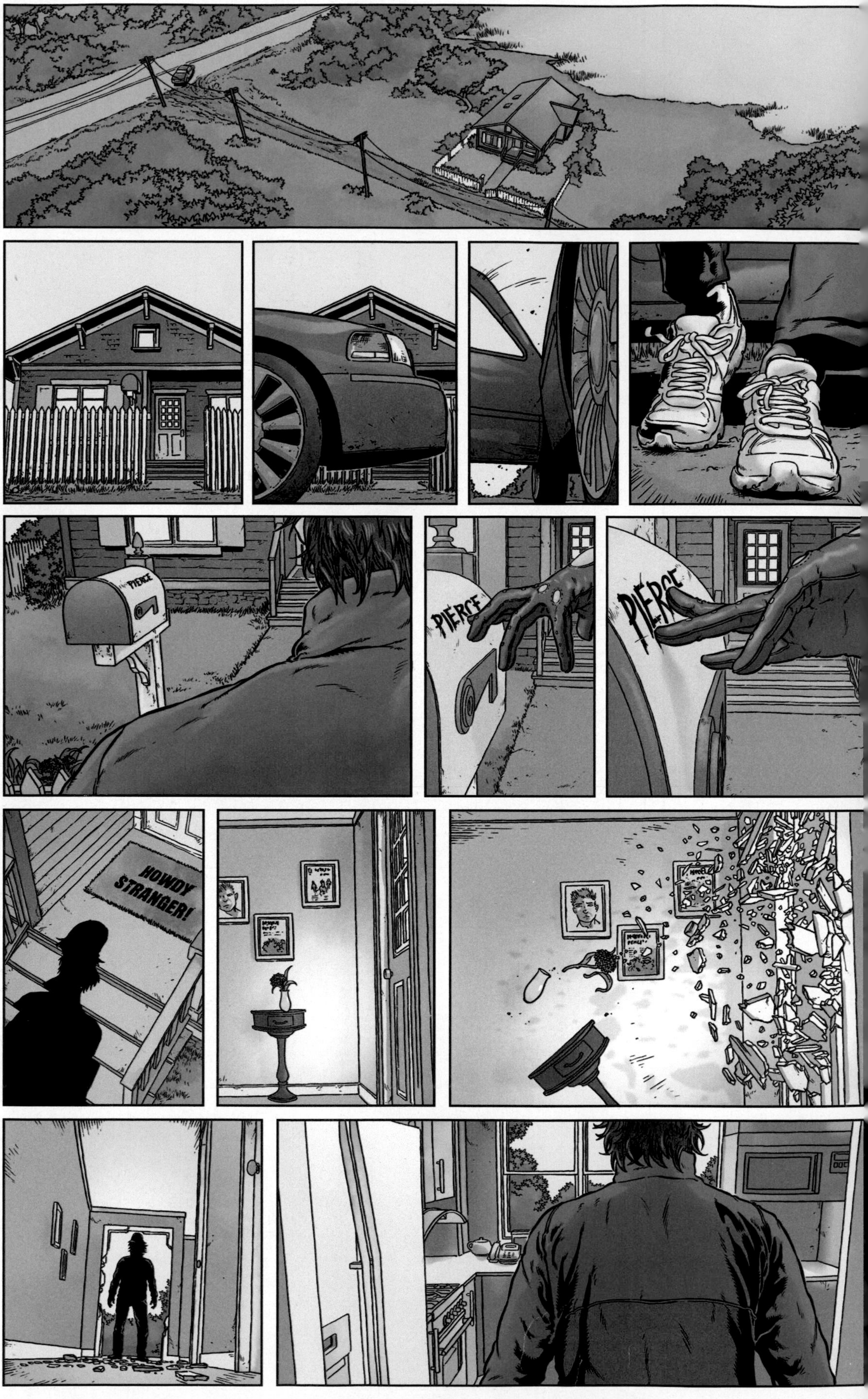
PIERCE
PIERCE
PIERCE
HOWDY
STRANGER!

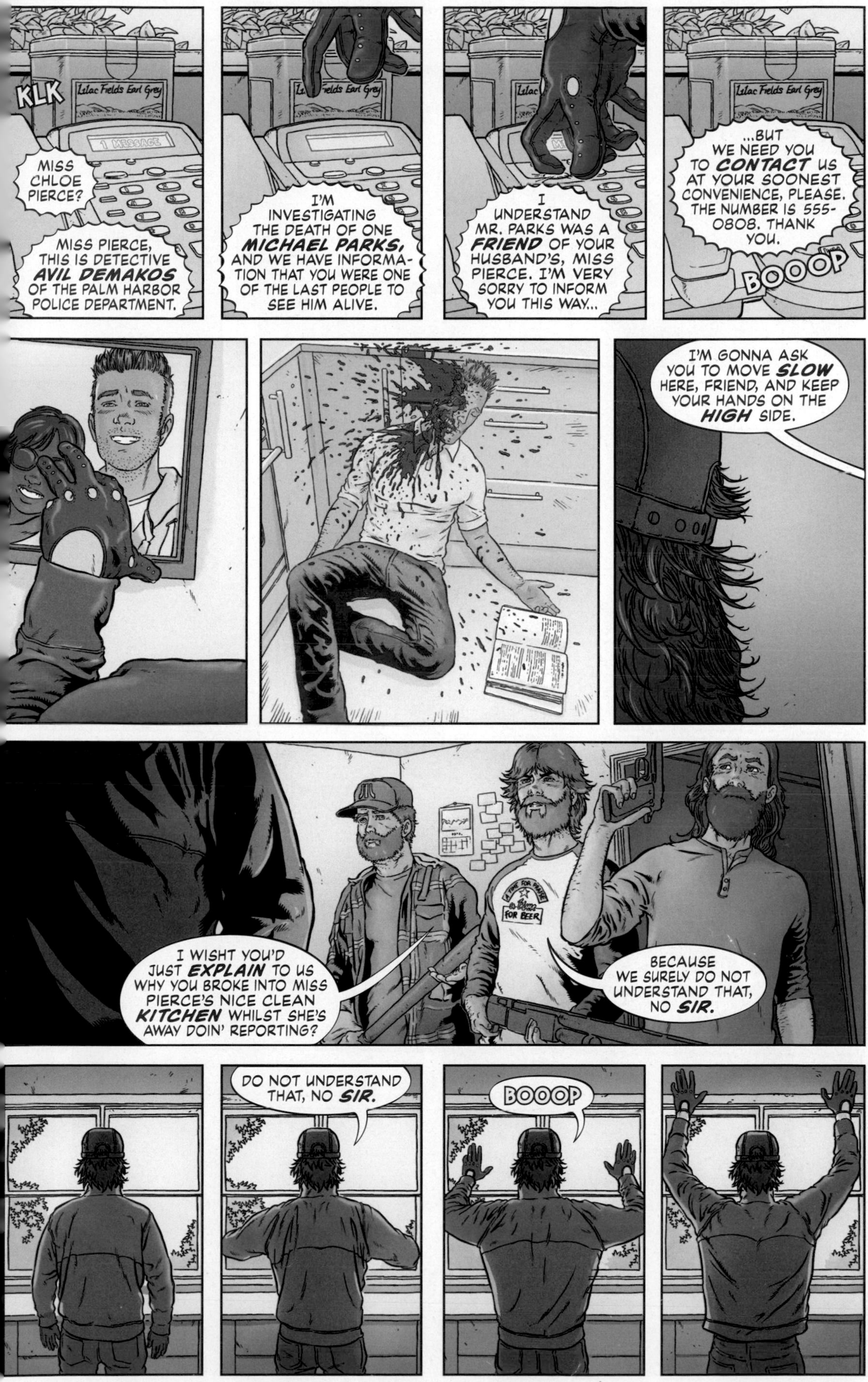

KLK
Lilac Fields Earl Grey
1 MESSAGE
MISS CHLOE PIERCE?
MISS PIERCE, THIS IS DETECTIVE AVIL DEMAKOS OF THE PALM HARBOR POLICE DEPARTMENT.
I'M INVESTIGATING THE DEATH OF ONE MICHAEL PARKS, AND WE HAVE INFORMATION THAT YOU WERE ONE OF THE LAST PEOPLE TO SEE HIM ALIVE.
I UNDERSTAND MR. PARKS WAS A FRIEND OF YOUR HUSBAND'S, MISS PIERCE. I'M VERY SORRY TO INFORM YOU THIS WAY...
...BUT WE NEED YOU TO CONTACT US AT YOUR SOONEST CONVENIENCE, PLEASE. THE NUMBER IS 555-0808. THANK YOU.
BOOOP
I'M GONNA ASK YOU TO MOVE SLOW HERE, FRIEND, AND KEEP YOUR HANDS ON THE HIGH SIDE.
FOR BEER
I WISHT YOU'D JUST EXPLAIN TO US WHY YOU BROKE INTO MISS PIERCE'S NICE CLEAN KITCHEN WHILST SHE'S AWAY DOIN' REPORTING?
BECAUSE WE SURELY DO NOT UNDERSTAND THAT, NO SIR.
DO NOT UNDERSTAND THAT, NO SIR.
BOOOP

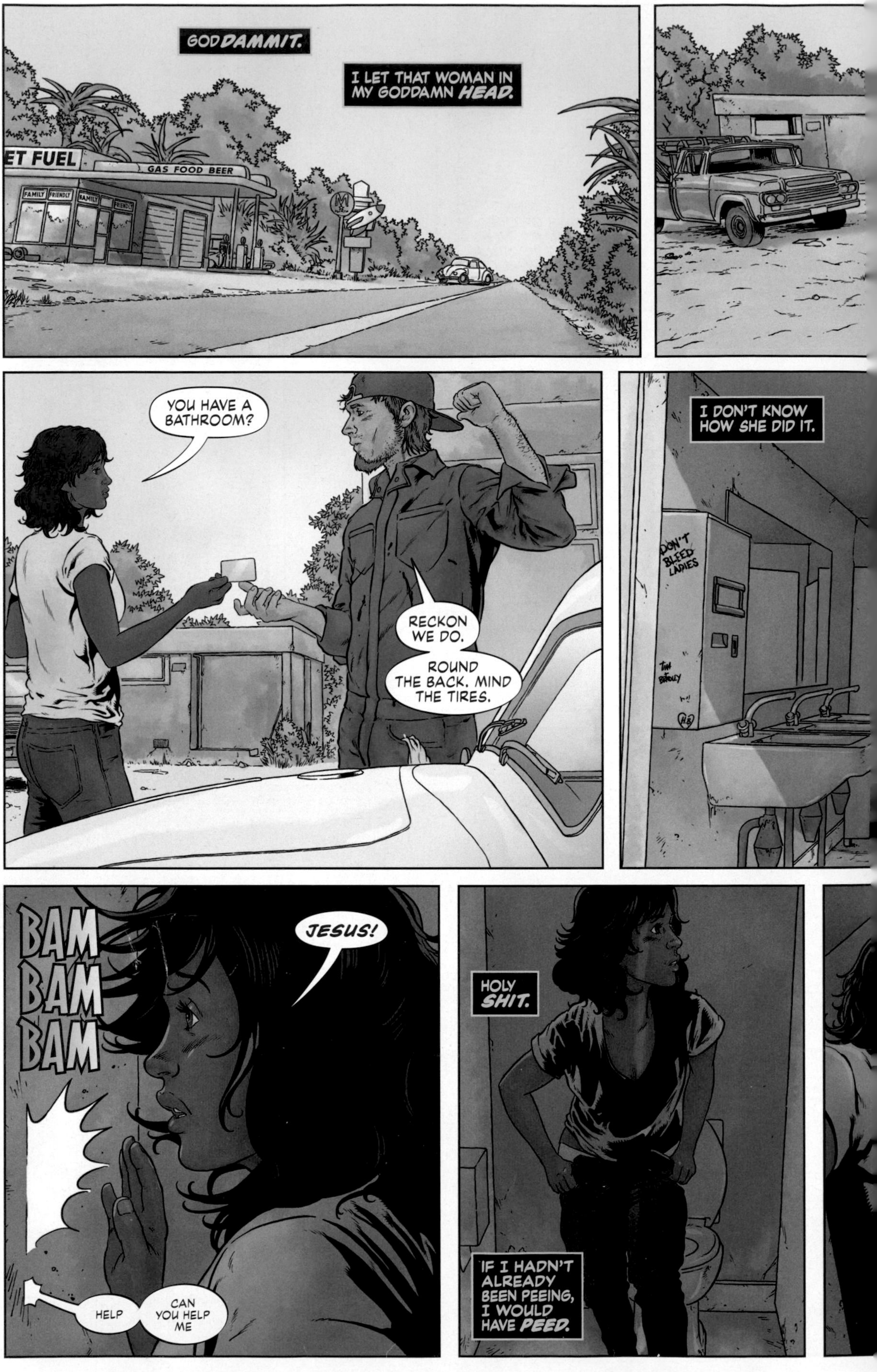
GOD DAMMIT.
I LET THAT WOMAN IN MY GODDAMN HEAD.
ET FUEL
GAS FOOD BEER
FAMILY FRIENDLY
FAMILY FRIENDLY
YOU HAVE A BATHROOM?
RECKON WE DO.
ROUND THE BACK. MIND THE TIRES.
I DON'T KNOW HOW SHE DID IT.
DON'T BLEED LADIES
BAM BAM BAM
JESUS!
HELP
CAN YOU HELP ME
HOLY SHIT.
IF I HADN'T ALREADY BEEN PEEING, I WOULD HAVE PEED.

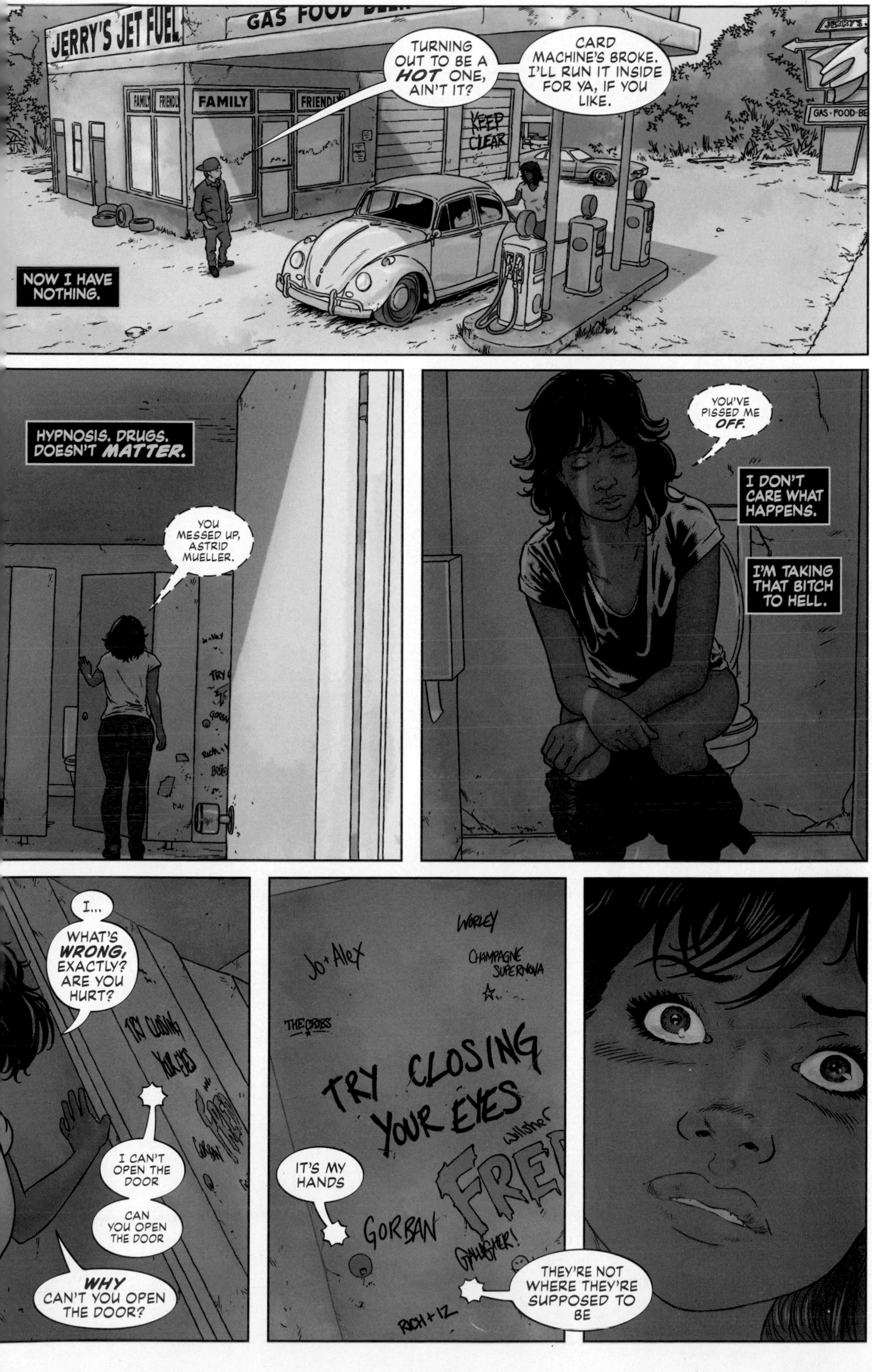
JERRY'S JET FUEL
FAMILY
FRIENDLY
KEEP CLEAR
TURNING OUT TO BE A HOT ONE, AIN'T IT?
CARD MACHINE'S BROKE. I'LL RUN IT INSIDE FOR YA, IF YOU LIKE.
NOW I HAVE NOTHING.
HYPNOSIS. DRUGS. DOESN'T MATTER.
YOU MESSED UP, ASTRID MUELLER.
YOU'VE PISSED ME OFF.
I DON'T CARE WHAT HAPPENS.
I'M TAKING THAT BITCH TO HELL.
I...
WHAT'S WRONG, EXACTLY? ARE YOU HURT?
TRY CLOSING YOUR EYES
I CAN'T OPEN THE DOOR
CAN YOU OPEN THE DOOR
WHY CAN'T YOU OPEN THE DOOR?
Worley
Jo+Alex
CHAMPAGNE SUPERNOVA
THE CRIBS
TRY CLOSING YOUR EYES
wilsher
GORBAN
GALLAGHER!
RICH + IZ
IT'S MY HANDS
THEY'RE NOT WHERE THEY'RE SUPPOSED TO BE

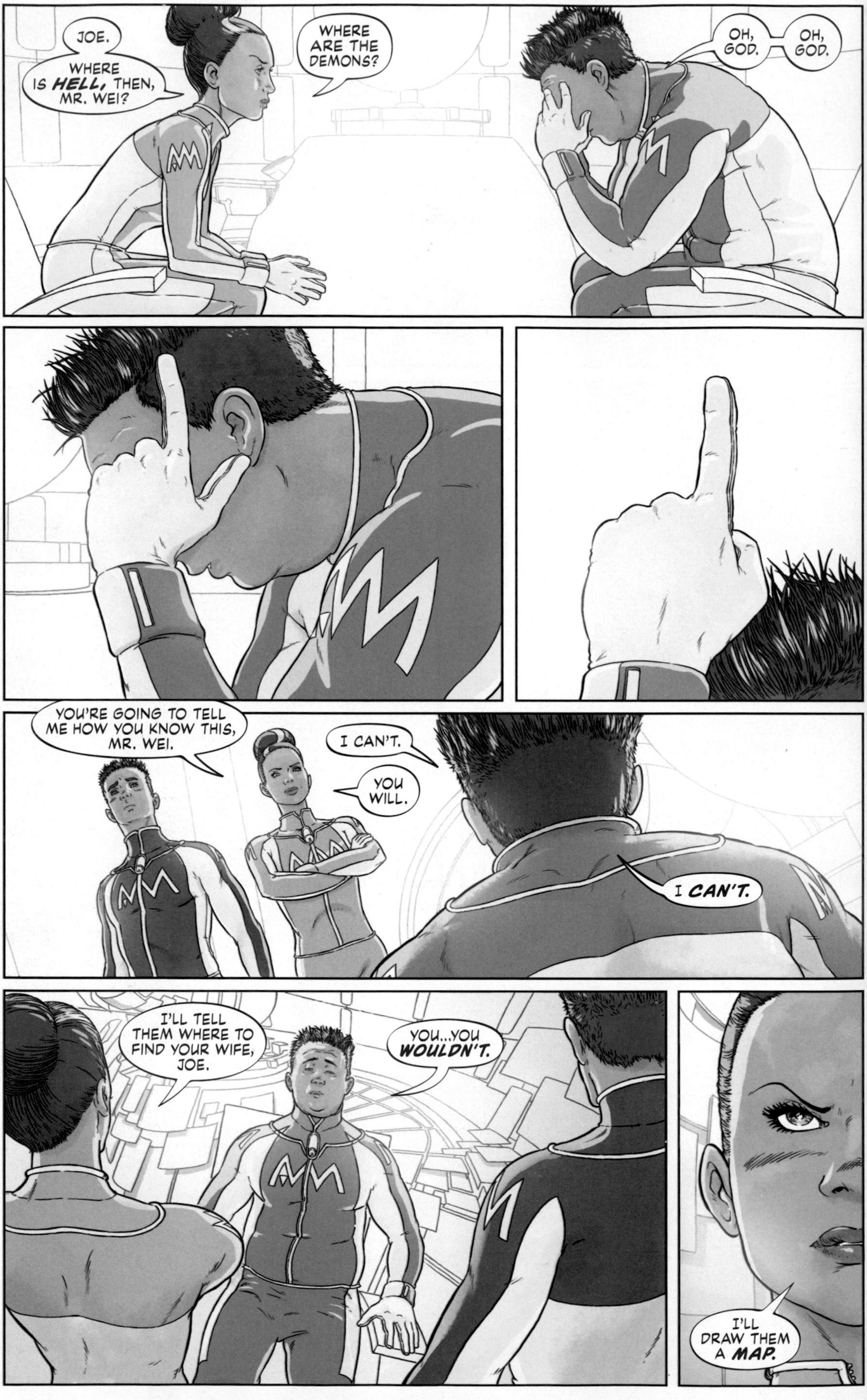
JOE.
WHERE IS HELL, THEN, MR. WEI?
WHERE ARE THE DEMONS?
OH, GOD.
OH, GOD.
YOU'RE GOING TO TELL ME HOW YOU KNOW THIS, MR. WEI.
I CAN'T.
YOU WILL.
I CAN'T.
I'LL TELL THEM WHERE TO FIND YOUR WIFE, JOE.
YOU...YOU WOULDN'T.
I'LL DRAW THEM A MAP.

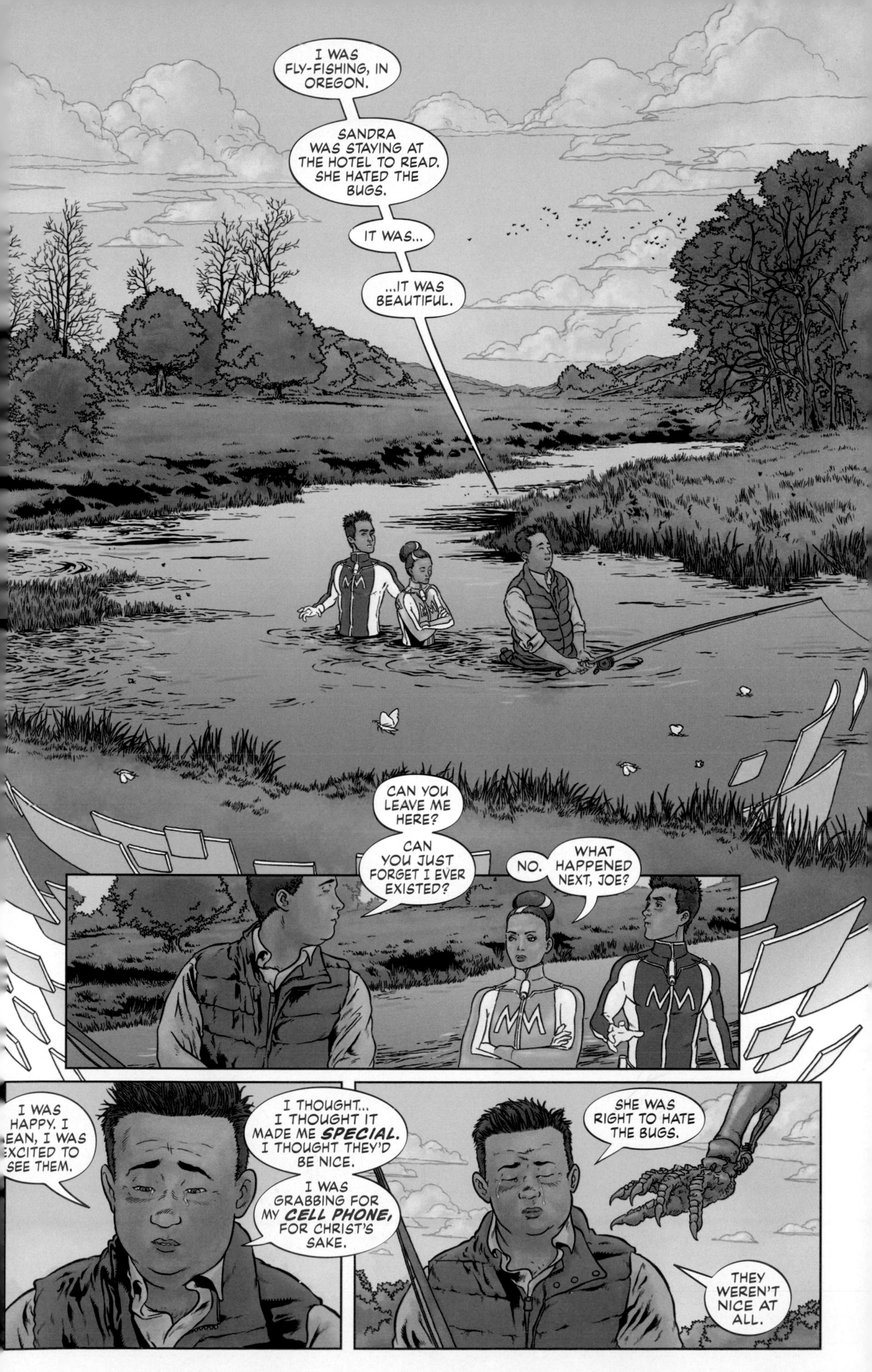
I WAS FLY-FISHING, IN OREGON.
SANDRA WAS STAYING AT THE HOTEL TO READ. SHE HATED THE BUGS.
IT WAS...
...IT WAS BEAUTIFUL.
CAN YOU LEAVE ME HERE?
CAN YOU JUST FORGET I EVER EXISTED?
NO.
WHAT HAPPENED NEXT, JOE?
I WAS HAPPY. I EAN, I WAS XCITED TO SEE THEM.
I THOUGHT... I THOUGHT IT MADE ME SPECIAL. I THOUGHT THEY'D BE NICE.
I WAS GRABBING FOR MY CELL PHONE, FOR CHRIST'S SAKE.
SHE WAS RIGHT TO HATE THE BUGS.
THEY WEREN'T NICE AT ALL.

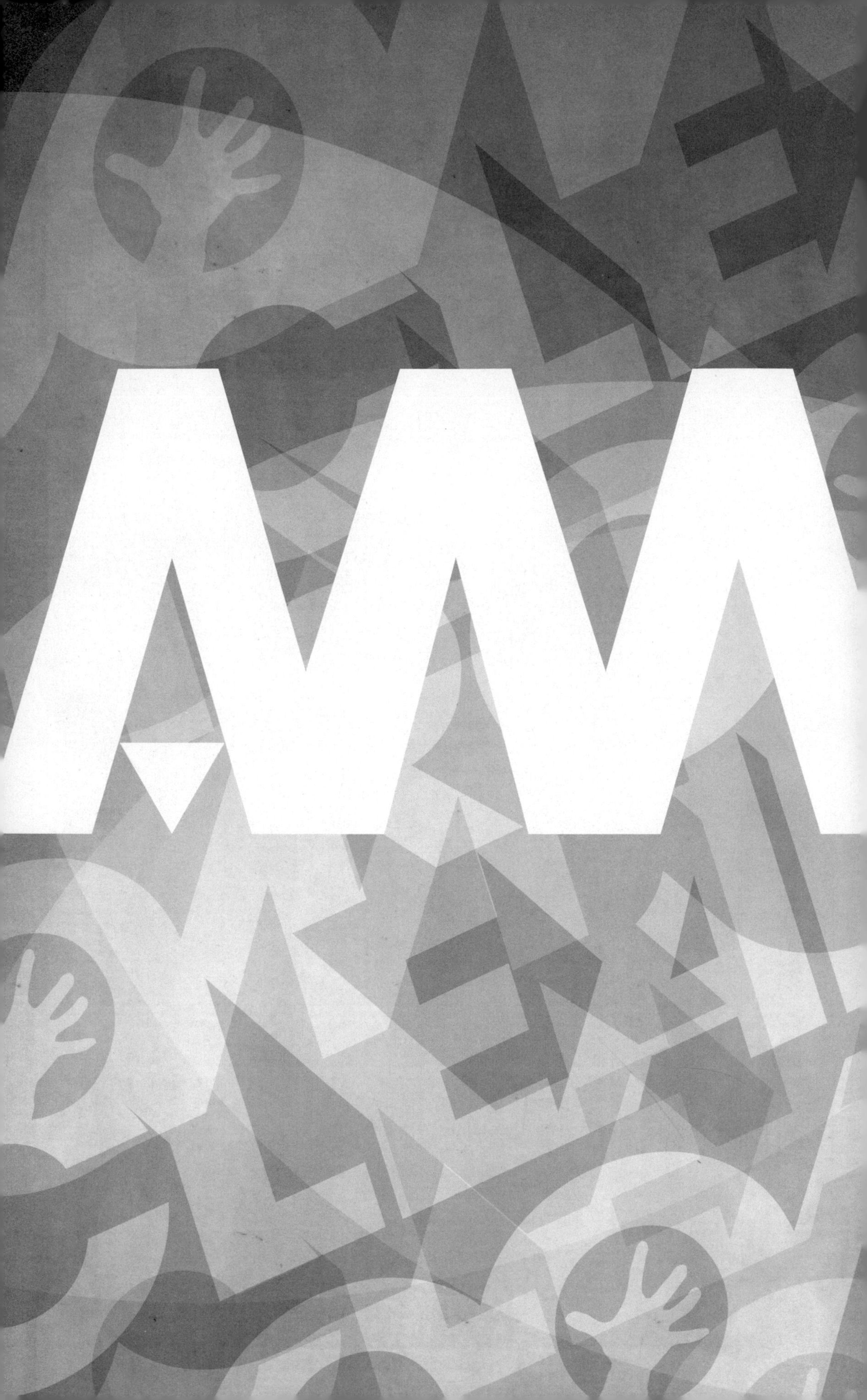

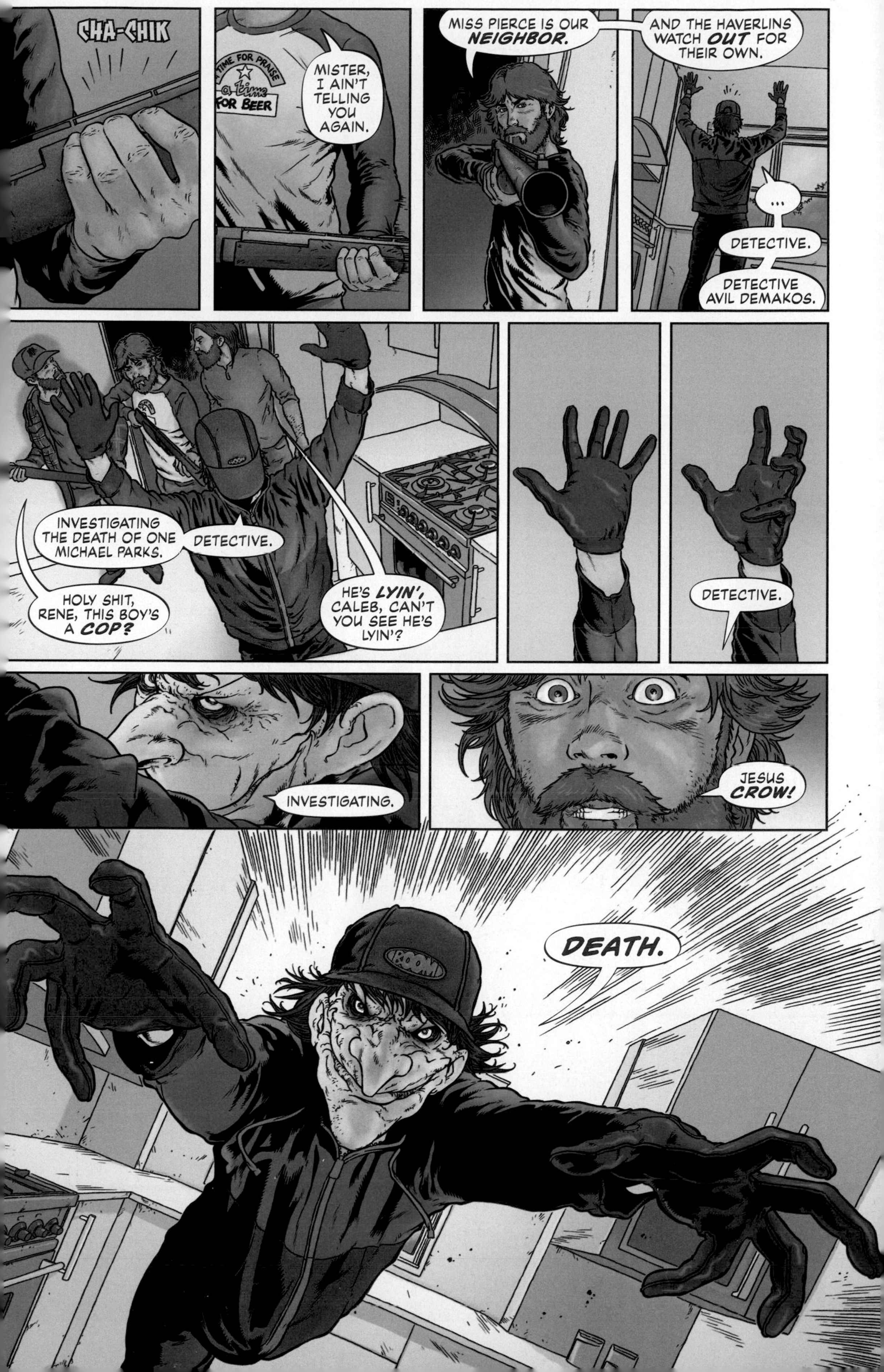
CHA-CHIK
A TIME FOR PRAISE
A TIME FOR BEER
MISTER, I AIN'T TELLING YOU AGAIN.
MISS PIERCE IS OUR NEIGHBOR.
AND THE HAVERLINS WATCH OUT FOR THEIR OWN.
...
DETECTIVE.
DETECTIVE AVIL DEMAKOS.
INVESTIGATING THE DEATH OF ONE MICHAEL PARKS.
DETECTIVE.
HOLY SHIT, RENE, THIS BOY'S A COP?
HE'S LYIN', CALEB, CAN'T YOU SEE HE'S LYIN'?
DETECTIVE.
INVESTIGATING.
JESUS CROW!
DEATH.

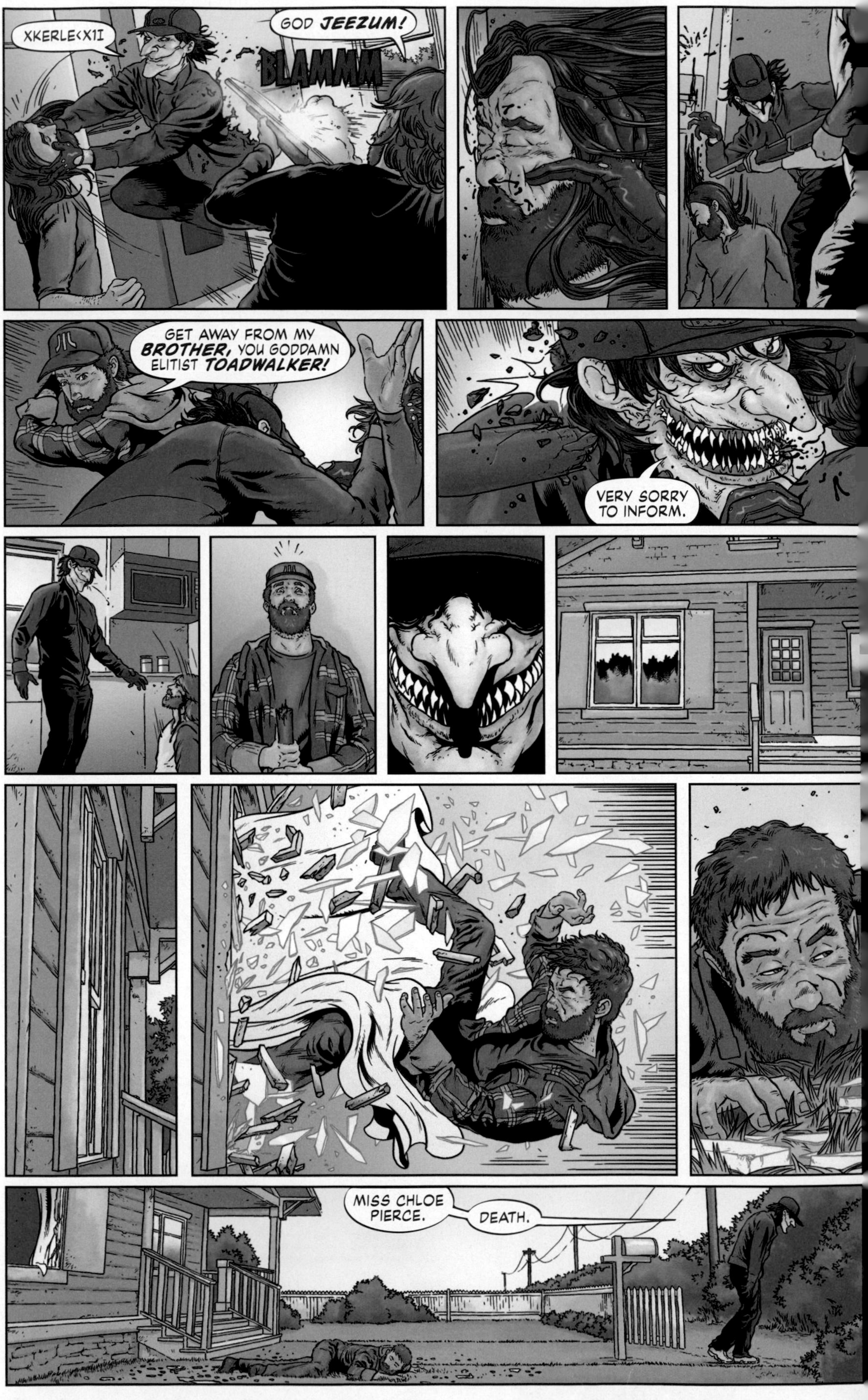
XKERLE<X1I
GOD JEEZUM!
BLAMMM
GET AWAY FROM MY BROTHER, YOU GODDAMN ELITIST TOADWALKER!
VERY SORRY TO INFORM.
MISS CHLOE PIERCE.
DEATH.

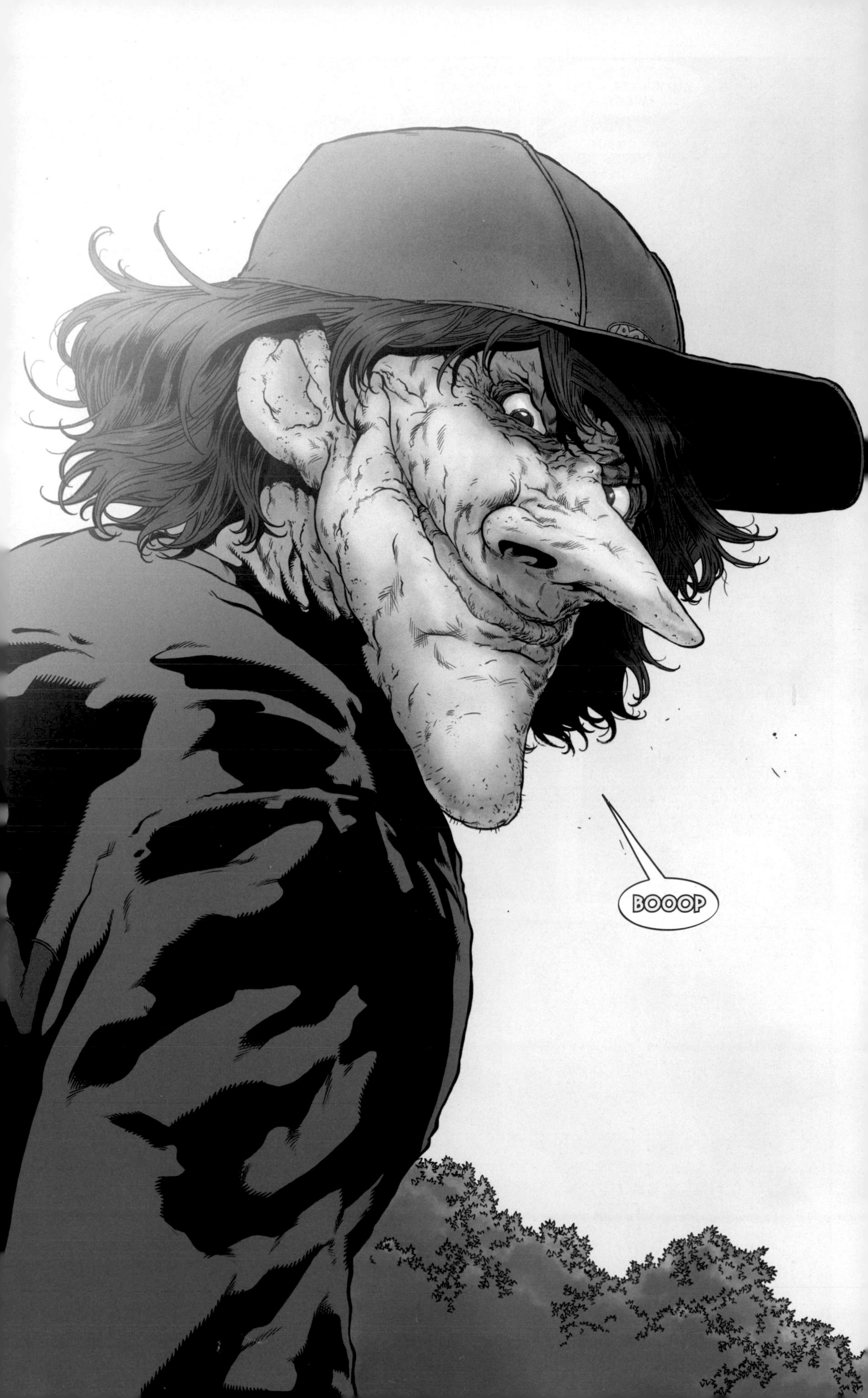
BOOOP

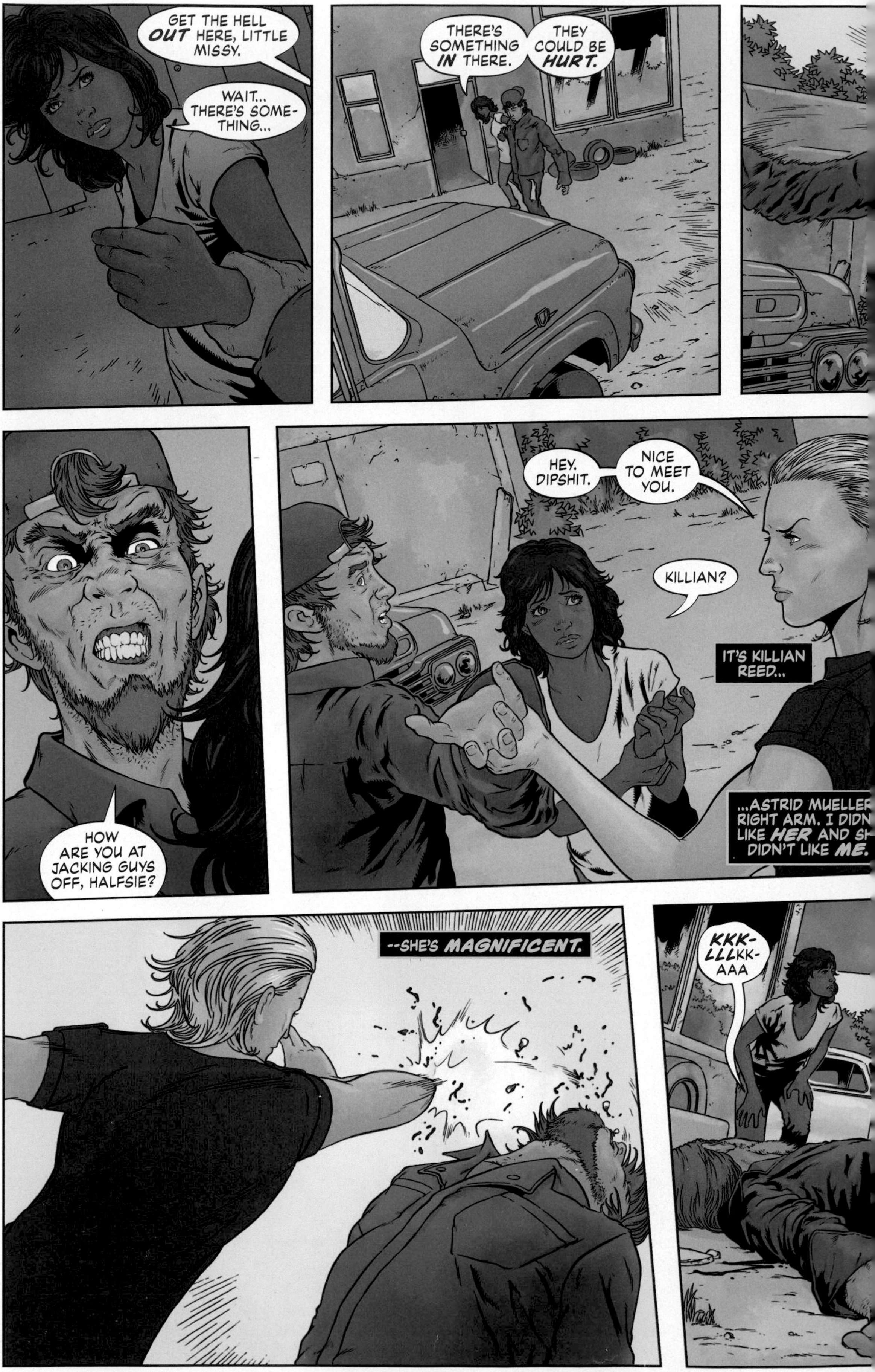
GET THE HELL OUT HERE, LITTLE MISSY.
WAIT... THERE'S SOME-THING...
THERE'S SOMETHING IN THERE.
THEY COULD BE HURT.
HOW ARE YOU AT JACKING GUYS OFF, HALFSIE?
HEY. DIPSHIT.
NICE TO MEET YOU.
KILLIAN?
IT'S KILLIAN REED...
...ASTRID MUELLER RIGHT ARM. I DIDN LIKE HER AND SH DIDN'T LIKE ME.
--SHE'S MAGNIFICENT.
KKK-LLLKK-AAA

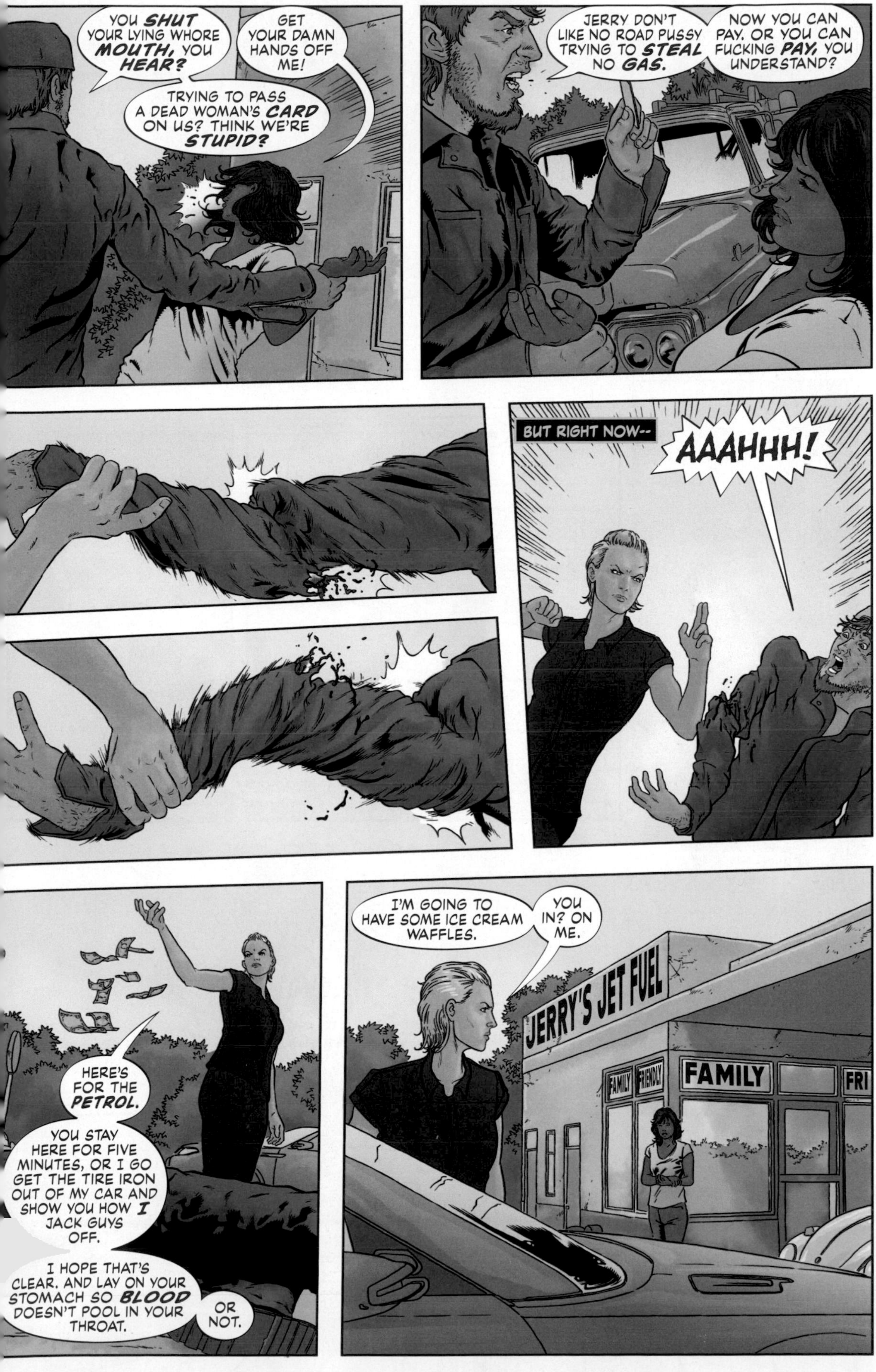
YOU SHUT YOUR LYING WHORE MOUTH, YOU HEAR?
GET YOUR DAMN HANDS OFF ME!
TRYING TO PASS A DEAD WOMAN'S CARD ON US? THINK WE'RE STUPID?
JERRY DON'T LIKE NO ROAD PUSSY TRYING TO STEAL NO GAS.
NOW YOU CAN PAY, OR YOU CAN FUCKING PAY, YOU UNDERSTAND?
BUT RIGHT NOW--
AAAHHH!
HERE'S FOR THE PETROL.
YOU STAY HERE FOR FIVE MINUTES, OR I GO GET THE TIRE IRON OUT OF MY CAR AND SHOW YOU HOW I JACK GUYS OFF.
I HOPE THAT'S CLEAR. AND LAY ON YOUR STOMACH SO BLOOD DOESN'T POOL IN YOUR THROAT.
OR NOT.
I'M GOING TO HAVE SOME ICE CREAM WAFFLES.
YOU IN? ON ME.
JERRY'S JET FUEL
FAMILY
FRIENDLY
FAMILY
FRI

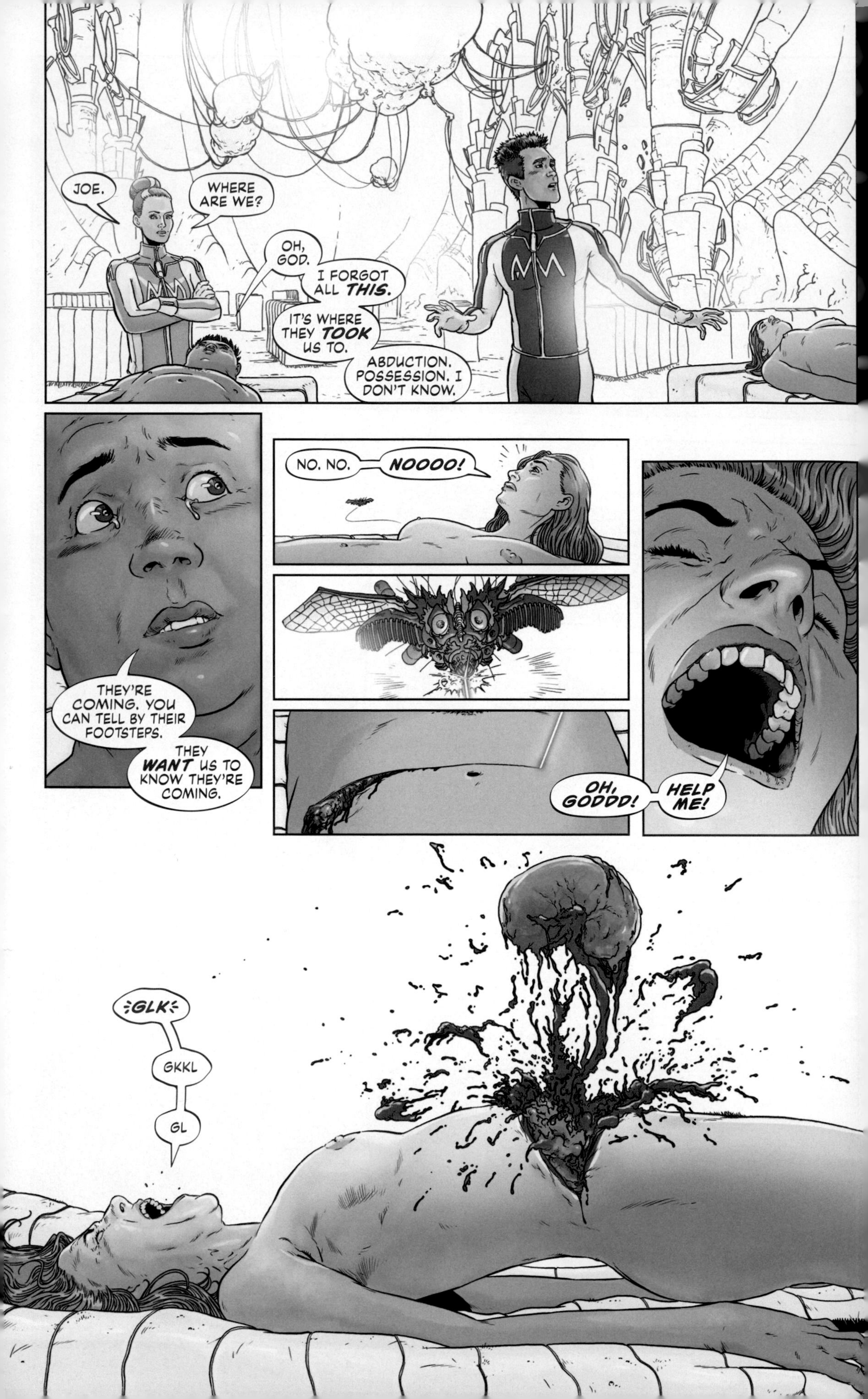
JOE.
WHERE ARE WE?
OH, GOD.
I FORGOT ALL THIS.
IT'S WHERE THEY TOOK US TO.
ABDUCTION. POSSESSION. I DON'T KNOW.
THEY'RE COMING. YOU CAN TELL BY THEIR FOOTSTEPS.
THEY WANT US TO KNOW THEY'RE COMING.
NO. NO.
NOOOO!
OH, GODDD!
HELP ME!
GLK
GKKL
GL

IT'S MY TURN. IT'S *MY TURN.*

ASTRID, WE HAVE TO *GO.* PLEASE!

JOE. I NEED TO SEE THEM. I NEED YOU TO *SEE* THEM.

OH.

TELL ME WHAT YOU *SEE.*

WHAT *ARE* THEY? WHAT *IS* THIS?

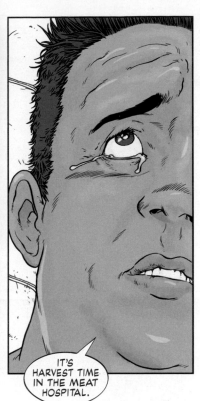

IT'S HARVEST TIME IN THE MEAT HOSPITAL.

WHOEVER, *WHATEVER* YOU ARE...

...I KNOW YOU'RE THERE.

YOU KNOW WHO I AM.

TELL YOUR MASTER I'M HERE TO *SEE* HIM.

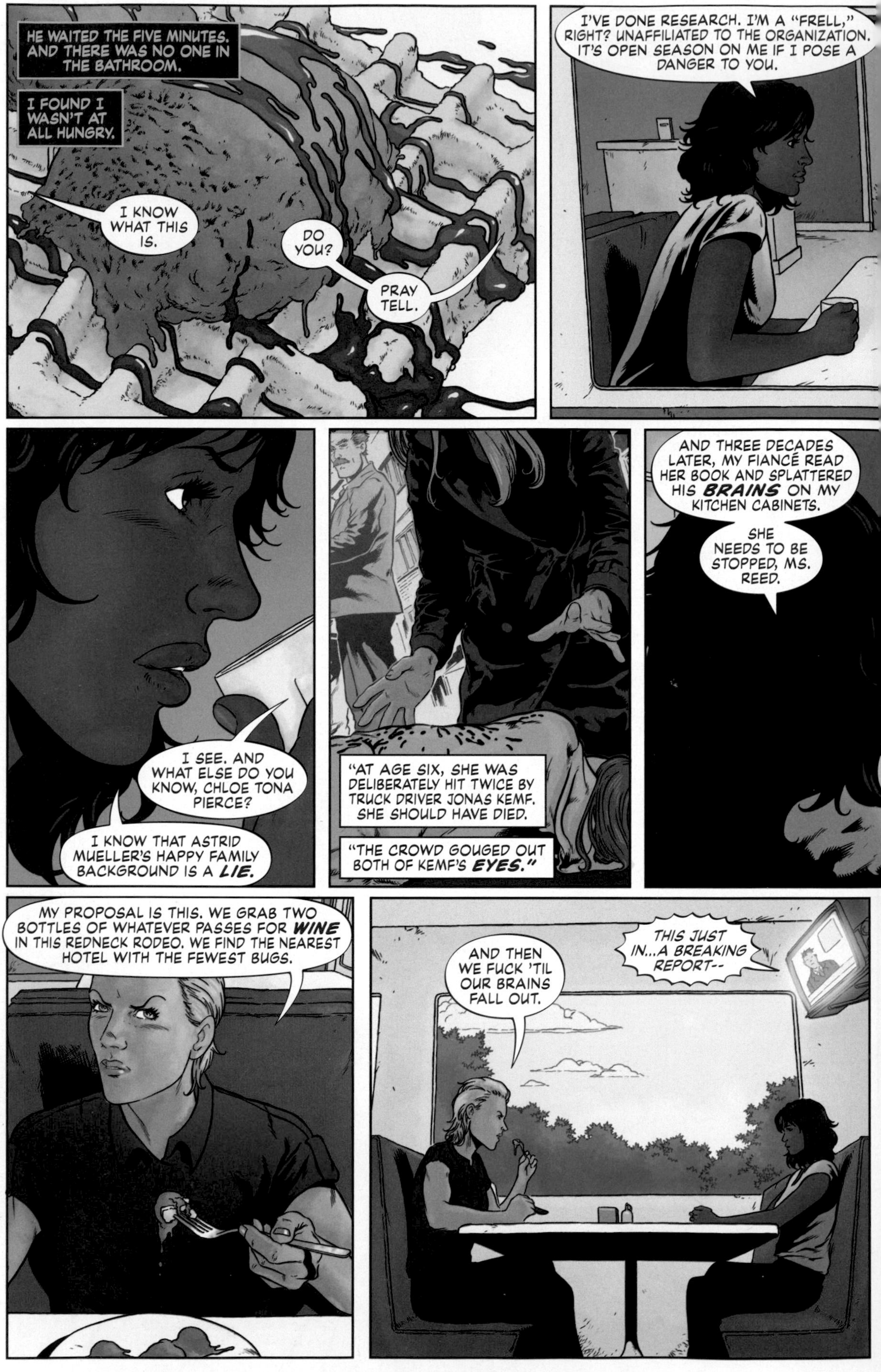
HE WAITED THE FIVE MINUTES. AND THERE WAS NO ONE IN THE BATHROOM.
I FOUND I WASN'T AT ALL HUNGRY.
I KNOW WHAT THIS IS.
DO YOU?
PRAY TELL.
I'VE DONE RESEARCH. I'M A "FRELL," RIGHT? UNAFFILIATED TO THE ORGANIZATION. IT'S OPEN SEASON ON ME IF I POSE A DANGER TO YOU.
I SEE. AND WHAT ELSE DO YOU KNOW, CHLOE TONA PIERCE?
I KNOW THAT ASTRID MUELLER'S HAPPY FAMILY BACKGROUND IS A LIE.
"AT AGE SIX, SHE WAS DELIBERATELY HIT TWICE BY TRUCK DRIVER JONAS KEMF. SHE SHOULD HAVE DIED.
"THE CROWD GOUGED OUT BOTH OF KEMF'S EYES."
AND THREE DECADES LATER, MY FIANCÉ READ HER BOOK AND SPLATTERED HIS BRAINS ON MY KITCHEN CABINETS.
SHE NEEDS TO BE STOPPED, MS. REED.
MY PROPOSAL IS THIS. WE GRAB TWO BOTTLES OF WHATEVER PASSES FOR WINE IN THIS REDNECK RODEO. WE FIND THE NEAREST HOTEL WITH THE FEWEST BUGS.
AND THEN WE FUCK 'TIL OUR BRAINS FALL OUT.
THIS JUST IN...A BREAKING REPORT--

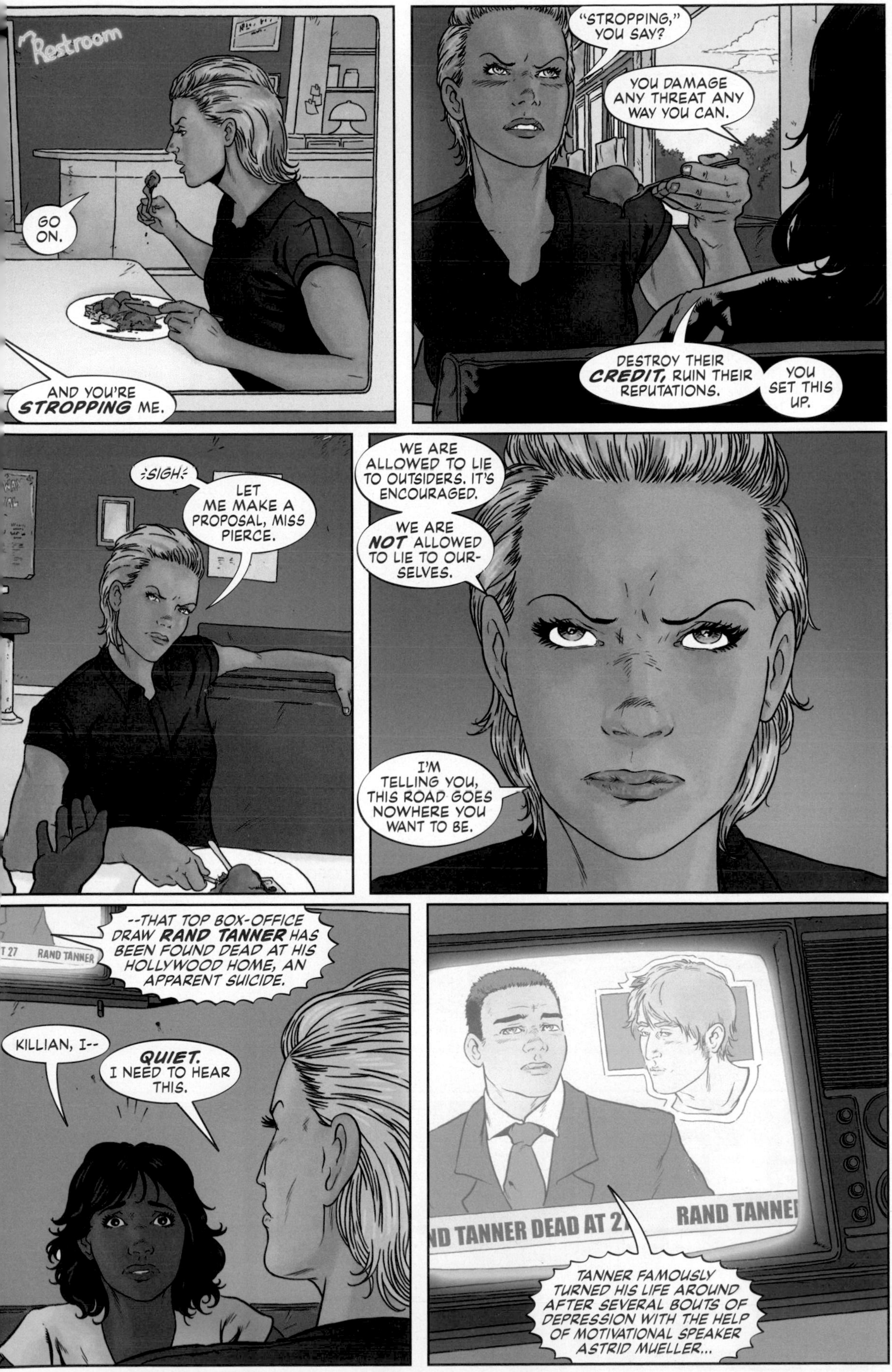
Restroom
GO ON.
AND YOU'RE STROPPING ME.
"STROPPING," YOU SAY?
YOU DAMAGE ANY THREAT ANY WAY YOU CAN.
DESTROY THEIR CREDIT, RUIN THEIR REPUTATIONS.
YOU SET THIS UP.
SIGH
LET ME MAKE A PROPOSAL, MISS PIERCE.
WE ARE ALLOWED TO LIE TO OUTSIDERS. IT'S ENCOURAGED.
WE ARE NOT ALLOWED TO LIE TO OURSELVES.
I'M TELLING YOU, THIS ROAD GOES NOWHERE YOU WANT TO BE.
RAND TANNER
--THAT TOP BOX-OFFICE DRAW RAND TANNER HAS BEEN FOUND DEAD AT HIS HOLLYWOOD HOME, AN APPARENT SUICIDE.
KILLIAN, I--
QUIET. I NEED TO HEAR THIS.
ND TANNER DEAD AT 27
RAND TANNE
TANNER FAMOUSLY TURNED HIS LIFE AROUND AFTER SEVERAL BOUTS OF DEPRESSION WITH THE HELP OF MOTIVATIONAL SPEAKER ASTRID MUELLER...

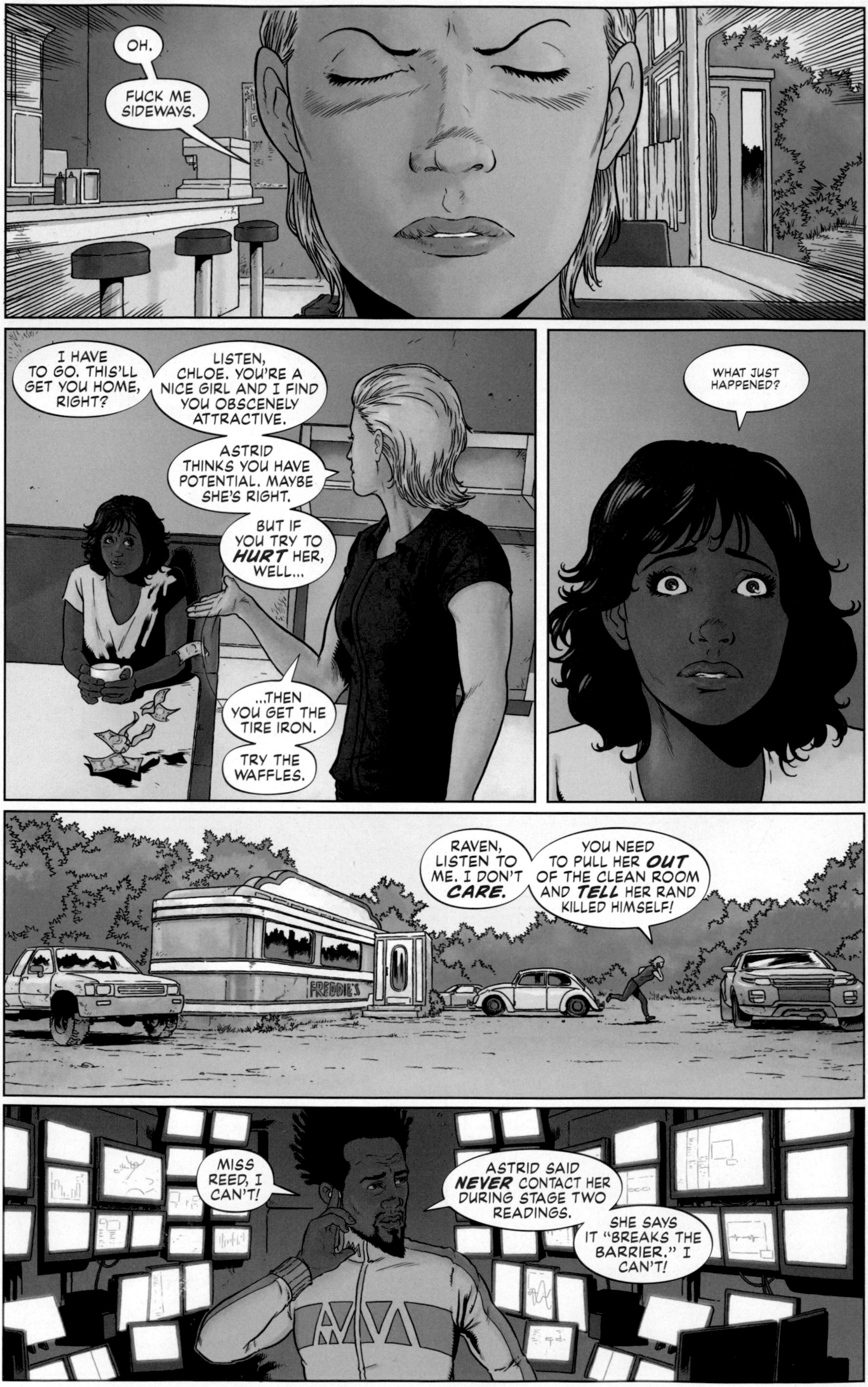
OH.
FUCK ME SIDEWAYS.
I HAVE TO GO. THIS'LL GET YOU HOME, RIGHT?
LISTEN, CHLOE. YOU'RE A NICE GIRL AND I FIND YOU OBSCENELY ATTRACTIVE.
ASTRID THINKS YOU HAVE POTENTIAL. MAYBE SHE'S RIGHT.
BUT IF YOU TRY TO **HURT** HER, WELL...
...THEN YOU GET THE TIRE IRON.
TRY THE WAFFLES.
WHAT JUST HAPPENED?
RAVEN, LISTEN TO ME. I DON'T **CARE.**
YOU NEED TO PULL HER **OUT** OF THE CLEAN ROOM AND **TELL** HER RAND KILLED HIMSELF!
FREDDIE'S
MISS REED, I CAN'T!
ASTRID SAID **NEVER** CONTACT HER DURING STAGE TWO READINGS.
SHE SAYS IT "BREAKS THE BARRIER." I CAN'T!

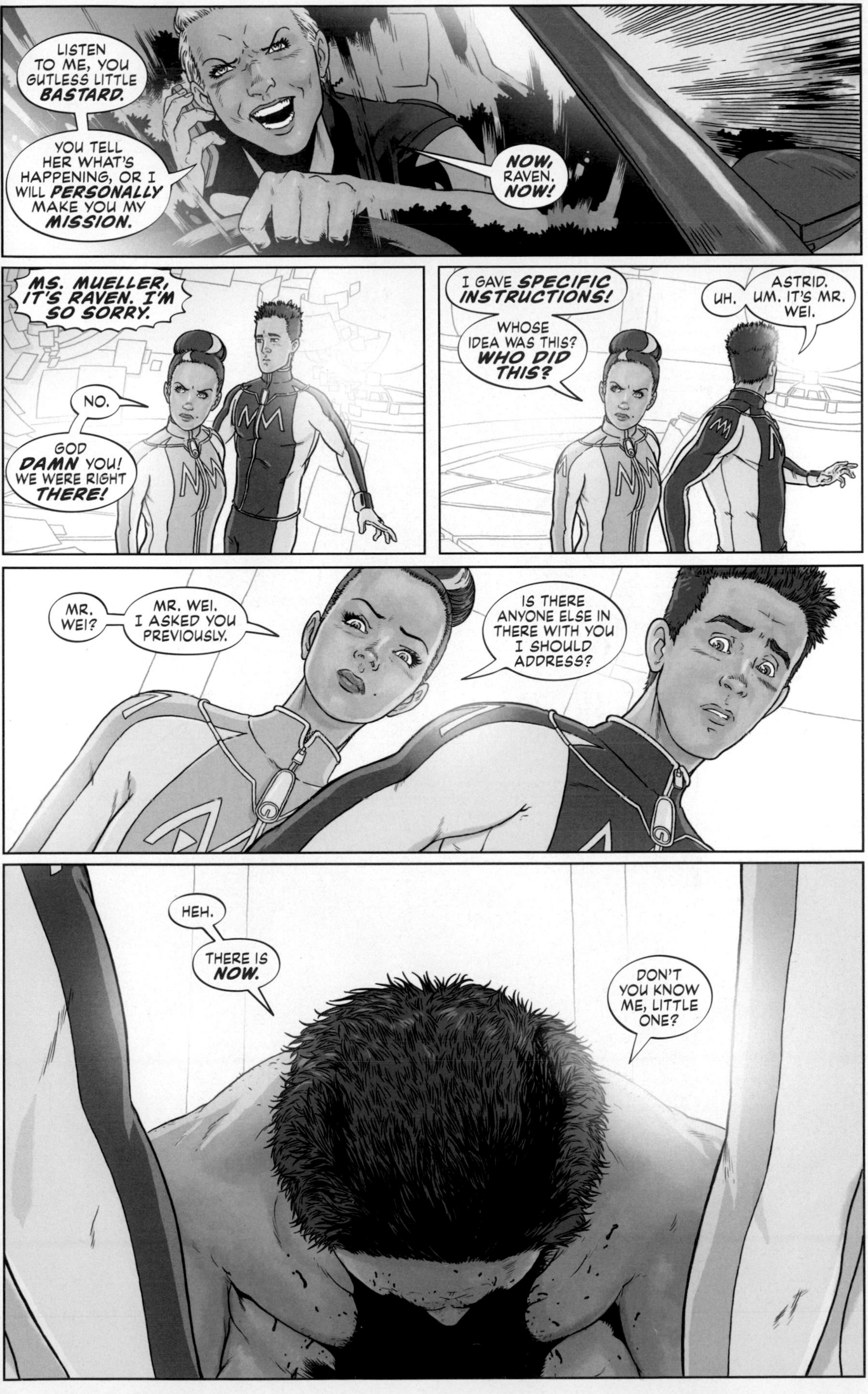
LISTEN TO ME, YOU GUTLESS LITTLE BASTARD.
YOU TELL HER WHAT'S HAPPENING, OR I WILL PERSONALLY MAKE YOU MY MISSION.
NOW, RAVEN. NOW!
MS. MUELLER, IT'S RAVEN. I'M SO SORRY.
NO.
GOD DAMN YOU! WE WERE RIGHT THERE!
I GAVE SPECIFIC INSTRUCTIONS!
WHOSE IDEA WAS THIS? WHO DID THIS?
UH.
ASTRID. UM. IT'S MR. WEI.
MR. WEI?
MR. WEI. I ASKED YOU PREVIOUSLY.
IS THERE ANYONE ELSE IN THERE WITH YOU I SHOULD ADDRESS?
HEH.
THERE IS NOW.
DON'T YOU KNOW ME, LITTLE ONE?

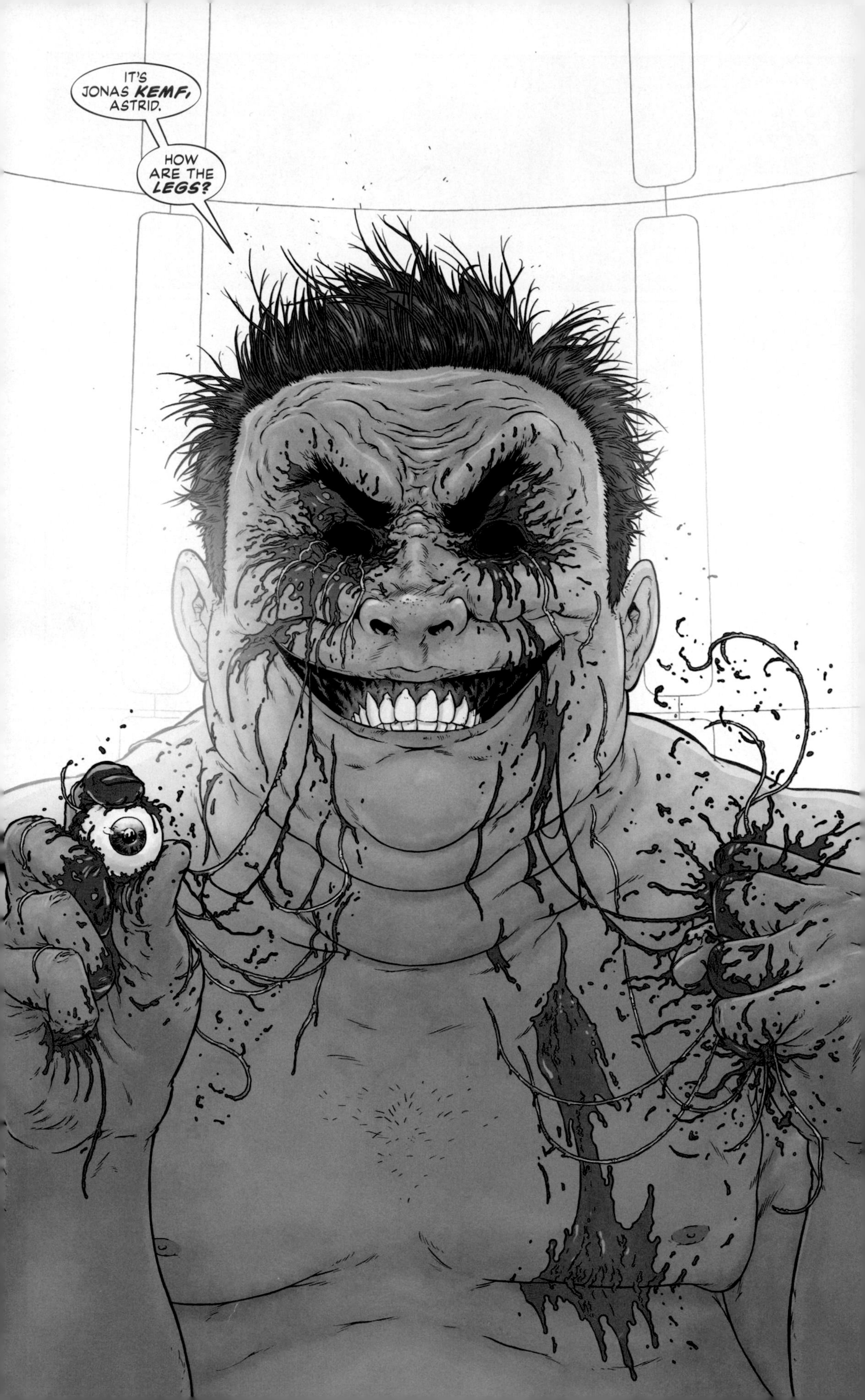
IT'S JONAS KEMF, ASTRID.
HOW ARE THE LEGS?

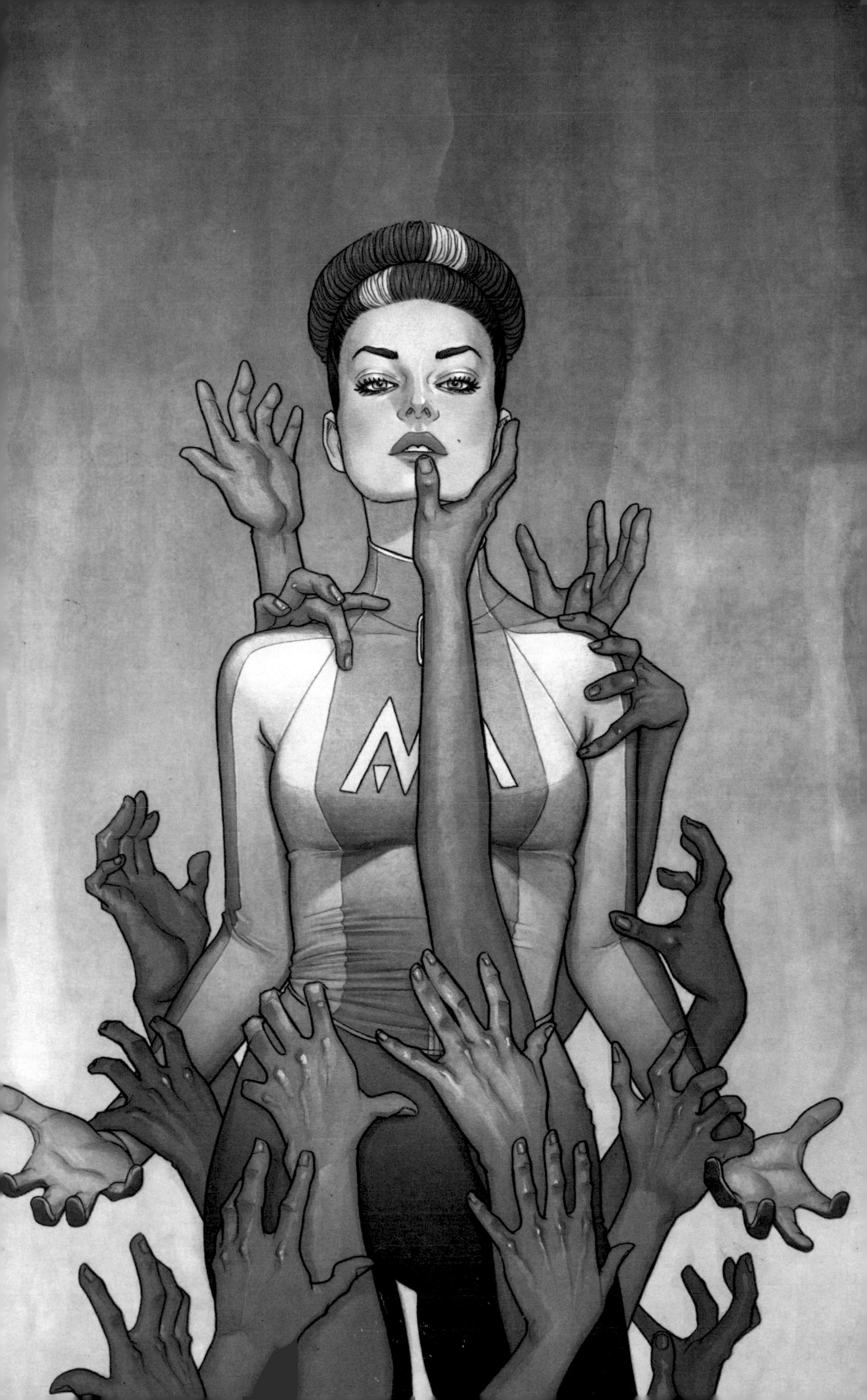

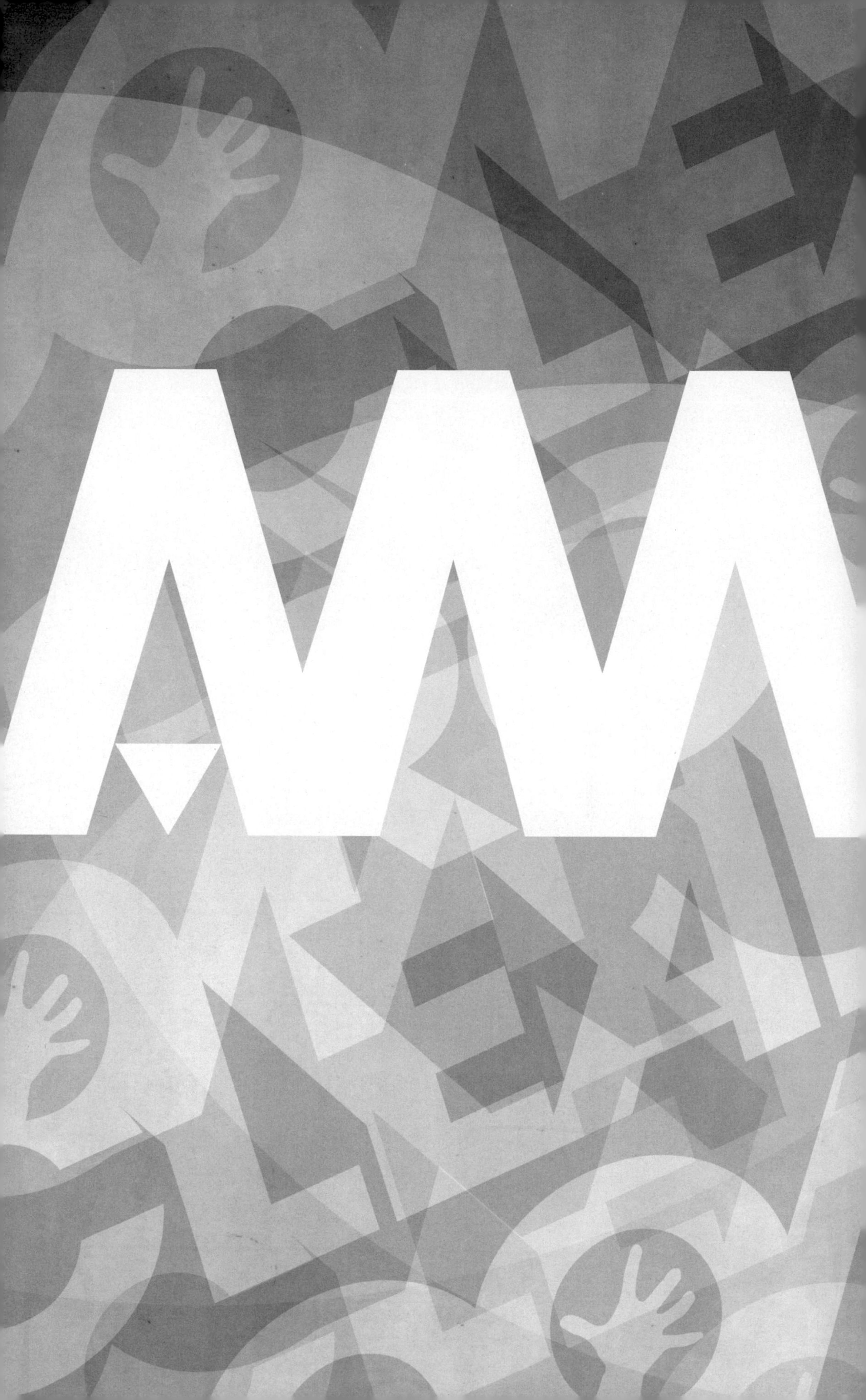

FIFTEEN YEARS AGO, IN NORWAY.
THIS IS GOOD.
THIS SPOT, I FEEL IT PULLING ME. TOUCHING ME.

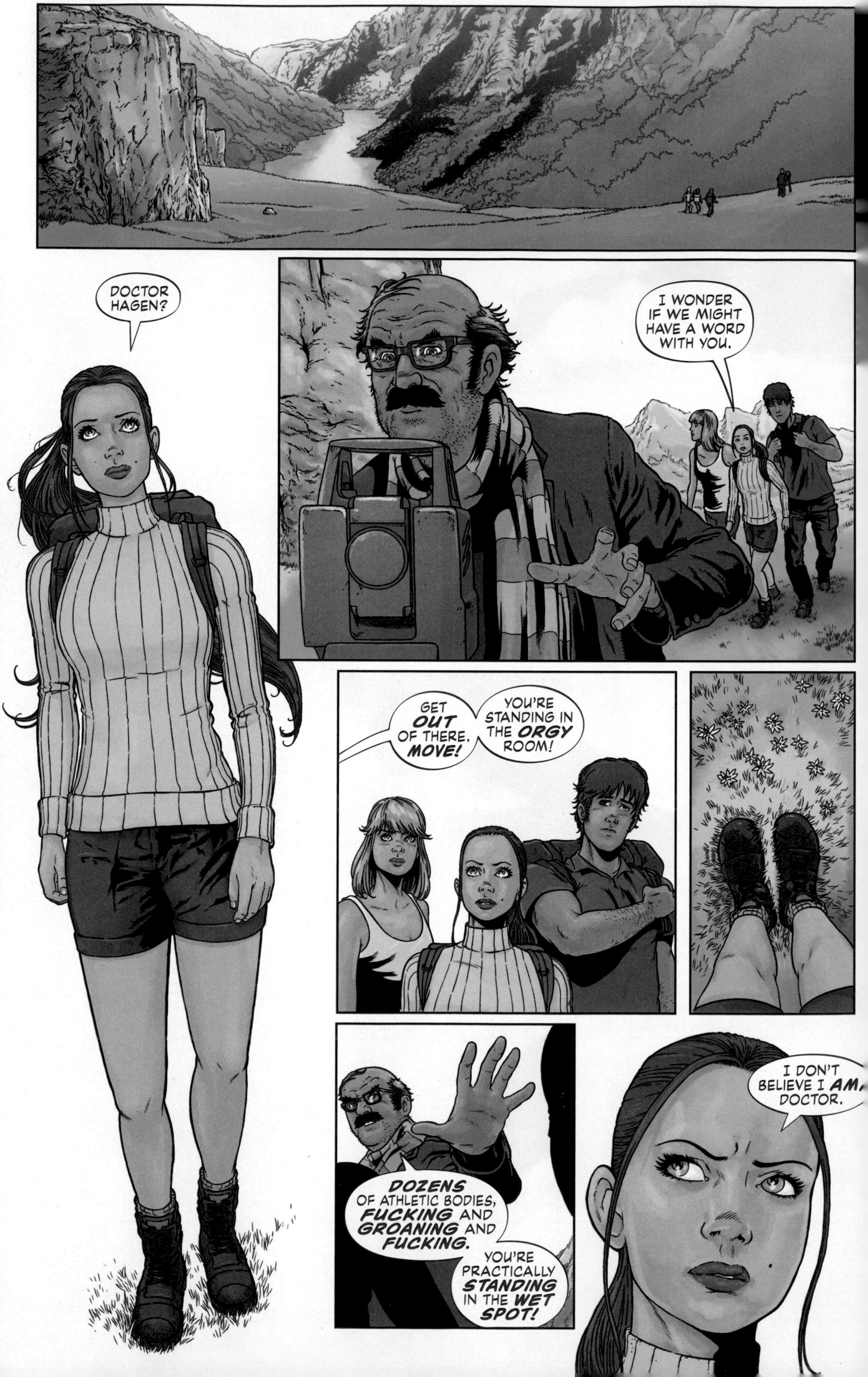

DOCTOR HAGEN?
I WONDER IF WE MIGHT HAVE A WORD WITH YOU.
GET OUT OF THERE. MOVE!
YOU'RE STANDING IN THE ORGY ROOM!
DOZENS OF ATHLETIC BODIES, FUCKING AND GROANING AND FUCKING.
YOU'RE PRACTICALLY STANDING IN THE WET SPOT!
I DON'T BELIEVE I AM, DOCTOR.

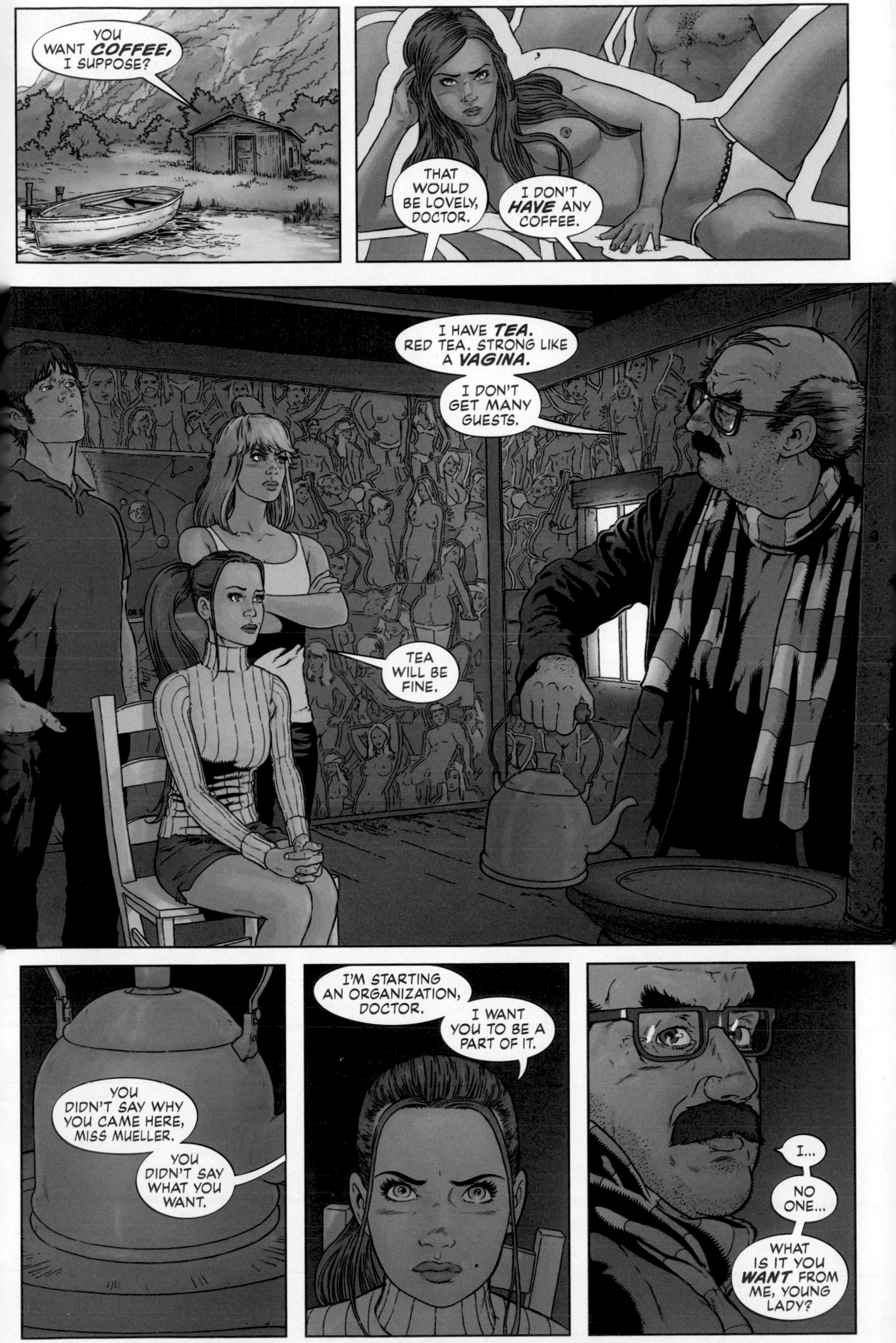
YOU WANT COFFEE, I SUPPOSE?
THAT WOULD BE LOVELY, DOCTOR.
I DON'T HAVE ANY COFFEE.
I HAVE TEA. RED TEA. STRONG LIKE A VAGINA.
I DON'T GET MANY GUESTS.
TEA WILL BE FINE.
YOU DIDN'T SAY WHY YOU CAME HERE, MISS MUELLER.
YOU DIDN'T SAY WHAT YOU WANT.
I'M STARTING AN ORGANIZATION, DOCTOR.
I WANT YOU TO BE A PART OF IT.
I...
NO ONE...
WHAT IS IT YOU WANT FROM ME, YOUNG LADY?

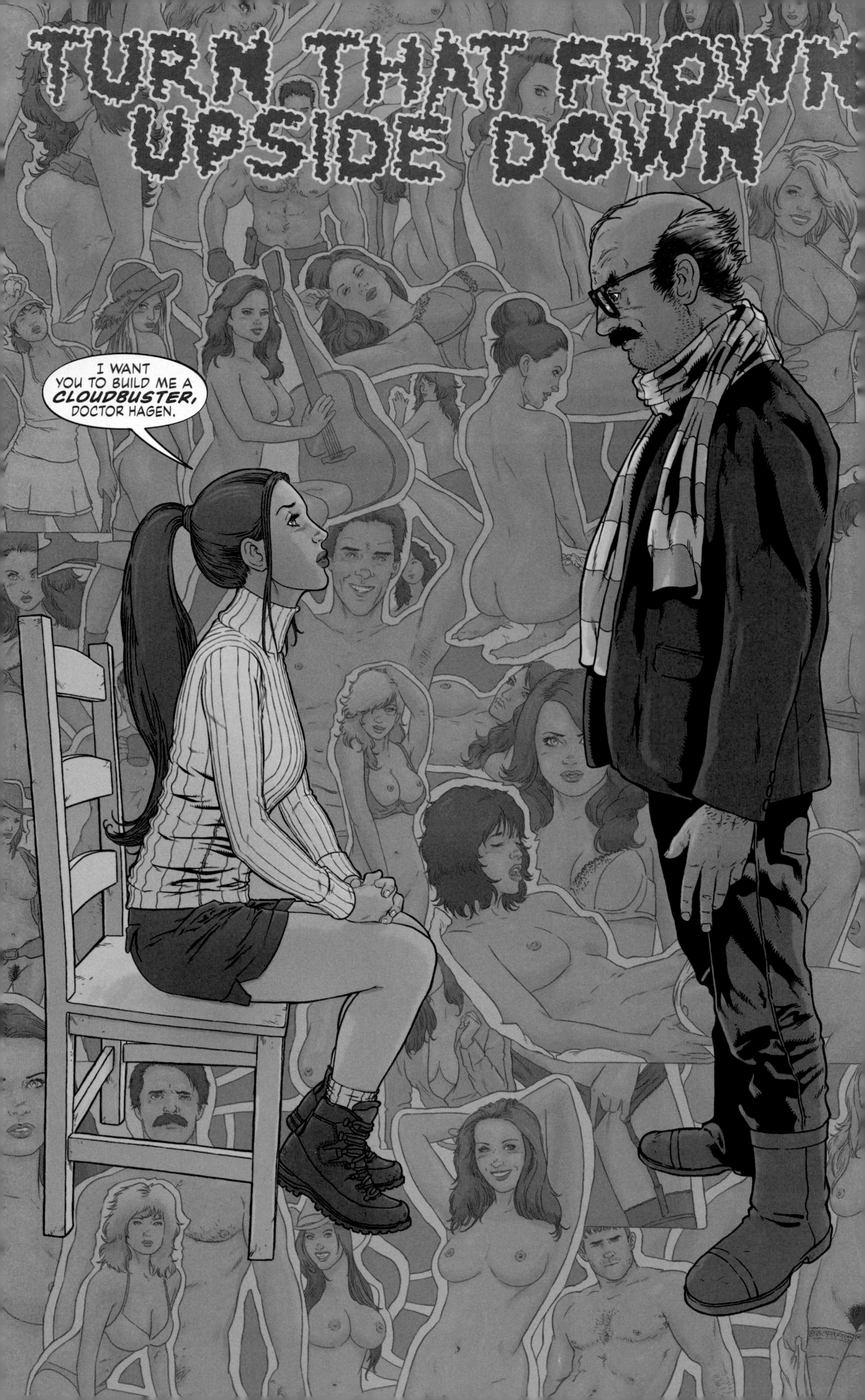
TURN THAT FROWN UPSIDE DOWN
I WANT YOU TO BUILD ME A CLOUDBUSTER, DOCTOR HAGEN.

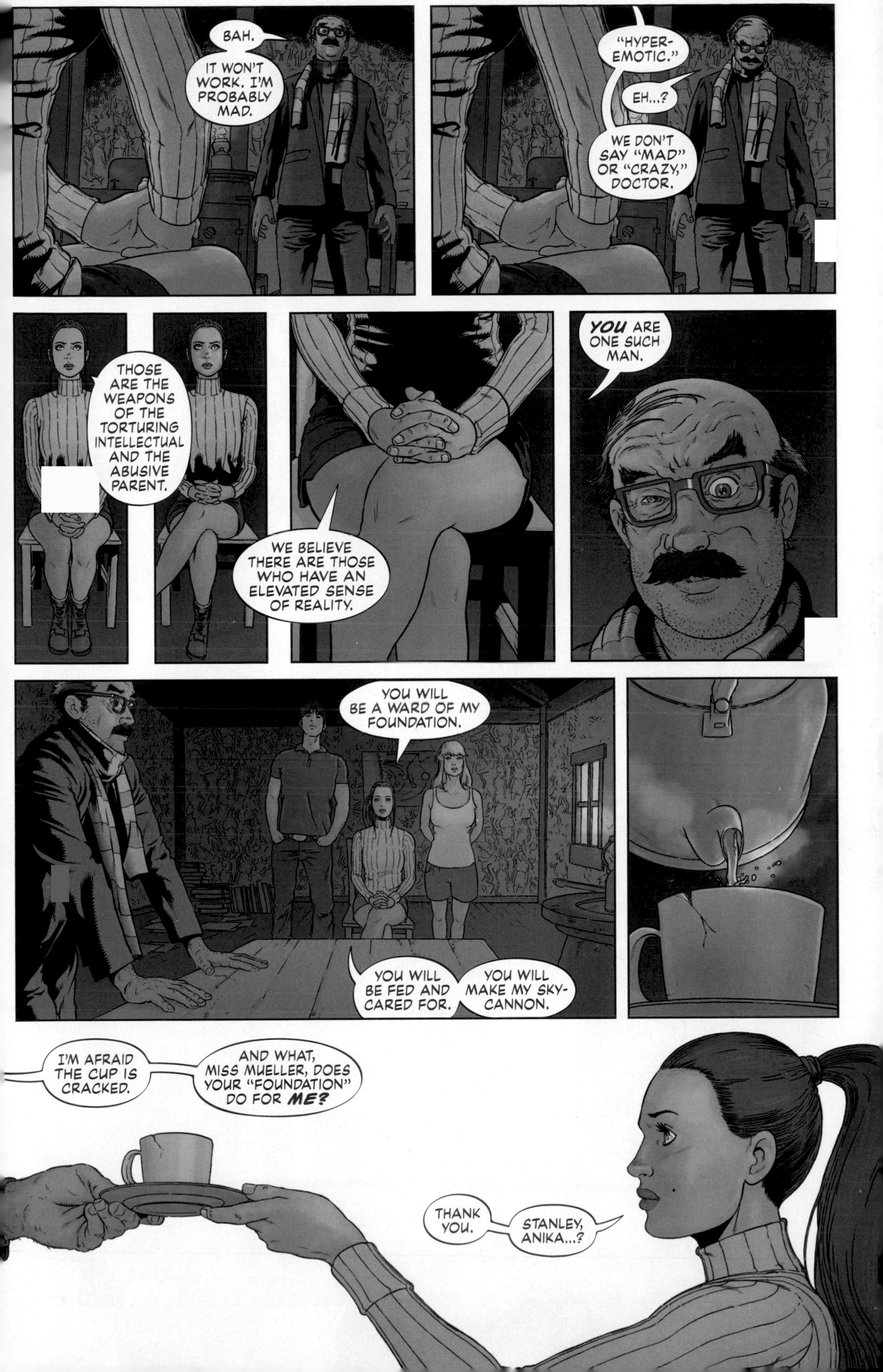
BAH.
IT WON'T WORK. I'M PROBABLY MAD.
"HYPER-EMOTIC."
EH...?
WE DON'T SAY "MAD" OR "CRAZY," DOCTOR.
THOSE ARE THE WEAPONS OF THE TORTURING INTELLECTUAL AND THE ABUSIVE PARENT.
WE BELIEVE THERE ARE THOSE WHO HAVE AN ELEVATED SENSE OF REALITY.
YOU ARE ONE SUCH MAN.
YOU WILL BE A WARD OF MY FOUNDATION.
YOU WILL BE FED AND CARED FOR.
YOU WILL MAKE MY SKY-CANNON.
I'M AFRAID THE CUP IS CRACKED.
AND WHAT, MISS MUELLER, DOES YOUR "FOUNDATION" DO FOR ME?
THANK YOU.
STANLEY, ANIKA...?

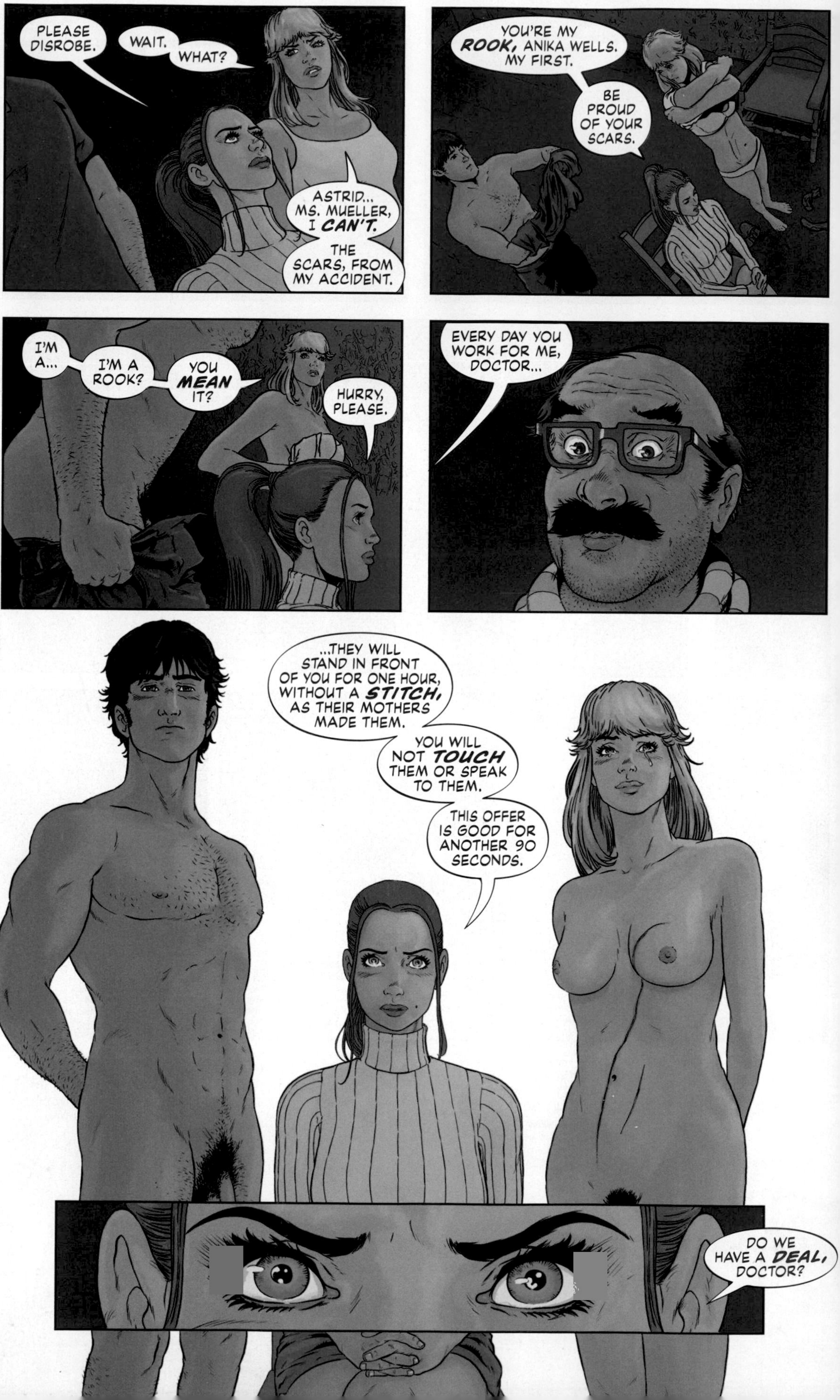
PLEASE DISROBE.
WAIT.
WHAT?
ASTRID... MS. MUELLER, I CAN'T.
THE SCARS, FROM MY ACCIDENT.
YOU'RE MY ROOK, ANIKA WELLS. MY FIRST.
BE PROUD OF YOUR SCARS.
I'M A...
I'M A ROOK?
YOU MEAN IT?
HURRY, PLEASE.
EVERY DAY YOU WORK FOR ME, DOCTOR...
...THEY WILL STAND IN FRONT OF YOU FOR ONE HOUR, WITHOUT A STITCH, AS THEIR MOTHERS MADE THEM.
YOU WILL NOT TOUCH THEM OR SPEAK TO THEM.
THIS OFFER IS GOOD FOR ANOTHER 90 SECONDS.
DO WE HAVE A DEAL, DOCTOR?

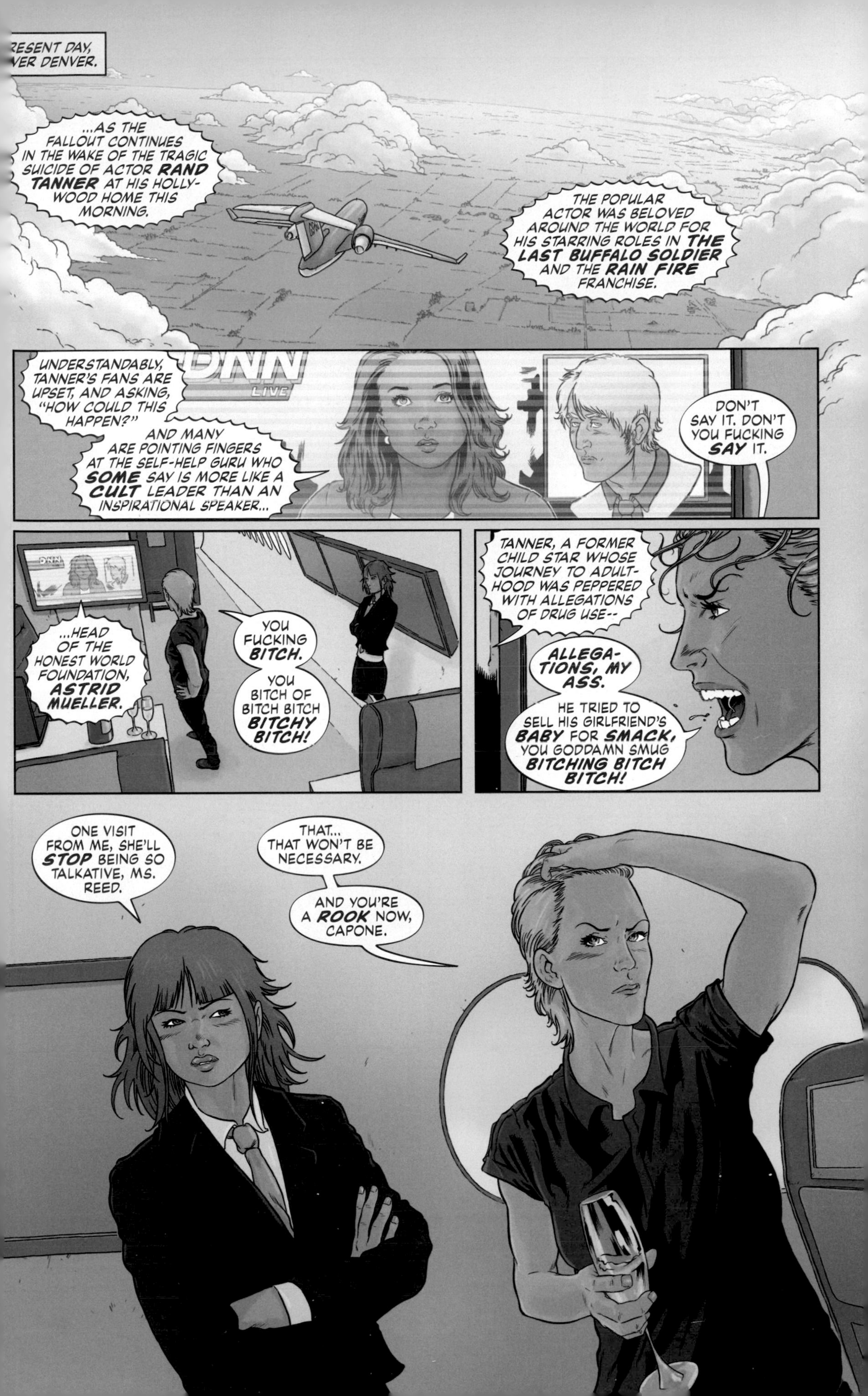

RESENT DAY, VER DENVER.
...AS THE FALLOUT CONTINUES IN THE WAKE OF THE TRAGIC SUICIDE OF ACTOR RAND TANNER AT HIS HOLLY-WOOD HOME THIS MORNING.
THE POPULAR ACTOR WAS BELOVED AROUND THE WORLD FOR HIS STARRING ROLES IN THE LAST BUFFALO SOLDIER AND THE RAIN FIRE FRANCHISE.
UNDERSTANDABLY, TANNER'S FANS ARE UPSET, AND ASKING, "HOW COULD THIS HAPPEN?"
AND MANY ARE POINTING FINGERS AT THE SELF-HELP GURU WHO SOME SAY IS MORE LIKE A CULT LEADER THAN AN INSPIRATIONAL SPEAKER...
DNN LIVE
DON'T SAY IT. DON'T YOU FUCKING SAY IT.
...HEAD OF THE HONEST WORLD FOUNDATION, ASTRID MUELLER.
YOU FUCKING BITCH.
YOU BITCH OF BITCH BITCH BITCHY BITCH!
TANNER, A FORMER CHILD STAR WHOSE JOURNEY TO ADULT-HOOD WAS PEPPERED WITH ALLEGATIONS OF DRUG USE--
ALLEGA-TIONS, MY ASS.
HE TRIED TO SELL HIS GIRLFRIEND'S BABY FOR SMACK, YOU GODDAMN SMUG BITCHING BITCH BITCH!
ONE VISIT FROM ME, SHE'LL STOP BEING SO TALKATIVE, MS. REED.
THAT... THAT WON'T BE NECESSARY.
AND YOU'RE A ROOK NOW, CAPONE.

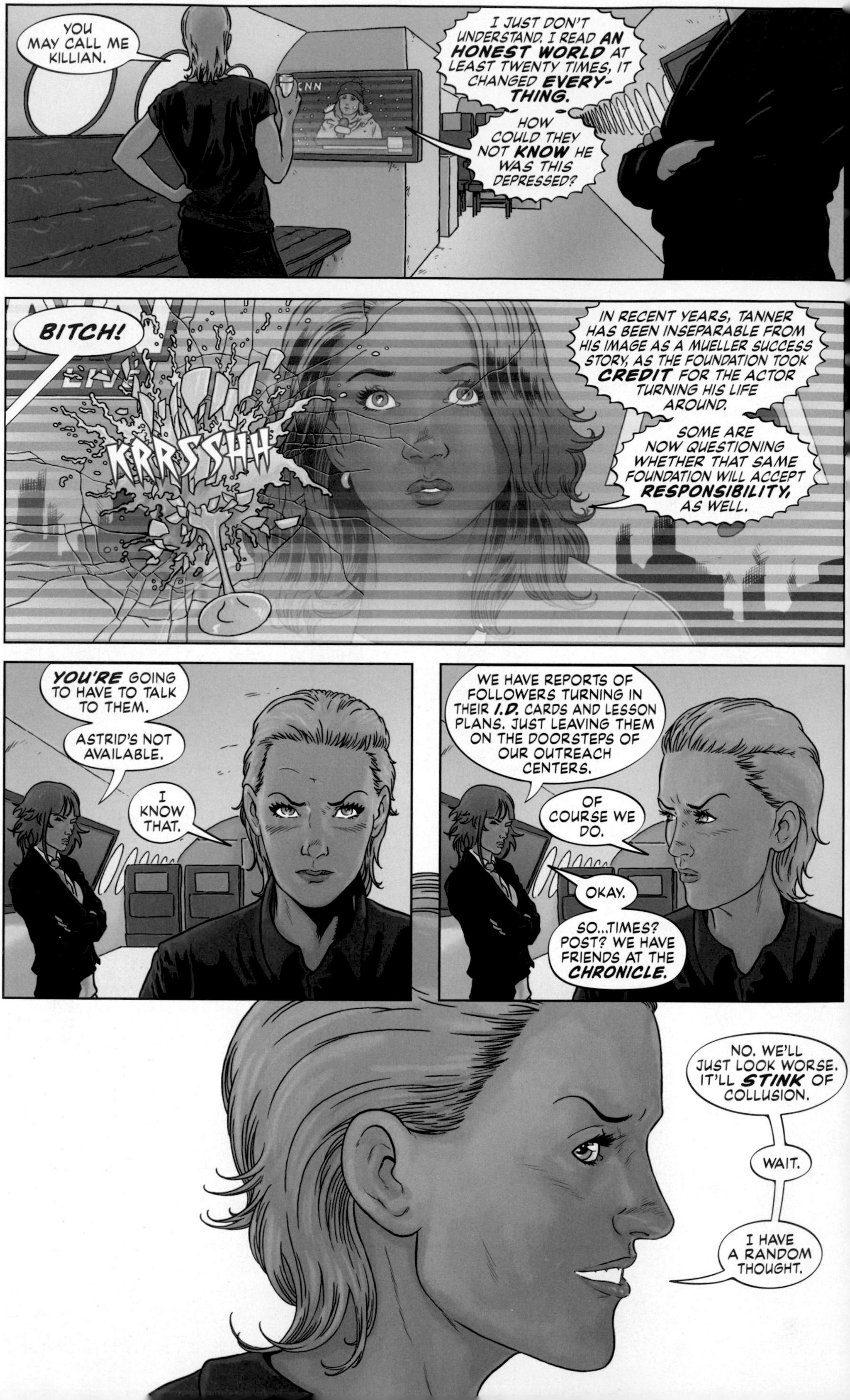
YOU MAY CALL ME KILLIAN.
I JUST DON'T UNDERSTAND. I READ AN HONEST WORLD AT LEAST TWENTY TIMES, IT CHANGED EVERYTHING.
HOW COULD THEY NOT KNOW HE WAS THIS DEPRESSED?
BITCH!
KRRSSHH
IN RECENT YEARS, TANNER HAS BEEN INSEPARABLE FROM HIS IMAGE AS A MUELLER SUCCESS STORY, AS THE FOUNDATION TOOK CREDIT FOR THE ACTOR TURNING HIS LIFE AROUND.
SOME ARE NOW QUESTIONING WHETHER THAT SAME FOUNDATION WILL ACCEPT RESPONSIBILITY, AS WELL.
YOU'RE GOING TO HAVE TO TALK TO THEM.
ASTRID'S NOT AVAILABLE.
I KNOW THAT.
WE HAVE REPORTS OF FOLLOWERS TURNING IN THEIR I.D. CARDS AND LESSON PLANS. JUST LEAVING THEM ON THE DOORSTEPS OF OUR OUTREACH CENTERS.
OF COURSE WE DO.
OKAY.
SO...TIMES? POST? WE HAVE FRIENDS AT THE CHRONICLE.
NO. WE'LL JUST LOOK WORSE. IT'LL STINK OF COLLUSION.
WAIT.
I HAVE A RANDOM THOUGHT.

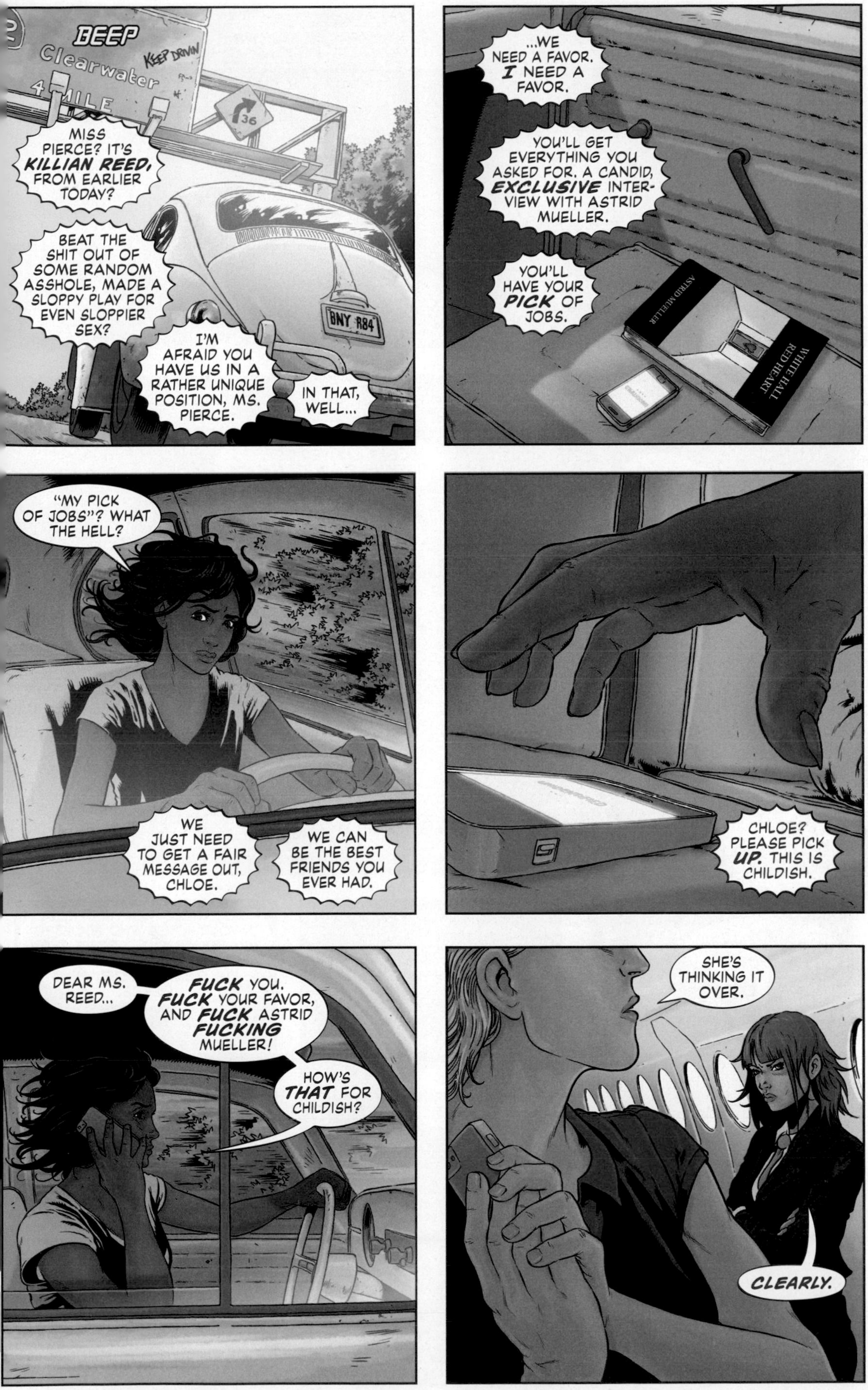
BEEP
Clearwater
4 MILE
KEEP DRIVIN
36
MISS PIERCE? IT'S KILLIAN REED, FROM EARLIER TODAY?
BEAT THE SHIT OUT OF SOME RANDOM ASSHOLE, MADE A SLOPPY PLAY FOR EVEN SLOPPIER SEX?
BNY R84
I'M AFRAID YOU HAVE US IN A RATHER UNIQUE POSITION, MS. PIERCE.
IN THAT, WELL...
...WE NEED A FAVOR. I NEED A FAVOR.
YOU'LL GET EVERYTHING YOU ASKED FOR. A CANDID, EXCLUSIVE INTERVIEW WITH ASTRID MUELLER.
YOU'LL HAVE YOUR PICK OF JOBS.
ASTRID MUELLER
WHITE HALL RED HEART
"MY PICK OF JOBS"? WHAT THE HELL?
WE JUST NEED TO GET A FAIR MESSAGE OUT, CHLOE.
WE CAN BE THE BEST FRIENDS YOU EVER HAD.
CHLOE? PLEASE PICK UP. THIS IS CHILDISH.
DEAR MS. REED...
FUCK YOU. FUCK YOUR FAVOR, AND FUCK ASTRID FUCKING MUELLER!
HOW'S THAT FOR CHILDISH?
SHE'S THINKING IT OVER.
CLEARLY.

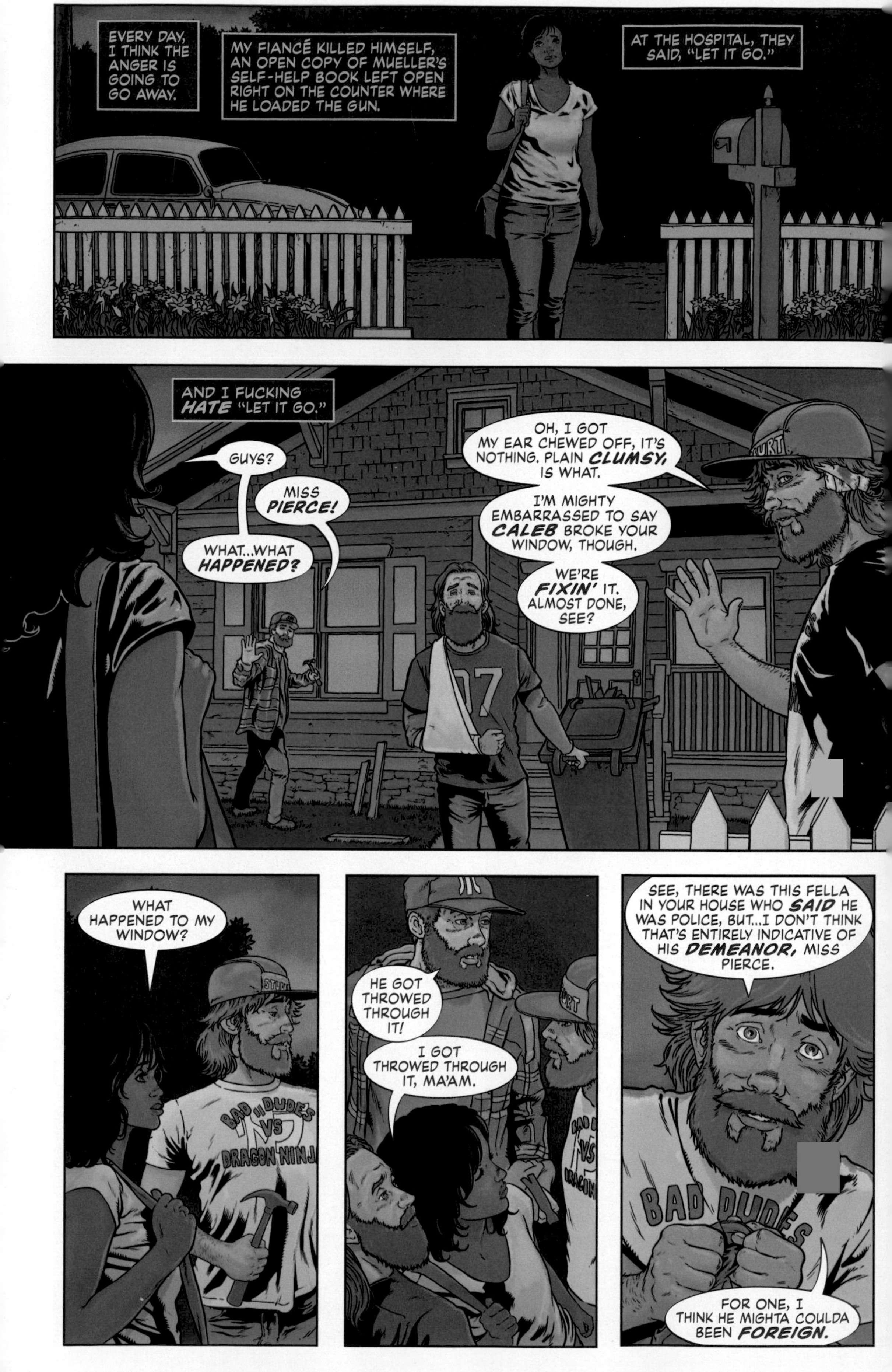
EVERY DAY, I THINK THE ANGER IS GOING TO GO AWAY.
MY FIANCÉ KILLED HIMSELF, AN OPEN COPY OF MUELLER'S SELF-HELP BOOK LEFT OPEN RIGHT ON THE COUNTER WHERE HE LOADED THE GUN.
AT THE HOSPITAL, THEY SAID, "LET IT GO."
AND I FUCKING HATE "LET IT GO."
GUYS?
WHAT...WHAT HAPPENED?
MISS PIERCE!
OH, I GOT MY EAR CHEWED OFF, IT'S NOTHING. PLAIN CLUMSY, IS WHAT.
I'M MIGHTY EMBARRASSED TO SAY CALEB BROKE YOUR WINDOW, THOUGH.
WE'RE FIXIN' IT. ALMOST DONE, SEE?
WHAT HAPPENED TO MY WINDOW?
HE GOT THROWED THROUGH IT!
I GOT THROWED THROUGH IT, MA'AM.
SEE, THERE WAS THIS FELLA IN YOUR HOUSE WHO SAID HE WAS POLICE, BUT...I DON'T THINK THAT'S ENTIRELY INDICATIVE OF HIS DEMEANOR, MISS PIERCE.
FOR ONE, I THINK HE MIGHTA COULDA BEEN FOREIGN.

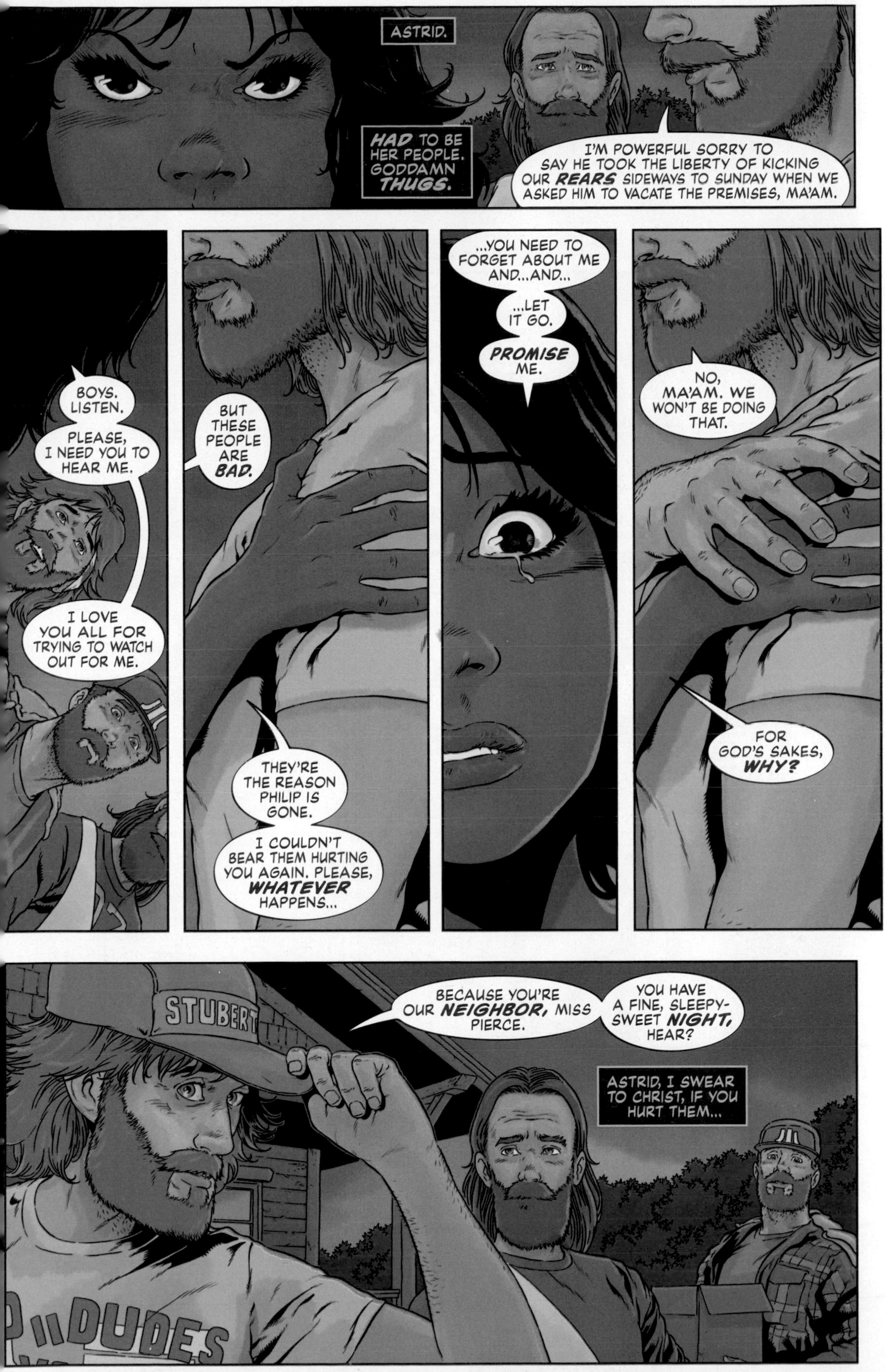
ASTRID.
HAD TO BE HER PEOPLE. GODDAMN THUGS.
I'M POWERFUL SORRY TO SAY HE TOOK THE LIBERTY OF KICKING OUR REARS SIDEWAYS TO SUNDAY WHEN WE ASKED HIM TO VACATE THE PREMISES, MA'AM.
BOYS. LISTEN.
PLEASE, I NEED YOU TO HEAR ME.
I LOVE YOU ALL FOR TRYING TO WATCH OUT FOR ME.
BUT THESE PEOPLE ARE BAD.
THEY'RE THE REASON PHILIP IS GONE.
I COULDN'T BEAR THEM HURTING YOU AGAIN. PLEASE, WHATEVER HAPPENS...
...YOU NEED TO FORGET ABOUT ME AND...AND...
...LET IT GO.
PROMISE ME.
NO, MA'AM. WE WON'T BE DOING THAT.
FOR GOD'S SAKES, WHY?
BECAUSE YOU'RE OUR NEIGHBOR, MISS PIERCE.
YOU HAVE A FINE, SLEEPY-SWEET NIGHT, HEAR?
ASTRID, I SWEAR TO CHRIST, IF YOU HURT THEM...
STUBERT
DUDES

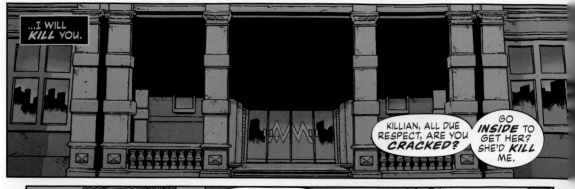

...I WILL *KILL* YOU.

KILLIAN, ALL DUE RESPECT, ARE YOU *CRACKED?*

GO *INSIDE* TO GET HER? SHE'D *KILL* ME.

MR. RAVEN. I WANT YOU TO UNDERSTAND ME VERY CLEARLY.

I AM ON A PLANE ON MY WAY THERE. I HAVE MS. *CAPONE* WITH ME.

LET'S NOT MAKE LIGHT CONVERSATION ABOUT *WHO* MIGHT KILL *WHOM.*

I'M SORRY, MISS REED.

BUT THERE'S SOMETHING IN *THERE* THAT'S WORSE EVEN THAN THAT PSYCHO *YOU'RE* WITH.

PLEASE HURRY.

"SHE *NEEDS* YOU."

MISS MUELLER. IT'S BEEN FOUR *HOURS.*

HUSH, PLEASE, TERRY.

PLEASE. HE'S...HE'S *GONE* SOMEWHERE.

I CAN'T--I HAVE TO GET *OUT.* I CAN'T BE IN HERE WITH...*THAT*... ANYMORE.

IF YOU CONTINUE TALKING, TERRY...

...I WON'T BE ABLE TO *PROTECT* YOU.

GIVE THAT THOUGHT A SPIN, WON'T YOU?

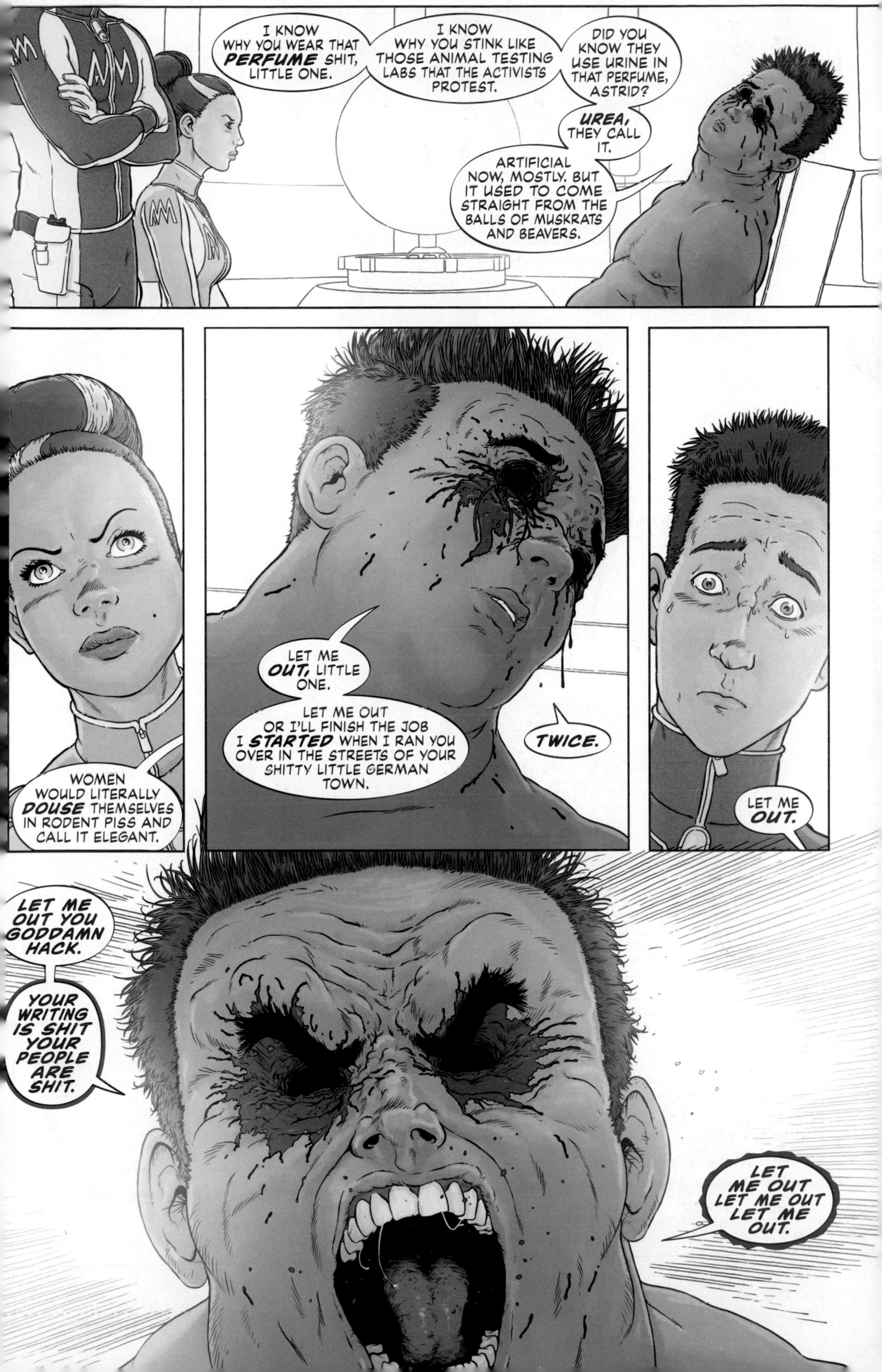
I KNOW WHY YOU WEAR THAT PERFUME SHIT, LITTLE ONE.
I KNOW WHY YOU STINK LIKE THOSE ANIMAL TESTING LABS THAT THE ACTIVISTS PROTEST.
DID YOU KNOW THEY USE URINE IN THAT PERFUME, ASTRID?
UREA, THEY CALL IT.
ARTIFICIAL NOW, MOSTLY. BUT IT USED TO COME STRAIGHT FROM THE BALLS OF MUSKRATS AND BEAVERS.
WOMEN WOULD LITERALLY DOUSE THEMSELVES IN RODENT PISS AND CALL IT ELEGANT.
LET ME OUT, LITTLE ONE.
LET ME OUT OR I'LL FINISH THE JOB I STARTED WHEN I RAN YOU OVER IN THE STREETS OF YOUR SHITTY LITTLE GERMAN TOWN.
TWICE.
LET ME OUT.
LET ME OUT YOU GODDAMN HACK.
YOUR WRITING IS SHIT YOUR PEOPLE ARE SHIT.
LET ME OUT LET ME OUT LET ME OUT.

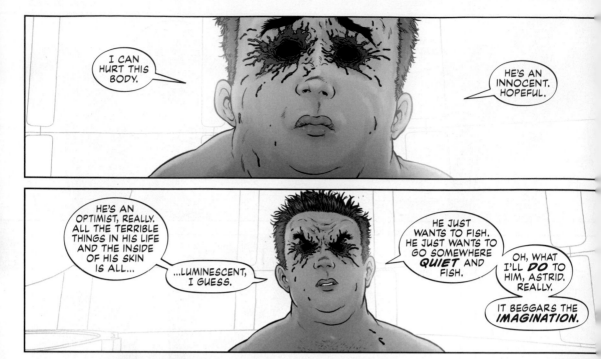

I CAN HURT THIS BODY.

HE'S AN INNOCENT. HOPEFUL.

HE'S AN OPTIMIST, REALLY. ALL THE TERRIBLE THINGS IN HIS LIFE AND THE INSIDE OF HIS SKIN IS ALL...

...LUMINESCENT, I GUESS.

HE JUST WANTS TO FISH. HE JUST WANTS TO GO SOMEWHERE *QUIET* AND FISH.

OH, WHAT I'LL *DO* TO HIM, ASTRID. REALLY.

IT BEGGARS THE *IMAGINATION.*

YOU'VE ALREADY GOUGED OUT HIS EYES, ENTITY.

I'D SAY HIS FISHING DAYS ARE OVER.

WHY ARE YOU SMILING?

OH, JUST THINKING.

YOUR TINY BODY MADE THE FUNNIEST LITTLE LUMP IN THE ROAD AS I RAN MY TIRES OVER IT.

YOUR BROTHER NEVER REALLY *DID* RECOVER, DID HE?

WHAT IS YOUR NAME, CREATURE?

WHAT ARE YOU *CALLED?*

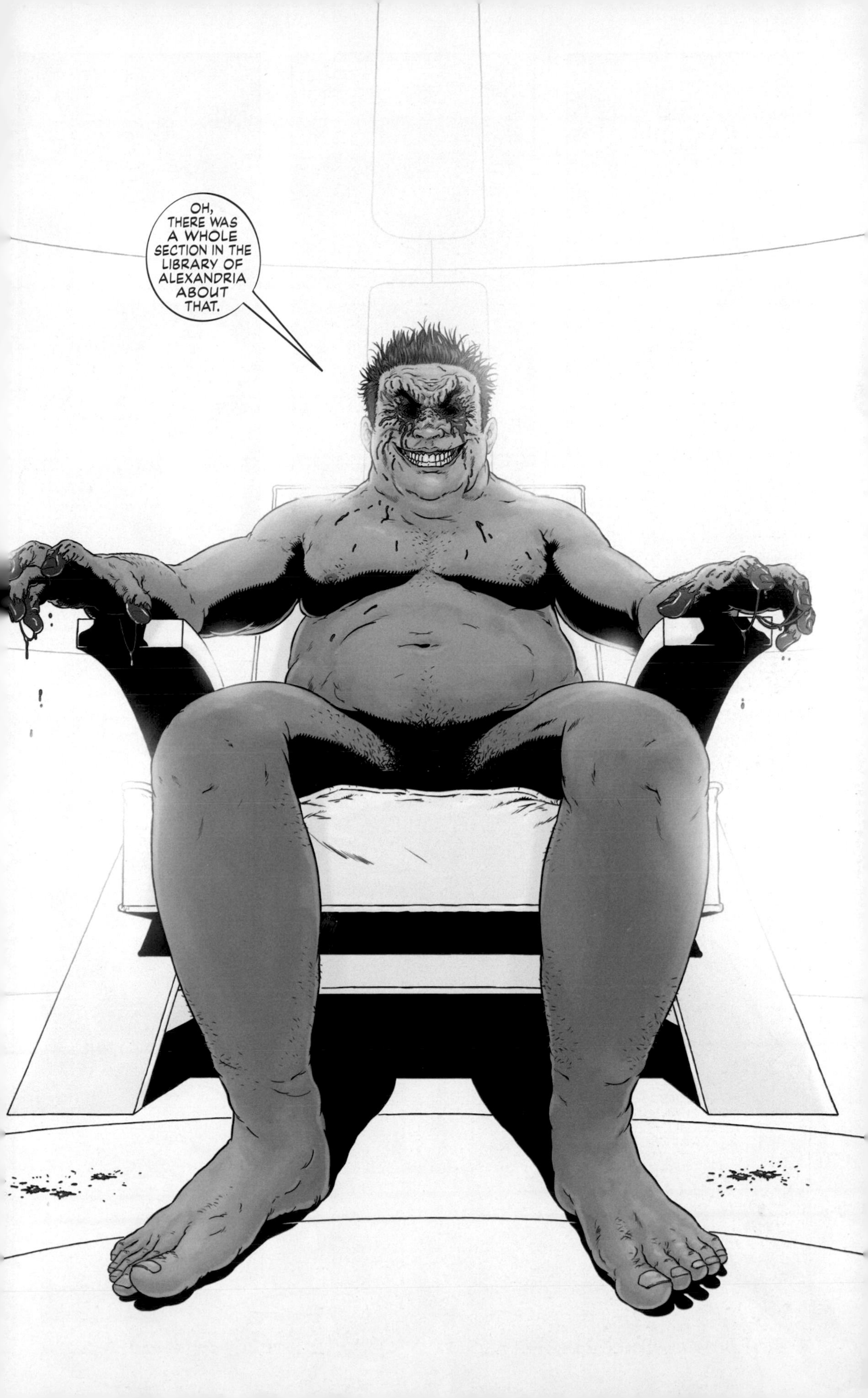
OH, THERE WAS A WHOLE SECTION IN THE LIBRARY OF ALEXANDRIA ABOUT THAT.

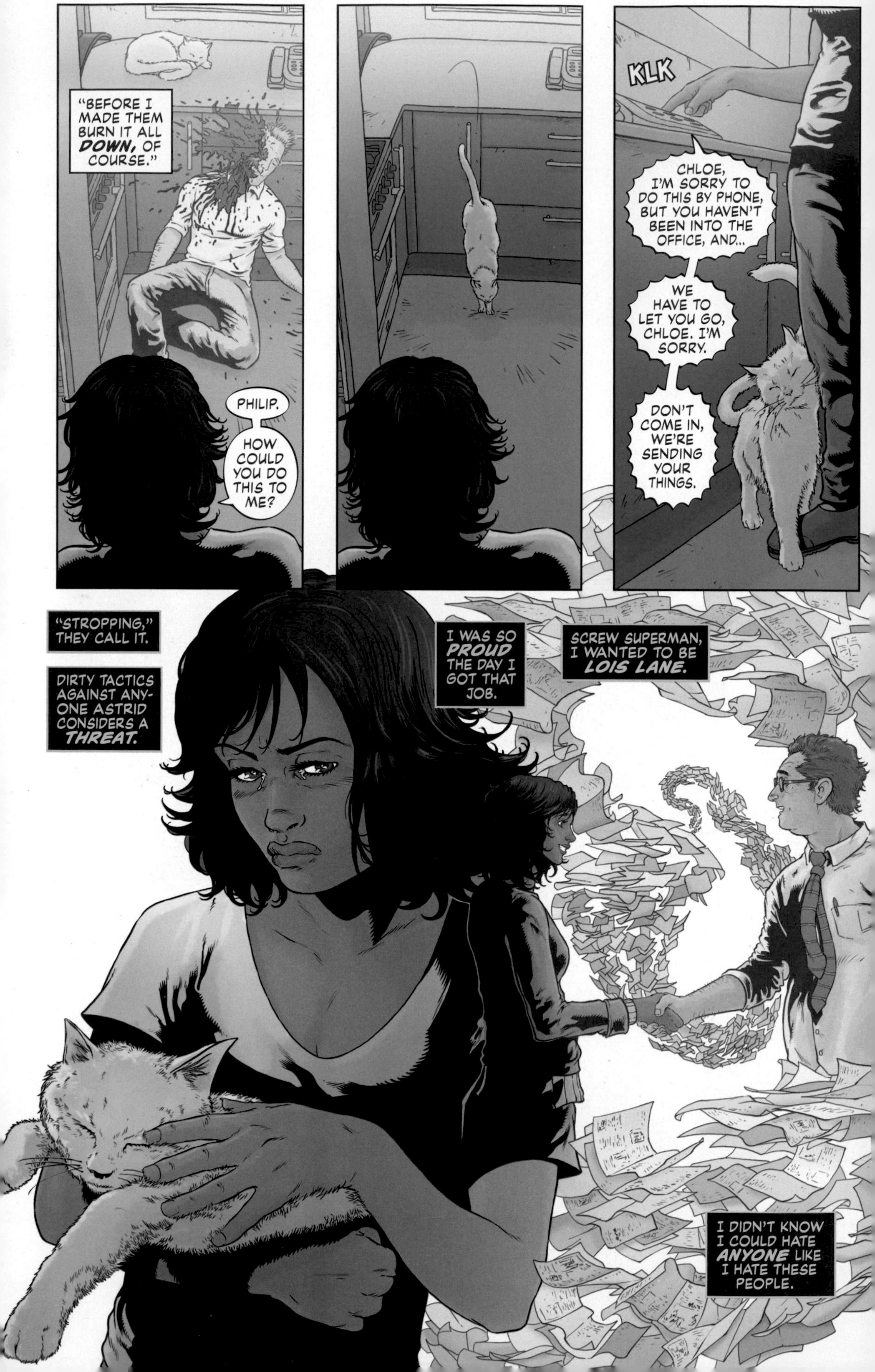
"BEFORE I MADE THEM BURN IT ALL DOWN, OF COURSE."
PHILIP.
HOW COULD YOU DO THIS TO ME?
KLK
CHLOE, I'M SORRY TO DO THIS BY PHONE, BUT YOU HAVEN'T BEEN INTO THE OFFICE, AND...
WE HAVE TO LET YOU GO, CHLOE. I'M SORRY.
DON'T COME IN, WE'RE SENDING YOUR THINGS.
"STROPPING," THEY CALL IT.
DIRTY TACTICS AGAINST ANY-ONE ASTRID CONSIDERS A THREAT.
I WAS SO PROUD THE DAY I GOT THAT JOB.
SCREW SUPERMAN, I WANTED TO BE LOIS LANE.
I DIDN'T KNOW I COULD HATE ANYONE LIKE I HATE THESE PEOPLE.

Where are the knives, sad one?

Where are all the knives?

WHO...?

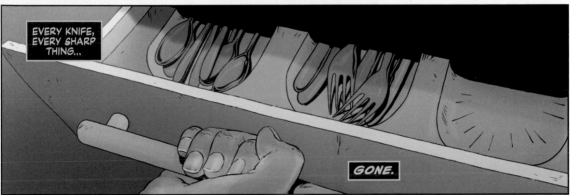

EVERY KNIFE, EVERY SHARP THING...

GONE.

WHO *ARE* YOU? WHAT ARE YOU DOING IN MY *HOUSE?*

I did the funniest thing with them.

Honestly, you'll *DIE.*

Check the *BATHROOM,* Chloe.

Oh, yes, *DO.*

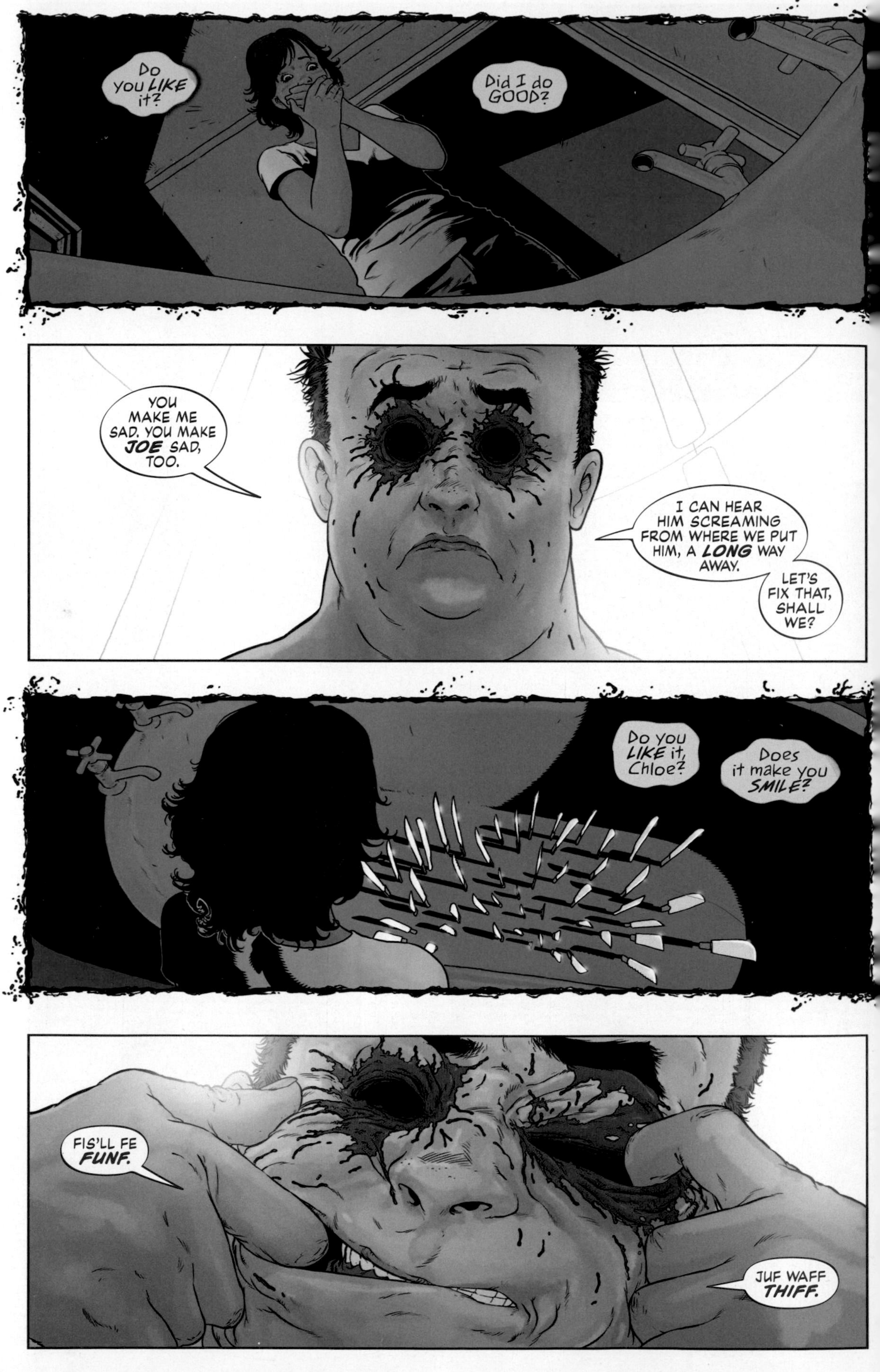
Do you LIKE it?
Did I do GOOD?
YOU MAKE ME SAD. YOU MAKE JOE SAD, TOO.
I CAN HEAR HIM SCREAMING FROM WHERE WE PUT HIM, A LONG WAY AWAY.
LET'S FIX THAT, SHALL WE?
Do you LIKE it, Chloe?
Does it make you SMILE?
FIS'LL FE FUNF.
JUF WAFF THIFF.

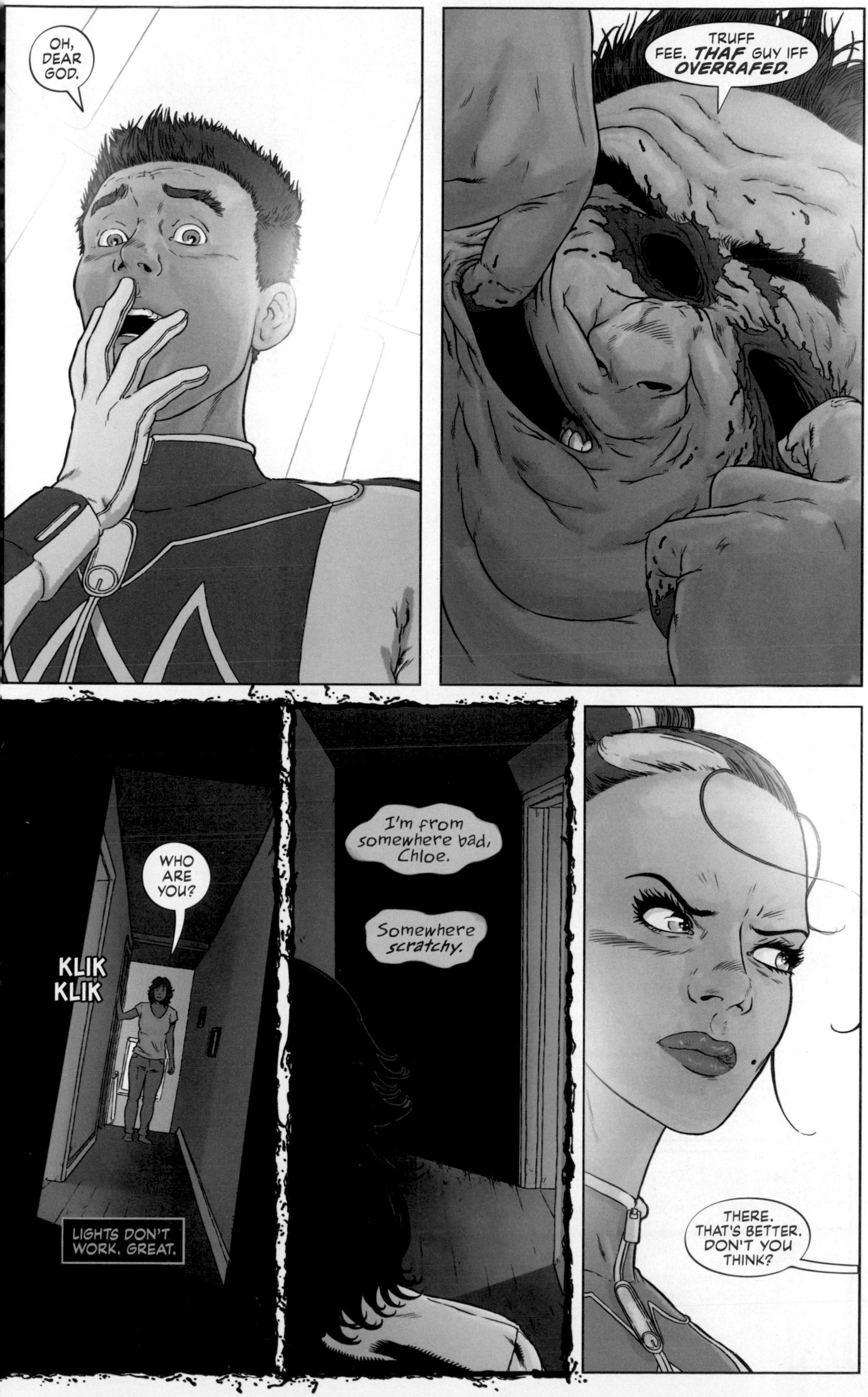
OH, DEAR GOD.
TRUFF FEE. THAF GUY IFF OVERRAFED.
WHO ARE YOU?
KLIK KLIK
LIGHTS DON'T WORK. GREAT.
I'm from somewhere bad, Chloe.
Somewhere scratchy.
THERE. THAT'S BETTER. DON'T YOU THINK?

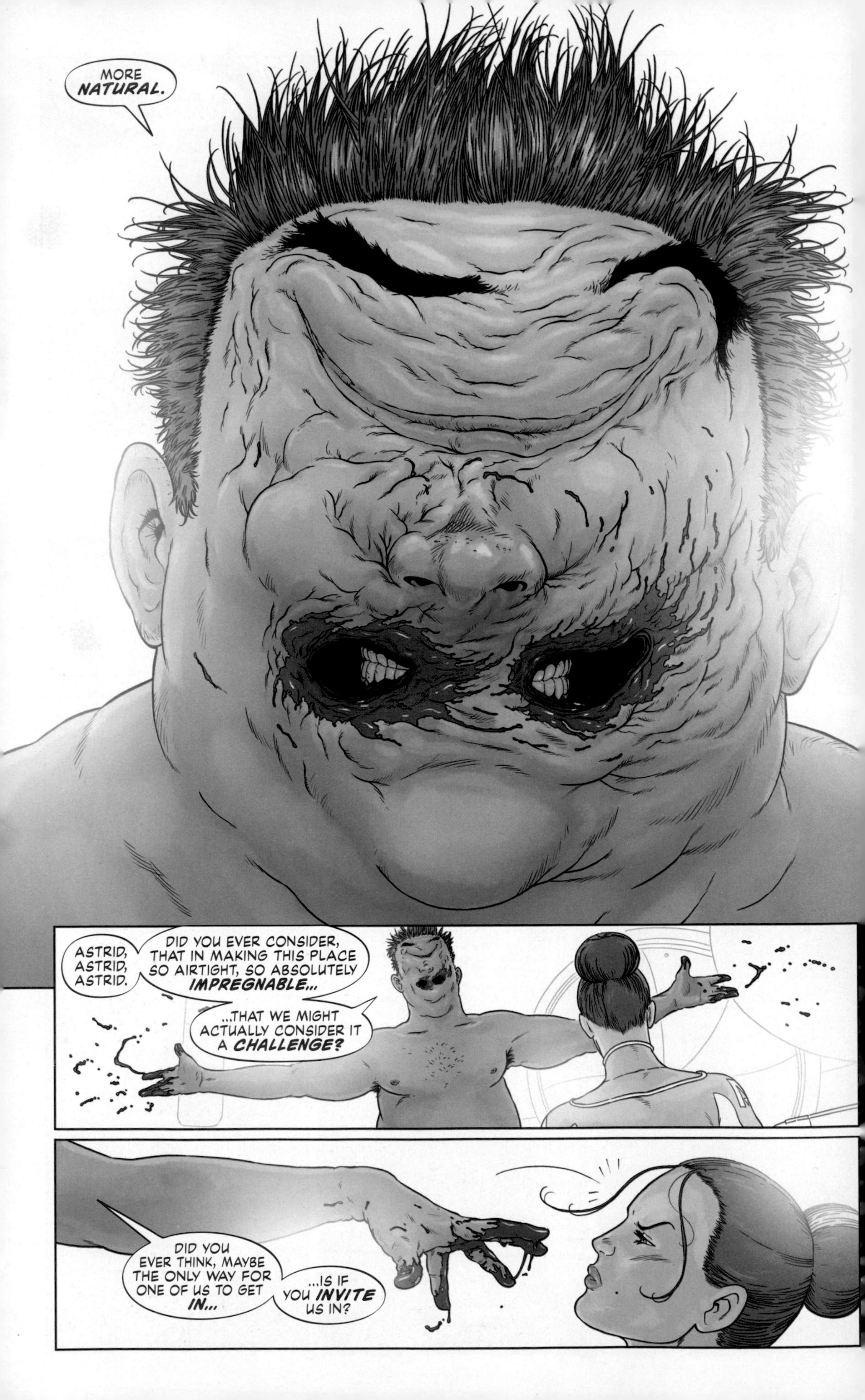
MORE NATURAL.
ASTRID, ASTRID, ASTRID.
DID YOU EVER CONSIDER, THAT IN MAKING THIS PLACE SO AIRTIGHT, SO ABSOLUTELY IMPREGNABLE...
...THAT WE MIGHT ACTUALLY CONSIDER IT A CHALLENGE?
DID YOU EVER THINK, MAYBE THE ONLY WAY FOR ONE OF US TO GET IN...
...IS IF YOU INVITE US IN?

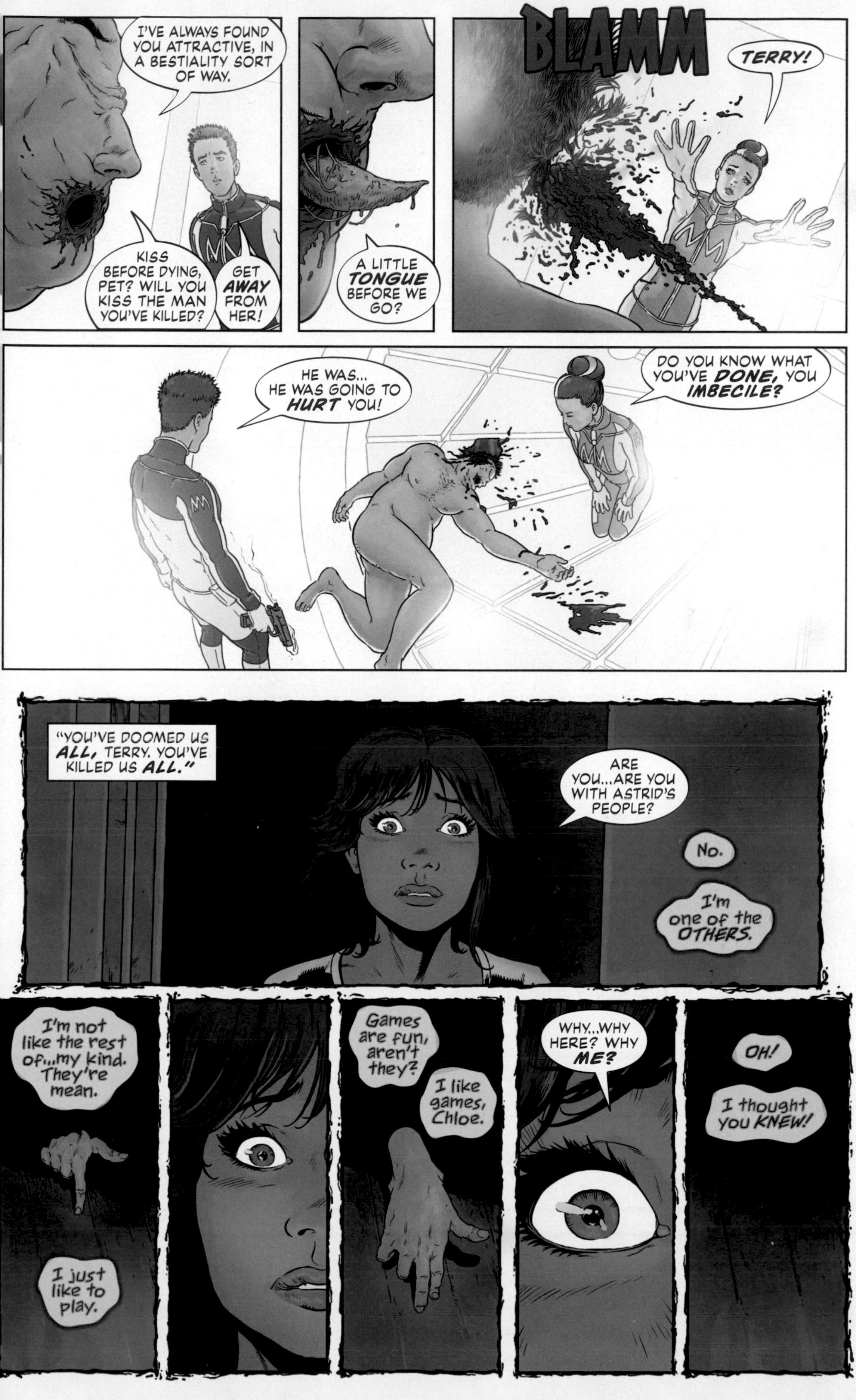
I'VE ALWAYS FOUND YOU ATTRACTIVE, IN A BESTIALITY SORT OF WAY.
KISS BEFORE DYING, PET? WILL YOU KISS THE MAN YOU'VE KILLED?
GET AWAY FROM HER!
A LITTLE TONGUE BEFORE WE GO?
BLAMM
TERRY!
HE WAS... HE WAS GOING TO HURT YOU!
DO YOU KNOW WHAT YOU'VE DONE, YOU IMBECILE?
"YOU'VE DOOMED US ALL, TERRY. YOU'VE KILLED US ALL."
ARE YOU...ARE YOU WITH ASTRID'S PEOPLE?
No.
I'm one of the OTHERS.
I'm not like the rest of...my kind. They're mean.
I just like to play.
Games are fun, aren't they?
I like games, Chloe.
WHY...WHY HERE? WHY ME?
OH!
I thought you KNEW!

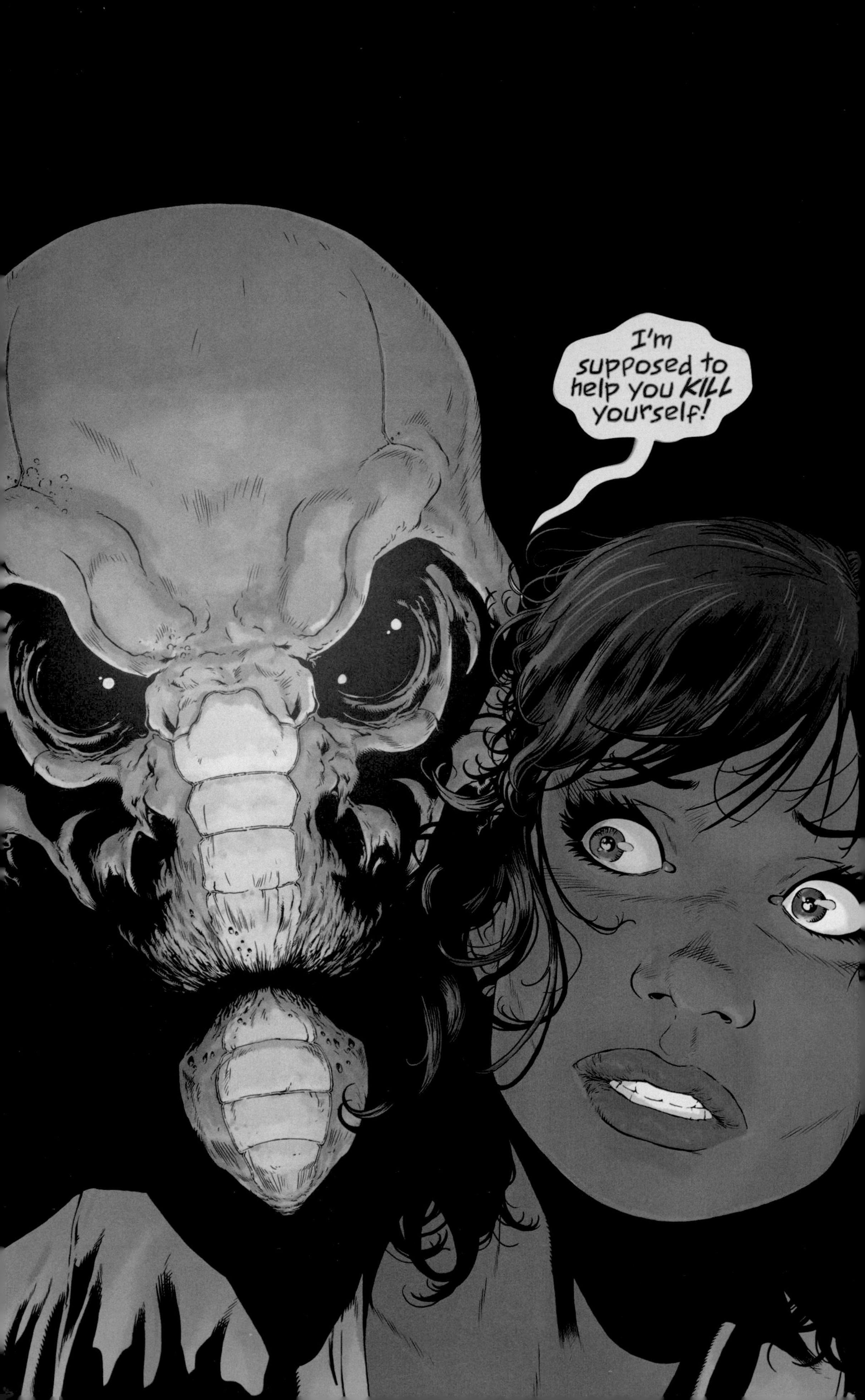
I'm supposed to help you KILL yourself!

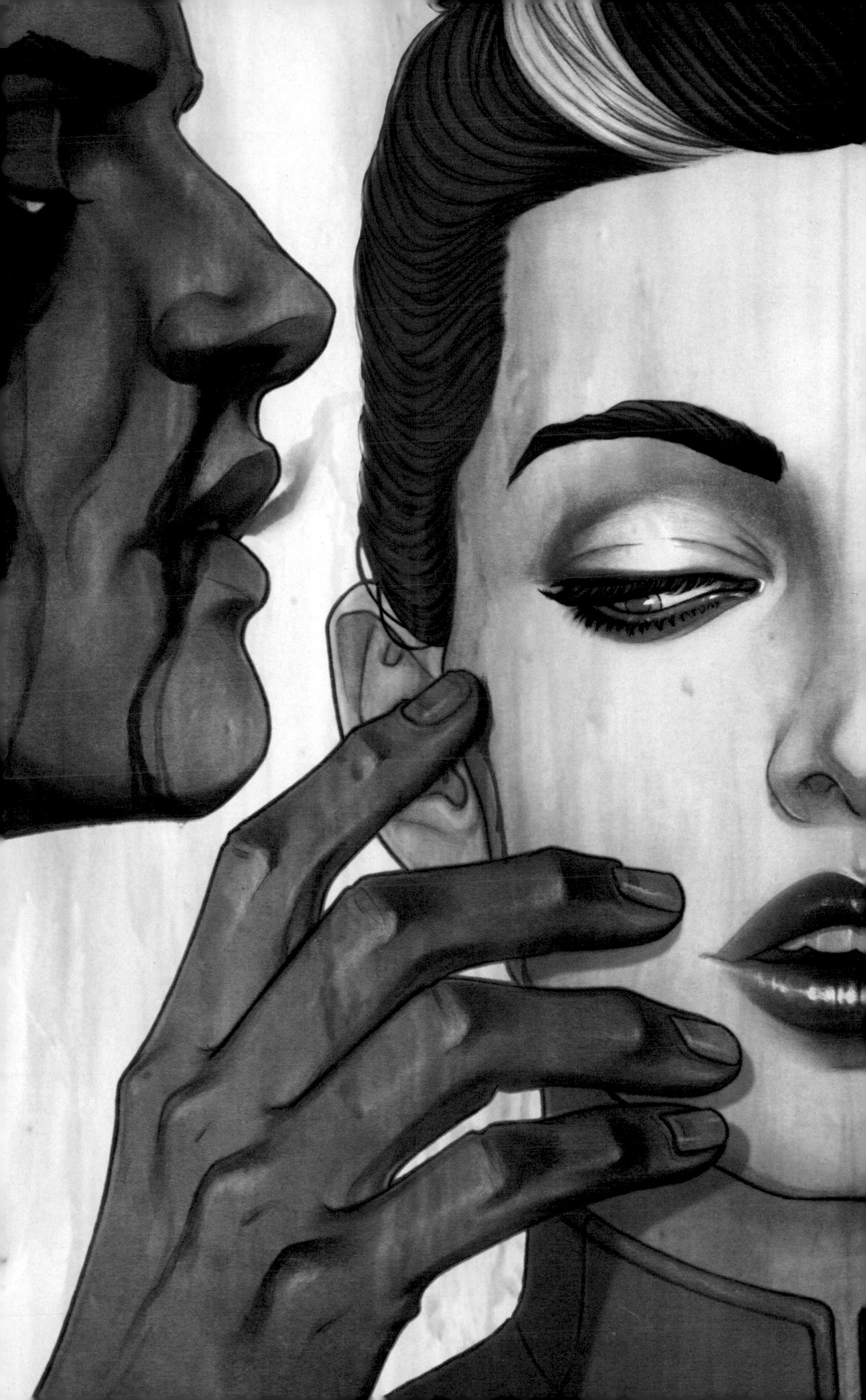

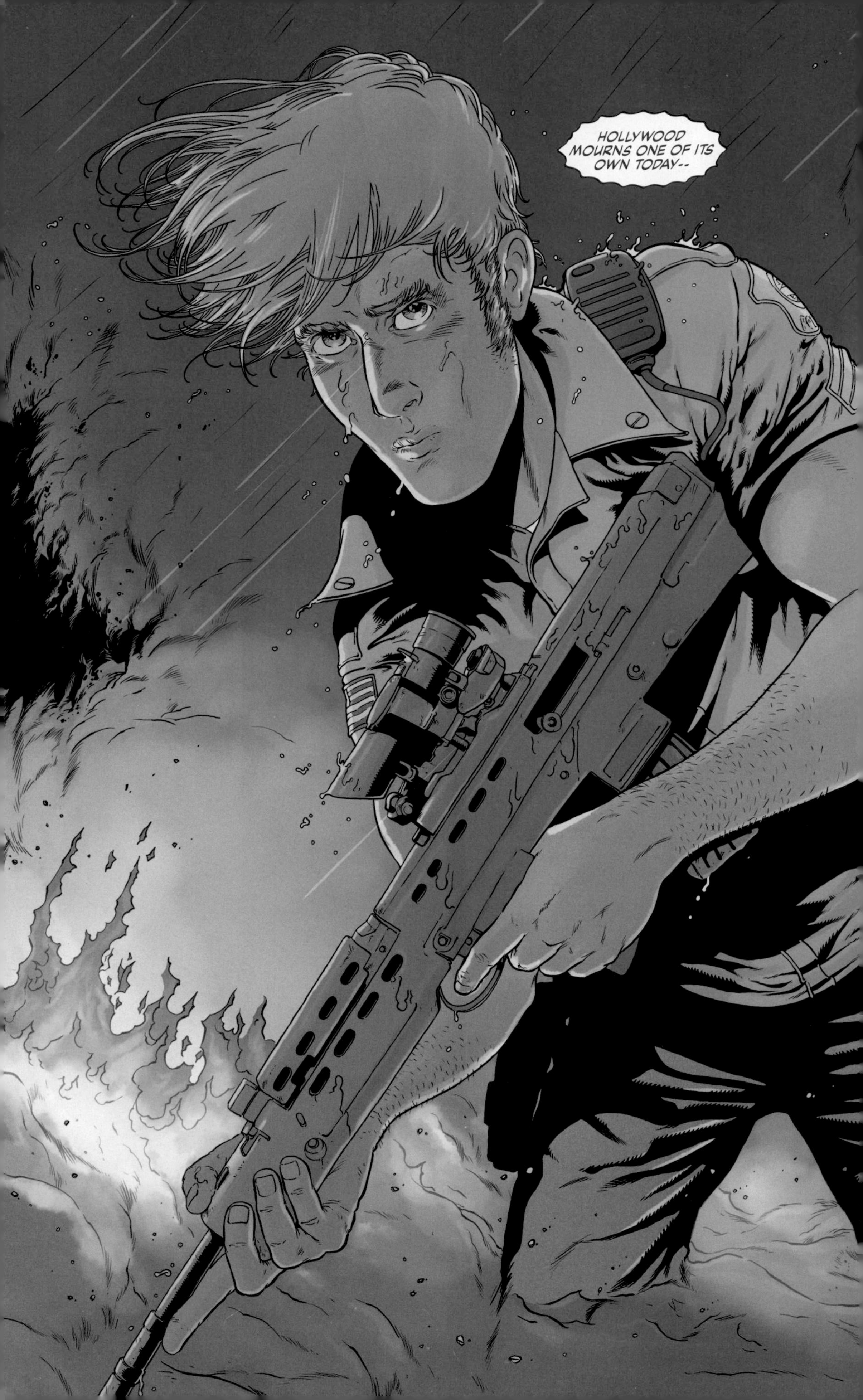
HOLLYWOOD MOURNS ONE OF ITS OWN TODAY--

--AS ONE OF THE BRIGHTEST AND MOST PROMISING YOUNG ACTION STARS HAS DIED, APPARENTLY OF AN OVERDOSE OF PRESCRIPTION MEDICATION.

RAND TANNER DEAD AT 33

HOLLYWOOD TONIGHT **HT**

TANNER HAD BEEN PERHAPS THE MOST PROMINENT SUCCESS STORY OF SELF-HELP GURU **ASTRID MUELLER,** CREDITED WITH TURNING THE YOUNG ACTOR'S LIFE AROUND.

BUT IN THE WAKE OF TRAGEDY, MANY ARE NOW ASKING WHAT THIS WOMAN AND HER ORGANIZATION ACTUALLY **DO.**

HOLLYWOOD TONIGHT **HT**   FRIEND OR FRAUD?

LONGTIME SPOKESPERSON FOR THE GROUP, **KILLIAN REED,** HAS RUSHED TO BE AT THE CORPORATE HEADQUARTERS RIGHT HERE IN CHICAGO...

...BUT OFFERED ONLY A TERSE "NO COMMENT," IN RESPONSE TO GROWING ACCUSATIONS OF INCOMPETENCE AND IMPROPRIETY.

HOLLYWOOD TONIGHT **HT**

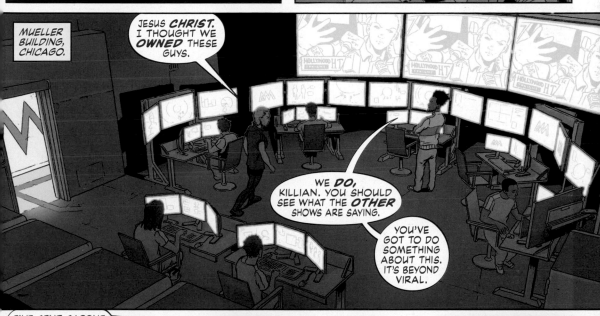

MUELLER BUILDING, CHICAGO.

JESUS **CHRIST.** I THOUGHT WE **OWNED** THESE GUYS.

WE **DO,** KILLIAN. YOU SHOULD SEE WHAT THE **OTHER** SHOWS ARE SAYING.

YOU'VE GOT TO DO SOMETHING ABOUT THIS. IT'S BEYOND VIRAL.

I'VE SENT CAPONE TO DEAL WITH IT.

CAPONE? YOU SENT **CAPONE?**

ALL DUE RESPECT...WAS THAT WISE?

ALMOST CERTAINLY NOT.

HOW LONG HAS ASTRID BEEN IN THE CLEAN ROOM, RAVEN?

SIX HOURS TOTAL.

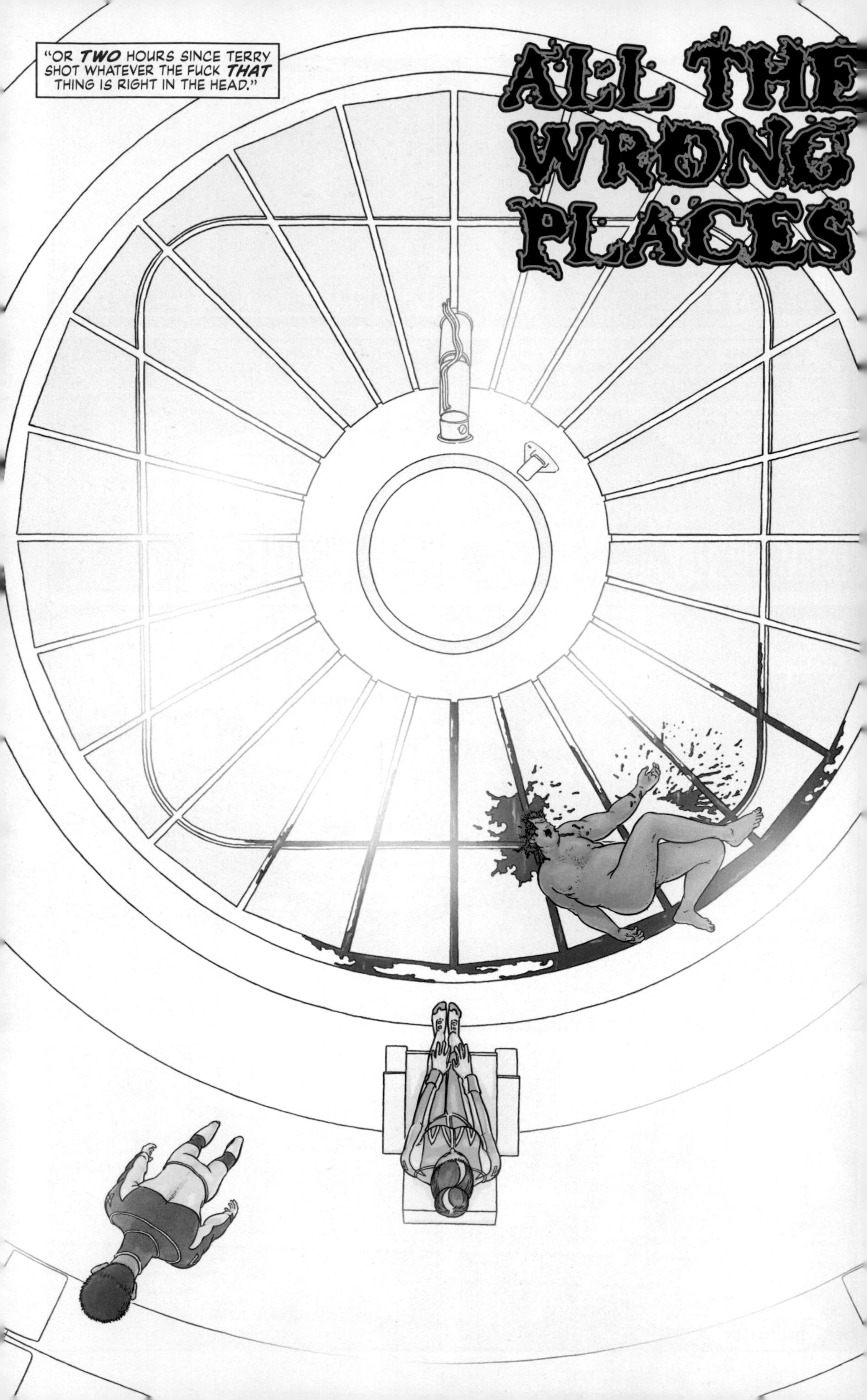
"OR TWO HOURS SINCE TERRY SHOT WHATEVER THE FUCK THAT THING IS RIGHT IN THE HEAD."
ALL THE WRONG PLACES

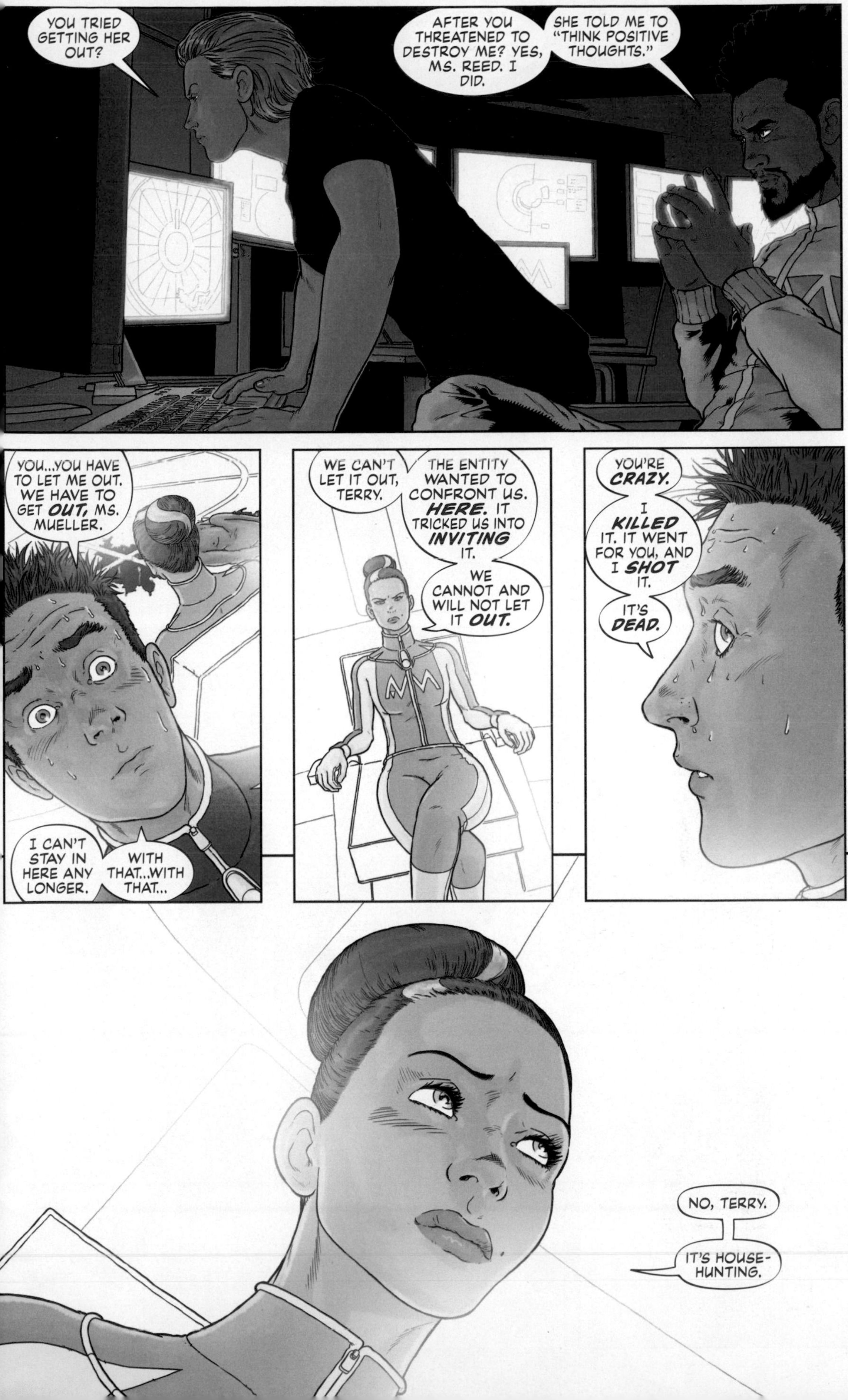
YOU TRIED GETTING HER OUT?
AFTER YOU THREATENED TO DESTROY ME? YES, MS. REED. I DID.
SHE TOLD ME TO "THINK POSITIVE THOUGHTS."
YOU...YOU HAVE TO LET ME OUT. WE HAVE TO GET OUT, MS. MUELLER.
I CAN'T STAY IN HERE ANY LONGER.
WITH THAT...WITH THAT...
WE CAN'T LET IT OUT, TERRY.
THE ENTITY WANTED TO CONFRONT US. HERE. IT TRICKED US INTO INVITING IT.
WE CANNOT AND WILL NOT LET IT OUT.
YOU'RE CRAZY.
I KILLED IT. IT WENT FOR YOU, AND I SHOT IT.
IT'S DEAD.
NO, TERRY.
IT'S HOUSE-HUNTING.

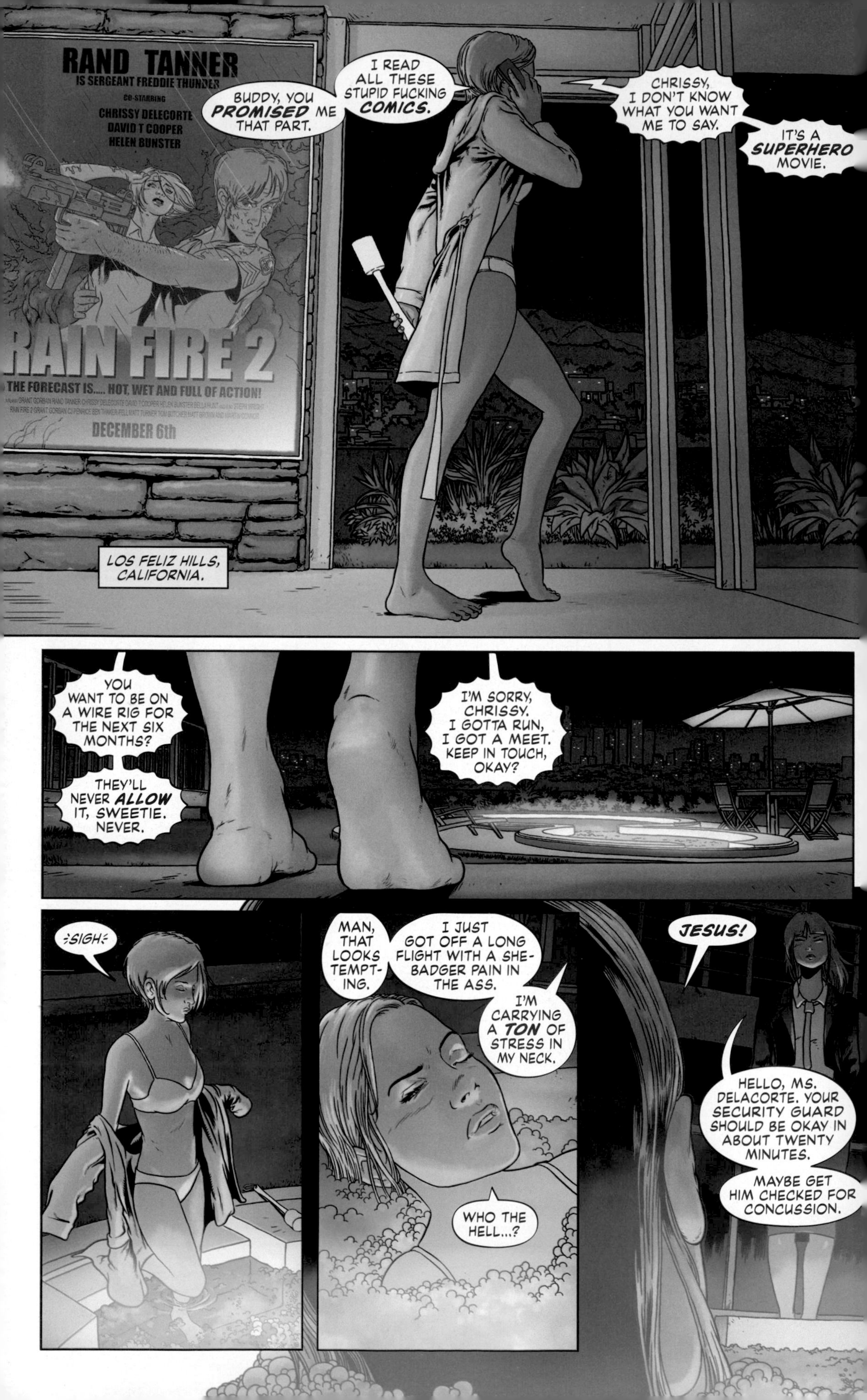
RAND TANNER
IS SERGEANT FREDDIE THUNDER
CO-STARRING
CHRISSY DELECORTE
DAVID T COOPER
HELEN BUNSTER
RAIN FIRE 2
THE FORECAST IS..... HOT, WET AND FULL OF ACTION!
DECEMBER 6th
LOS FELIZ HILLS, CALIFORNIA.
BUDDY, YOU PROMISED ME THAT PART.
I READ ALL THESE STUPID FUCKING COMICS.
CHRISSY, I DON'T KNOW WHAT YOU WANT ME TO SAY.
IT'S A SUPERHERO MOVIE.
YOU WANT TO BE ON A WIRE RIG FOR THE NEXT SIX MONTHS?
THEY'LL NEVER ALLOW IT, SWEETIE. NEVER.
I'M SORRY, CHRISSY. I GOTTA RUN, I GOT A MEET. KEEP IN TOUCH, OKAY?
SIGH
MAN, THAT LOOKS TEMPT-ING.
I JUST GOT OFF A LONG FLIGHT WITH A SHE-BADGER PAIN IN THE ASS.
I'M CARRYING A TON OF STRESS IN MY NECK.
WHO THE HELL...?
JESUS!
HELLO, MS. DELACORTE. YOUR SECURITY GUARD SHOULD BE OKAY IN ABOUT TWENTY MINUTES.
MAYBE GET HIM CHECKED FOR CONCUSSION.

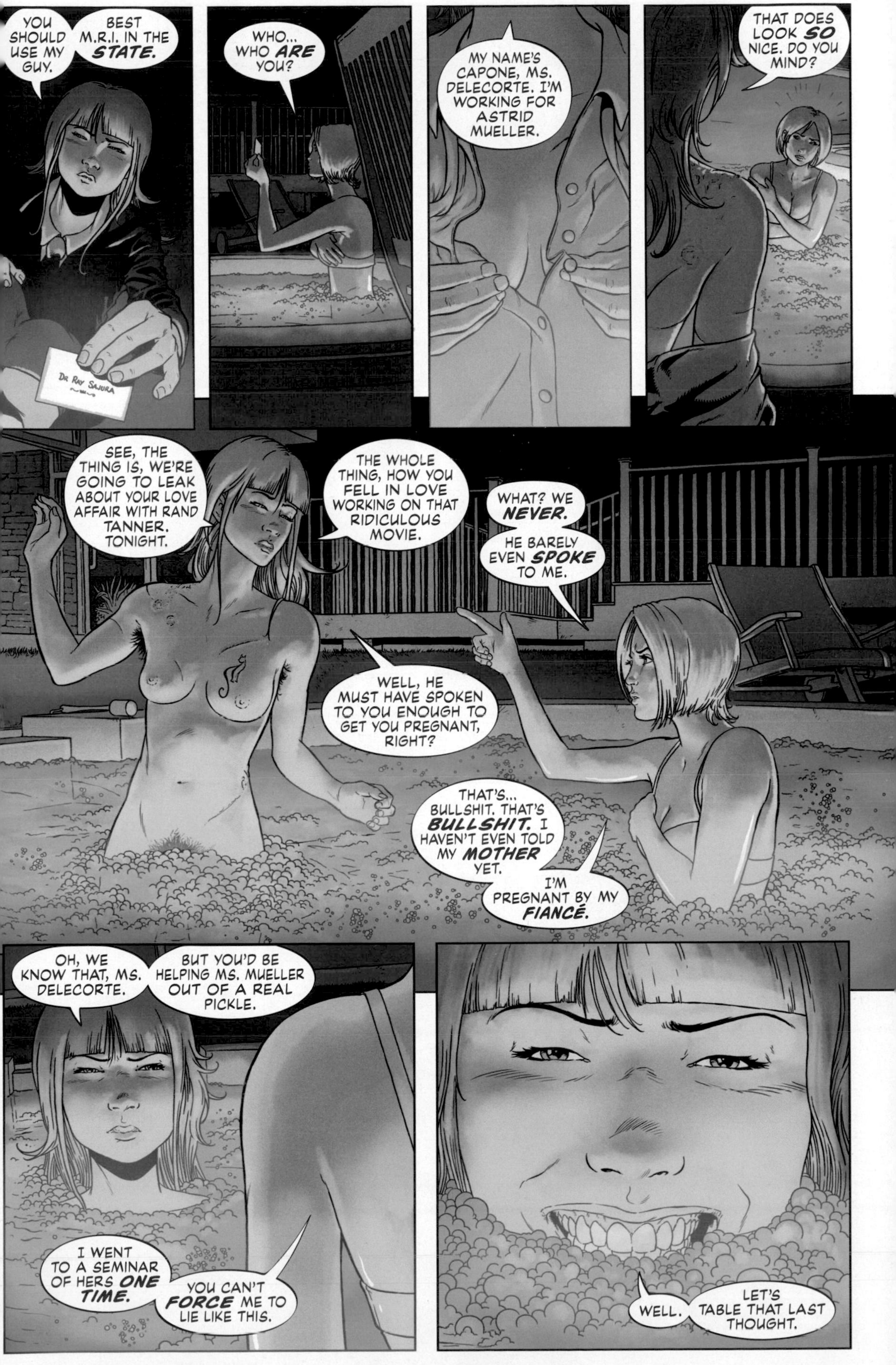
YOU SHOULD USE MY GUY.
BEST M.R.I. IN THE STATE.
DR RAY SAJURA
WHO... WHO ARE YOU?
MY NAME'S CAPONE, MS. DELECORTE. I'M WORKING FOR ASTRID MUELLER.
THAT DOES LOOK SO NICE. DO YOU MIND?
SEE, THE THING IS, WE'RE GOING TO LEAK ABOUT YOUR LOVE AFFAIR WITH RAND TANNER. TONIGHT.
THE WHOLE THING, HOW YOU FELL IN LOVE WORKING ON THAT RIDICULOUS MOVIE.
WHAT? WE NEVER.
HE BARELY EVEN SPOKE TO ME.
WELL, HE MUST HAVE SPOKEN TO YOU ENOUGH TO GET YOU PREGNANT, RIGHT?
THAT'S... BULLSHIT. THAT'S BULLSHIT. I HAVEN'T EVEN TOLD MY MOTHER YET.
I'M PREGNANT BY MY FIANCÉ.
OH, WE KNOW THAT, MS. DELECORTE.
BUT YOU'D BE HELPING MS. MUELLER OUT OF A REAL PICKLE.
I WENT TO A SEMINAR OF HERS ONE TIME.
YOU CAN'T FORCE ME TO LIE LIKE THIS.
WELL.
LET'S TABLE THAT LAST THOUGHT.

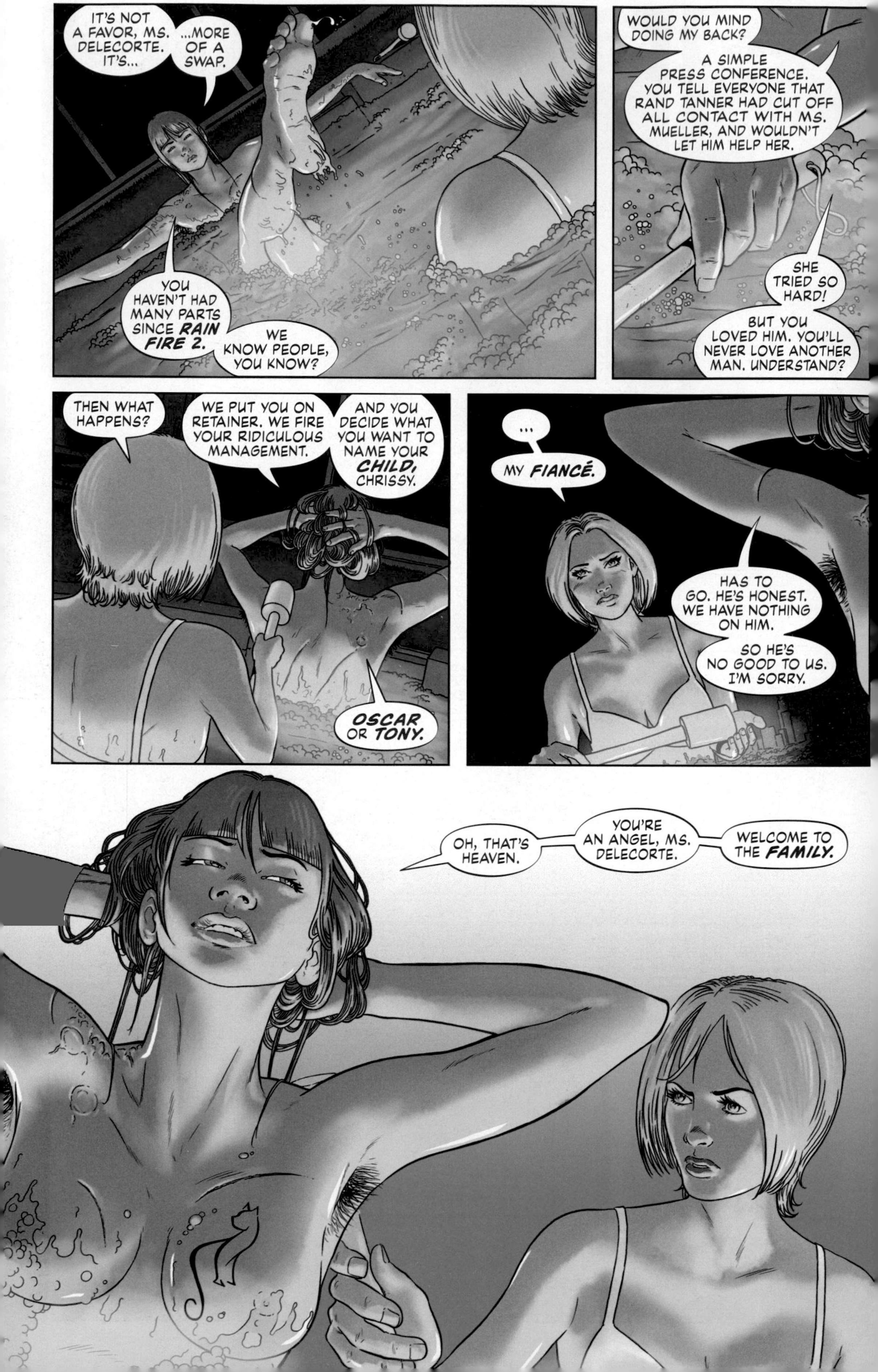

IT'S NOT A FAVOR, MS. DELECORTE. IT'S...
...MORE OF A SWAP.
YOU HAVEN'T HAD MANY PARTS SINCE RAIN FIRE 2.
WE KNOW PEOPLE, YOU KNOW?
WOULD YOU MIND DOING MY BACK?
A SIMPLE PRESS CONFERENCE. YOU TELL EVERYONE THAT RAND TANNER HAD CUT OFF ALL CONTACT WITH MS. MUELLER, AND WOULDN'T LET HIM HELP HER.
SHE TRIED SO HARD!
BUT YOU LOVED HIM. YOU'LL NEVER LOVE ANOTHER MAN. UNDERSTAND?
THEN WHAT HAPPENS?
WE PUT YOU ON RETAINER. WE FIRE YOUR RIDICULOUS MANAGEMENT.
AND YOU DECIDE WHAT YOU WANT TO NAME YOUR CHILD, CHRISSY.
OSCAR OR TONY.
...
MY FIANCÉ.
HAS TO GO. HE'S HONEST. WE HAVE NOTHING ON HIM.
SO HE'S NO GOOD TO US. I'M SORRY.
OH, THAT'S HEAVEN.
YOU'RE AN ANGEL, MS. DELECORTE.
WELCOME TO THE FAMILY.

I DREAMED OF A DEMON.

HELLO.

GAAAHHH!

FLORIDA, HOME OF CHLOE PIERCE.

JESUS! WHAT THE *FUCK?!*

Chloe.

Chloe Chloe Chloe.

You went to that place you all go sometimes until you go there forever.

YOU'RE *REAL.*

I'm *SPARK.*

I am making you anxiety. Aren't I?

You are nerves.

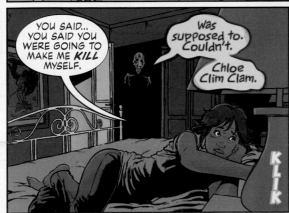

YOU SAID... YOU SAID YOU WERE GOING TO MAKE ME *KILL* MYSELF.

Was supposed to. Couldn't.

Chloe Clim Clam.

KLIK

WHO WANTED YOU TO HURT ME?

Spark is failure. I try to be anger, I really do.

But I was *EXORCISED.*

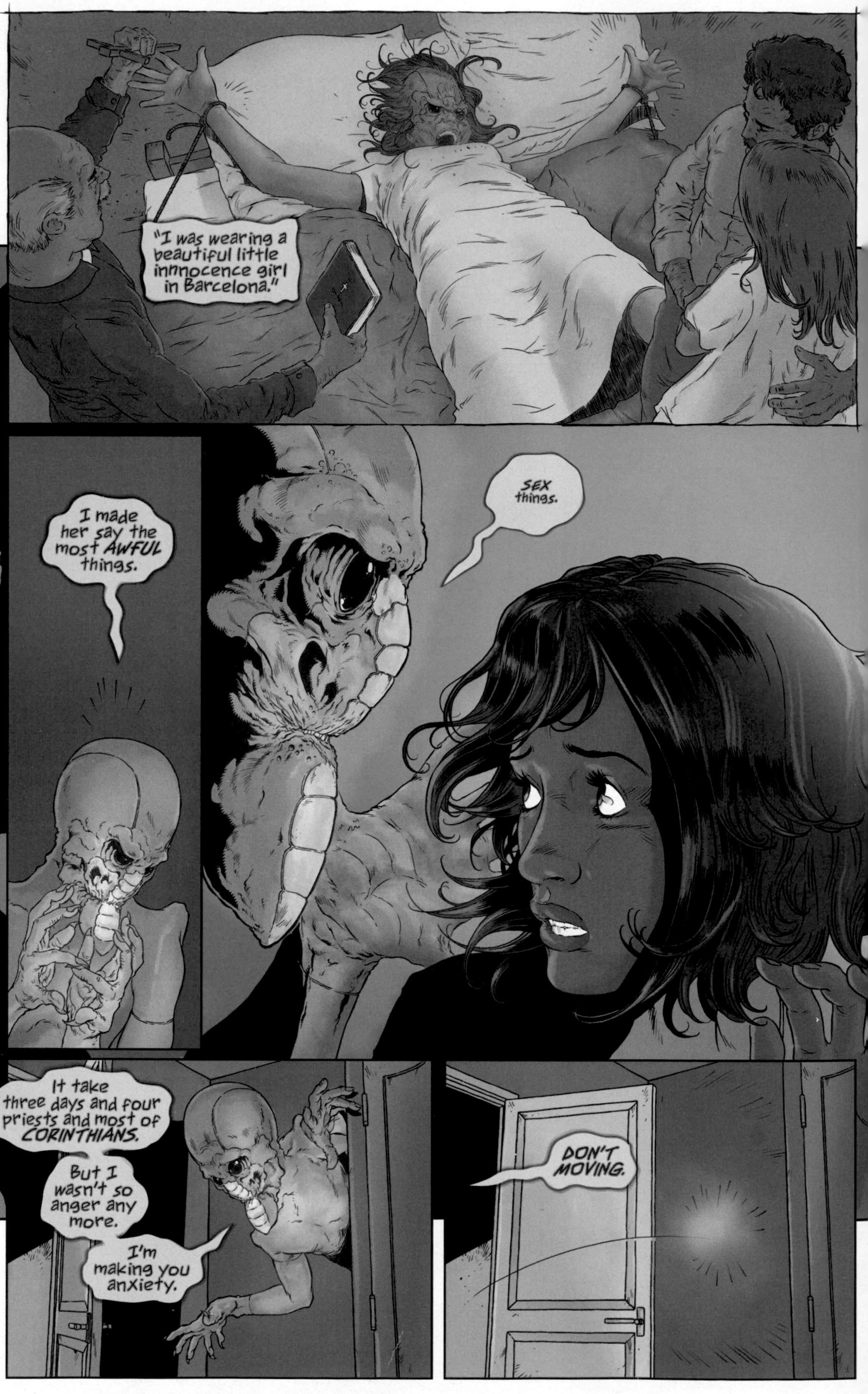
"I was wearing a beautiful little innocence girl in Barcelona."
I made her say the most AWFUL things.
SEX things.
It take three days and four priests and most of CORINTHIANS.
But I wasn't so anger any more.
I'm making you anxiety.
DON'T MOVING.

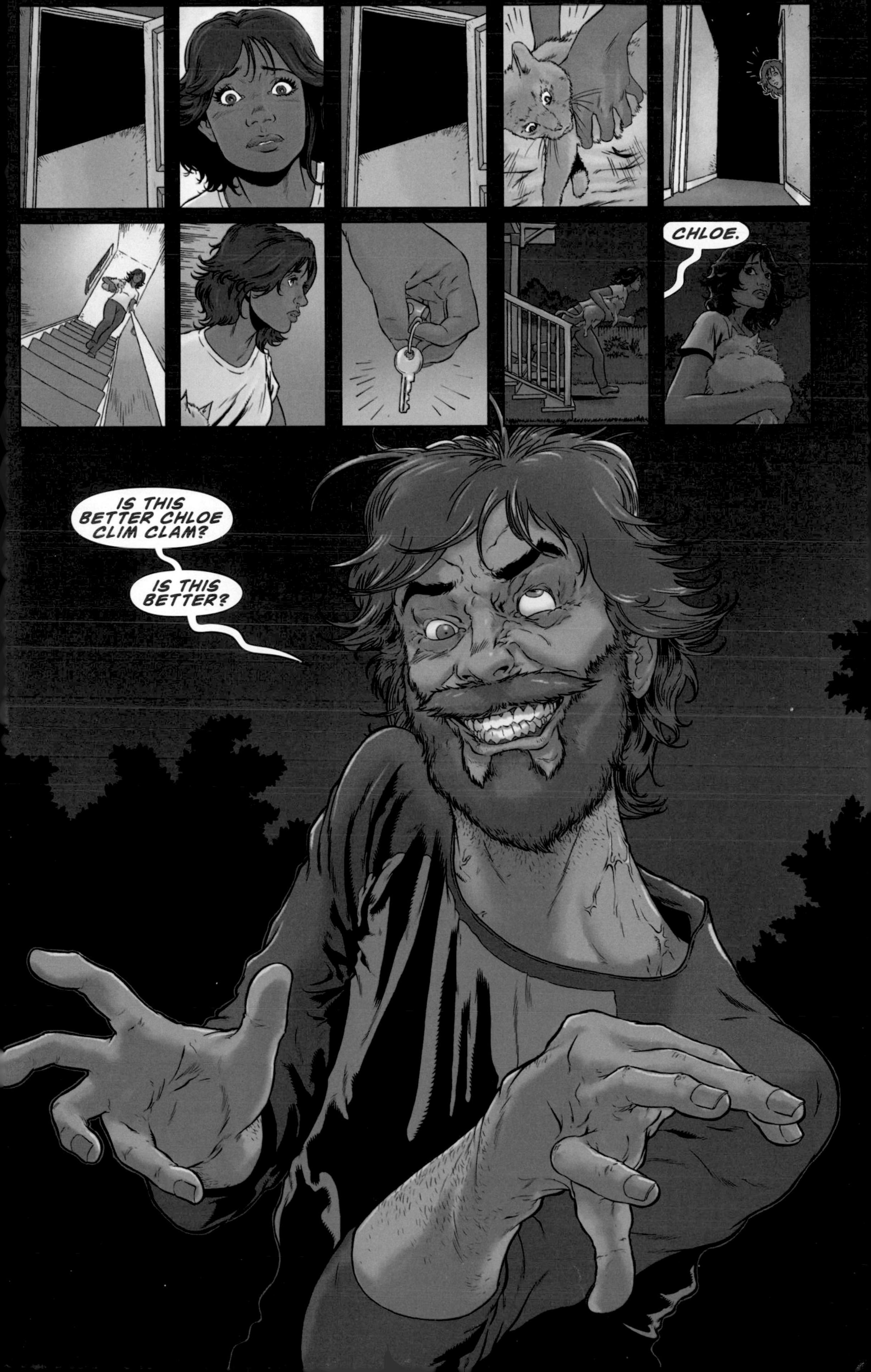
CHLOE.
IS THIS BETTER CHLOE CLIM CLAM?
IS THIS BETTER?

TERRY. ARE YOU FEELING ANY BETTER?

HEH. SORT OF.

MS. MUELLER.

YES?

DO YOU KNOW WHAT TIME IT IS?

YOU KNOW TIME-PIECES ARE NOT ALLOWED IN THE--

DO YOU KNOW...

...WHAT TIME IT IS, ASTRID?

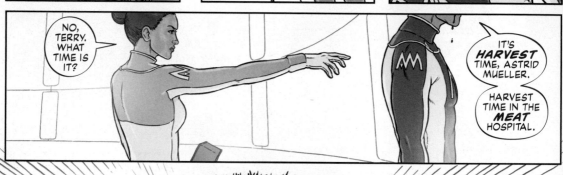

NO, TERRY. WHAT TIME IS IT?

IT'S HARVEST TIME, ASTRID MUELLER.

HARVEST TIME IN THE MEAT HOSPITAL.

FOR EVERY LAST FUCKING ONE OF YOU VERMIN.

TERRY. I'M GOING TO WALK OUT OF THIS ROOM, NOW.

DO YOU UNDERSTAND?

I'M AFRAID I CAN'T ALLOW THAT, MS. MUELLER.

IT'S IN HIM.

KEMF IS IN TERRY.

YOU THINK?

I'M GOING IN.

YOU CAN'T.

SHE SET THE PROTOCOL HERSELF.

YES, I DID, RAVEN. KILLIAN, I WONDER IF YOU'D BE A DEAR AND GO FETCH TERRY WHITCOMB'S LIFEBOX, PLEASE.

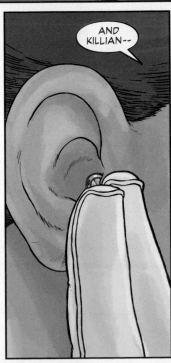

AND KILLIAN--

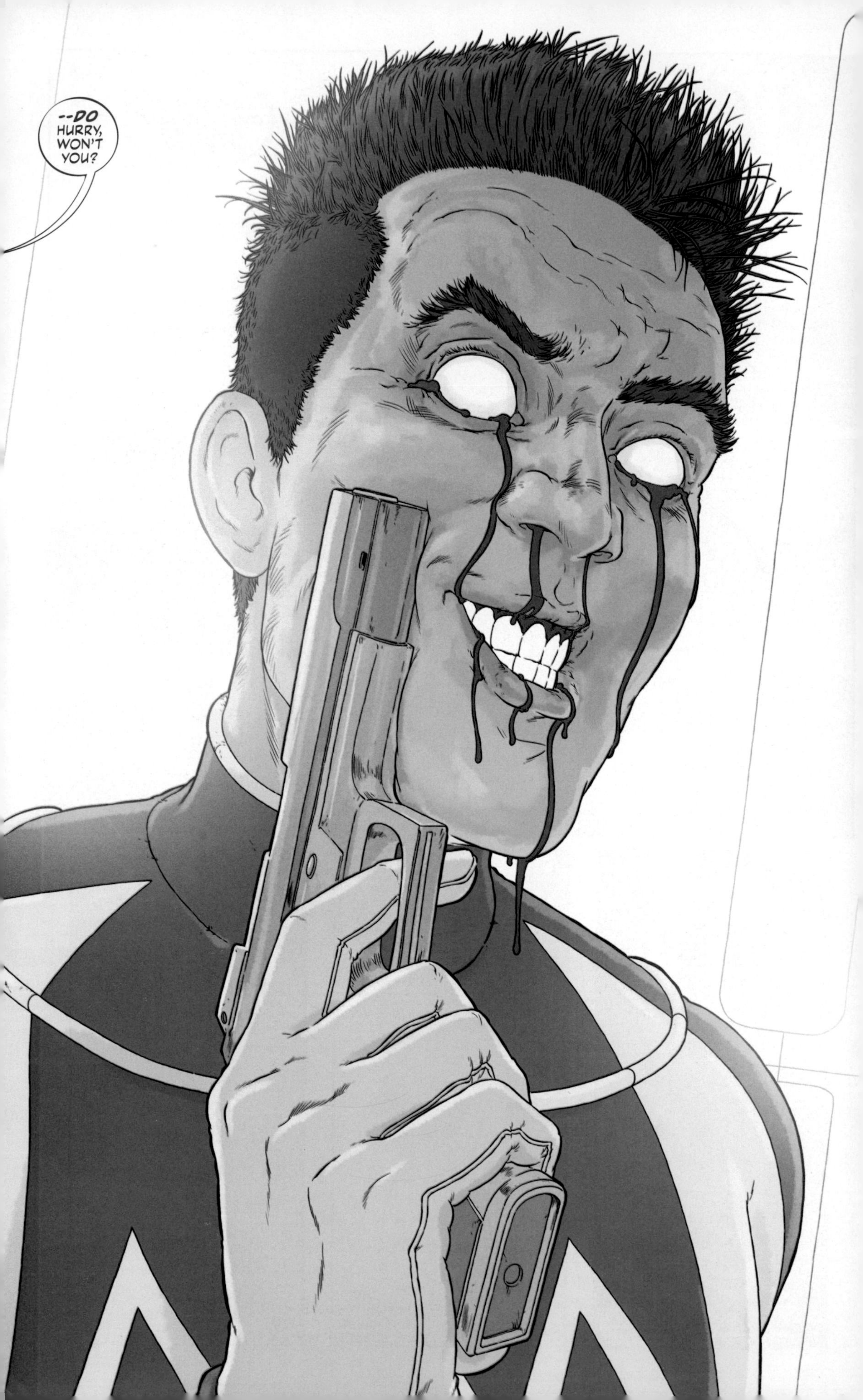
--DO HURRY, WON'T YOU?

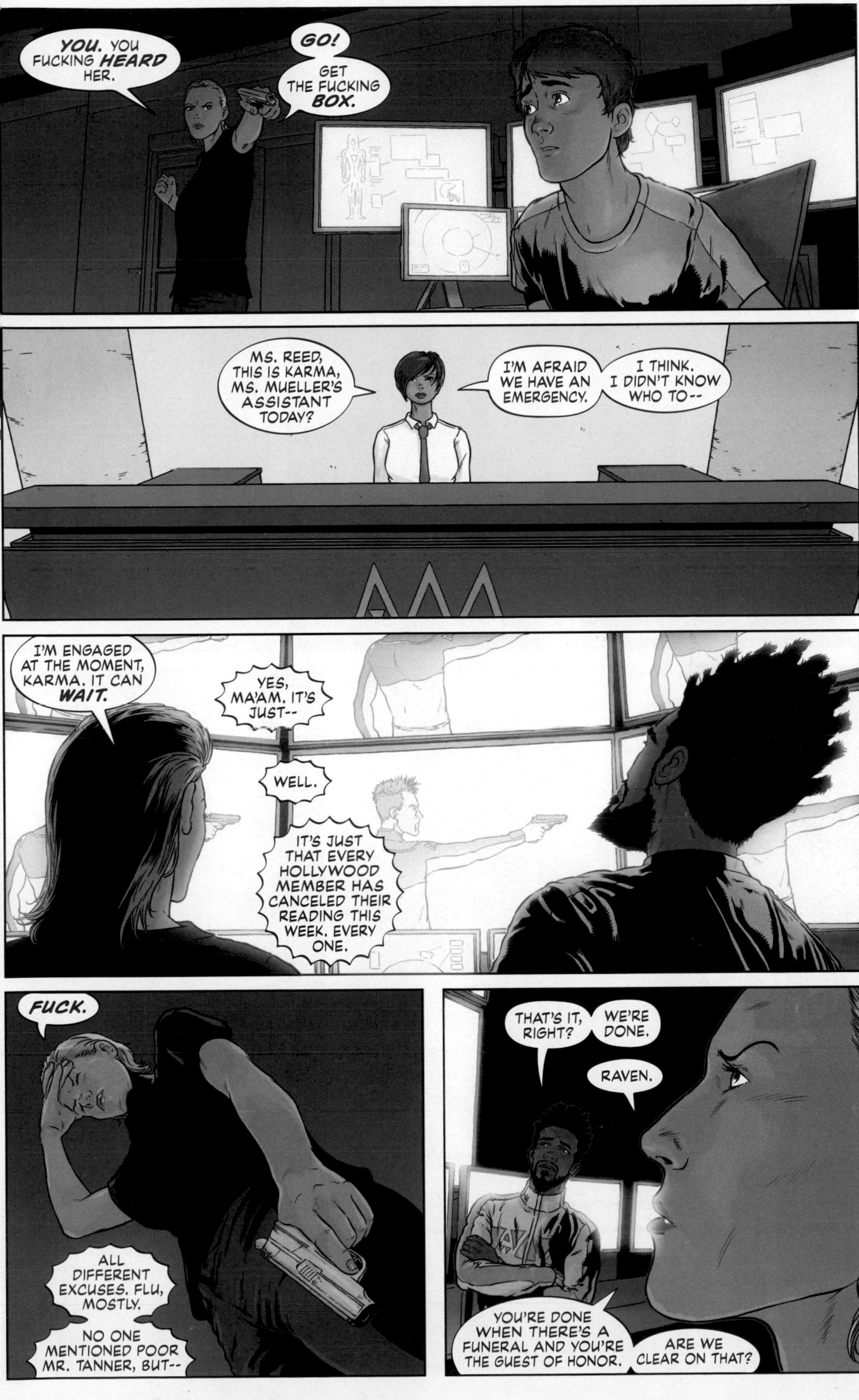
YOU. YOU FUCKING HEARD HER.
GO!
GET THE FUCKING BOX.
MS. REED, THIS IS KARMA, MS. MUELLER'S ASSISTANT TODAY?
I'M AFRAID WE HAVE AN EMERGENCY.
I THINK. I DIDN'T KNOW WHO TO--
I'M ENGAGED AT THE MOMENT, KARMA. IT CAN WAIT.
YES, MA'AM. IT'S JUST--
WELL.
IT'S JUST THAT EVERY HOLLYWOOD MEMBER HAS CANCELED THEIR READING THIS WEEK. EVERY ONE.
FUCK.
ALL DIFFERENT EXCUSES. FLU, MOSTLY.
NO ONE MENTIONED POOR MR. TANNER, BUT--
THAT'S IT, RIGHT?
WE'RE DONE.
RAVEN.
YOU'RE DONE WHEN THERE'S A FUNERAL AND YOU'RE THE GUEST OF HONOR.
ARE WE CLEAR ON THAT?

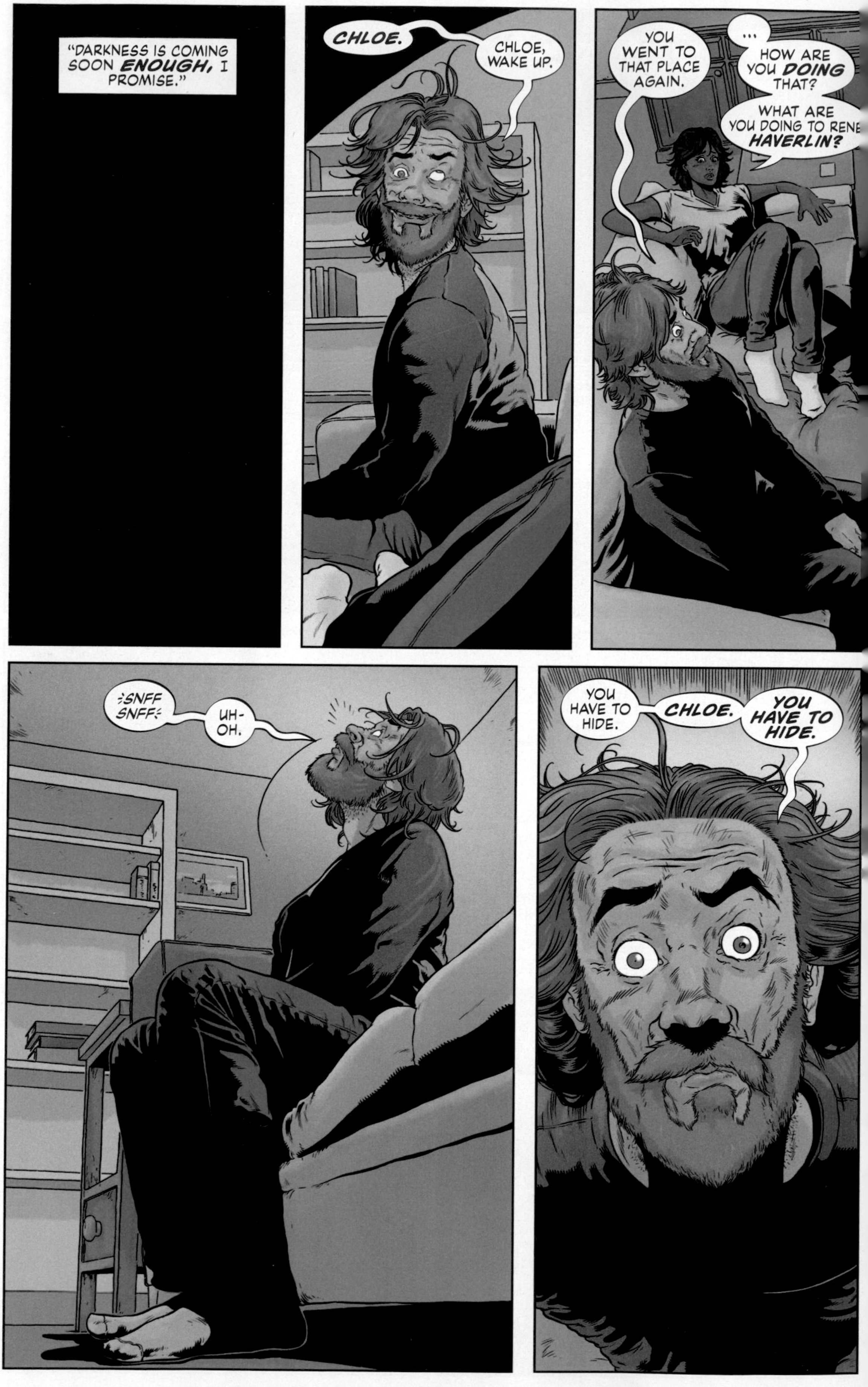
"DARKNESS IS COMING SOON ENOUGH, I PROMISE."
CHLOE.
CHLOE, WAKE UP.
YOU WENT TO THAT PLACE AGAIN.
...
HOW ARE YOU DOING THAT?
WHAT ARE YOU DOING TO RENE HAVERLIN?
SNFF SNFF
UH-OH.
YOU HAVE TO HIDE.
CHLOE.
YOU HAVE TO HIDE.

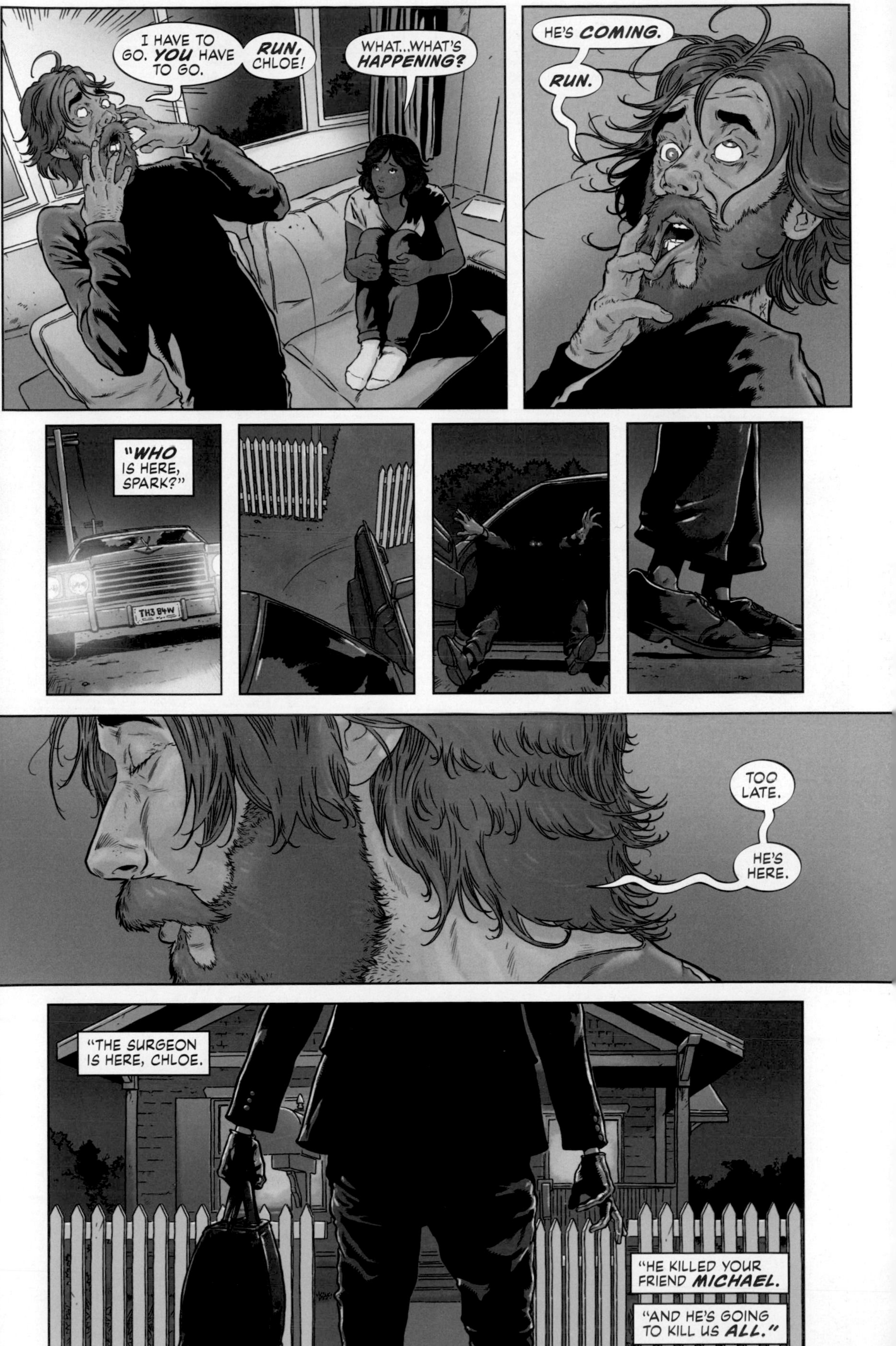
I HAVE TO GO. YOU HAVE TO GO.
RUN, CHLOE!
WHAT...WHAT'S HAPPENING?
HE'S COMING.
RUN.
"WHO IS HERE, SPARK?"
TH3 84W
TOO LATE.
HE'S HERE.
"THE SURGEON IS HERE, CHLOE.
"HE KILLED YOUR FRIEND MICHAEL.
"AND HE'S GOING TO KILL US ALL."

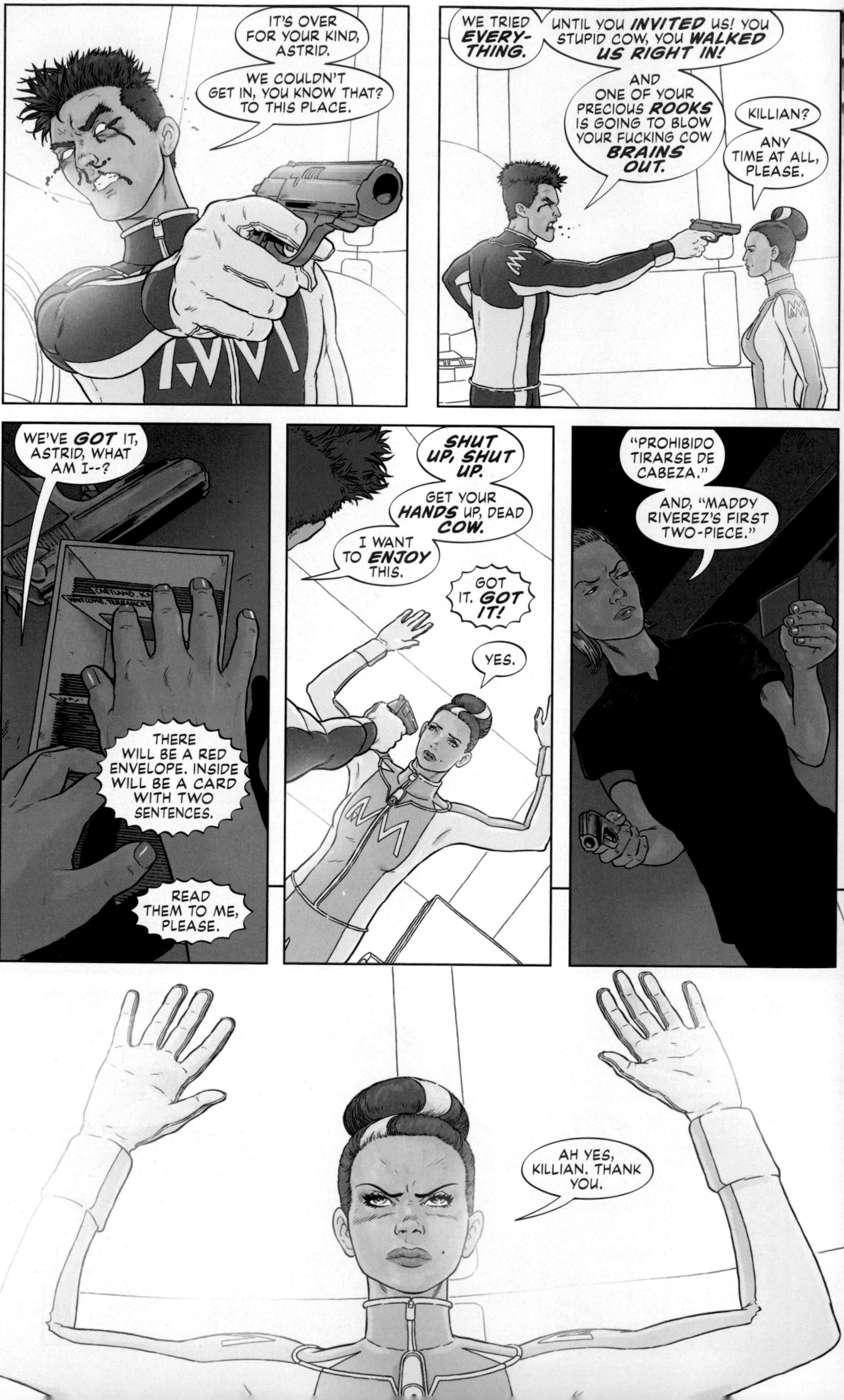
IT'S OVER FOR YOUR KIND, ASTRID.
WE COULDN'T GET IN, YOU KNOW THAT? TO THIS PLACE.
WE TRIED EVERY-THING.
UNTIL YOU INVITED US! YOU STUPID COW, YOU WALKED US RIGHT IN!
AND ONE OF YOUR PRECIOUS ROOKS IS GOING TO BLOW YOUR FUCKING COW BRAINS OUT.
KILLIAN?
ANY TIME AT ALL, PLEASE.
WE'VE GOT IT, ASTRID, WHAT AM I--?
THERE WILL BE A RED ENVELOPE. INSIDE WILL BE A CARD WITH TWO SENTENCES.
READ THEM TO ME, PLEASE.
SHUT UP, SHUT UP.
GET YOUR HANDS UP, DEAD COW.
I WANT TO ENJOY THIS.
GOT IT. GOT IT!
YES.
"PROHIBIDO TIRARSE DE CABEZA."
AND, "MADDY RIVEREZ'S FIRST TWO-PIECE."
AH YES, KILLIAN. THANK YOU.

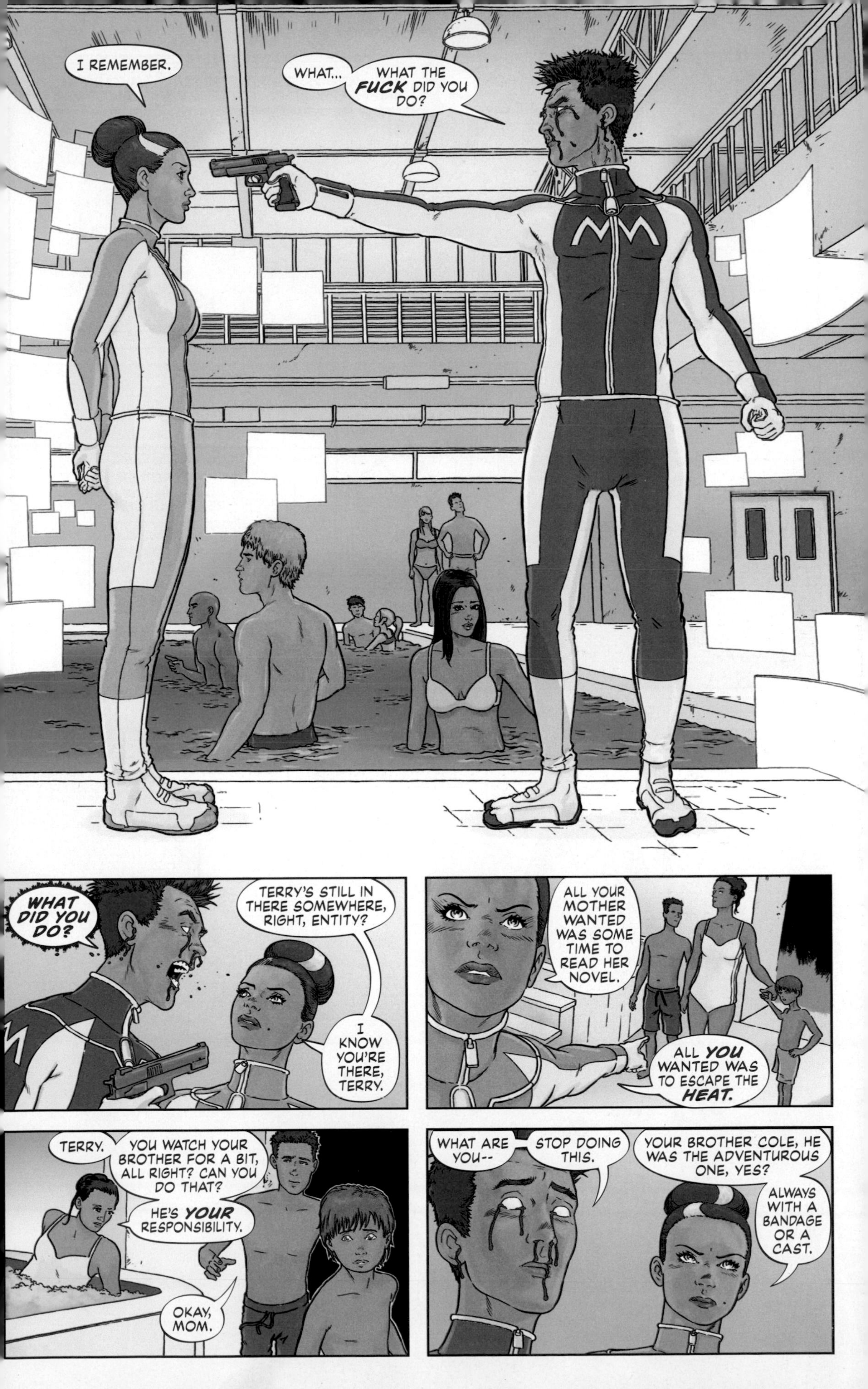
I REMEMBER.
WHAT...
WHAT THE *FUCK* DID YOU DO?
WHAT DID YOU DO?
TERRY'S STILL IN THERE SOMEWHERE, RIGHT, ENTITY?
I KNOW YOU'RE THERE, TERRY.
ALL YOUR MOTHER WANTED WAS SOME TIME TO READ HER NOVEL.
ALL *YOU* WANTED WAS TO ESCAPE THE *HEAT.*
TERRY.
YOU WATCH YOUR BROTHER FOR A BIT, ALL RIGHT? CAN YOU DO THAT?
HE'S *YOUR* RESPONSIBILITY.
OKAY, MOM.
WHAT ARE YOU--
STOP DOING THIS.
YOUR BROTHER COLE, HE WAS THE ADVENTUROUS ONE, YES?
ALWAYS WITH A BANDAGE OR A CAST.

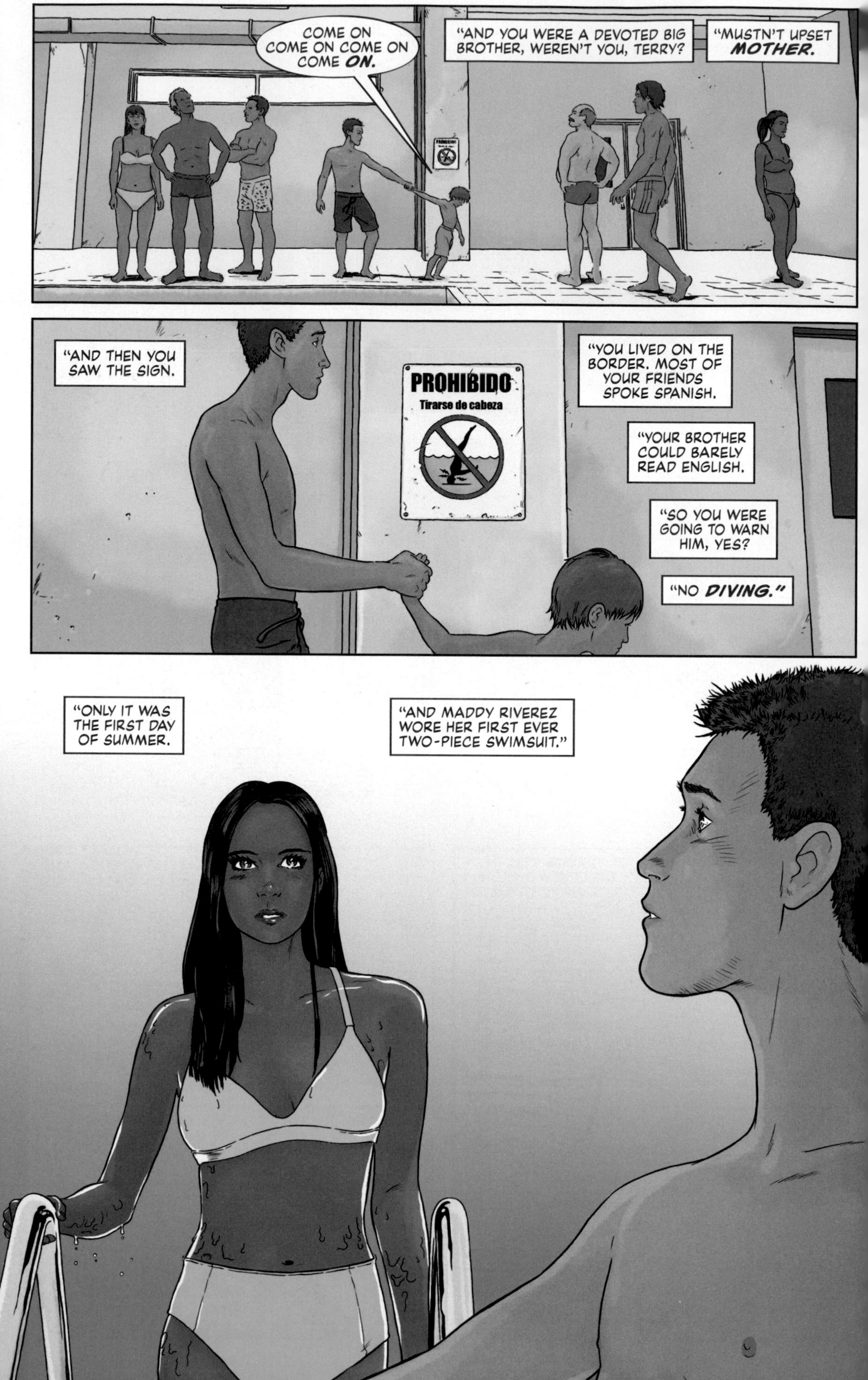
COME ON COME ON COME ON COME ON.
"AND YOU WERE A DEVOTED BIG BROTHER, WEREN'T YOU, TERRY?
"MUSTN'T UPSET MOTHER.
"AND THEN YOU SAW THE SIGN.
PROHIBIDO
Tirarse de cabeza
"YOU LIVED ON THE BORDER. MOST OF YOUR FRIENDS SPOKE SPANISH.
"YOUR BROTHER COULD BARELY READ ENGLISH.
"SO YOU WERE GOING TO WARN HIM, YES?
"NO DIVING."
"ONLY IT WAS THE FIRST DAY OF SUMMER.
"AND MADDY RIVEREZ WORE HER FIRST EVER TWO-PIECE SWIMSUIT."

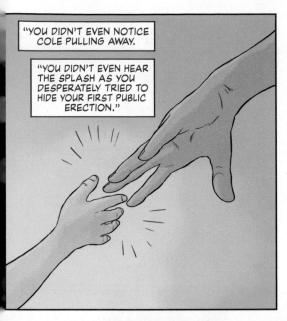

"YOU DIDN'T EVEN NOTICE COLE PULLING AWAY."

"YOU DIDN'T EVEN HEAR THE SPLASH AS YOU DESPERATELY TRIED TO HIDE YOUR FIRST PUBLIC ERECTION."

BUT YOU HEARD YOUR MOTHER **SCREAM**, DIDN'T YOU, TERRY?

RIGHT UP UNTIL THE **EMT**s SHOT HER FULL OF PROPOFOL.

NO. **NO**.

YOU SAID, IN MY READING.

YOU SAID I WAS **INNOCENT**. I WAS JUST A **KID**.

NO.

I SAID GUILT WAS SELFISH.

OF COURSE IT WAS YOUR FAULT. HE WAS YOUR **RESPONSIBILITY**.

STOP IT.

I'LL LET YOU IN ON A LITTLE SECRET, TERRY.

I DON'T CHOOSE MY ROOKS FOR THEIR INVULNERABILITY.

IT'S IMPORTANT THAT I HAVE A FAIL-SAFE, DO YOU UNDERSTAND?

I NEED TO BE ABLE TO BREAK THEM.

SO I LEAVE A CRACK IN THE TEACUP.

TERRY...?

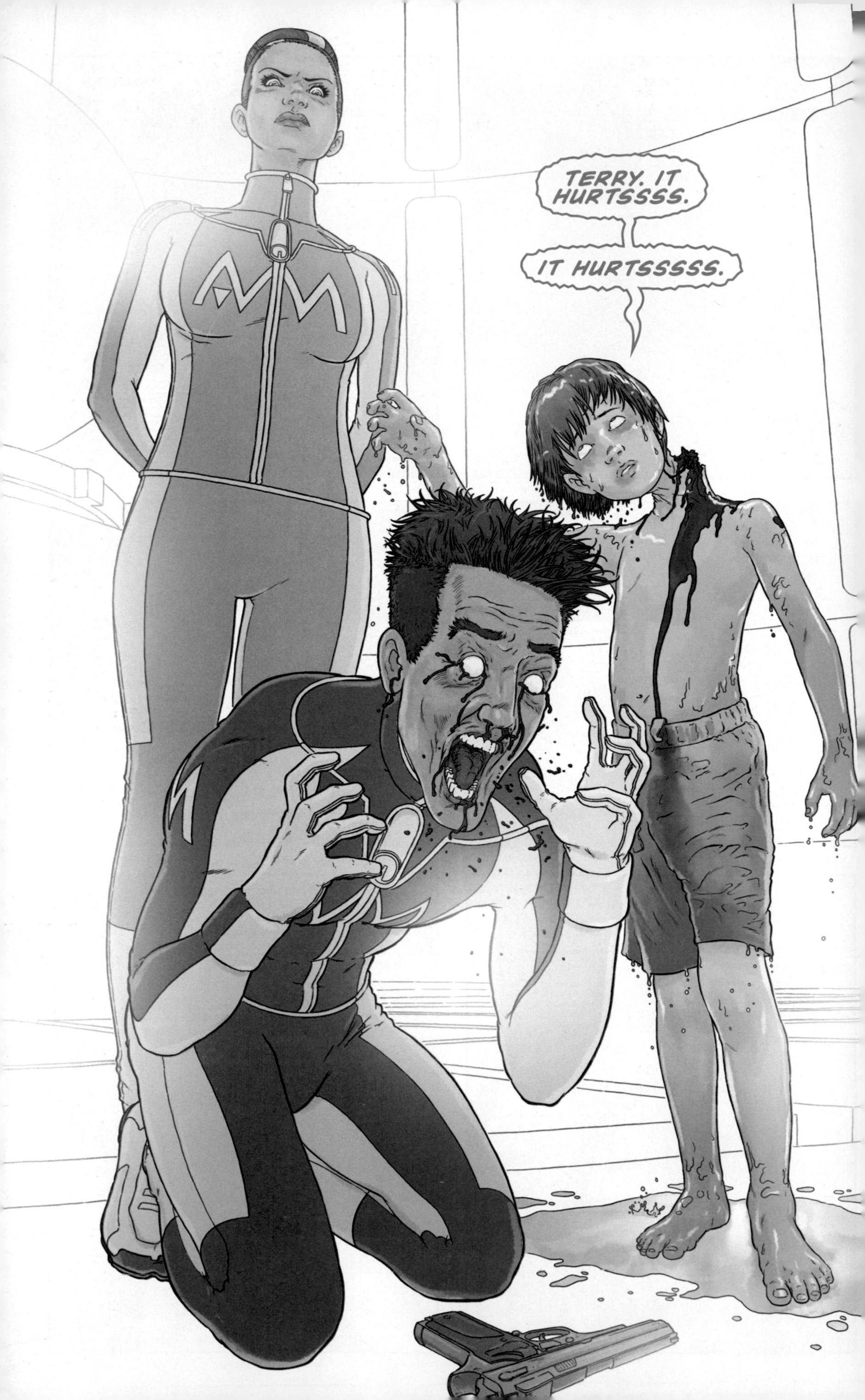
TERRY. IT HURTSSSS.
IT HURTSSSSS.

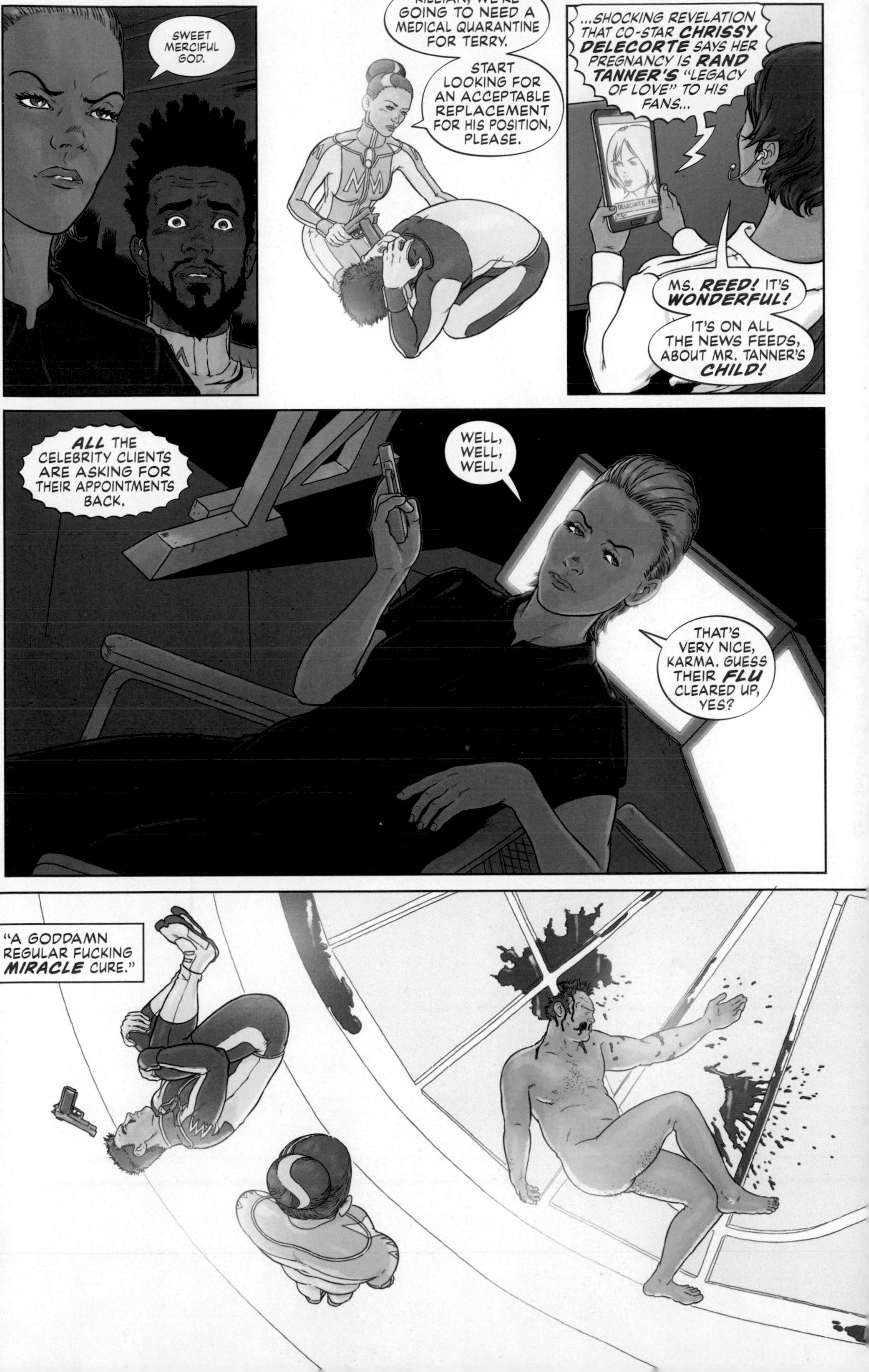
SWEET MERCIFUL GOD.
KILLIAN, WE'RE GOING TO NEED A MEDICAL QUARANTINE FOR TERRY.
START LOOKING FOR AN ACCEPTABLE REPLACEMENT FOR HIS POSITION, PLEASE.
...SHOCKING REVELATION THAT CO-STAR CHRISSY DELECORTE SAYS HER PREGNANCY IS RAND TANNER'S "LEGACY OF LOVE" TO HIS FANS...
MS. REED! IT'S WONDERFUL!
IT'S ON ALL THE NEWS FEEDS, ABOUT MR. TANNER'S CHILD!
ALL THE CELEBRITY CLIENTS ARE ASKING FOR THEIR APPOINTMENTS BACK.
WELL, WELL, WELL.
THAT'S VERY NICE, KARMA. GUESS THEIR FLU CLEARED UP, YES?
"A GODDAMN REGULAR FUCKING MIRACLE CURE."

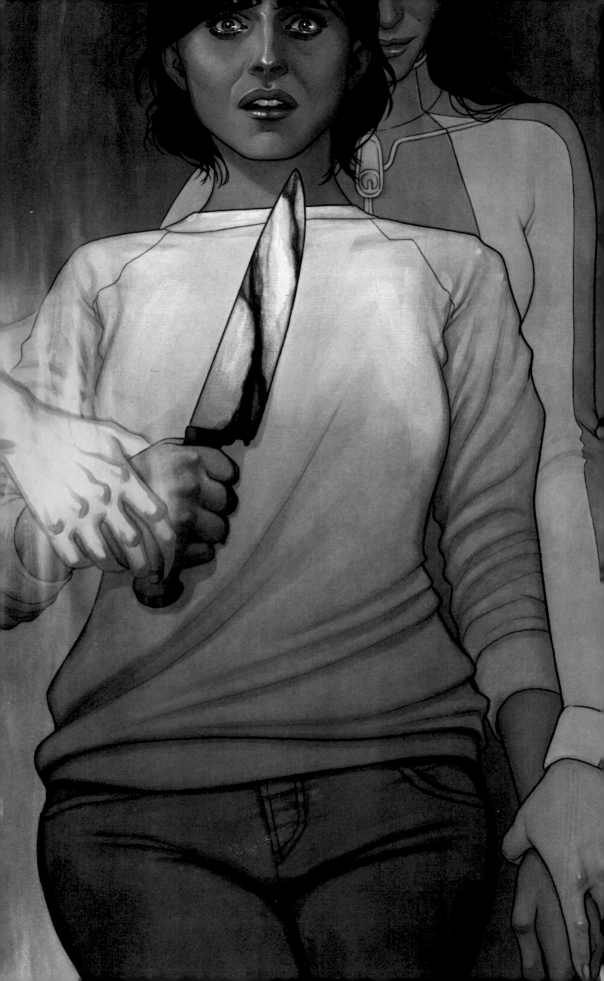

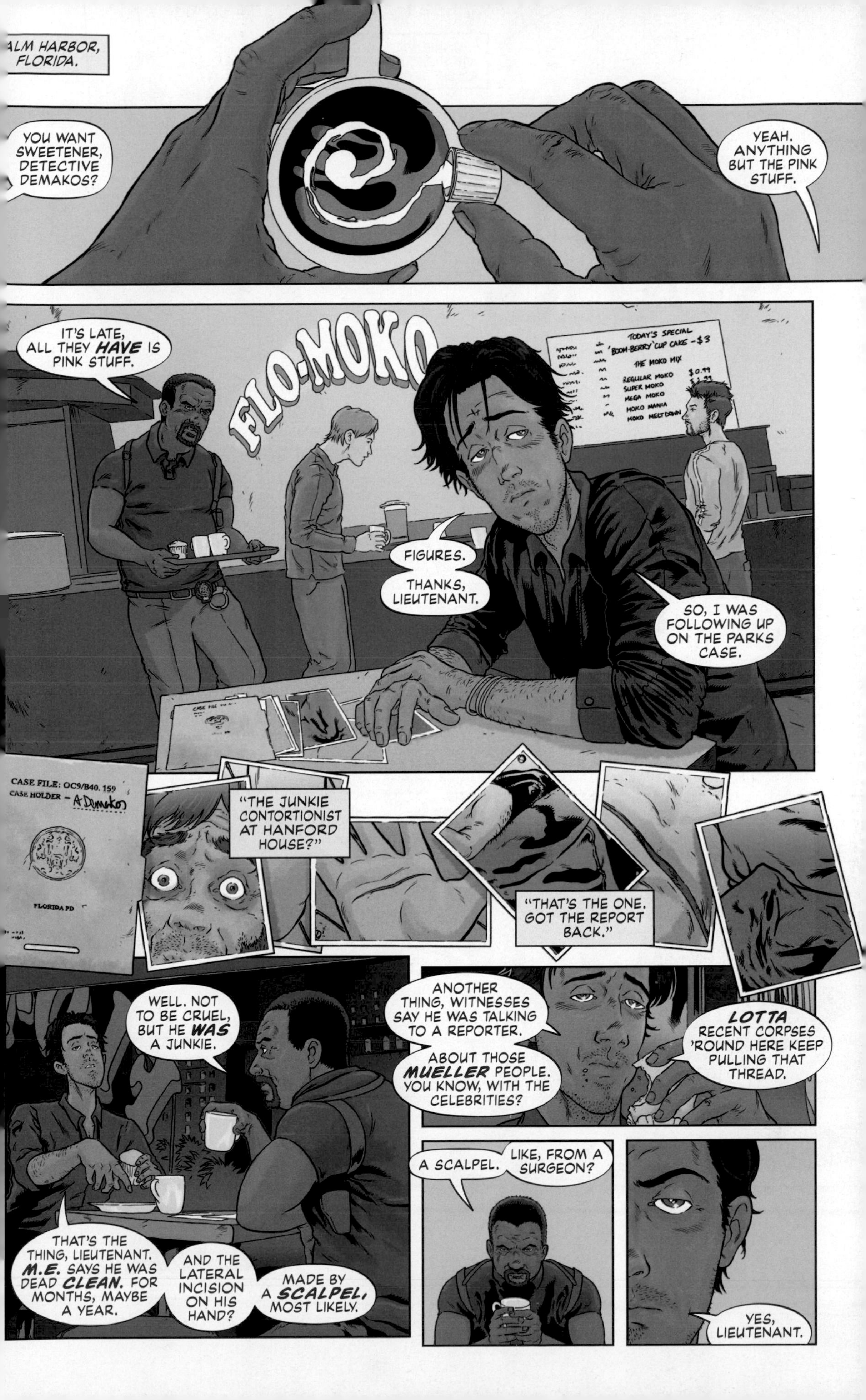
ALM HARBOR, FLORIDA.
YOU WANT SWEETENER, DETECTIVE DEMAKOS?
YEAH. ANYTHING BUT THE PINK STUFF.
IT'S LATE, ALL THEY HAVE IS PINK STUFF.
FLO-MOKO
TODAY'S SPECIAL 'BOOM-BERRY' CUP CAKE - $3
THE MOKO MIX
REGULAR MOKO
SUPER MOKO
MEGA MOKO
MOKO MANIA
MOKO MELTDOWN
FIGURES.
THANKS, LIEUTENANT.
SO, I WAS FOLLOWING UP ON THE PARKS CASE.
CASE FILE: OC9/B40. 159
CASE HOLDER – A. Demakos
FLORIDA PD
"THE JUNKIE CONTORTIONIST AT HANFORD HOUSE?"
"THAT'S THE ONE. GOT THE REPORT BACK."
WELL. NOT TO BE CRUEL, BUT HE WAS A JUNKIE.
THAT'S THE THING, LIEUTENANT. M.E. SAYS HE WAS DEAD CLEAN. FOR MONTHS, MAYBE A YEAR.
AND THE LATERAL INCISION ON HIS HAND?
MADE BY A SCALPEL, MOST LIKELY.
ANOTHER THING, WITNESSES SAY HE WAS TALKING TO A REPORTER.
ABOUT THOSE MUELLER PEOPLE. YOU KNOW, WITH THE CELEBRITIES?
LOTTA RECENT CORPSES 'ROUND HERE KEEP PULLING THAT THREAD.
A SCALPEL.
LIKE, FROM A SURGEON?
YES, LIEUTENANT.

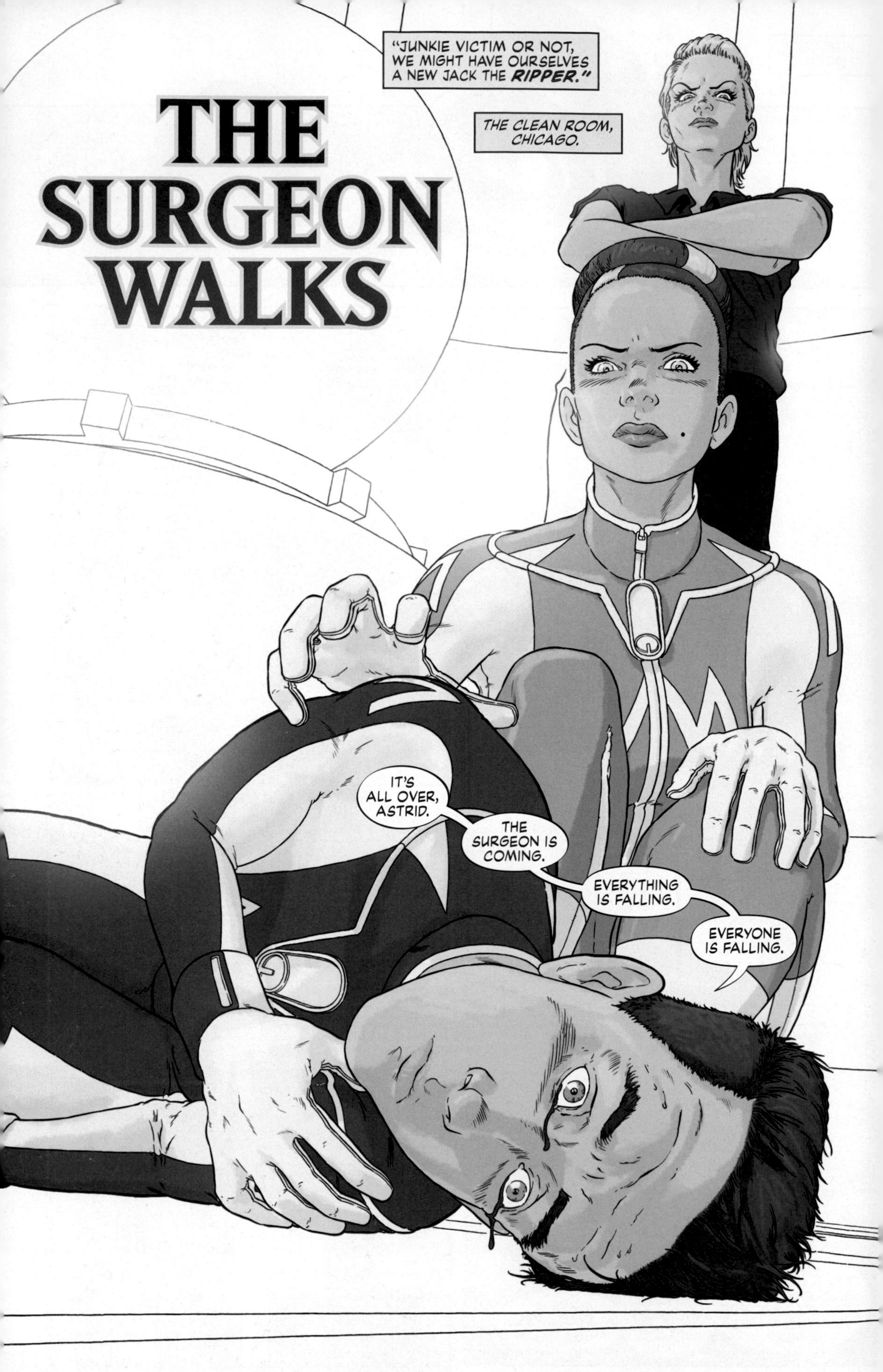
"JUNKIE VICTIM OR NOT, WE MIGHT HAVE OURSELVES A NEW JACK THE RIPPER."
THE CLEAN ROOM, CHICAGO.
THE SURGEON WALKS
IT'S ALL OVER, ASTRID.
THE SURGEON IS COMING.
EVERYTHING IS FALLING.
EVERYONE IS FALLING.

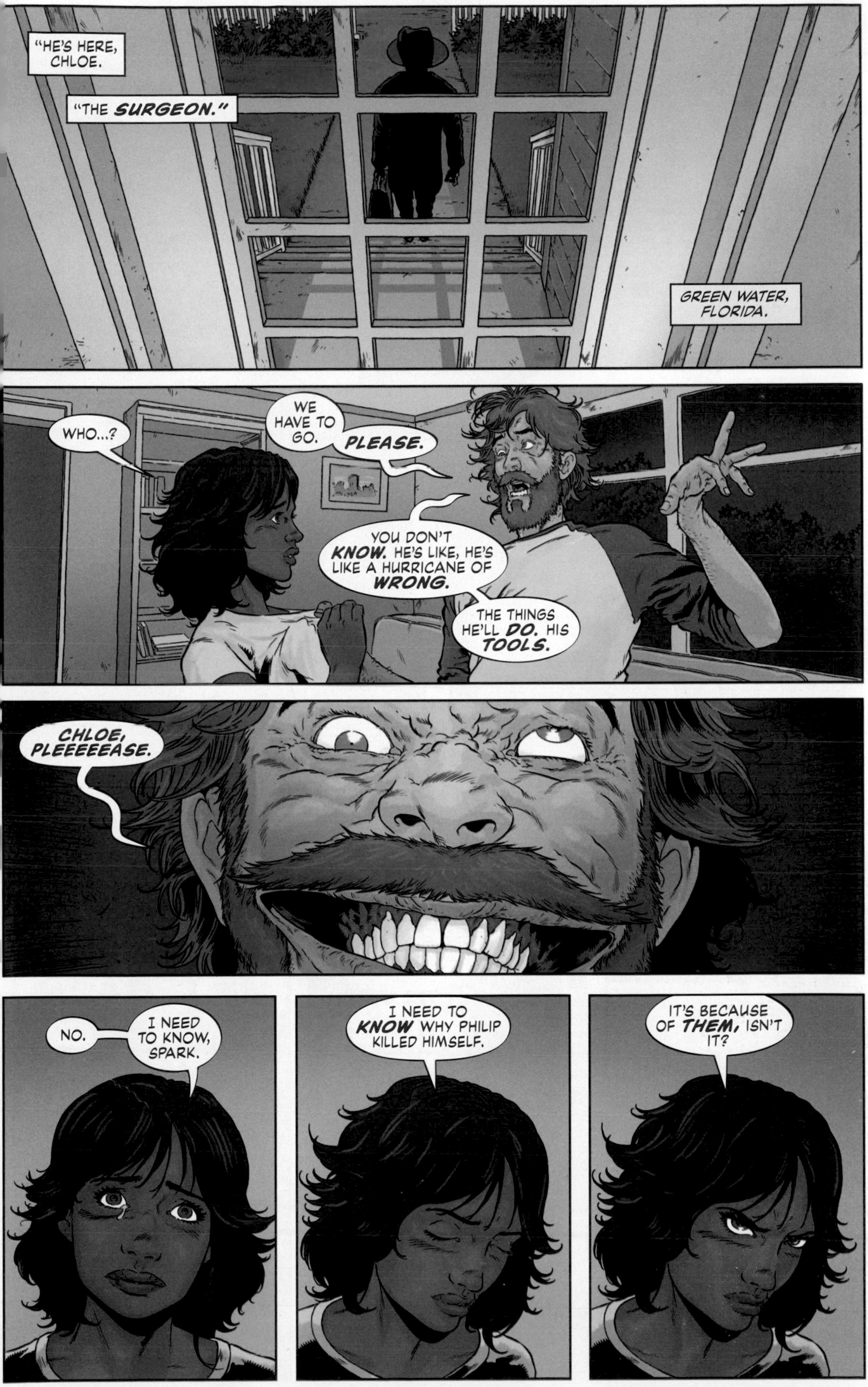
"HE'S HERE, CHLOE.
"THE SURGEON."
GREEN WATER, FLORIDA.
WHO...?
WE HAVE TO GO.
PLEASE.
YOU DON'T KNOW. HE'S LIKE, HE'S LIKE A HURRICANE OF WRONG.
THE THINGS HE'LL DO. HIS TOOLS.
CHLOE, PLEEEEEASE.
NO.
I NEED TO KNOW, SPARK.
I NEED TO KNOW WHY PHILIP KILLED HIMSELF.
IT'S BECAUSE OF THEM, ISN'T IT?

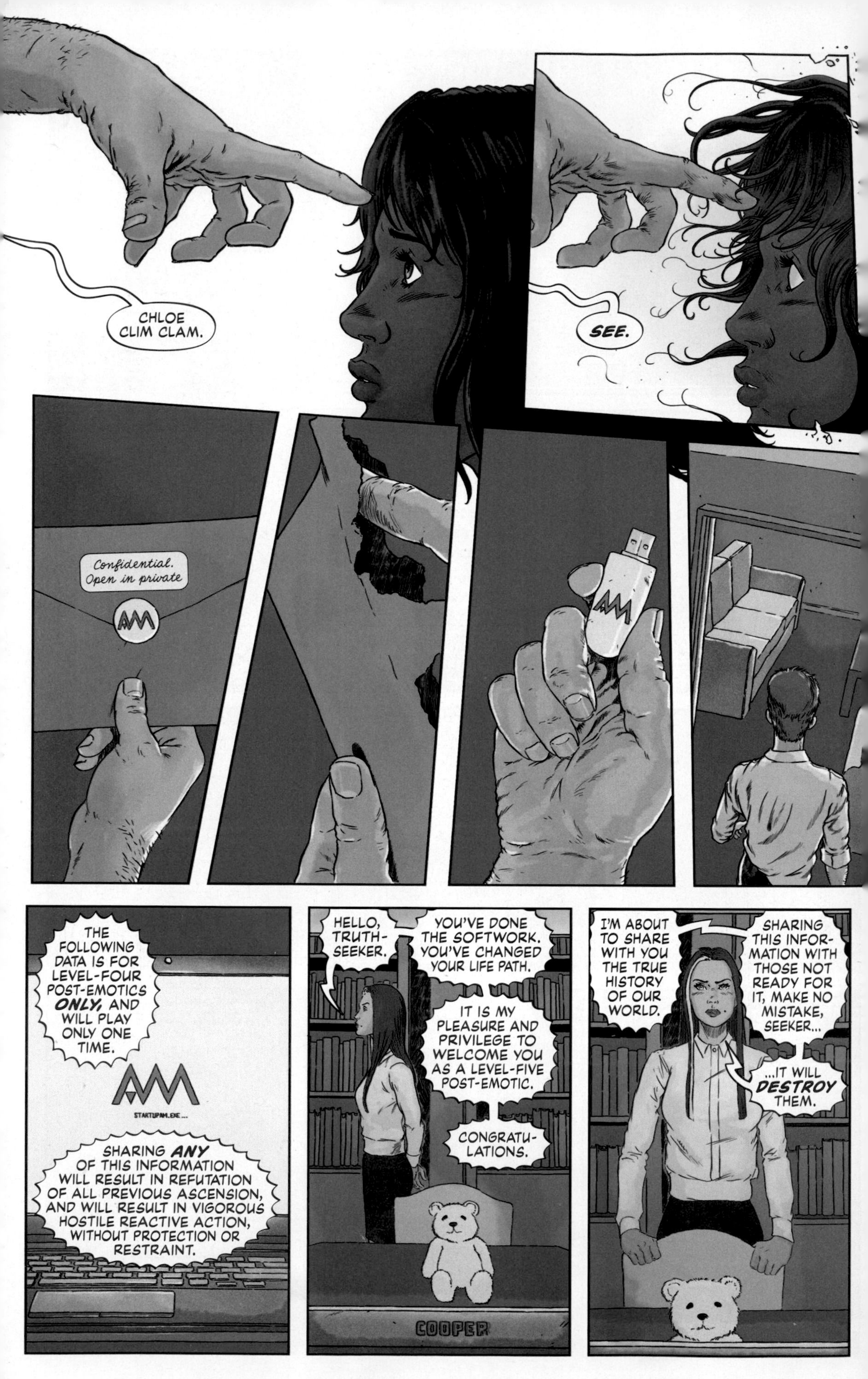
CHLOE
CLIM CLAM.
SEE.
Confidential.
Open in private
AM
THE FOLLOWING DATA IS FOR LEVEL-FOUR POST-EMOTICS ONLY, AND WILL PLAY ONLY ONE TIME.
AM
STARTUPAM.EXE ...
SHARING ANY OF THIS INFORMATION WILL RESULT IN REFUTATION OF ALL PREVIOUS ASCENSION, AND WILL RESULT IN VIGOROUS HOSTILE REACTIVE ACTION, WITHOUT PROTECTION OR RESTRAINT.
HELLO, TRUTH-SEEKER.
YOU'VE DONE THE SOFTWORK. YOU'VE CHANGED YOUR LIFE PATH.
IT IS MY PLEASURE AND PRIVILEGE TO WELCOME YOU AS A LEVEL-FIVE POST-EMOTIC.
CONGRATU-LATIONS.
COOPER
I'M ABOUT TO SHARE WITH YOU THE TRUE HISTORY OF OUR WORLD.
SHARING THIS INFOR-MATION WITH THOSE NOT READY FOR IT, MAKE NO MISTAKE, SEEKER...
...IT WILL DESTROY THEM.

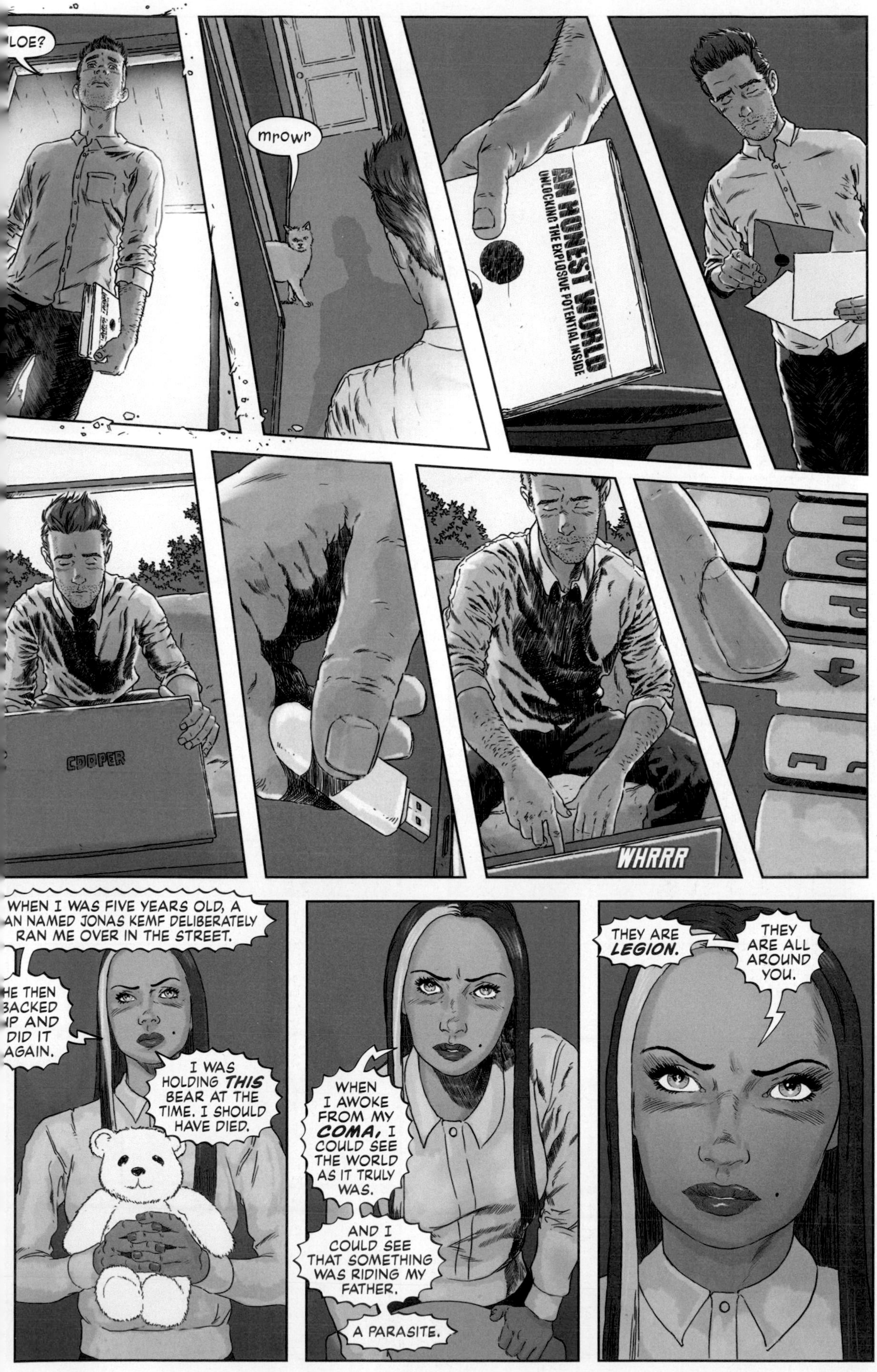

LOE?
mrowr
AN HONEST WORLD
UNLOCKING THE EXPLOSIVE POTENTIAL INSIDE
COOPER
WHRRR
WHEN I WAS FIVE YEARS OLD, A
AN NAMED JONAS KEMF DELIBERATELY
RAN ME OVER IN THE STREET.
HE THEN BACKED IP AND DID IT AGAIN.
I WAS HOLDING THIS BEAR AT THE TIME. I SHOULD HAVE DIED.
WHEN I AWOKE FROM MY COMA, I COULD SEE THE WORLD AS IT TRULY WAS.
AND I COULD SEE THAT SOMETHING WAS RIDING MY FATHER.
A PARASITE.
THEY ARE LEGION.
THEY ARE ALL AROUND YOU.

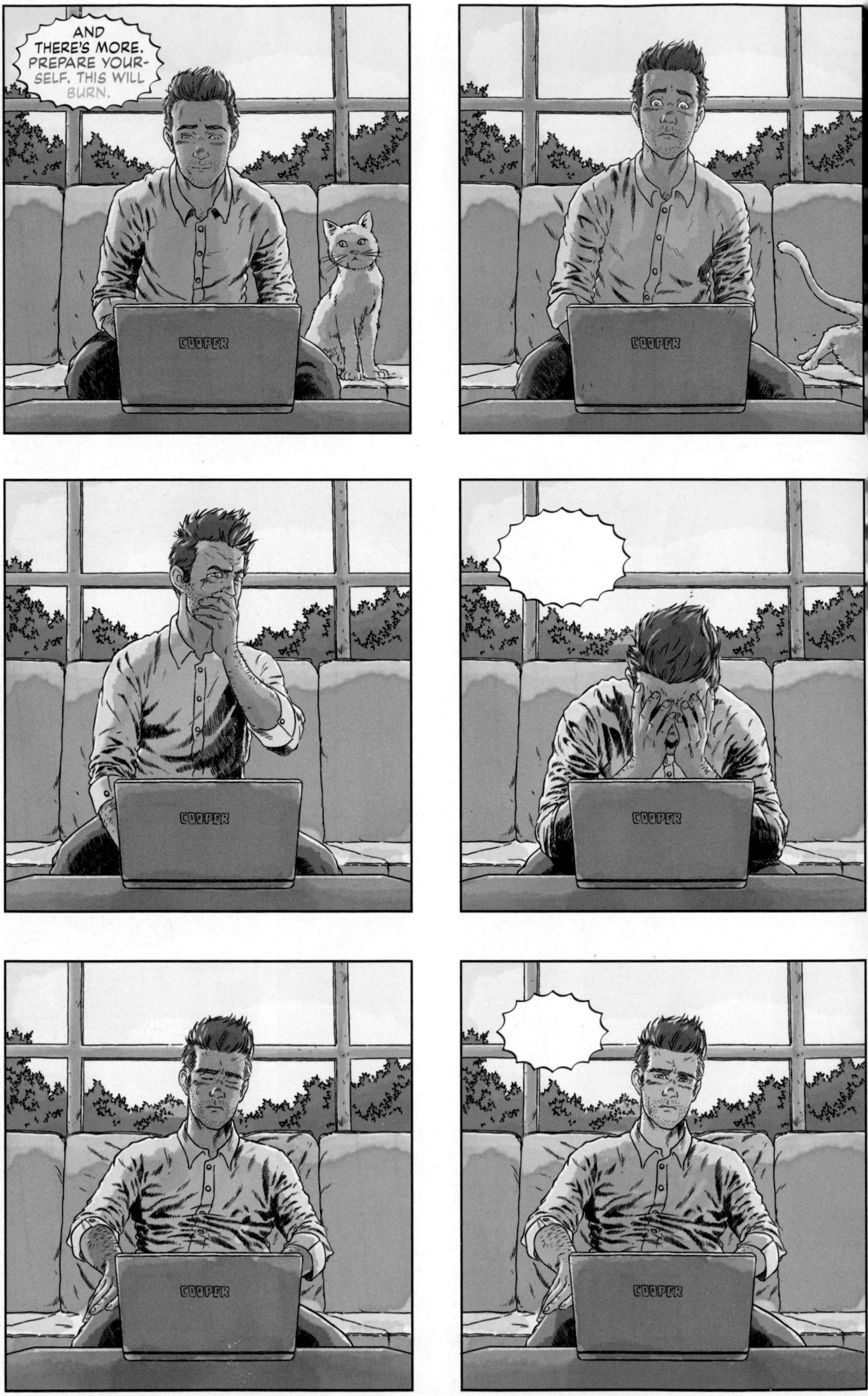
AND THERE'S MORE. PREPARE YOURSELF. THIS WILL BURN.
COOPER
COOPER
COOPER
COOPER
COOPER
COOPER

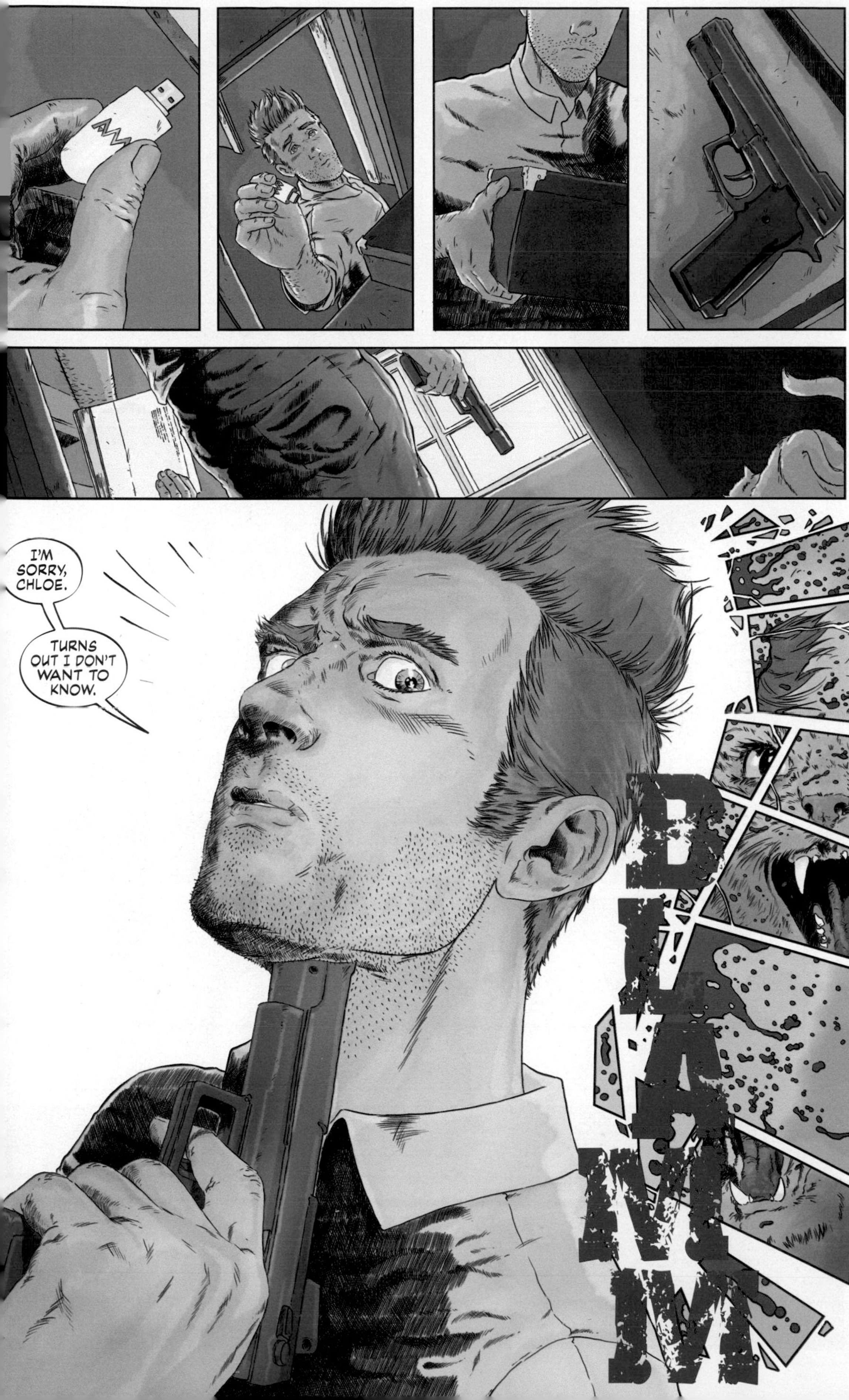
I'M SORRY, CHLOE.
TURNS OUT I DON'T WANT TO KNOW.
BLAM

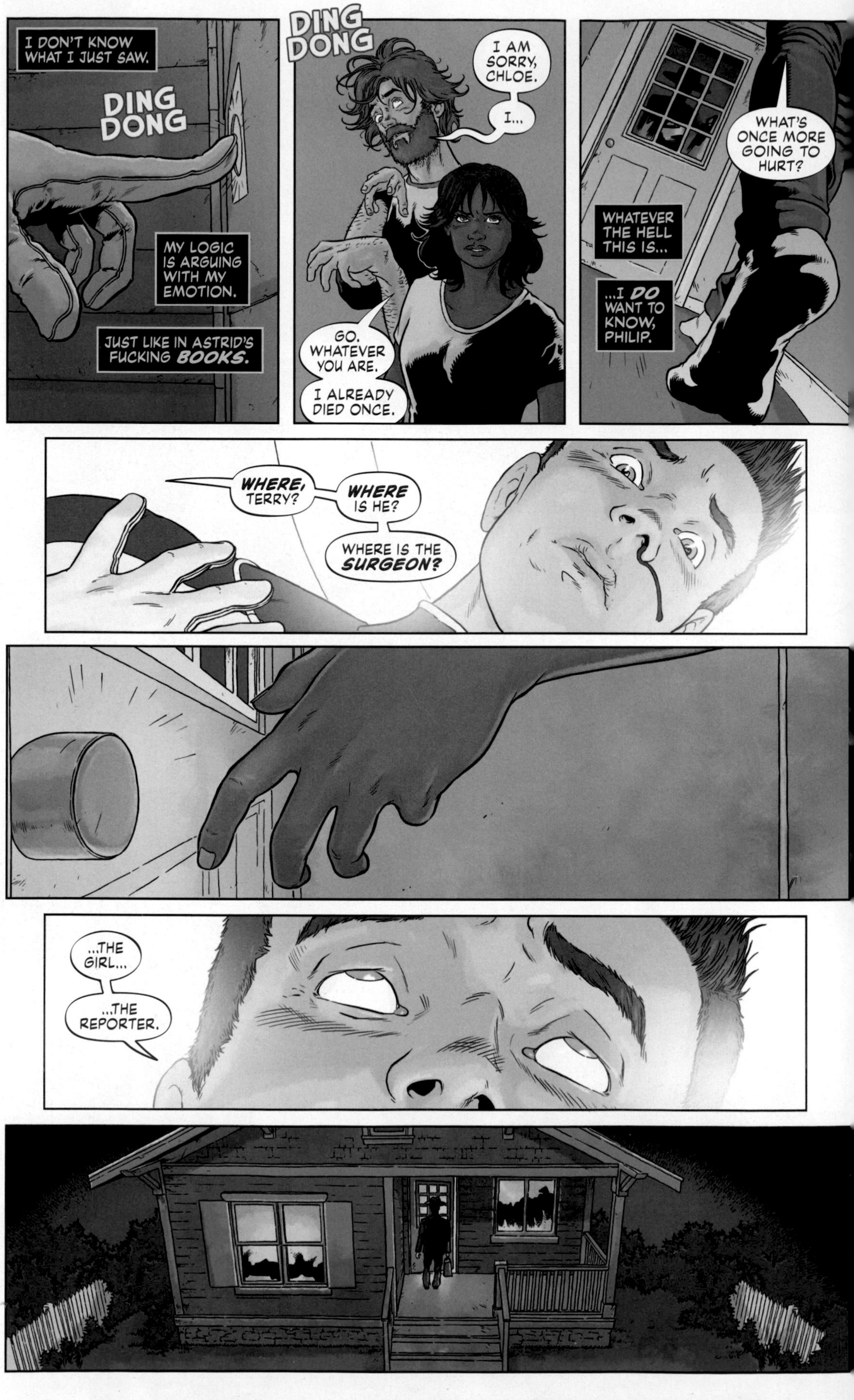
I DON'T KNOW WHAT I JUST SAW.
DING DONG
MY LOGIC IS ARGUING WITH MY EMOTION.
JUST LIKE IN ASTRID'S FUCKING BOOKS.
DING DONG
I AM SORRY, CHLOE.
I...
GO. WHATEVER YOU ARE.
I ALREADY DIED ONCE.
WHAT'S ONCE MORE GOING TO HURT?
WHATEVER THE HELL THIS IS...
...I DO WANT TO KNOW, PHILIP.
WHERE, TERRY?
WHERE IS HE?
WHERE IS THE SURGEON?
...THE GIRL...
...THE REPORTER.

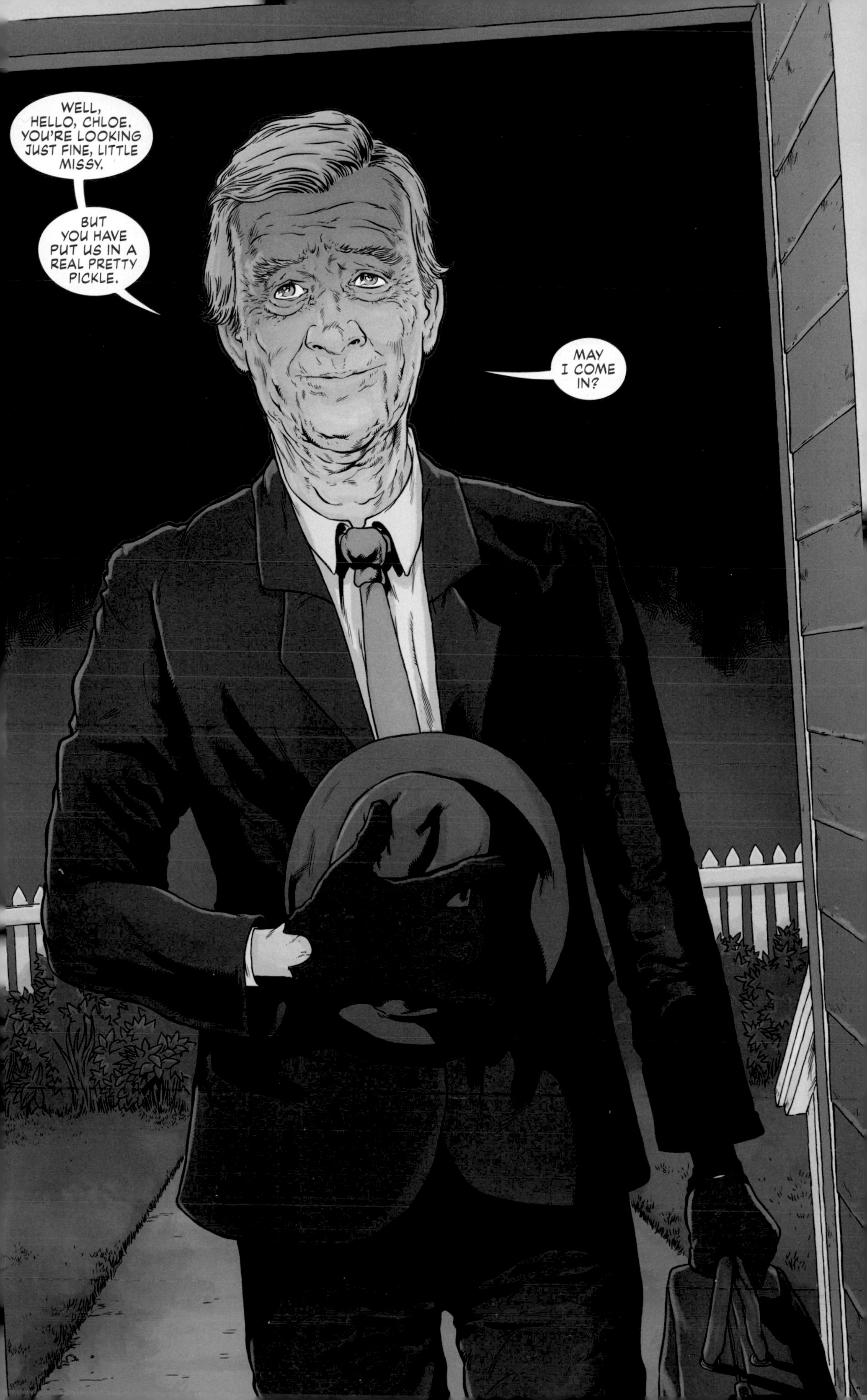
WELL, HELLO, CHLOE. YOU'RE LOOKING JUST FINE, LITTLE MISSY.
BUT YOU HAVE PUT US IN A REAL PRETTY PICKLE.
MAY I COME IN?

YOU DON'T HAPPEN TO HAVE ANY LEMONADE, DO YOU?

A MAN GETS PARCHED ON THAT DUSTY ROAD.

...

WHO *ARE* YOU?

OH, CHLOE. DON'T YOU KNOW ME?

I'M YOUR *DOCTOR,* SWEETIE.

BEEN YOUR DOCTOR SINCE YOU...

...WELL, TRIED TO HURT YOURSELF.

NO.

BULLSHIT.

IT'S TRUE, MISS PIERCE.

TRY TO *REMEMBER.*

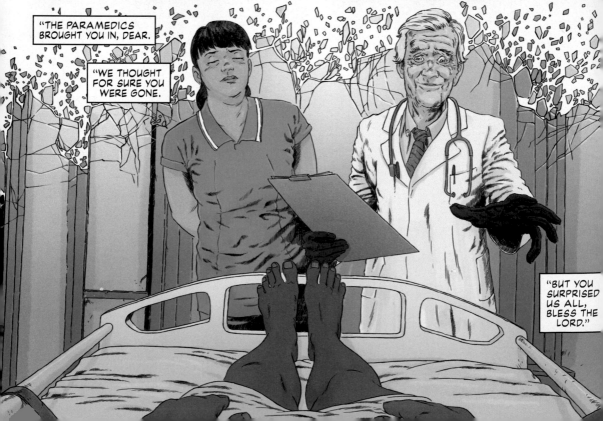

"THE PARAMEDICS BROUGHT YOU IN, DEAR.

"WE THOUGHT FOR SURE YOU WERE GONE.

"BUT YOU SURPRISED US ALL, BLESS THE LORD."

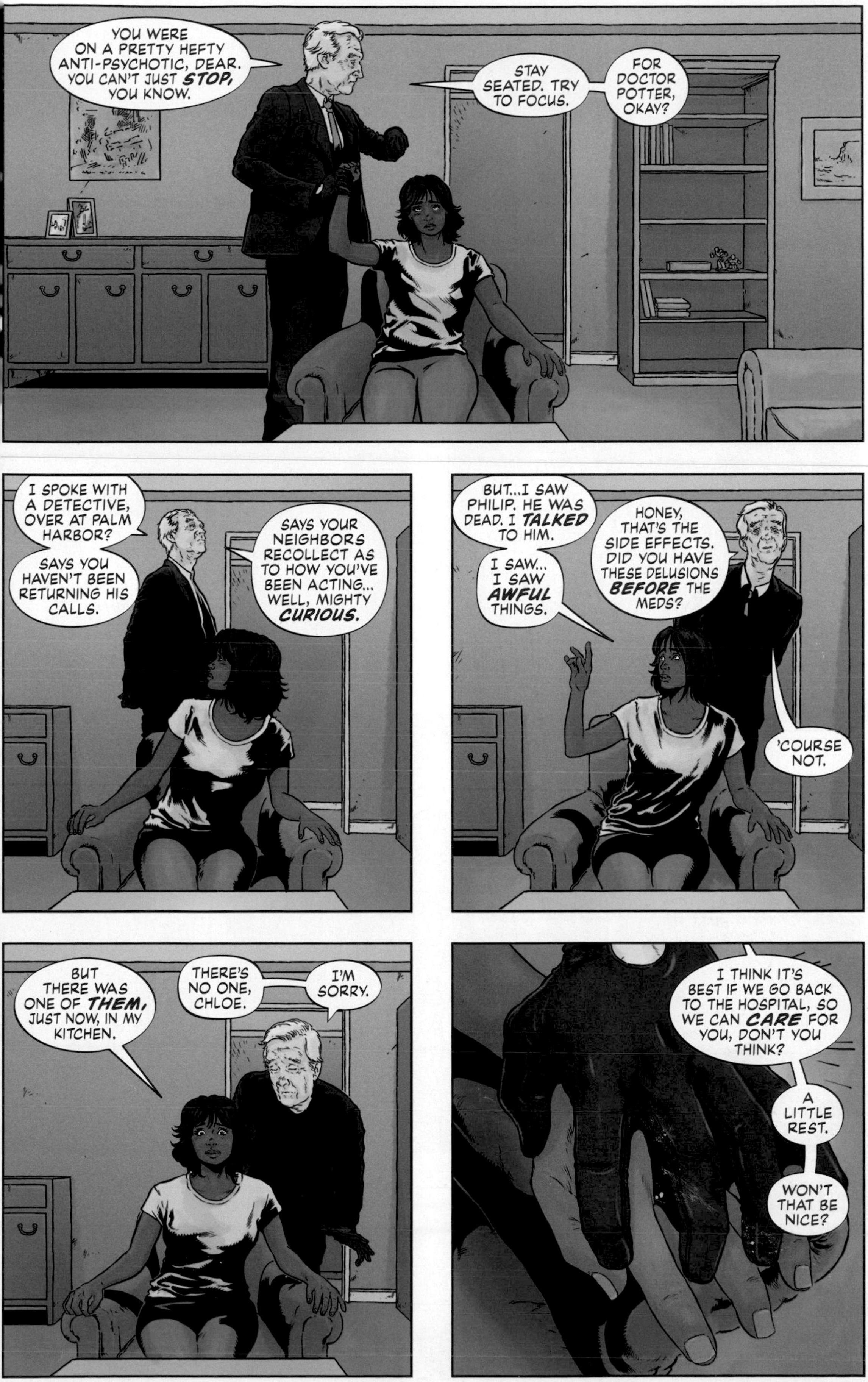
YOU WERE ON A PRETTY HEFTY ANTI-PSYCHOTIC, DEAR. YOU CAN'T JUST STOP, YOU KNOW.
STAY SEATED. TRY TO FOCUS.
FOR DOCTOR POTTER, OKAY?
I SPOKE WITH A DETECTIVE, OVER AT PALM HARBOR?
SAYS YOU HAVEN'T BEEN RETURNING HIS CALLS.
SAYS YOUR NEIGHBORS RECOLLECT AS TO HOW YOU'VE BEEN ACTING... WELL, MIGHTY CURIOUS.
BUT...I SAW PHILIP. HE WAS DEAD. I TALKED TO HIM.
I SAW... I SAW AWFUL THINGS.
HONEY, THAT'S THE SIDE EFFECTS. DID YOU HAVE THESE DELUSIONS BEFORE THE MEDS?
'COURSE NOT.
BUT THERE WAS ONE OF THEM, JUST NOW, IN MY KITCHEN.
THERE'S NO ONE, CHLOE.
I'M SORRY.
I THINK IT'S BEST IF WE GO BACK TO THE HOSPITAL, SO WE CAN CARE FOR YOU, DON'T YOU THINK?
A LITTLE REST.
WON'T THAT BE NICE?

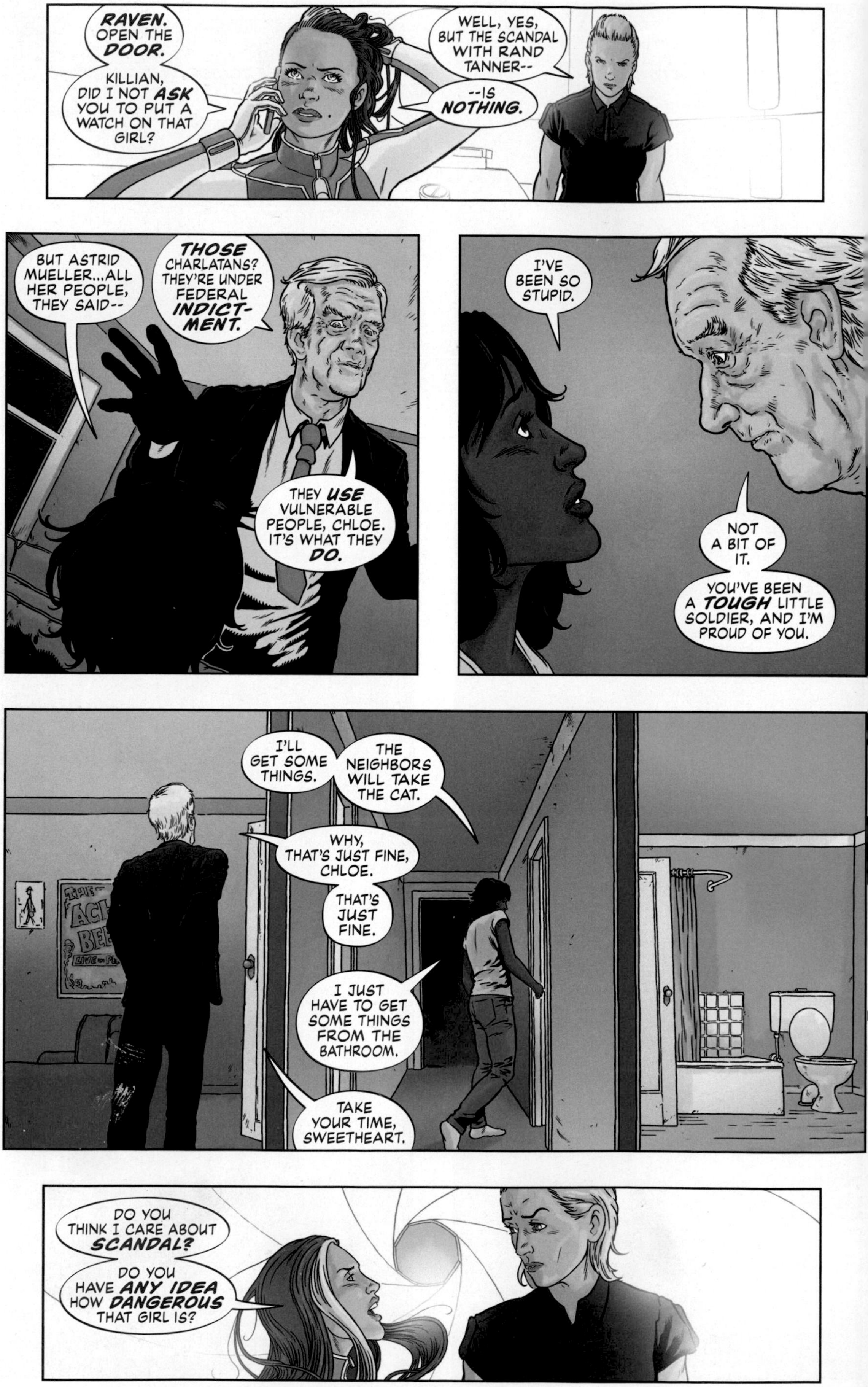
RAVEN. OPEN THE DOOR.
KILLIAN, DID I NOT ASK YOU TO PUT A WATCH ON THAT GIRL?
WELL, YES, BUT THE SCANDAL WITH RAND TANNER--
--IS NOTHING.
BUT ASTRID MUELLER...ALL HER PEOPLE, THEY SAID--
THOSE CHARLATANS? THEY'RE UNDER FEDERAL INDICT-MENT.
THEY USE VULNERABLE PEOPLE, CHLOE. IT'S WHAT THEY DO.
I'VE BEEN SO STUPID.
NOT A BIT OF IT.
YOU'VE BEEN A TOUGH LITTLE SOLDIER, AND I'M PROUD OF YOU.
I'LL GET SOME THINGS.
THE NEIGHBORS WILL TAKE THE CAT.
WHY, THAT'S JUST FINE, CHLOE.
THAT'S JUST FINE.
I JUST HAVE TO GET SOME THINGS FROM THE BATHROOM.
TAKE YOUR TIME, SWEETHEART.
DO YOU THINK I CARE ABOUT SCANDAL?
DO YOU HAVE ANY IDEA HOW DANGEROUS THAT GIRL IS?

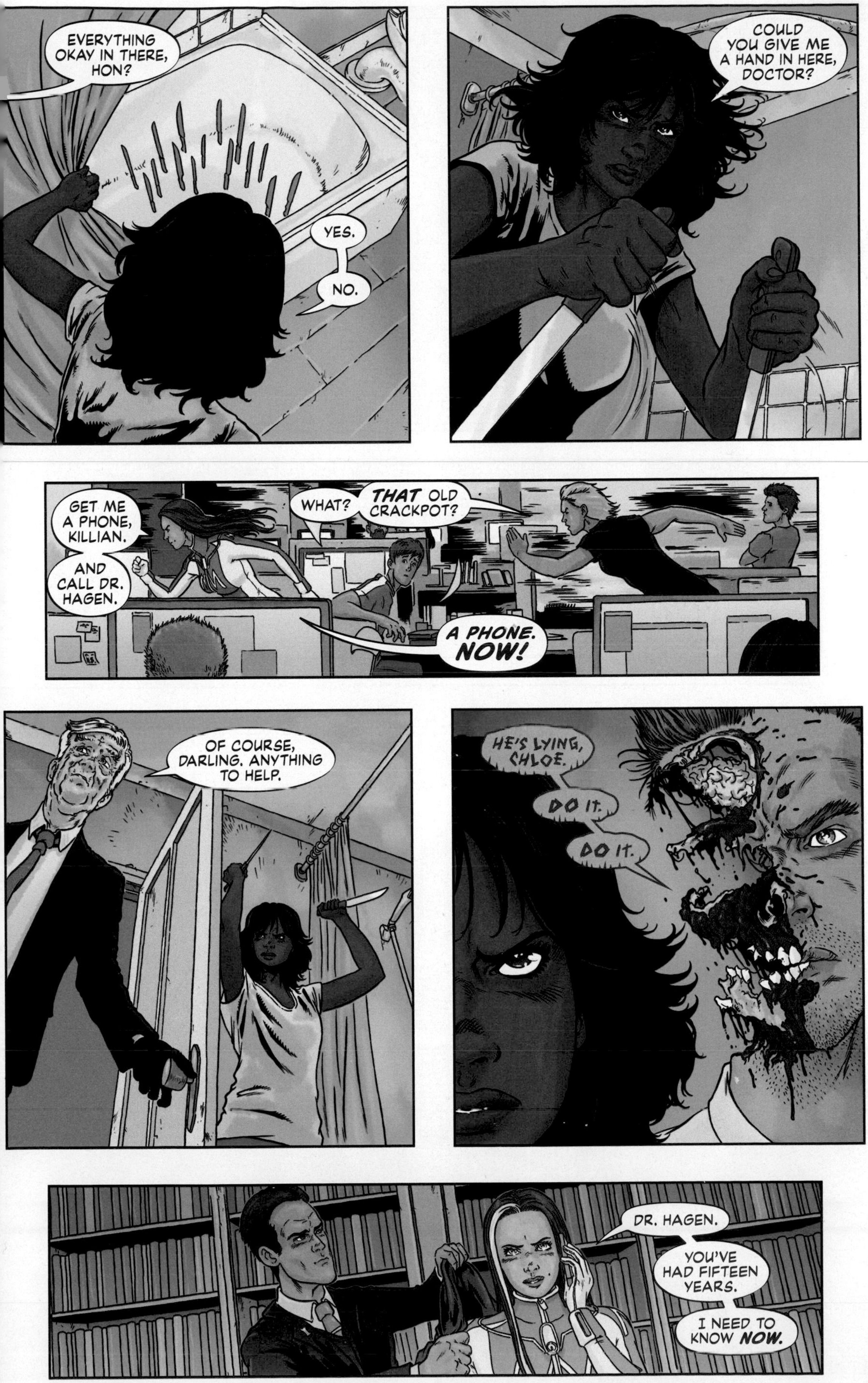
EVERYTHING OKAY IN THERE, HON?
YES.
NO.
COULD YOU GIVE ME A HAND IN HERE, DOCTOR?
GET ME A PHONE, KILLIAN.
AND CALL DR. HAGEN.
WHAT? THAT OLD CRACKPOT?
A PHONE. NOW!
OF COURSE, DARLING. ANYTHING TO HELP.
HE'S LYING, CHLOE.
DO IT.
DO IT.
DR. HAGEN.
YOU'VE HAD FIFTEEN YEARS.
I NEED TO KNOW NOW.

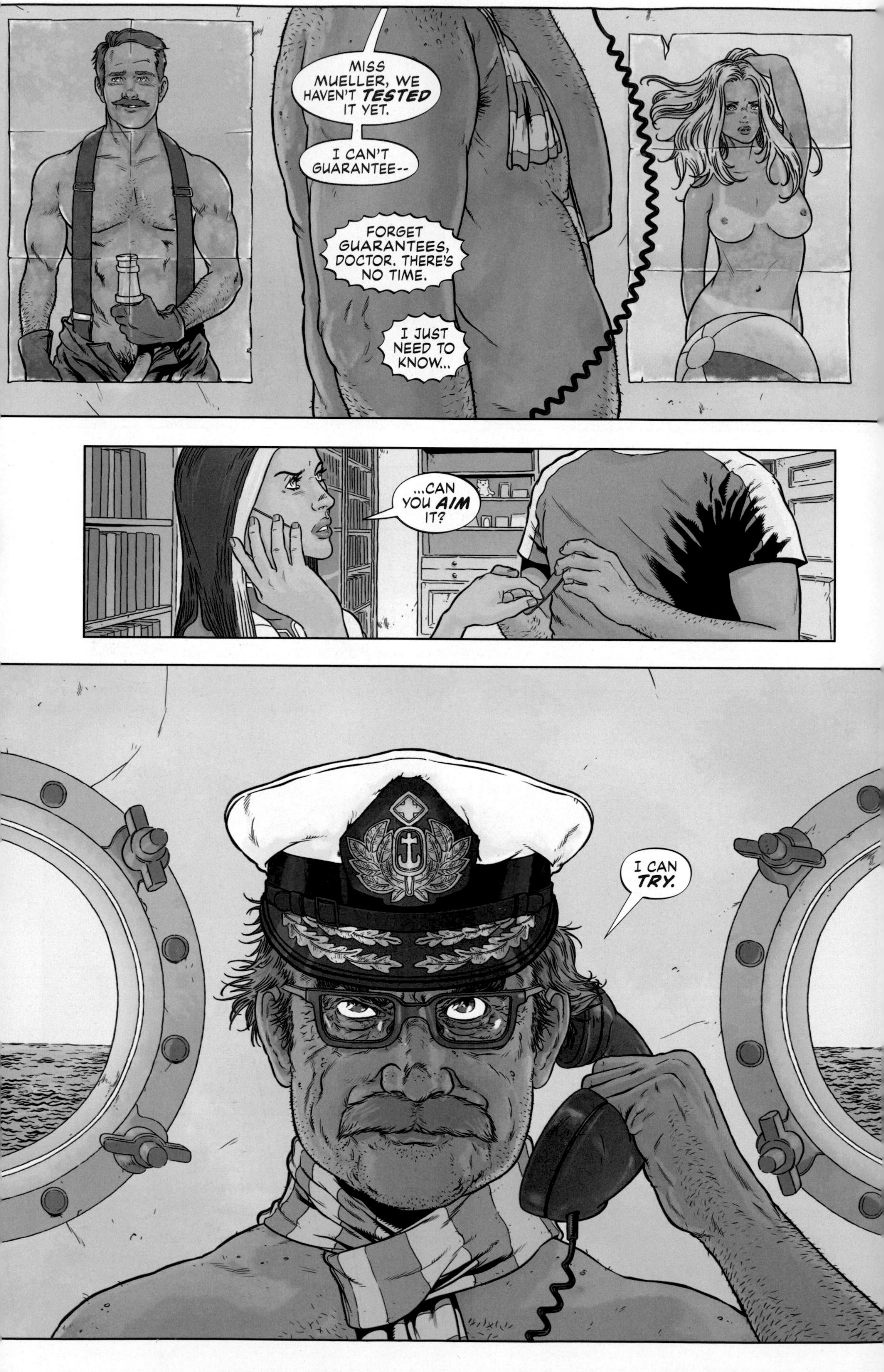
MISS MUELLER, WE HAVEN'T TESTED IT YET.
I CAN'T GUARANTEE--
FORGET GUARANTEES, DOCTOR. THERE'S NO TIME.
I JUST NEED TO KNOW...
...CAN YOU AIM IT?
I CAN TRY.

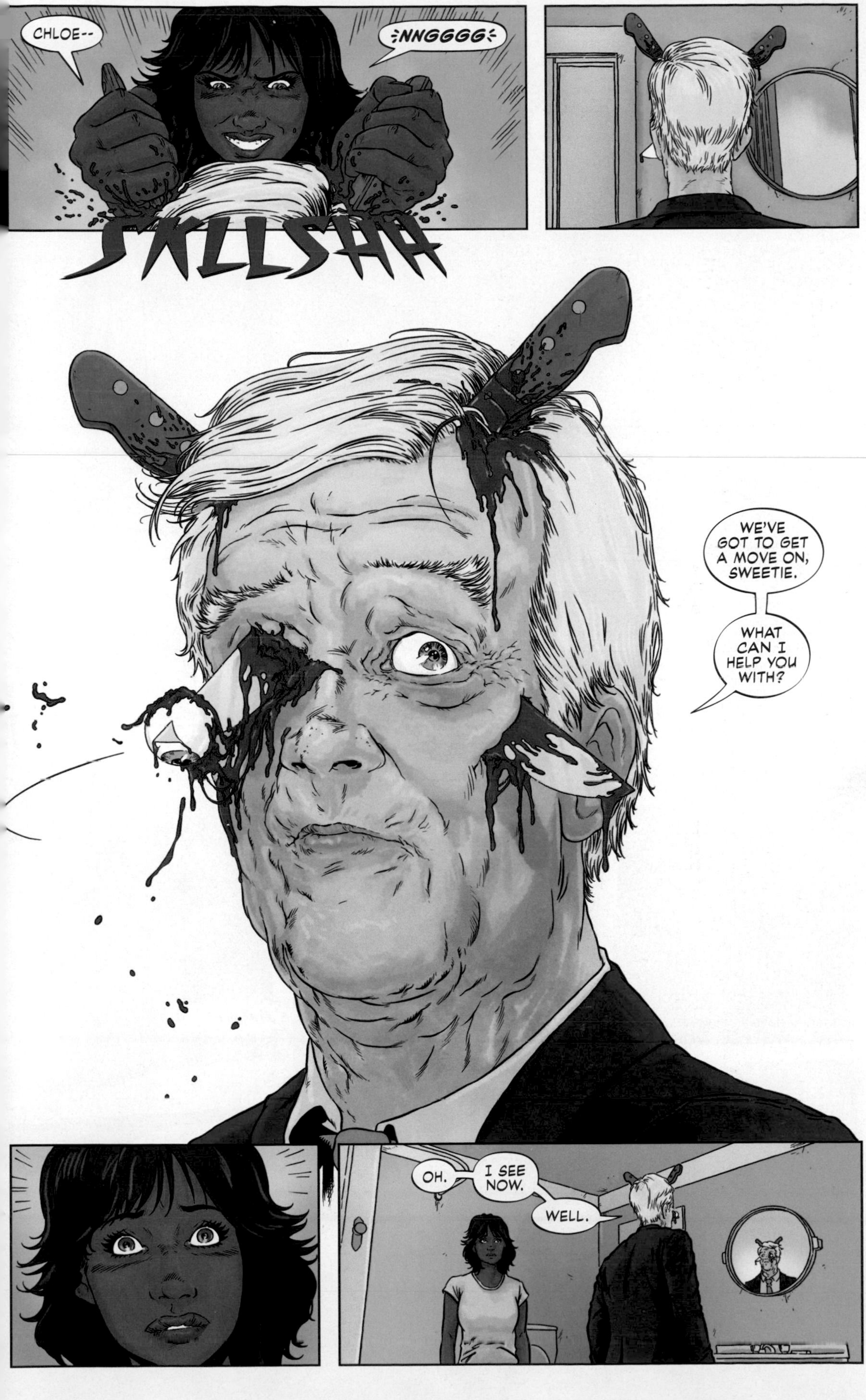
CHLOE--
NNGGGG
SKLLSHA
WE'VE GOT TO GET A MOVE ON, SWEETIE.
WHAT CAN I HELP YOU WITH?
OH.
I SEE NOW.
WELL.

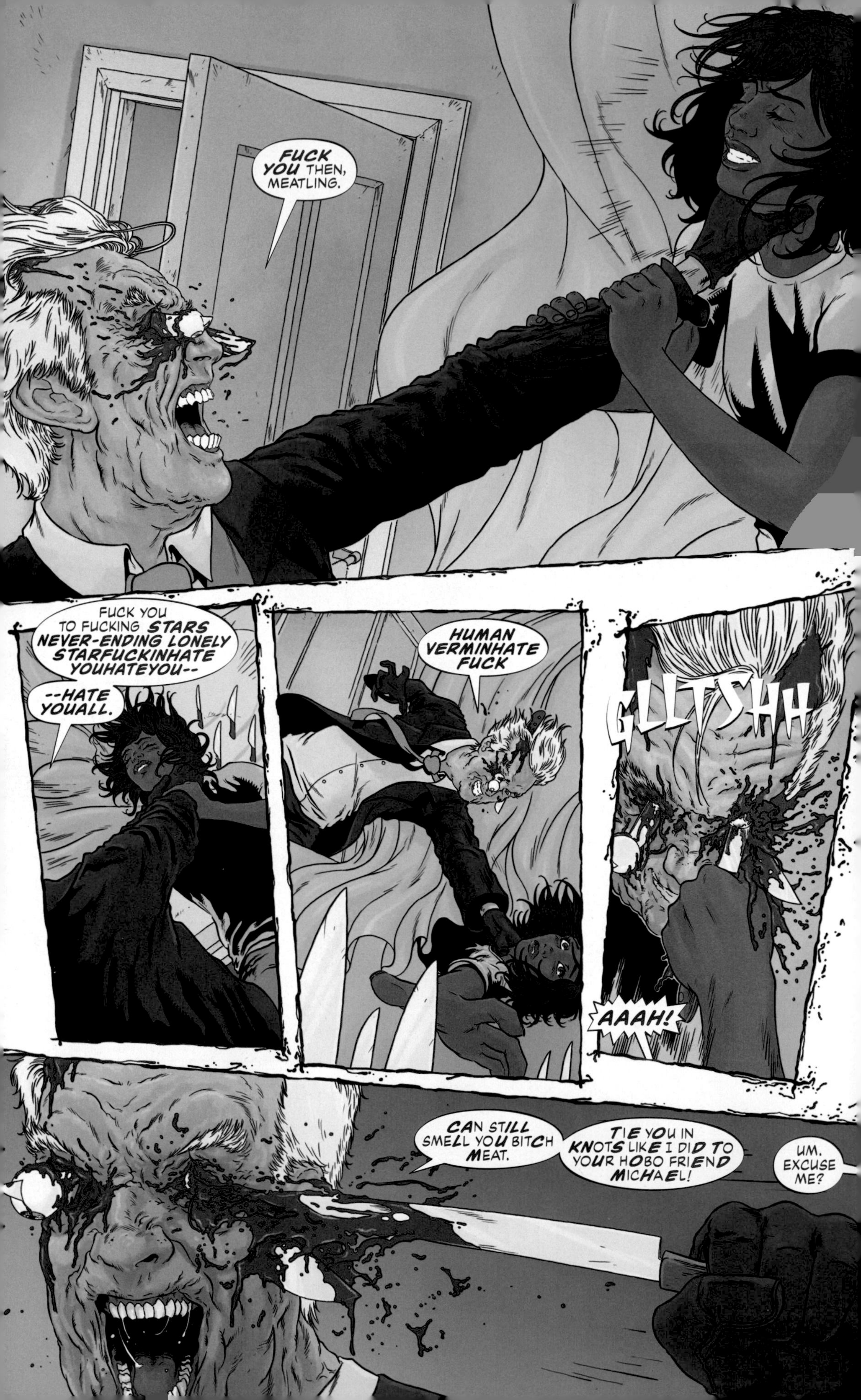
FUCK YOU THEN, MEATLING.
FUCK YOU TO FUCKING STARS NEVER-ENDING LONELY STARFUCKINHATE YOUHATEYOU--
--HATE YOUALL.
HUMAN VERMINHATE FUCK
GLLTSHH
AAAH!
CAN STILL SMELL YOU BITCH MEAT.
TIE YOU IN KNOTS LIKE I DID TO YOUR HOBO FRIEND MICHAEL!
UM. EXCUSE ME?

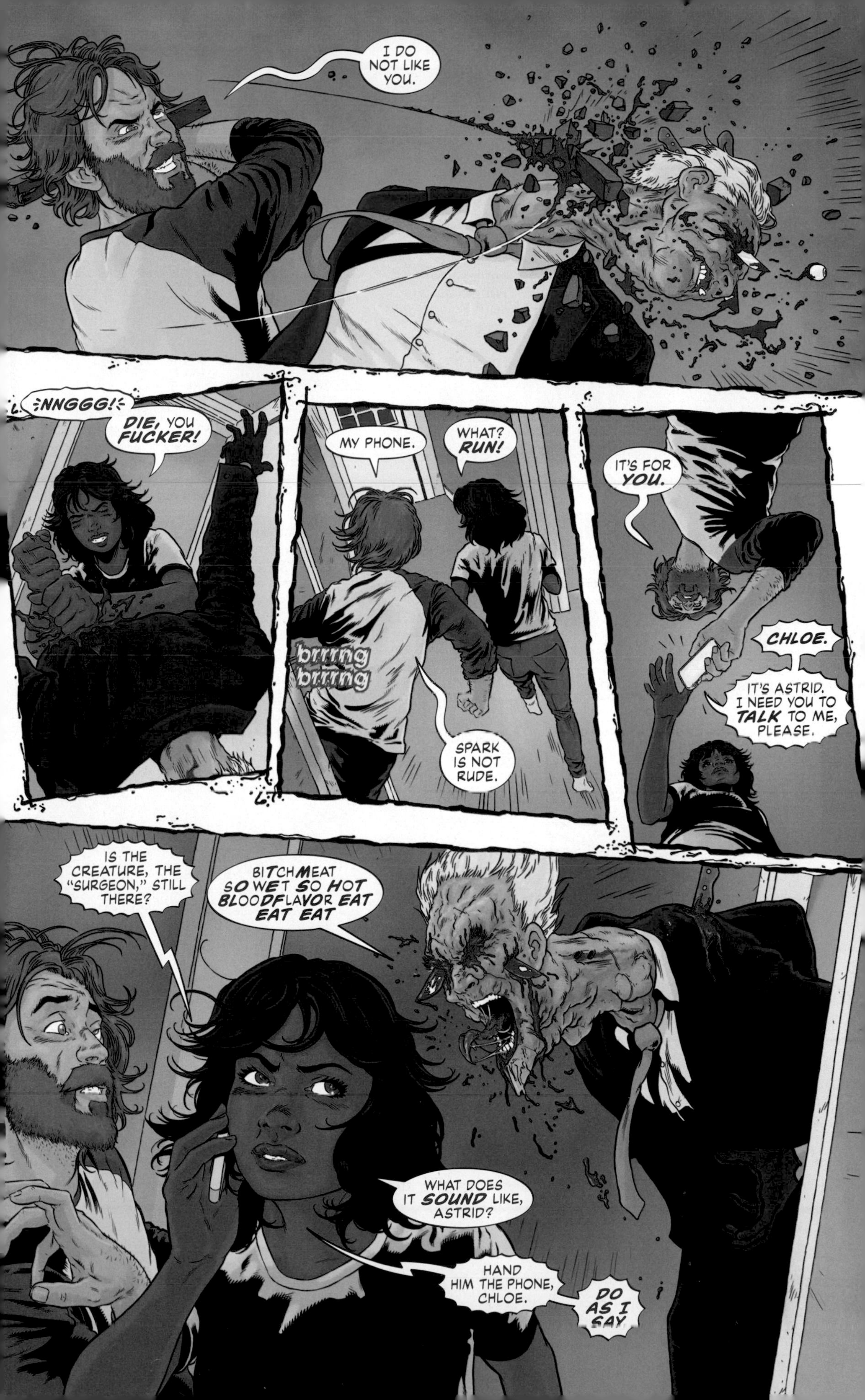
I DO NOT LIKE YOU.
NNGGG!
DIE, YOU FUCKER!
MY PHONE.
WHAT? RUN!
brrrng brrrng
SPARK IS NOT RUDE.
IT'S FOR YOU.
CHLOE.
IT'S ASTRID. I NEED YOU TO TALK TO ME, PLEASE.
IS THE CREATURE, THE "SURGEON," STILL THERE?
BITCHMEAT SO WET SO HOT BLOODFLAVOR EAT EAT EAT
WHAT DOES IT SOUND LIKE, ASTRID?
HAND HIM THE PHONE, CHLOE.
DO AS I SAY

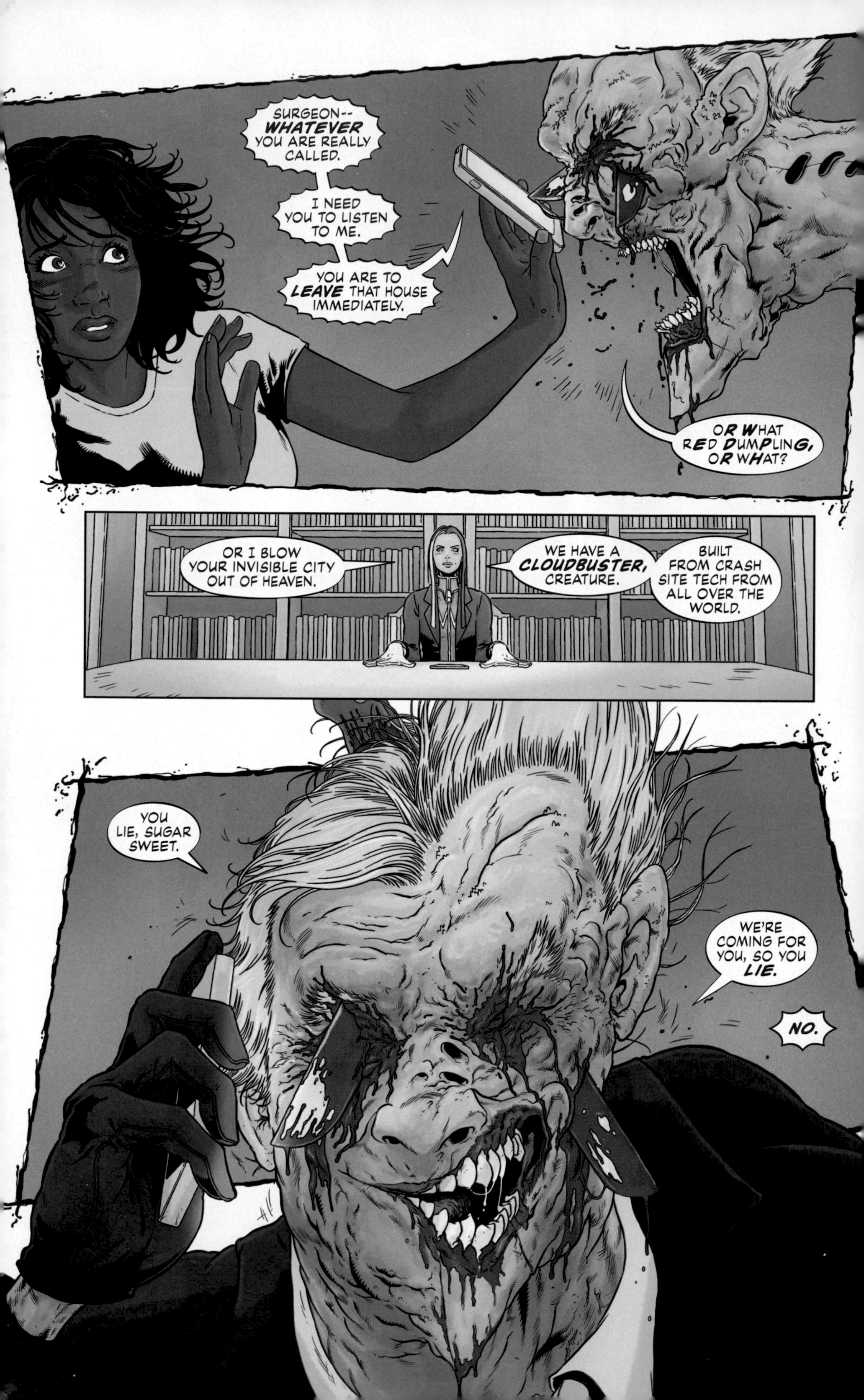
SURGEON-- WHATEVER YOU ARE REALLY CALLED.
I NEED YOU TO LISTEN TO ME.
YOU ARE TO LEAVE THAT HOUSE IMMEDIATELY.
OR WHAT RED DUMPLING, OR WHAT?
OR I BLOW YOUR INVISIBLE CITY OUT OF HEAVEN.
WE HAVE A CLOUDBUSTER, CREATURE.
BUILT FROM CRASH SITE TECH FROM ALL OVER THE WORLD.
YOU LIE, SUGAR SWEET.
WE'RE COMING FOR YOU, SO YOU LIE.
NO.

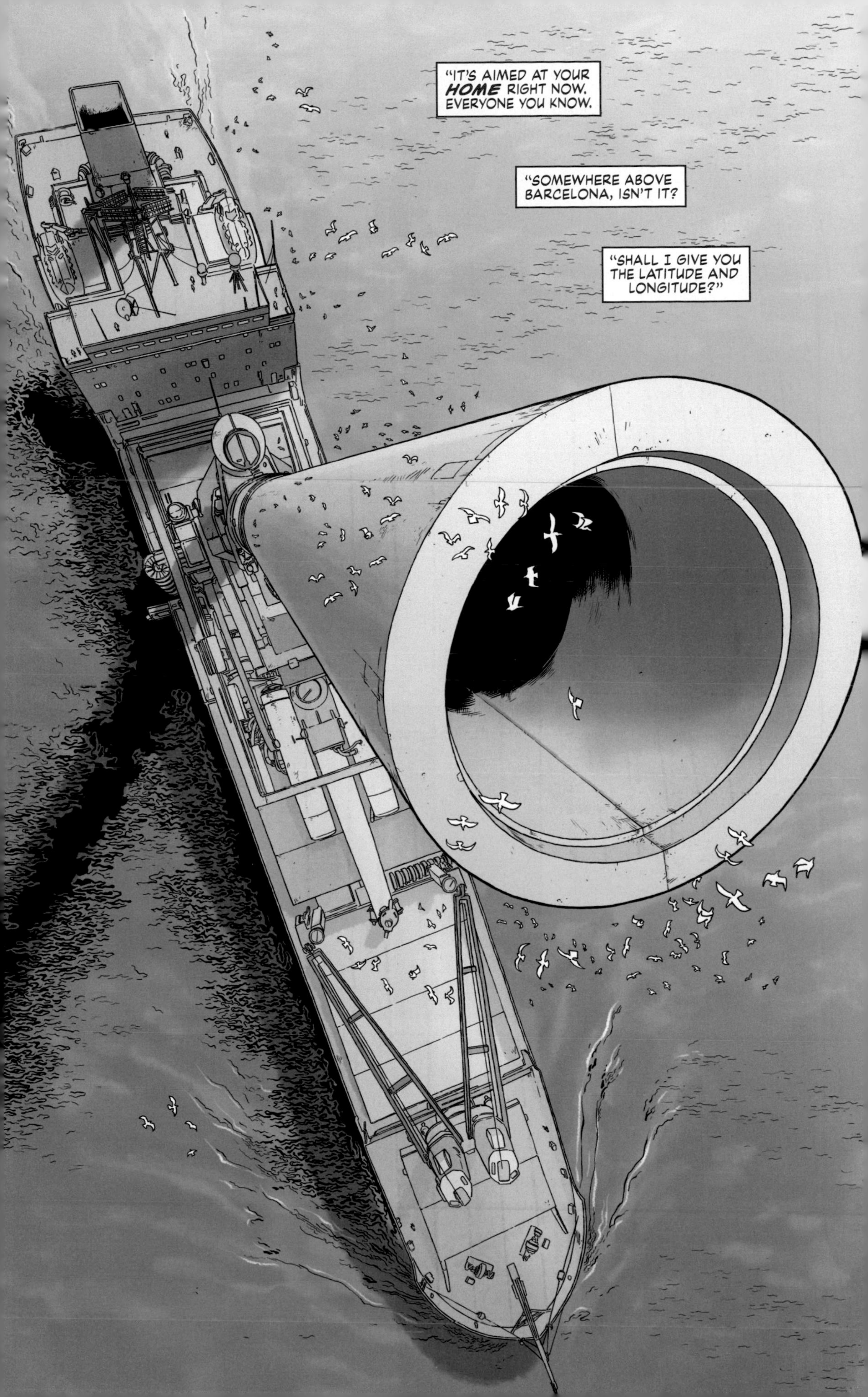
"IT'S AIMED AT YOUR **HOME** RIGHT NOW. EVERYONE YOU KNOW.
"SOMEWHERE ABOVE BARCELONA, ISN'T IT?
"SHALL I GIVE YOU THE LATITUDE AND LONGITUDE?"

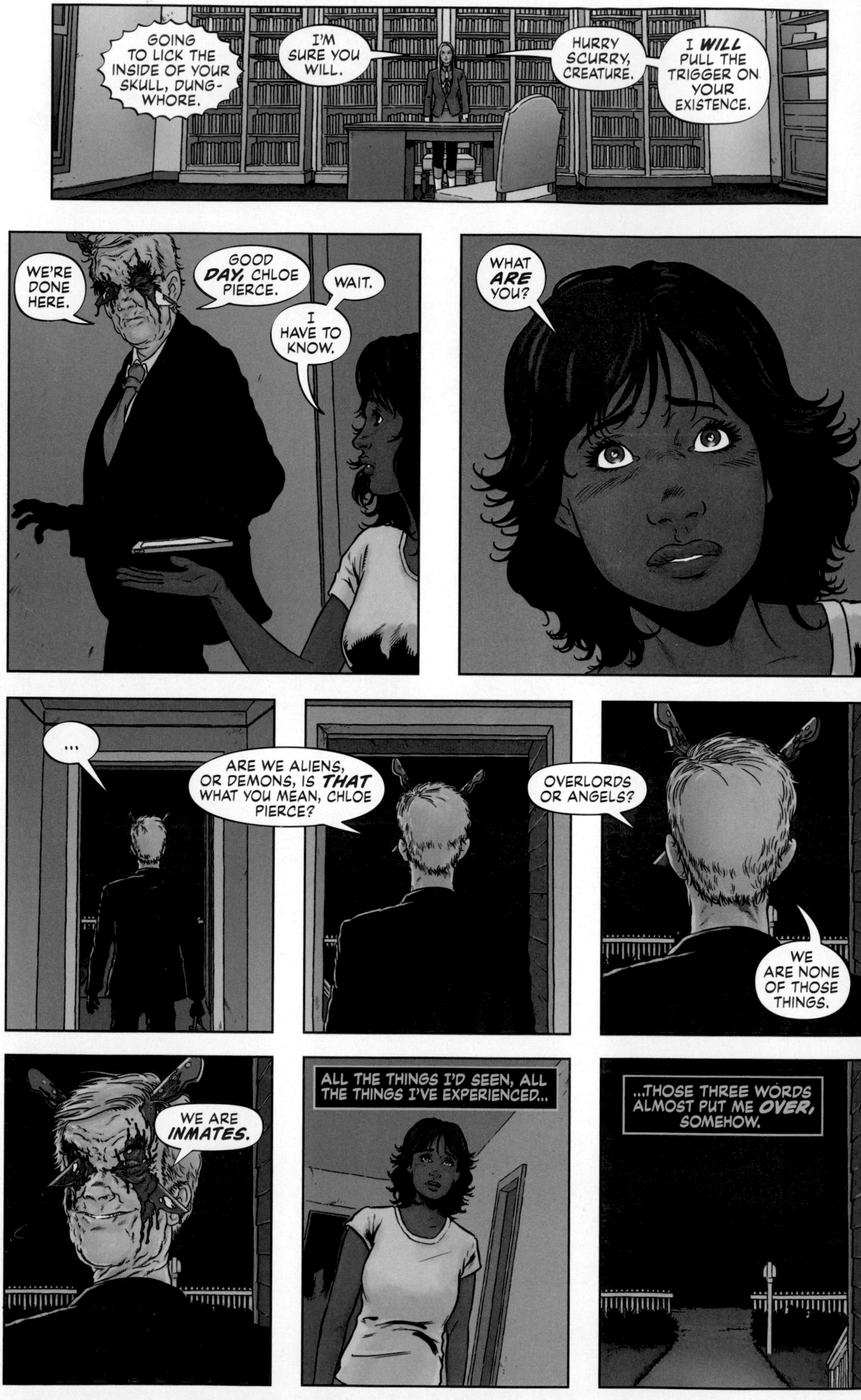
GOING TO LICK THE INSIDE OF YOUR SKULL, DUNG-WHORE.
I'M SURE YOU WILL.
HURRY SCURRY, CREATURE.
I **WILL** PULL THE TRIGGER ON YOUR EXISTENCE.
WE'RE DONE HERE.
GOOD **DAY,** CHLOE PIERCE.
WAIT.
I HAVE TO KNOW.
WHAT **ARE** YOU?
...
ARE WE ALIENS, OR DEMONS, IS **THAT** WHAT YOU MEAN, CHLOE PIERCE?
OVERLORDS OR ANGELS?
WE ARE NONE OF THOSE THINGS.
WE ARE **INMATES.**
ALL THE THINGS I'D SEEN, ALL THE THINGS I'VE EXPERIENCED...
...THOSE THREE WORDS ALMOST PUT ME **OVER,** SOMEHOW.

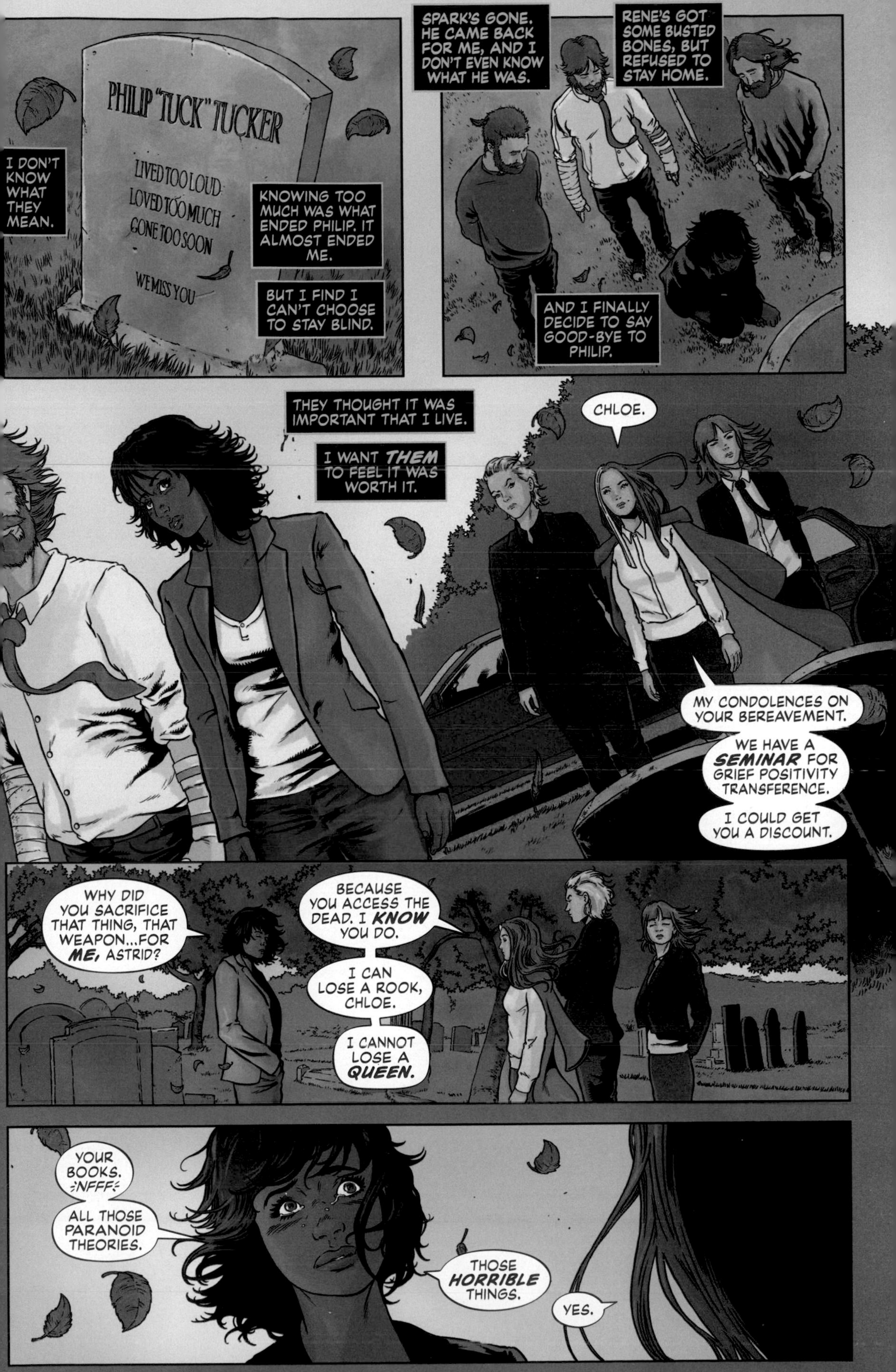
PHILIP "TUCK" TUCKER
LIVED TOO LOUD
LOVED TOO MUCH
GONE TOO SOON
WE MISS YOU
I DON'T KNOW WHAT THEY MEAN.
KNOWING TOO MUCH WAS WHAT ENDED PHILIP. IT ALMOST ENDED ME.
BUT I FIND I CAN'T CHOOSE TO STAY BLIND.
SPARK'S GONE. HE CAME BACK FOR ME, AND I DON'T EVEN KNOW WHAT HE WAS.
RENE'S GOT SOME BUSTED BONES, BUT REFUSED TO STAY HOME.
AND I FINALLY DECIDE TO SAY GOOD-BYE TO PHILIP.
THEY THOUGHT IT WAS IMPORTANT THAT I LIVE.
I WANT THEM TO FEEL IT WAS WORTH IT.
CHLOE.
MY CONDOLENCES ON YOUR BEREAVEMENT.
WE HAVE A SEMINAR FOR GRIEF POSITIVITY TRANSFERENCE.
I COULD GET YOU A DISCOUNT.
WHY DID YOU SACRIFICE THAT THING, THAT WEAPON...FOR ME, ASTRID?
BECAUSE YOU ACCESS THE DEAD. I KNOW YOU DO.
I CAN LOSE A ROOK, CHLOE.
I CANNOT LOSE A QUEEN.
YOUR BOOKS. NFFF
ALL THOSE PARANOID THEORIES.
THOSE HORRIBLE THINGS.
YES.

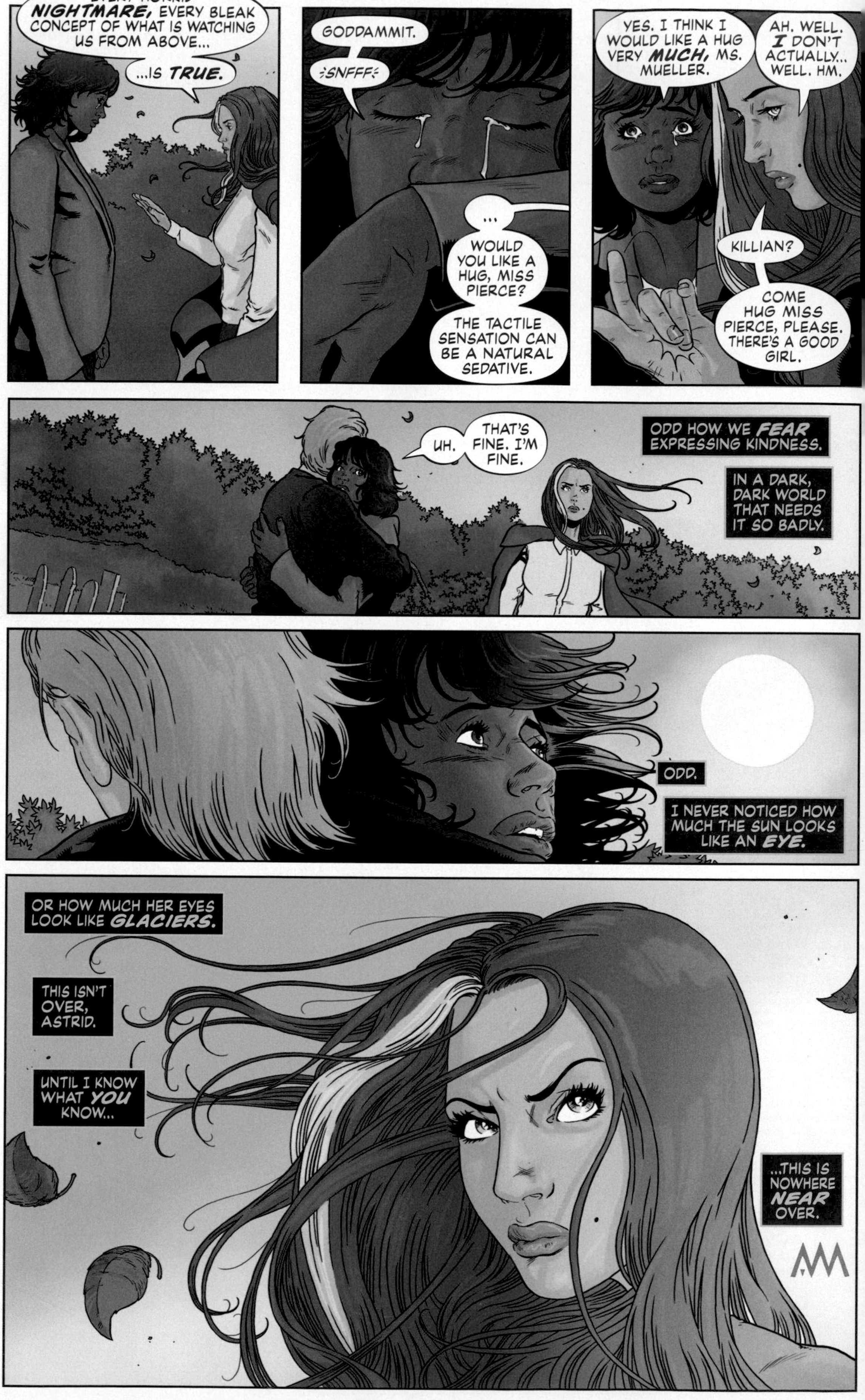
EVERY HORRID NIGHTMARE, EVERY BLEAK CONCEPT OF WHAT IS WATCHING US FROM ABOVE...
...IS TRUE.
GODDAMMIT.
SNFFF
...
WOULD YOU LIKE A HUG, MISS PIERCE?
THE TACTILE SENSATION CAN BE A NATURAL SEDATIVE.
YES. I THINK I WOULD LIKE A HUG VERY MUCH, MS. MUELLER.
AH. WELL. I DON'T ACTUALLY... WELL. HM.
KILLIAN?
COME HUG MISS PIERCE, PLEASE. THERE'S A GOOD GIRL.
UH.
THAT'S FINE. I'M FINE.
ODD HOW WE FEAR EXPRESSING KINDNESS.
IN A DARK, DARK WORLD THAT NEEDS IT SO BADLY.
ODD.
I NEVER NOTICED HOW MUCH THE SUN LOOKS LIKE AN EYE.
OR HOW MUCH HER EYES LOOK LIKE GLACIERS.
THIS ISN'T OVER, ASTRID.
UNTIL I KNOW WHAT YOU KNOW...
...THIS IS NOWHERE NEAR OVER.

DRAWING ROOM

Character sketches by Jon Davis-Hunt

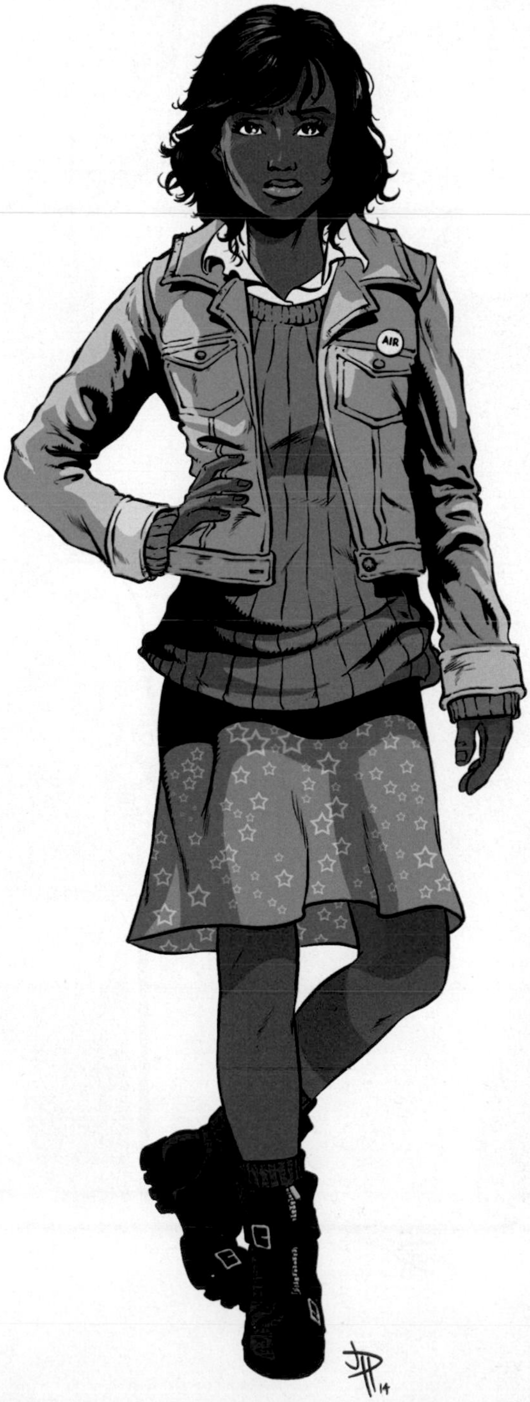
AIR

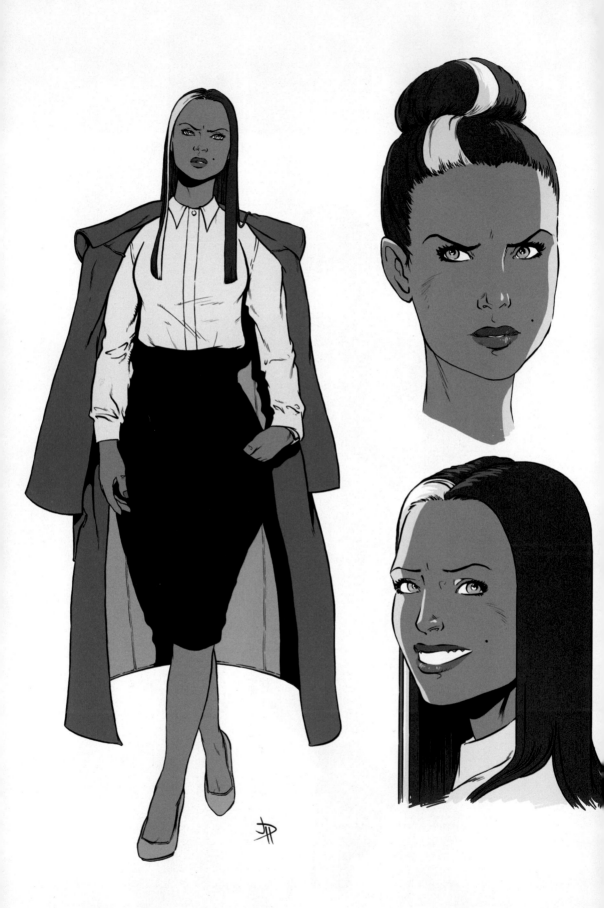

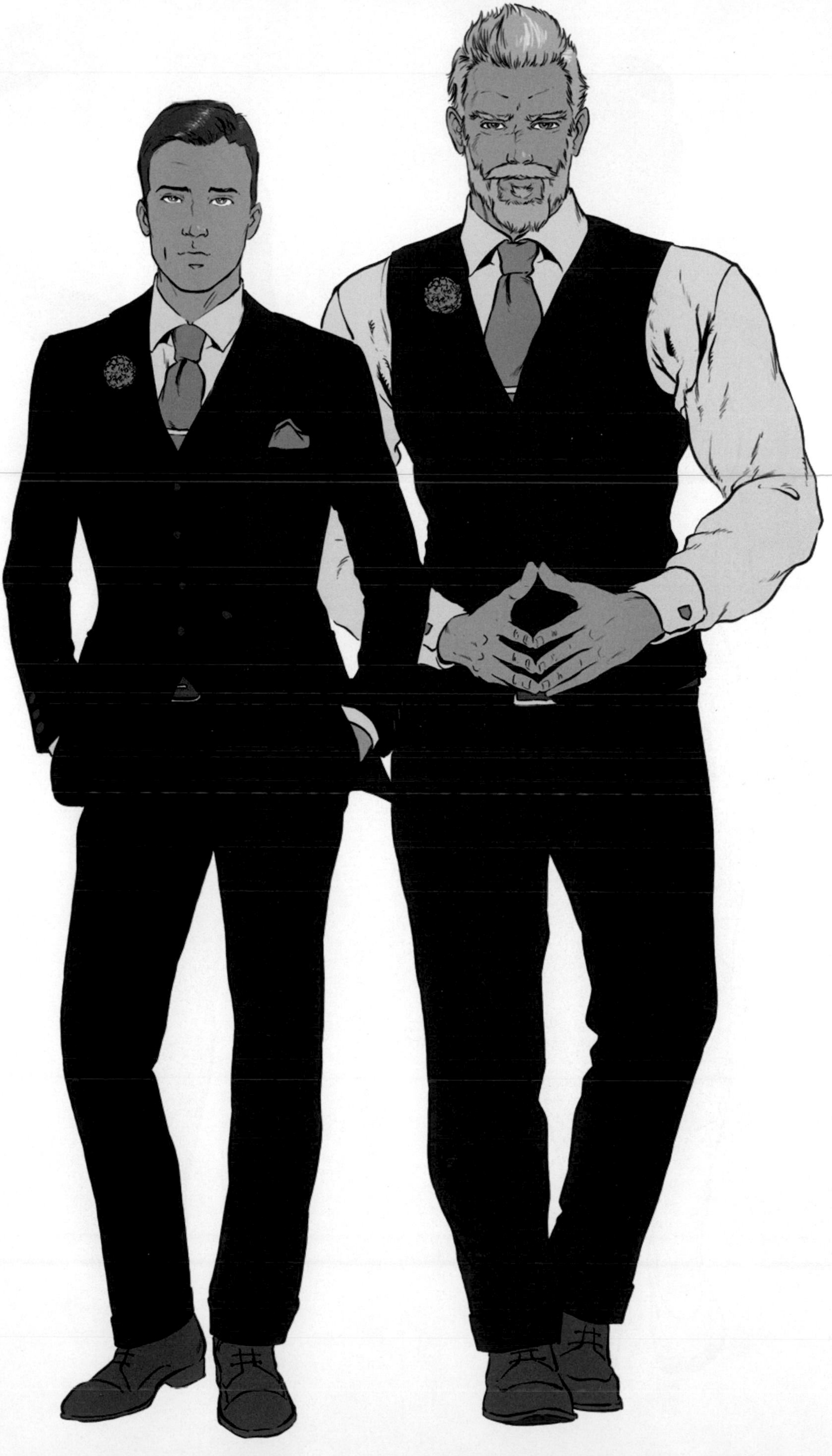

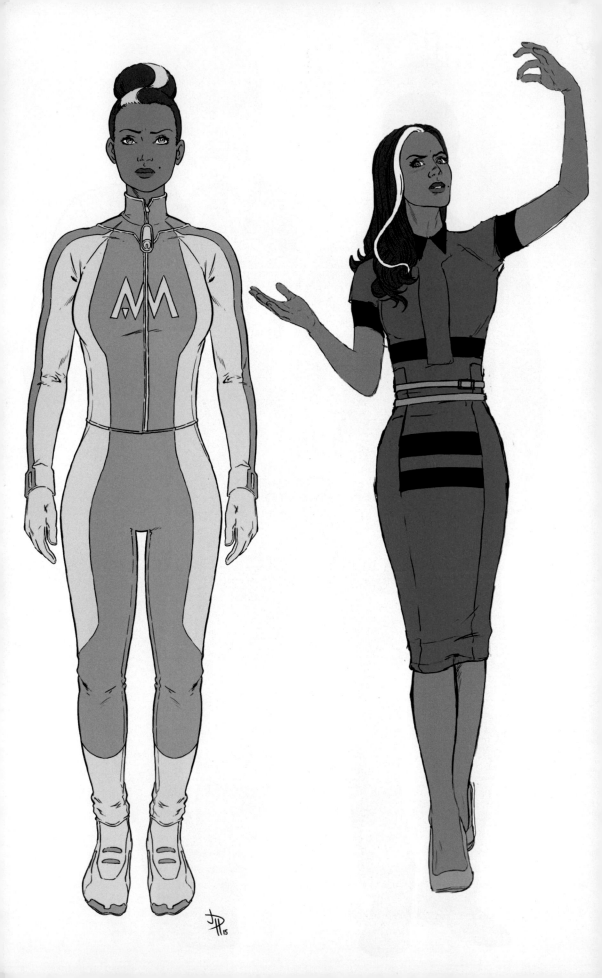

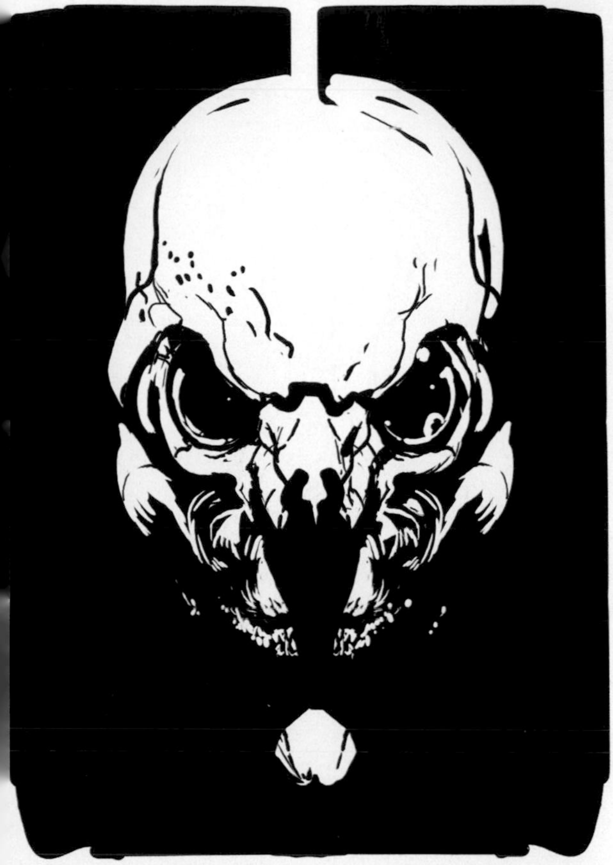

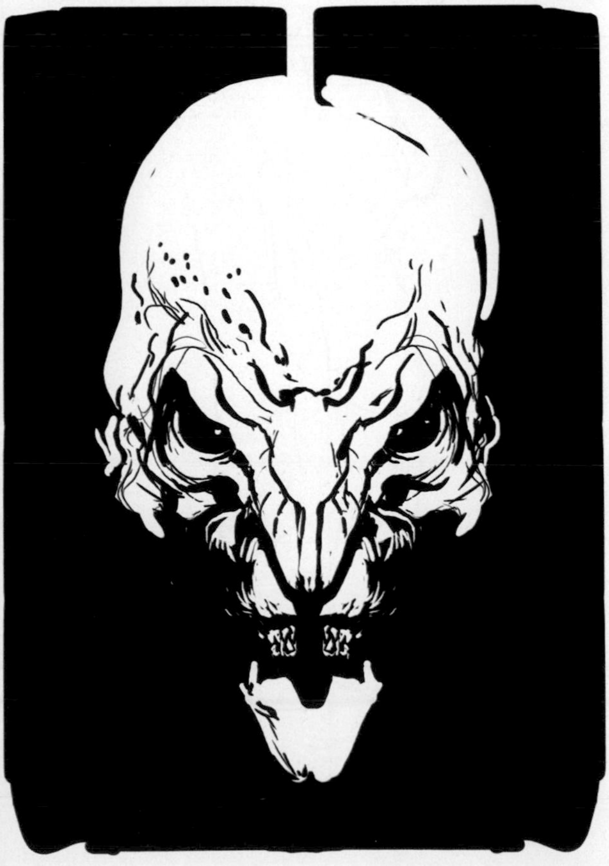

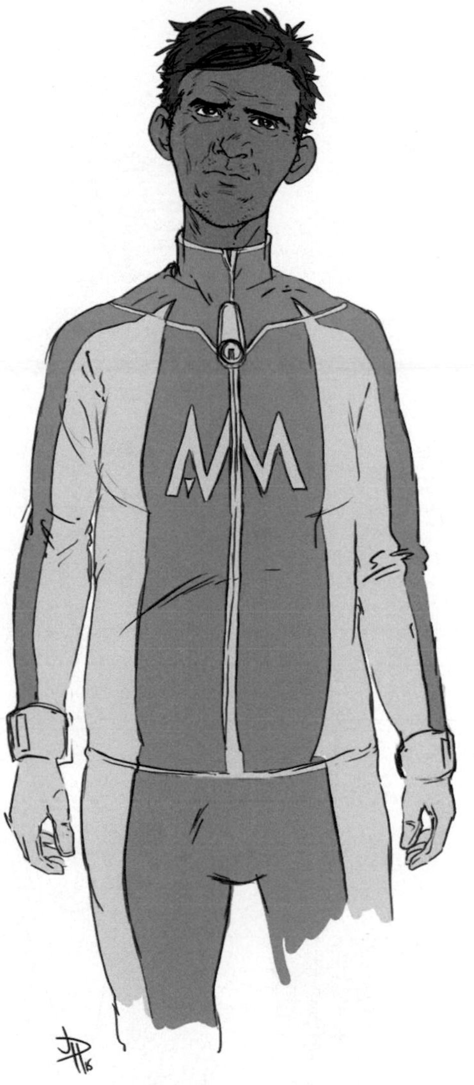

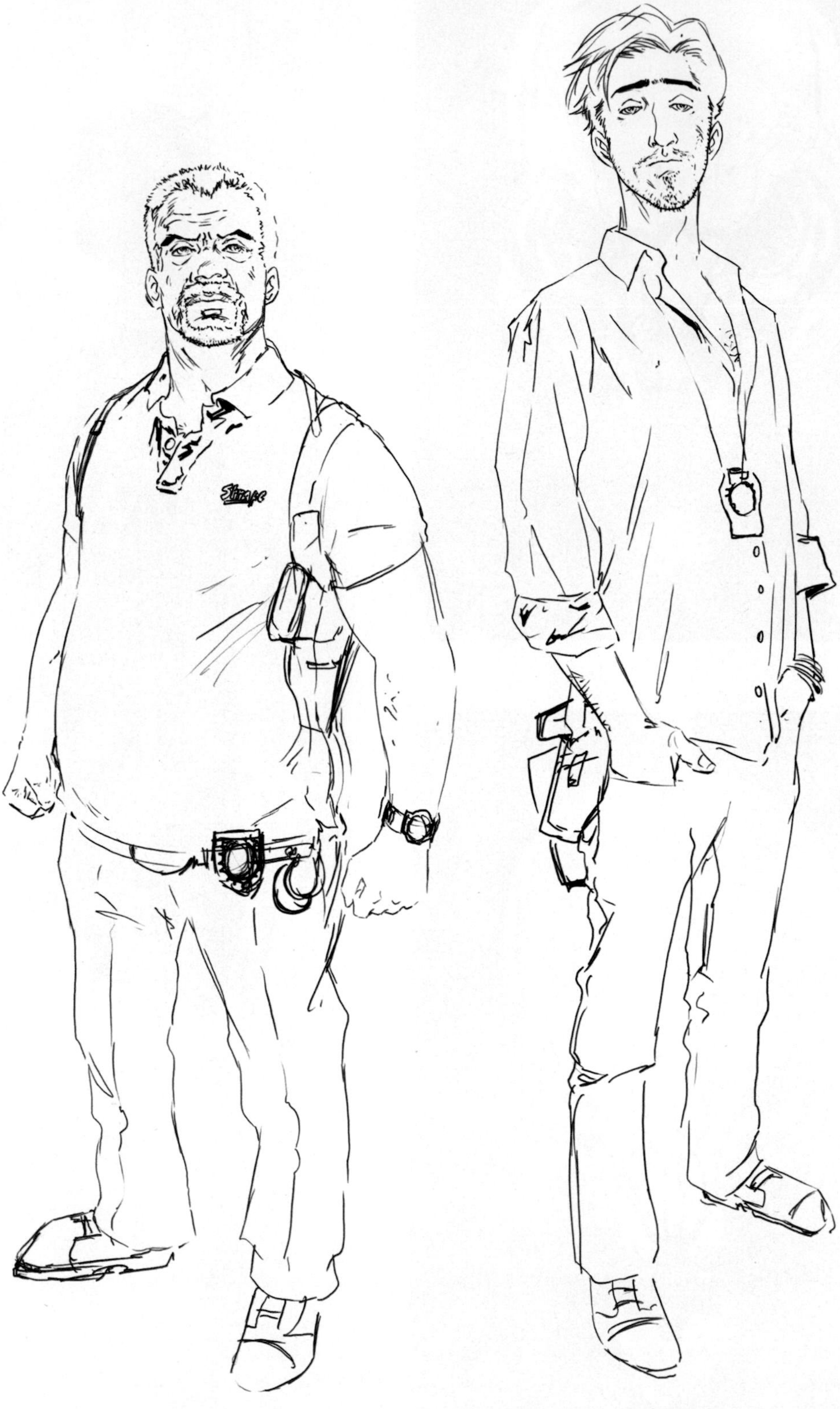

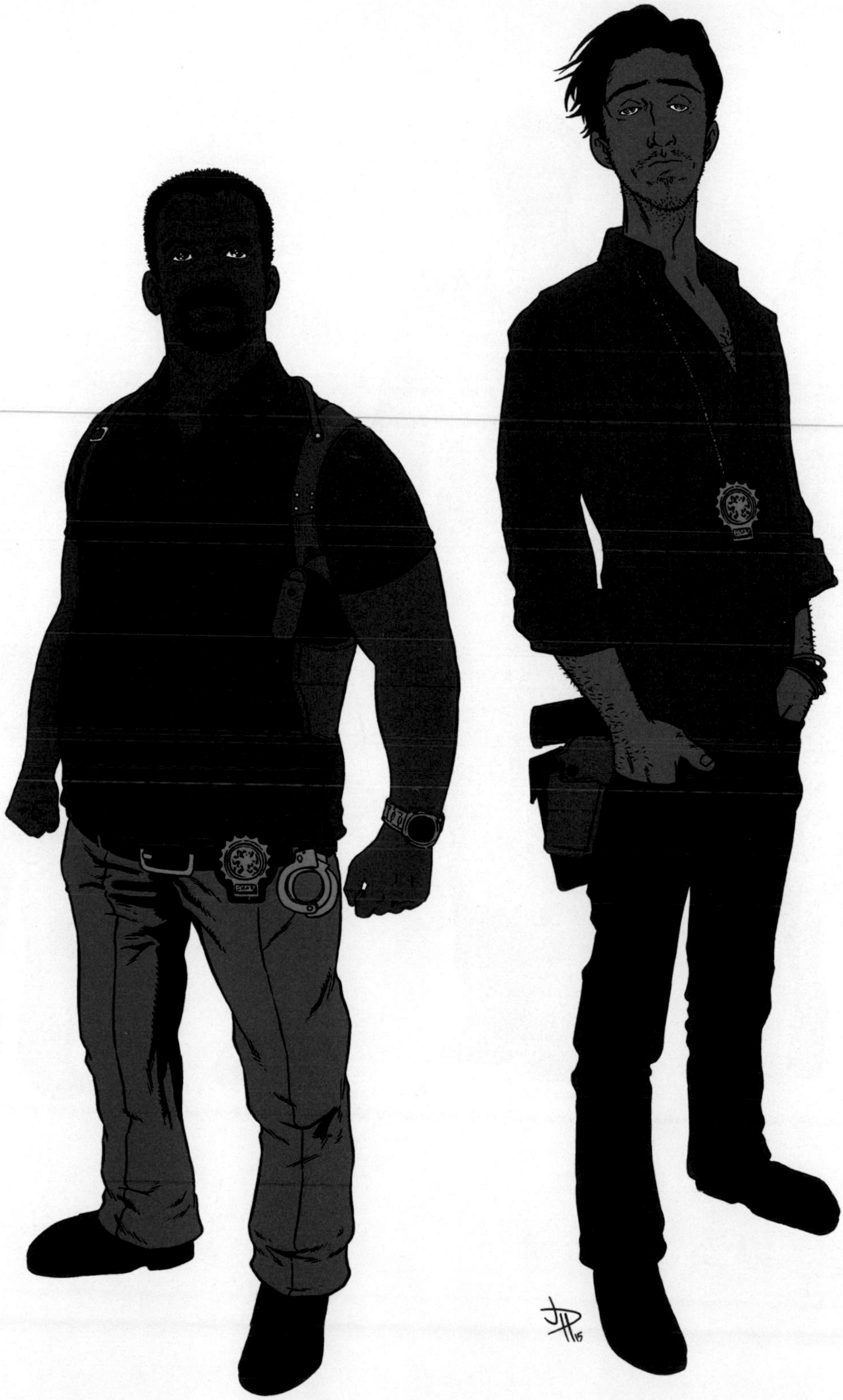

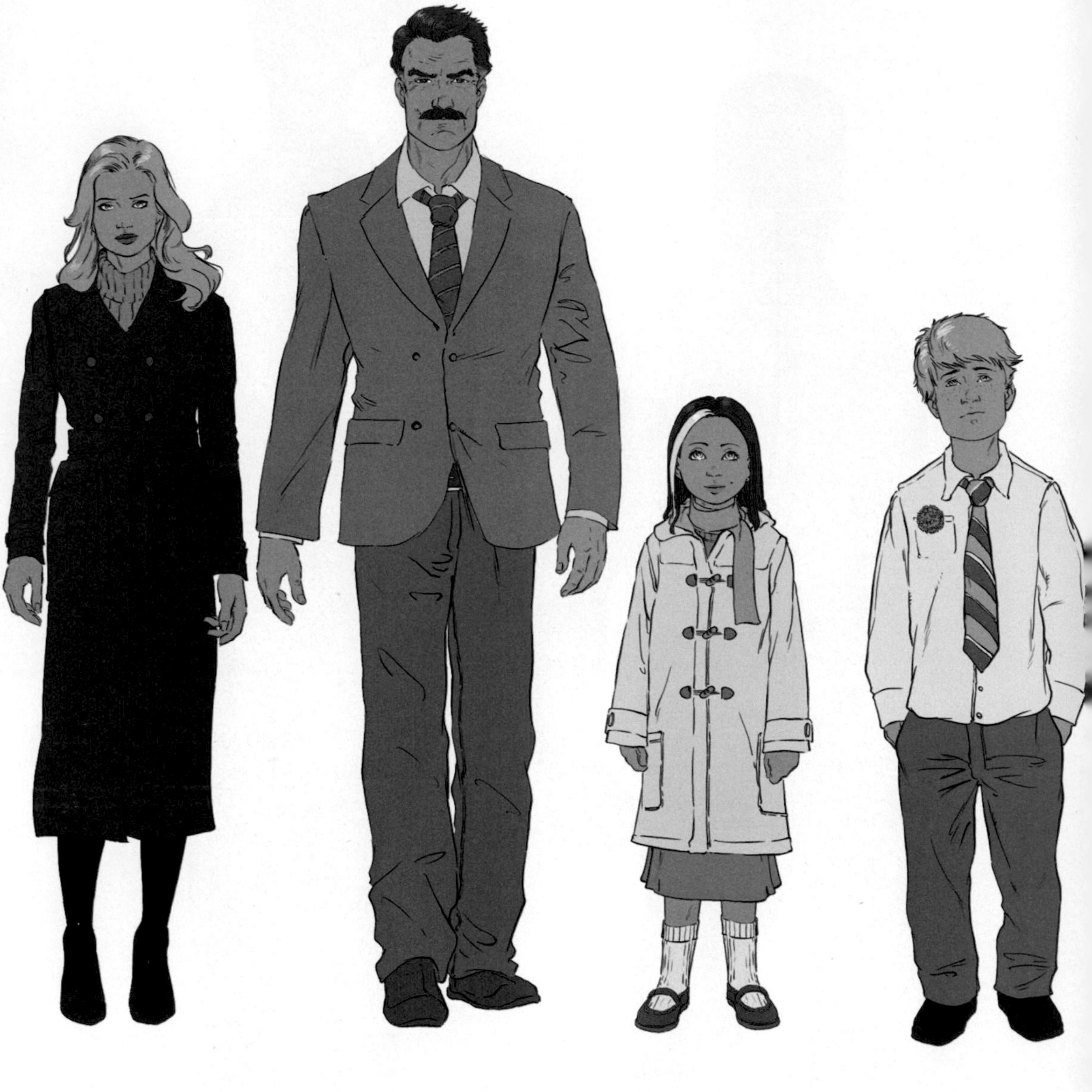

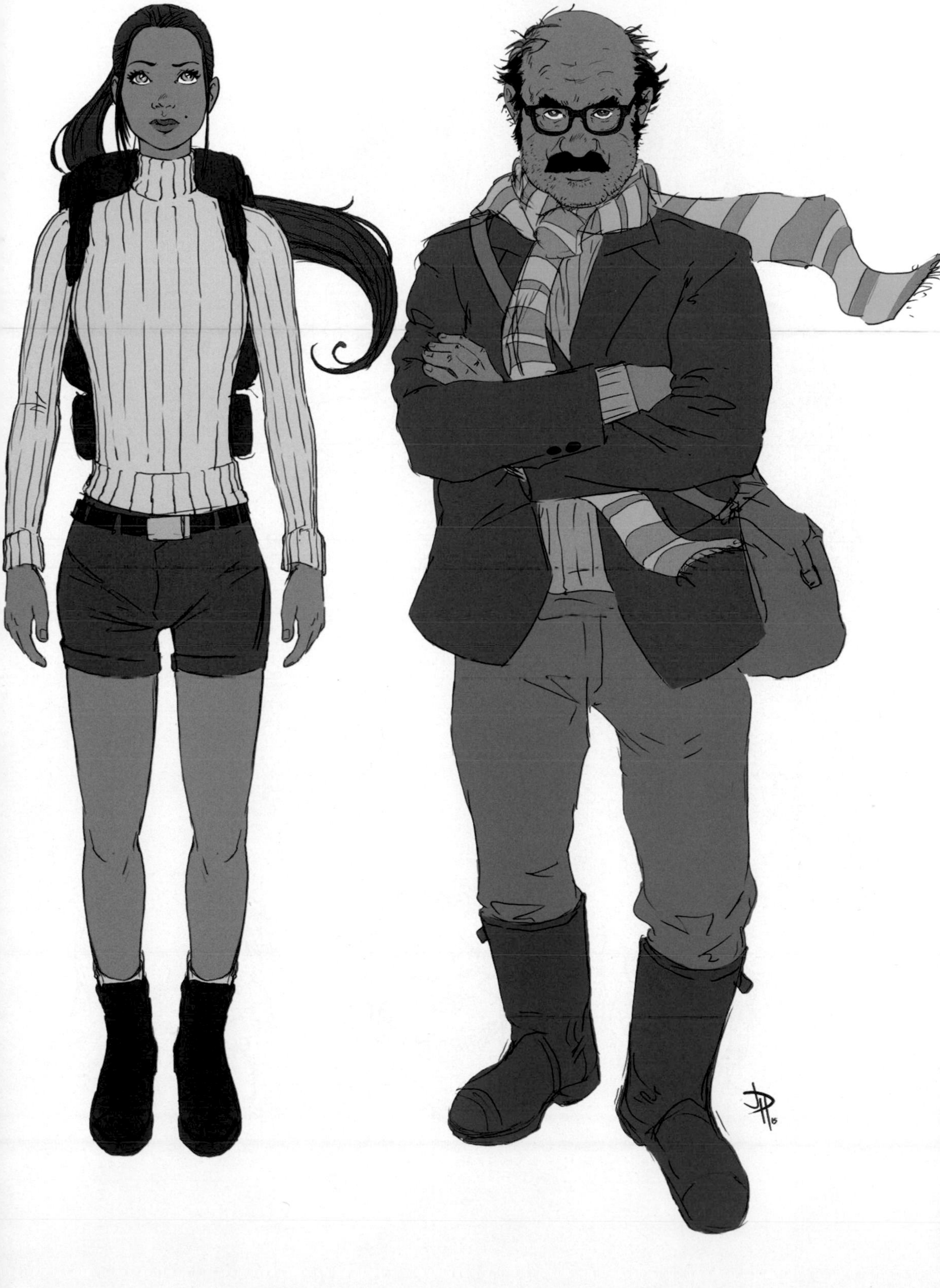

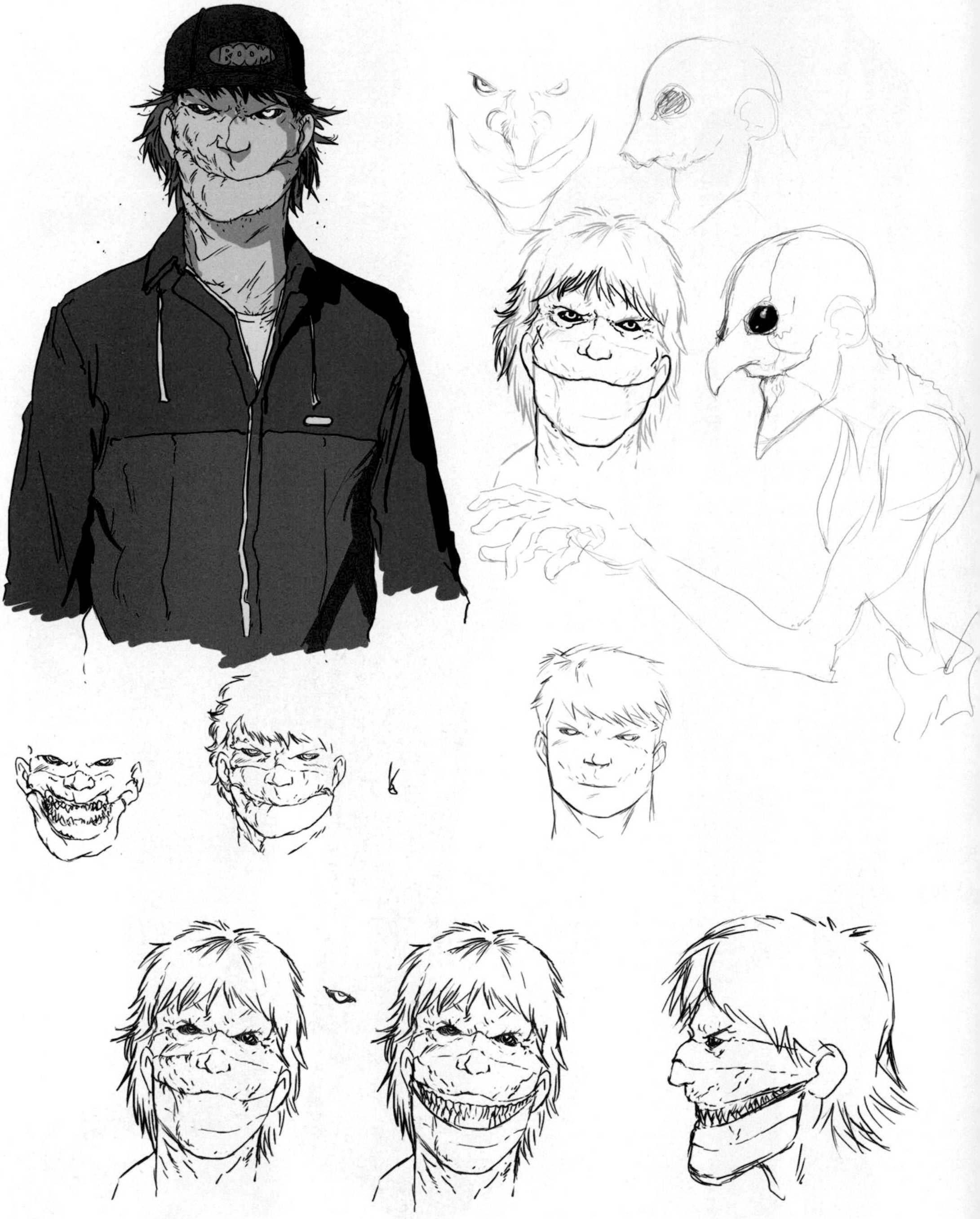
BOOM

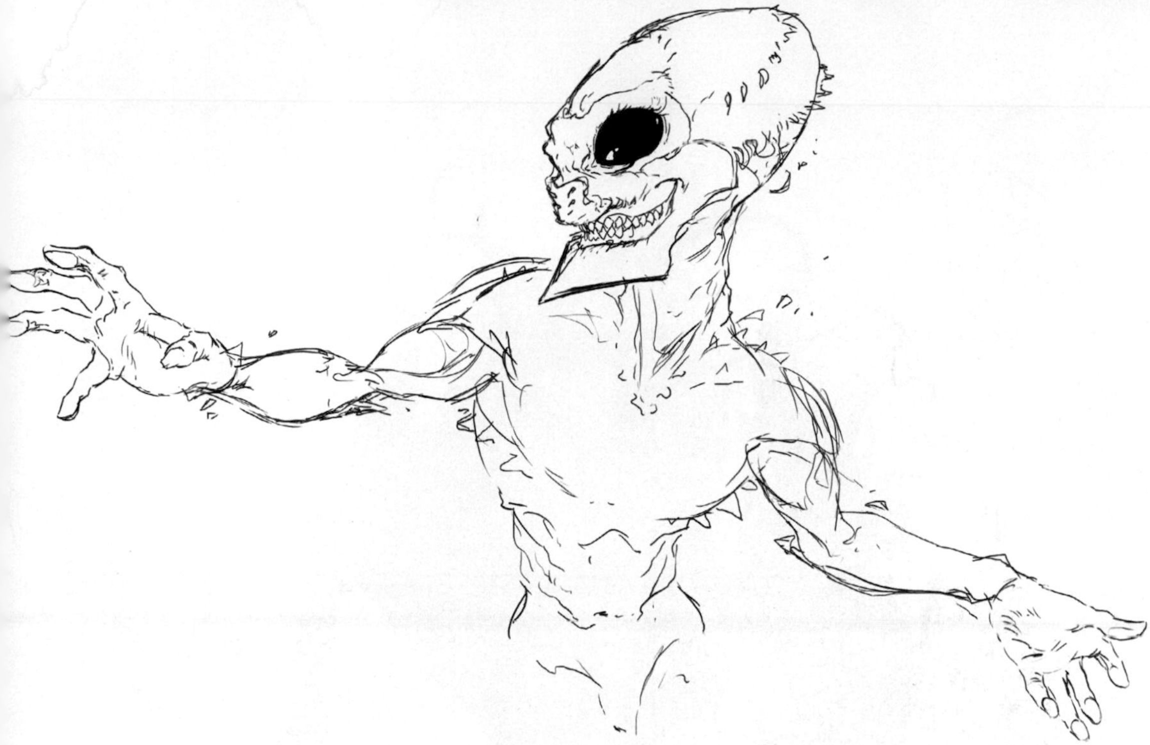

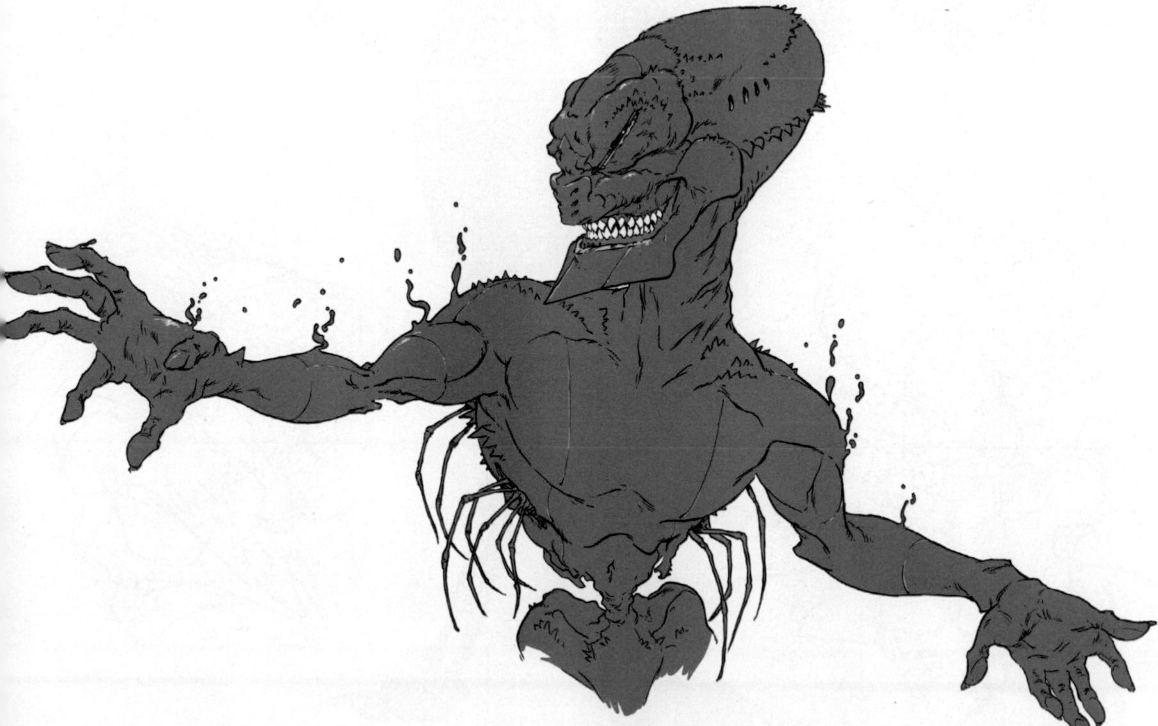

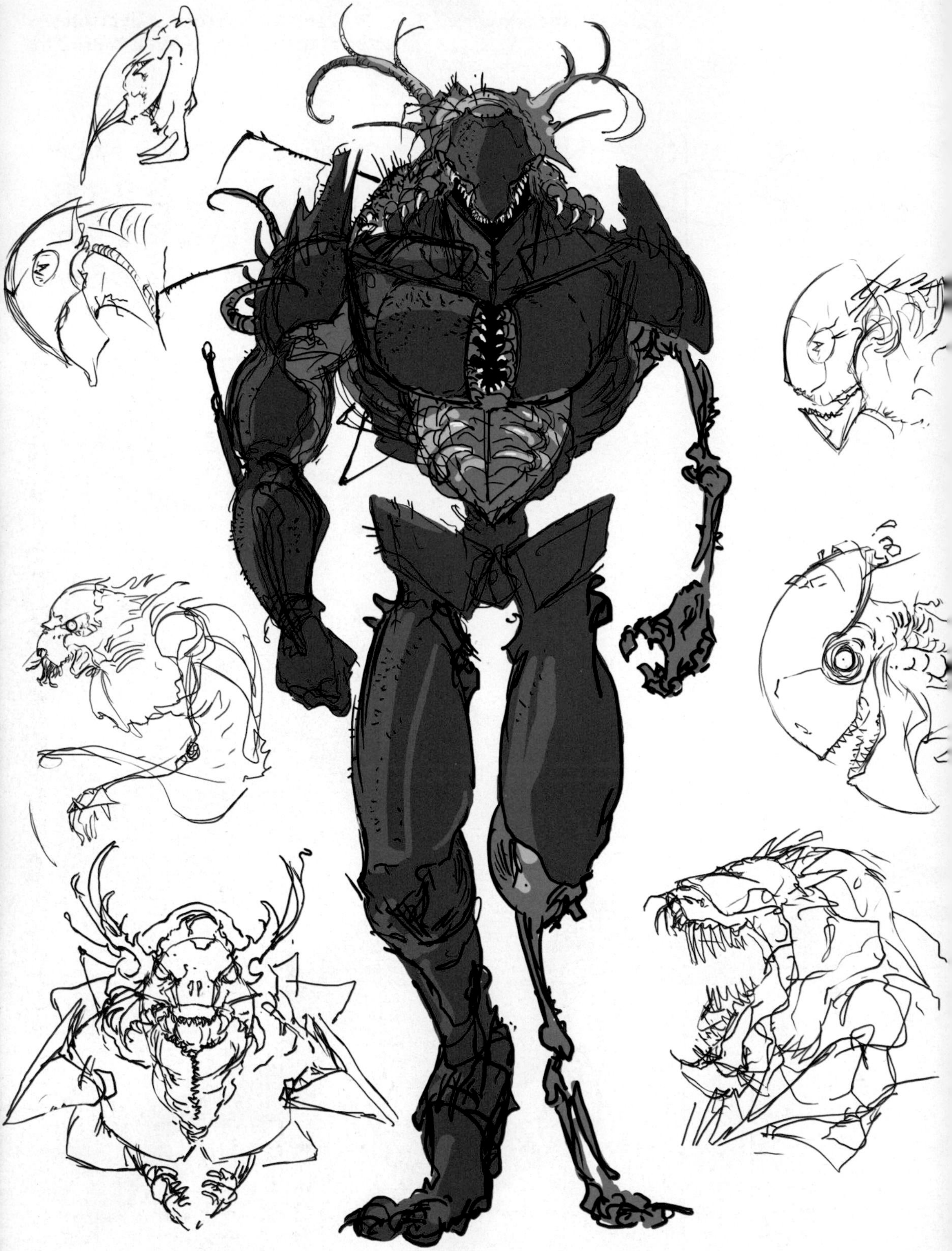

FROM THE WRITER OF *ANIMAL MAN*
JAMIE DELANO
with JOHN RIDGWAY, ALFREDO ALCALA and others

JOHN CONSTANTINE

HELLBLAZER
ORIGINAL SINS

VERTIGO

Jamie Delano   John Ridgway
Alfredo Alcala   Rick Veitch   Tom Mandrake

VERTIGO

"The most intense adult comic in ages."
—SPIN MAGAZINE

"Cool."
—ENTERTAINMENT WEEKLY

"Far and away the best example of the genre I have ever seen."
—THE GUARDIAN

READ THE ENTIRE SERIES!

PREACHER VOL. 3: PROUD AMERICANS

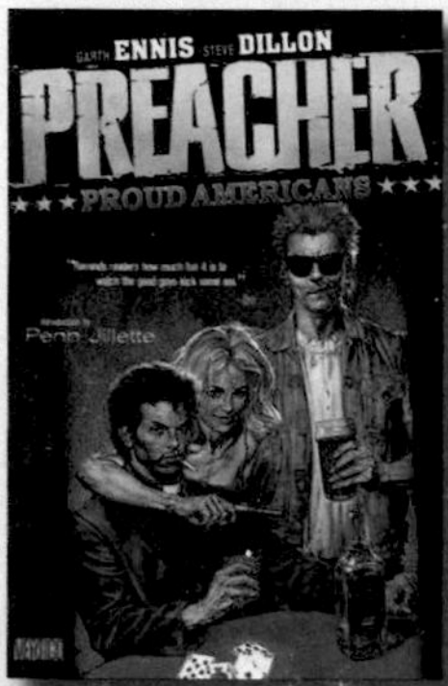
GARTH ENNIS STEVE DILLON
PREACHER
PROUD AMERICANS
Penn Jillette

PREACHER VOL. 6: WAR IN THE SUN

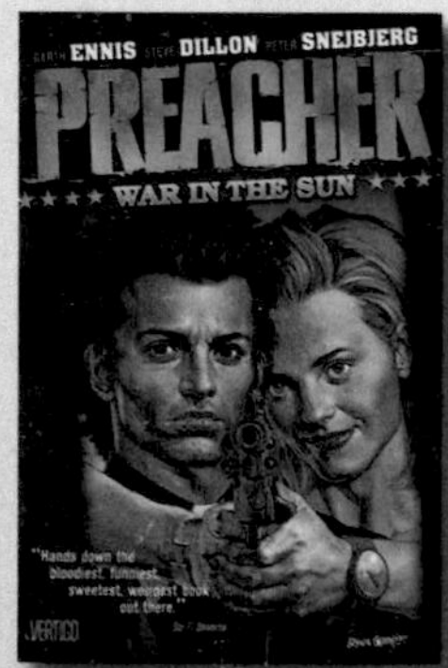
GARTH ENNIS STEVE DILLON PETER SNEJBJERG
PREACHER
WAR IN THE SUN
VERTIGO

PREACHER VOL. 1: GONE TO TEXAS

PREACHER VOL. 2: UNTIL THE END OF THE WORLD

PREACHER VOL. 3: PROUD AMERICANS

PREACHER VOL. 4: ANCIENT HISTORY

PREACHER VOL. 5: DIXIE FRIED

PREACHER VOL. 6: WAR IN THE SUN

PREACHER VOL. 7: SALVATION

PREACHER VOL. 8: ALL HELL'S A-COMING

PREACHER VOL. 9: ALAMO

GARTH ENNIS
with STEVE DILLON

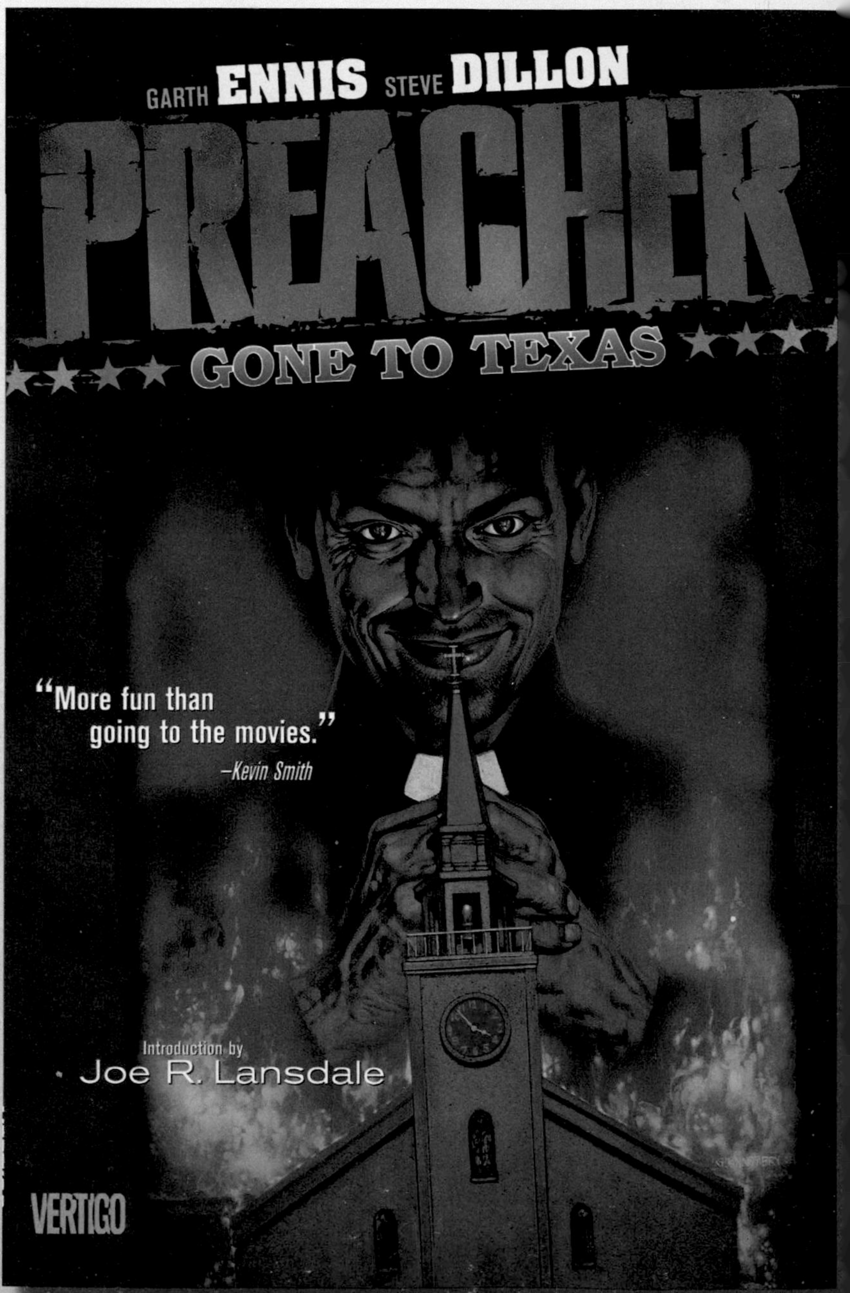
GARTH ENNIS STEVE DILLON
PREACHER
GONE TO TEXAS
"More fun than going to the movies."
–Kevin Smith
Introduction by
Joe R. Lansdale
VERTIGO